ATLAS OF WORLD HISTORY

ATLAS OF WORLD HISTORY

Edited by Kate Santon and Liz McKay

p

This is a Parragon Publishing Book
This edition published in 2006

Parragon Publishing
Queen Street House
4 Queen Street
Bath, BA1 1HE, UK

Copyright © Parragon Books Ltd 2005
Photographs courtesy of Getty Images. For full details see page 320
Produced by Atlantic Publishing

ISBN 1-40545-914-X

Printed in Malaysia

Contents

VICEROYALTY OF NEW SPAIN

Audiencia of Nueva Galicia

- Monterrey
- Saltillo
Durango •
San Luis Potosí
Guadalajara ■
Guanajuato •
Mexico ■ • Tampico
Veracruz
Mérida •
Audiencia of Mexico
• Oaxaca
• Campeche
Audiencia of Guatemala
Guatemala •
Granada •

Gulf of Mexico

St. Augustine •

Havana •

Audiencia of Santo Domingo

Santiago •

Santo Domingo •

Caribbean Sea

Maracaibo •
Santa Marta •
Cartagena ■
Coro •
• Mérida
Caracas •
Cumaná •

Audiencia of Santa

Panamá •

Audiencia of Panamá

Cali •
■ Bogotá
• Popayán
• Pasto
■ Quito
• Guayaquil
• Tumbes
• Moyobamba
Cajamarca •
Trujillo •

Audiencia of Quito

unexplored Spanish territory

Amazon

VICEROYALTY

unexplored Spanish territory

OF PERU

Audiencia of Lima

Lima •
• Cuzco
Arequipa •
Arica •
■ La Paz
La Plata
• Potosí

Audiencia of Charcas

• Salta
Asunción •
• Tucumán
Corrientes •

Mendoza •
• Córdoba
Valparaiso •
■ Santiago
Buenos Aires •
Audiencia of Chile
Concepción •

NORTH ATLANTIC OCEAN

PACIFIC OCEAN

N

0   500 km
0   500 miles

SOUTH ATLANTIC OCEAN

Introduction

The *Atlas of World History* looks at the broad sweep of human history, from our earliest beginnings in Africa to the world at the start of the twenty-first century. Truly international, it examines regions and events in a combination of specially drawn, full-color maps, fascinating text and lavish illustrations.

Together they combine to present a picture of a changing world. A world in which empires grow, struggle for dominance and decline; a world in which some individuals have had a global impact, whether they be conquerors like Alexander the Great, emperors like Süleyman the Magnificent and Akbar, or individuals like Gandhi. But there is also information about the things that affected everyday life, whether that be religion or culture, the impact of epidemics or a desire for independence.

Here you will find details of exploration and discoveries, not only of different lands and cultures but of scientific and technological advances too. Particular themes and topics are explored, and important buildings—such as Hagia Sofia, Versailles and the Great Wall—are described in a context which makes it possible to appreciate their significance.

From archaeological discoveries to contemporary affairs, *Atlas of World History* presents a twenty-first century view of the history of the whole world. It mirrors a growing understanding of the globe and presents a way for readers to understand—and appreciate—the world we live in today.

The Origins of Man

Ancestors of modern humans first appeared in Africa more than two million years ago. As they evolved and developed skills, they ranged further afield.

Homo erectus

Mankind's earliest ancestors are generally believed to be a species of pre-human, or hominid, called *Homo habilis*. Living between three and one million years ago, *Homo habilis* was distinguished from more ape-like hominids by its larger brain and its ability to make crude tools from stone. Found mainly in eastern and southern Africa, *Homo habilis* did not migrate beyond this region which, unlike other parts of the planet, was warm and easily habitable.

Approximately 1.6 million years ago, at the start of the Pleistocene Age, *Homo habilis* was succeeded by a more skilled hominid, *Homo erectus*. *Homo erectus* was taller and, as its name suggests, more upright than *Homo habilis*. Its skull was also wider and larger, evidence of a larger brain, and despite having a less prominent jaw its facial characteristics would have remained quite ape-like. The tools that *Homo erectus*

developed were more sophisticated; in particular flint hand axes which had two cutting edges and would have been used not only to kill animals but also to butcher meat. Homo erectus is also believed to have discovered fire, which would have improved its living conditions as well as its ability to hunt, since fire could be used as an effective weapon. Perhaps because of these features, this species of hominid is known to have ventured beyond Africa and evidence of its presence has been found in locations as far apart as northern Europe, Asia and eastern China.

Neanderthal Man

In about 200,000 BC *Homo neanderthalensis* appeared. It was shorter and stockier in build than *Homo erectus*, with a flat skull, a steeply receding forehead, and a thick brow ridge. However, despite their appearance, Neanderthals were biologically much closer to modern humans. Like *Homo erectus*, Neanderthals crafted tools for different purposes, but these items had become more specialized; they used their intelligence to make spears, chisels, and borers. They also buried their dead with some degree of ritual; skeletons have been found which have been encircled by stones or accompanied with animal horns. In one discovery in modern Iraq, pollen evidence suggests that a male skeleton had possibly been strewn with flowers at burial. Neanderthals appear to have lived in social communities, and skeletons which show signs of advanced bone diseases such as arthritis suggest that some individuals may well have been looked after by other members of their group. Confined to Europe and the Middle East, Neanderthal man appears to have died out in 35,000 BC, possibly as a result of competition with another species, *Homo sapiens* or modern man.

Above: The caves of Lascaux, France, c.15,000–3,000 BC, *are one of the most famous examples of Paleolithic art. The nomad lifestyle is illustrated with images of animals such as cows, bulls, horses, and deer.*
Opposite: Close view of the fossilized skull of a Homo erectus found in Java.

Homo sapiens

From the heart of Africa a new species emerged in 100,000 BC that, like *Homo erectus* and *Homo neanderthalensis*, migrated to other parts of the globe. *Homo sapiens*, or "wise man," is the species that we recognize today as ourselves. They did not have the flat, ape-like facial appearance of *Homo erectus*, and had a dome-like skull that could hold a larger brain rather than the flattened skull of the Neanderthals; the skull itself was longer and the eyebrow ridges were less pronounced. *Homo sapiens* would eventually evolve variations in height, coloring, and physiognomical features. These people were far more advanced than the Neanderthals, having developed projectile weapons such as spears which would have reduced the number of injuries sustained in bringing down a large animal.

They lived in caves but were also capable of building shelters and teepee-type huts; they also built more sophisticated hearths for keeping fires alight. Tools were crafted from a range of different materials, including needles made from bone, and rope and threads constructed from animal and plant fibers. Their clothing would probably have been tailored to cope with the extreme weather conditions of the Ice Age and some items were even decorated with beading.

In around 60,000 BC, a group of *Homo sapiens* moved out of Africa into Asia to become ancestors of the Mongoloid peoples. In roughly 40,000 BC, another group spread into Europe and western Asia to become the forebears of the Caucasian type. Those who remained in Africa were the ancestors of the Negroid peoples.

Global Spread of Homo sapiens

Human development gathered pace, and with climatic change modern humans were able to migrate to new areas of the world.

The Ice Age

The last great Ice Age ended around 13,000 years ago and signaled the end of the Pleistocene which had lasted for two million years. This period was marked by extreme variations in temperature across the planet, including a series of ice ages. Temperatures fell to such an extent that glaciers and ice sheets covered much of Europe, Asia, and North America. It was during this period that early man began to evolve more quickly, perhaps as a result of the difficult living conditions: their ability to adapt and change would have given them an advantage over other, less intelligent species. *Homo sapiens* was the species most able to cope with the extremities of life during the Pleistocene and, although confined to warmer areas during great freezes, they were able to migrate and colonize new regions whenever the ice retreated.

The existence of ice sheets in northern Europe and northern America meant that sea levels were much lower, exposing land bridges that linked most of the continents. These bridges linked north-eastern Asia to the Americas, Japan, and Indonesia to Asia, and Britain to Europe, and crucially provided migration routes for both humans and animals. The Australian continent remained separated from Asia by around 40 miles of deep water and so those people who traveled to Australia around 60,000 BC must have done so by boat, since there was no evidence of the simultaneous movement of animals. The mammals of Asia, such as monkeys and tigers, are not found in Australia; marsupials fill their roles on the Australian continent.

Migration into America

With the beginning of the thaw around 13,000 years ago, the ice plains on the Bering land bridge opened up to provide passage into Alaska. This, and the opening of the Canadian ice corridor, enabled people to migrate into the hitherto uninhabited continent. The first humans to advance into America were Mongoloid peoples from Siberian Asia who were well adapted for life in the harsh conditions of northern America. The lack of vegetation meant that they relied upon fishing, but they would have been drawn south by the better climate and more abundant food. The glaciers had not reached central and southern parts of the continent and as a result the rich grasslands and plains were teeming with big game: giant bison, mammoths, giant sloth, musk oxen, and

Out of Africa
c.100,000 – 10,000 BC

→ Possible human colonization route

● Major site

ICELAND

Svalbard

Novaya Zemlya

NORWAY SWEDEN FINLAND

UNITED KINGDOM

DEN.

EST.
LAT.
LITH.

IRELAND

NETH.
B. GER.
LUX.

POLAND

BELORUSSIA

● Kostienki

Sakhalin

RUSSIAN FEDERATION

KAZAKHSTAN

MONGOLIA

Hokkaido

Cro-Magnon ● FRANCE SWITZ. CZECH. SLK. UKRAINE REP. MOLD.
AUS. HUN. ROM.
SLV. CR.
B.H. YUG. BULG.
ITALY ALB.
GREECE

GEORGIA
ARM. AZER.
TURKEY TURKMEN.

UZBEKISTAN

KYRGYZ.

TAJIK.

Zhoukoudran ●

N. KOREA
S. KOREA

JAPAN

Honshu

● Hoshino

PORT. SPAIN

Las Palomas ●

TUNISIA

CYPRUS
LEB.
SYRIA
ISRAEL
JORDAN

IRAQ

Shanidar ●

IRAN

AFGHAN.

CHINA

Taiwan

MOROCCO

ALGERIA LIBYA EGYPT

SAUDI
KUWAIT
BAHRAIN
QATAR
A.E.

PAKISTAN

NEPAL
BHUTAN

BURMA

Hainan

WESTERN SAHARA

MAURITANIA MALI NIGER CHAD

ARABIA

OMAN

● Bhimbetka

INDIA
BANGLADESH

LAOS

VIETNAM

Luzon

PHILIPPINES

Mindanao

SENEGAL
GAMBIA
JINEA-BISSAU
GUINEA
SIERRA LEONE
LIBERIA

BURKINA FASO

NIGERIA

TOGO
BENIN

CENTRAL AFRICAN REPUBLIC

ERITREA

SUDAN

YEMEN

DJIBOUTI

ETHIOPIA

THAI.

CAMB.

SOMALIA

SRI LANKA

BRUNEI

MALAYSIA ● Niah Cave

IVORY COAST
GHANA

CAMEROON

GABON
REP. CONGO

DEM. REP. OF CONGO

UGANDA
RWANDA
BURUNDI

KENYA

● Olduvai Gorge

Sumatra

Borneo

Sulawesi

INDONESIA

Java

Timor-Leste

● Nombé
PAPUA NEW GUINEA

SOLOMON ISLANDS

TANZANIA

ANGOLA

MALAWI

ZAMBIA

MOZAMBIQUE

MADAGASCAR

ZIMBABWE

NAMIBIA

BOTSWANA

AUSTRALIA

● Kenniff Cave

SWAZILAND
● Border Cave

SOUTH AFRICA ● LESOTHO

● Klasies River Mouth

NEW ZEALAND

moose. Within a short period most of these animals were extinct, either as a result of overkill or climate change, or possibly a combination of the two. Many of the vast woodland areas became arid deserts and their new inhabitants either learned to adapt or continued to move south. In this way humankind moved into all parts of the American continent. The abundance of grazing

animals on the Great Plains meant that the peoples who inhabited this area found that they could sustain their hunter-gatherer lifestyle; they became the ancestors of Native Americans. The distinct societies that developed remained unchanged for thousands of years until relatively modern times.

The First Europeans

In around 43,000 BC, *Homo sapiens* made the move out of Africa and into Europe through the Near East. Remains of early Europeans have been found in clustered sites in modern Eastern Europe, suggesting the route that may have been taken by these people. Archeological discoveries in the Dordogne region of France have led to Early Europeans being called Cro-Magnons, a name derived from the places their settlements were found. They were skilled toolmakers and used bone and antlers to make spear tips and harpoons, with particularly sophisticated points that detached after striking, in order to cause more damage. Living in tents and shelters, the Cro-Magnons were nomadic hunter-gatherers who spread across northern Europe; their major food sources would have been reindeer, mammoth, and wild oxen.

As the world began to warm up both the landscape and resources began to change. Northern Europe gradually became an area of dense woodlands and mixed forests inhabited by pig, boar, and deer; consequently different methods of hunting were required. The inhabitants used the rivers as a means of traveling inland from the coastal areas through the thick forests and gradually people began to settle in various regions. Settlement and the warming of the climate had an important effect on the development of humankind. As the giant animals that had survived on the tundra died out and food sources became less readily available people learned to domesticate animals and tend crops, and in approximately 10,000 BC the Neolithic or agricultural age began.

The Rise of Agriculture

The Origins of Agriculture

The realization by humans that other species could be harnessed and utilized for the sole benefit of themselves was the first and most crucial step towards modern civilization. The retreat of the ice in western Asia and the Near East had opened up vast expanses of grassland, in particular of the edible varieties emmer and einkorn. These areas attracted large numbers of grazing mammals such as goats, gazelle, cattle, and horses, and the human population made full use of these animals. As early as 10,000 BC, people in this area on the eastern side of the Mediterranean began to domesticate and selectively breed both cereals and animals. They started to herd goats and sheep which could be used to provide not only meat but also wool and milk, and this was eventually followed by the breeding of pigs and cattle. The cultivation of crops such as beans, lentils, and peas followed, and where these were successful the process spread. By 4000 BC farming had replaced hunting as the main source of food in all parts of the world except the Pacific islands and the Arctic tundra. Because farming offered a reliable supply of food in one area, people were no longer forced to move from region to region, and by settling in one place they were able to build larger and stronger communities.

The Cultivation of Plants

Different parts of the world benefited from the growth of their own staple crops. In the Middle East, or the Fertile Crescent, the principal cereals became wheat and barley. A descendent of wild einkorn, wheat was selectively bred so that its ears were held up by stronger stalks and its seeds were larger. These grain crops were ground to become flour which could then be used for a variety of cooking needs, the most common being making bread. Fruits like figs, olives, and dates were also harvested. In the more eastern reaches of Asia, and in China, the staple grains were millet and rice which grew particularly well in waterlogged soil. In South and Central America maize was cultivated to produce larger and more vigorous varieties and this was accompanied by crops such as squashes, potatoes, and tomatoes.

The Domestication of Animals

All over the world animals could be exploited for a range of purposes, not only for the supply of meat. Cattle, goats, and sheep were also useful for their milk. Sheep, llamas and alpacas were providers of wool, and cattle and oxen supplied leather. Dogs had been used by people in the Middle East since 11,000 BC for hunting, and eventually other animals were employed to help increase productivity. Cattle and asses were used to pull plows and carts. Camels and yaks could carry heavy loads and the horse became a means of transportation. In the Americas the domestication of animals was not as prevalent as in other parts of the world. This was mainly because the animals available tended to be more difficult to control and hunting remained a more profitable exercise than herding.

Below: *Axes were buried on Mittelberg Hill near the town of Nebra, Germany, in 1600 BC.*
Opposite: *Neolithic Stonehenge on Salisbury Plain, England, is probably the most impressive megalithic building in Europe.*

Developing Cultures

Human societies became more sophisticated, with increasingly complex art and evidence of rituals. The beginnings of metalworking led to major changes.

Worship and Megaliths

One of the clearest indications of developing cultural awareness is the evidence of simple worship rituals. Early forms of worship seem to be the burial rituals performed by Neanderthals and early *Homo sapiens*. Grave sites often contained simple offerings such as colored stones, seeds and animal bones. Later on personal possessions were used and the corpses were often laid out in deliberate positions, perhaps curled up or in a sleeping position. Such rituals suggest that early man may have had an interest in some sort of afterlife, and perhaps demonstrates a growing spiritual awareness. The production of both fixed and portable works of art also suggest that other forms of worship had begun. The discovery of a number of similarly styled figurines dating from 23,000 BC, collectively called Venus figurines, may be part of an early form of fertility or goddess worship. These simply carved figures depict female forms with enlarged bellies and breasts and could be emblems of fertility or success.

By 4000 BC, the first megaliths were being built in Europe. These were constructions made of huge stones that were placed in significant patterns. Although their use is not fully understood, megalithic structures, such as Stonehenge in Britain, were probably used for ceremonial or burial purposes. Many of the stones align with the movements of the sun and stars and so were likely to have been linked to the calendar. By the time of the first great cities, more organized forms of religious worship were being practiced.

Art

Early humans had been expressing themselves artistically from as early as 30,000 years ago. Cave paintings found in France are among the oldest surviving examples of art. The paintings depict animals such as reindeer and horses, mammoths and birds. Some images are merely outlines, while others are more sophisticated with shading used to give a three-dimensional impression. The materials the artists used were found in their environment: ochre, iron oxide, chalk, charcoal, and even blood were used as paints. Hand stencils, found in Europe, Africa, and Australia,

were made by placing the hand on the cave wall then spraying the pigment over and around the hand.

Early Aboriginal art in Australia is mostly in the form of rock paintings, or petroglyphs. Many show the bones and organs of the animals they depict while others employ geometrical figures and lines to represent the landscape. They show a clearly developing system of belief with images such as rainbow serpents appearing in paintings dating from 6000 BC; the rainbow serpent myth tells how the slithering of the serpent created the landscape.

Numerous images of hunters chasing their quarry have been found in the Kalahari desert, dating from as far back as 20,000 BC. These cave paintings and petroglyphs, like the others, may have been used to convey impressions of the environment or to mark ceremonial hunting rites.

As human culture became more sophisticated, so the media for producing artistic images changed and the possible uses for art developed. The introduction of clay pottery, although functional, also provided a medium for expressing artistic style. Decorated pieces may have been used to denote social importance or even wealth. Many pieces of clayware, pots, and sculptures would have been used for ritual purposes and ancient examples have been found as part of funeral offerings at burial sites. Weaponry could also be decorated with simple markings, which became more elaborate as techniques in metallurgy developed.

Metallurgy

An important technological development was the ability to extract metal from rock or ore. Gold and copper deposits would have been visible to early humans in the rocks surrounding them but extracting them was difficult. In Asia, in approximately 9000 BC, copper was being used for tools and so some understanding of the process of smelting had been achieved. With the knowledge of smelting came the ability to work large amounts of metal by hammering and beating, and by 4000 BC copperworking had spread to North Africa and Europe. Mining for surface ores such as malachite was extensive in the Middle East and it was here that technologies such as casting were first effectively employed. Initially used mainly for decorative purposes, gold and copper were vital trade objects and certainly contributed to the development of economically powerful cultures which began to appear at this time. Although prized, both copper and gold were too soft to be suitable for heavier purposes, such as weaponry. However, the experience of working with copper led to a better understanding of the properties of metals in general and eventually copper was mixed with tin to produce a much stronger alloy, bronze. Because tin only occurred in certain areas, the Middle East, China, and the north-west of Europe, the Bronze Age only occurred in these regions. Elsewhere, as in Africa, the Americas and Australia, working stone remained the most effective means of tool production until the arrival of iron. The efficiency of bronze resulted in a surplus of tools, weapons, ceremonial objects, and luxury goods, which must have contributed to the increased wealth of certain communities.

The First Settlements

The impact of agriculture on mankind was vital in the establishment of larger, more concentrated populations. Inevitably, in more fertile areas where farming could easily sustain greater numbers of people, large settlements began to flourish. The most fertile areas were in the Middle East and north-east China, where the temperate climate and adequate water supply provided ideal conditions. Rivers and lakes were particularly popular areas for settlement, as apart from the regular supply of water, the quality of the soil was usually better. As farming populations moved into the alluvial plains, the areas around the major rivers—the Euphrates, the Tigris, the Nile and the Yellow River—became centers of population.

The first major settlements in the Middle East were Jericho in the Jordan valley and Çatal Hüyük in central Turkey. In 9000 BC Jericho had begun to develop from a small settlement into a larger, more organized community. The site of the town was surrounded by a man-made ditch and a tall stone wall, in all possibility used for defense. The wall was interrupted by a large, circular stone tower, which may have acted as a watchtower. The existence of shrines, containing plaster statues, and decorated skulls, suggests that the town had both public and private buildings. Çatal Hüyük was a far larger site, covering thirty-two acres. Unlike Jericho, it was not surrounded by defensive structures, but was far more densely populated. The dwellings were so close together that entry into them was made through the roof. The inhabitants practiced pottery, basketwork, and weaving, and some objects suggest that it engaged in trade with societies in other places. As at Jericho, shrines were common, with some evidence that bulls were worshiped. During this time, neither Jericho nor Çatal Hüyük can be technically described as a center of civilization since they existed before the development of writing, considered one of the features of a civilized society. Çatal Hüyük had declined by 5000 BC, whereas Jericho grew slowly over several millennia, despite earthquakes and invasions, to become a city.

The discovery of "Peking Man" at Zhoukoudien near present-day Beijing proves that China had been inhabited by _Homo erectus_ since around 500,000 BC; however, the first agricultural communities date from 4000 BC. The late Neolithic peoples, the Lung-shan, lived in settlements and villages throughout the Yellow River area and the south-east. Although Chinese legend refers to a Xia dynasty, it wasn't until the second millennium BC that true civilization arrived with the emergence of the Shang Dynasty.

Mesoamerica
_c. 5000_ BCE

OLMECS
_c. 1200_ BCE

ATLANTIC OCEAN

CHAVIN
_c. 900_ BCE

Peru
_c. 4000_ BCE

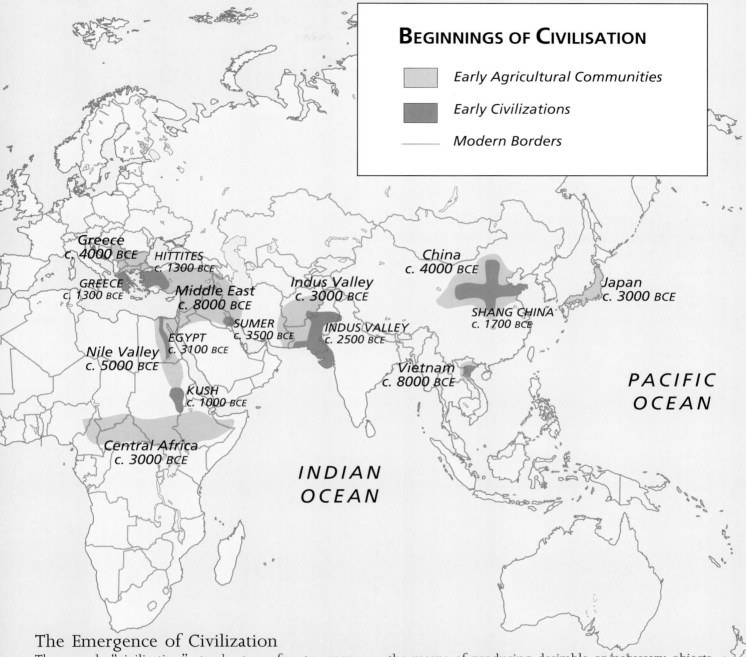

BEGINNINGS OF CIVILISATION

- Early Agricultural Communities
- Early Civilizations
- Modern Borders

Greece
c. 4000 BCE

HITTITES
c. 1300 BCE

GREECE
c. 1300 BCE

Middle East
c. 8000 BCE

China
c. 4000 BCE

Indus Valley
c. 3000 BCE

Japan
c. 3000 BCE

SHANG CHINA
c. 1700 BCE

SUMER
c. 3500 BCE

INDUS VALLEY
c. 2500 BCE

EGYPT
c. 3100 BCE

Nile Valley
c. 5000 BCE

KUSH
c. 1000 BCE

Vietnam
c. 8000 BCE

PACIFIC
OCEAN

Central Africa
c. 3000 BCE

INDIAN
OCEAN

The Emergence of Civilization

The word "civilization" tends to refer to more complex societies. In these, individuals began to belong to organized cultures with public bodies such as military forces and governing administrations, and with places of worship. People also began to be organized into a class system, where some members of society had more wealth, power and status than others. One development that hastened the onset of civilization was trade; the two technologies that were particularly important to the growth of trade during this period were metallurgy and pottery. Artisans with the means of producing desirable or necessary objects benefited in early barter economies. In addition to this, communities where agricultural productivity was particularly high tended to have an advantage over others. In some regions, the development of irrigation was a vital tool in ensuring a regularly high yield.

Crucially, civilization relies upon the development of both technology and a means of recording changes, rules, and rites—writing. The first true civilizations in the ancient world all demonstrate the beginning of writing systems.

Early Empires of Mesopotamia

Increasingly complex civilizations grew out of early city states between the Tigris and Euphrates Rivers, leaving written records behind them.

Mesopotamia

The melting of the ice sheets had caused global water levels to rise steadily, flooding a number of land bridges and changing the face of the planet. Much of the American coastline disappeared and the Bering Strait was created as the land bridge between Alaska and Asia was submerged. Britain was separated from Europe by the Atlantic, creating the North Sea and the English Channel. In approximately 5600 BC the waters of the Mediterranean burst through the land bridge joining Turkey to Bulgaria, creating the Bosporus and flooding and expanding the small freshwater lake to create the saltwater Black Sea.

This catastrophic event resulted in the displacement of huge numbers of people who had lived on the shores of the freshwater lake; many headed towards Egypt while others moved south toward the fertile lands between the rivers Euphrates and Tigris. It was in this area that the first collection of city states fully emerged. Mesopotamia is the name used for the area between the Euphrates and the Tigris in what is now Iraq. Farmers and fishermen, known as Sumerians, had already begun to settle in this region which, with its rich land watered by both rivers and their tributaries, provided enough food to sustain even larger populations. Gradually a number of cities grew up: as populations expanded, temples and monumental buildings were built and complex social systems developed. In particular, the world's first writing system—"cuneiform" script—was invented and used to record the flow of goods and products as trade flourished. Mesopotamia is now considered to be the first example of a true civilization: not one large city, but a region dominated by city states linked by common culture and commercial interests.

Sumer and Akkad

Two cultural groups made up the majority of the population of Mesopotamia before 2340 BC, the Sumerians and the Akkadians. The southern part of Mesopotamia was dominated by the Sumerians, who had probably migrated from Persia. These were a sophisticated people, who introduced the first writing system into the area, built up large centers of worship

Below: The famous ziggurat, a three-tiered edifice dating back to 2113 BC, stands more than 55ft. high in the ancient city of Ur in southern Iraq. The remains of the biblical birthplace of Abraham also lie at the archeological site.

Above: One of 300 Archaemenian clay tablets, in the Elamite scripts, which were written in cuneiform writing. The tablets record the workings of the Persian administration—including details such as the daily food rations given to workers—but perhaps more importantly they provide one of the few original sources of information on the Persian Empire from about 500 BC.

and introduced an irrigation technique that would ensure water supply in times of drought. The first Sumerian city was Uruk, which stood on the banks of the Euphrates from at least 3500 BC. It was dominated by a huge pyramid-shaped temple called a ziggurat, which was dedicated to their god, Anu. Situated in the heart of a religious complex, the ziggurat was entered by a staircase which only priests were permitted to climb. By the end of the fourth millennium BC, Uruk was the largest city in the world but others had begun to grow in its wake. The two other notable Sumerian cities were Eridu and Ur which, like Uruk, consisted of tightly packed mud and brick buildings surrounding a central ziggurat, each of which was dedicated to one of the gods in the Sumerian pantheon. The wealth of one of these city states was demonstrated by the discovery of a series of royal tombs. The burial site at Ur contained sixteen tombs, each containing precious possessions such as jewels, golden artefacts, musical instruments, ornate clothes, and cosmetics. Most

remarkable, however, was the large number of human remains found. Beside many were small chalices that may well have contained poison; these bodies are believed to be those of servants, soldiers, and harpists who were sacrificed in order to accompany the royal figures on their journey into the afterlife. The city states were separated from each other by uncultivated land which became a source of conflict as each city grew. During the period known as the Early Dynastic Age (2900–2340 BC) they were almost constantly at war or engaged in forming strategic alliances.

In 2340 BC, Sumer was conquered by Sargon, the ruler of the Akkad region to the north of Mesopotamia, and the warring states were brought under the control of one dynasty. The Akkadians had been a semi-nomadic people who had gradually begun to settle and build their own powerful communities. Sargad ruled from his capital, Agade, which is believed to have been close to the site of present-day Baghdad. Agade became the center of trade and administration in the region and the Semitic language, Akkadian, was adopted as the official language in preference to Sumerian. During the Third Dynasty (2112–2004 BC) power shifted back to the city of Ur under the rule of Ur-Nammu. However, this centralized empire only lasted until approximately 2000 BC, when internal rivalries and pressure from invading tribes forced its collapse.

The Origins of Writing

The most important development to emerge from Mesopotamian culture was the invention of writing. The earliest form of writing comes from Uruk, where clay tablets bearing pictographic script, dating from approximately 3300 BC, were used to record quantities of goods. Plain clay tokens had initially been used to count agricultural goods, but to keep a record of the number of tokens exchanged the Sumerians began to seal them up in clay containers, or envelopes. In order to show how many tokens were inside the envelopes, they impressed pictures of the tokens onto the clay with a wedge-shaped stylus. In time, they dispensed with the tokens and envelopes and used only the impressions on simple clay surfaces. The "word pictures" represented objects, such as "sheep" or "grains," and symbols to count the number of objects were developed. Gradually, the pictographs developed into cuneiform, a series of wedge-shaped signs that consisted of ideographs (ideas as well as objects) and phonograms (representing sounds.) Once this system of writing had been invented it was used for many more purposes, such as recording events and myths. The Sumerian writing system was adopted and adapted by the Akkadians and later by the Babylonians. Although the spoken language had died out by 2000 BC, Sumerian cuneiform became the language of scholarship and was used by the scribal élite. Other civilized cultures, such as the Egyptians, and the Minoans on Crete, developed their own writing systems, though they may well have been influenced by the Mesopotamian tradition. Eventually alphabetic systems were developed by all these cultures and in time the alphabet adopted by the Greeks became the ancestor of all modern European script.

Babylonia

The appearance of written texts greatly helps the understanding of periods after the Early Dynastic Age, in particular the rise and fall in fortunes of various kingdoms, rulers, and empires. In 2004 BC, the fall of the city of Ur marked the end of the Early Dynastic Period and a new age began, referred to as the Old Babylonian. For the next 400 years, a series of rival dynasties, each ruling over the cities of the region—Babylon, Ashur, Mari, Larsa, and Isin—would struggle for control over the entire Mesopotamian region. These dynasties were all of Amorite descent, Semitic tribes that had settled in Mesopotamia during the third millennium BC. The two most important Amorite kingdoms were Babylon and Assyria. Assyria rose to power under the leadership of Shamshi-Adad I (1813–1781 BC) who, building upon strong trading links to the north with Anatolia, created the most powerful state in Mesopotamia. With Assyria's gradual decline, the city state of Babylon to the south began to rise under the reign of Hammurabi (1792–1750 BC), a scholarly ruler. Hammurabi is famed for his series of law codes, a range of regulations which dealt with topics as varied as the fixed prices of agricultural goods and punishments designed to fit specific crimes. One of these punishments was the river ordeal, where the accused was required to swim underwater for a designated distance; survival meant vindication. Hammurabi's reign also saw the introduction of many new forms of science and learning, such as astronomy and mathematics. This included a numbering system based on groups of sixty, from where we now get the sixty-minute hour and the 360-degree circle.

The division of Mesopotamia into Assyria in the north and Babylonia in the south was not permanent.

Babylonian society was gradually assimilated into the wealthier Assyrian culture, although sophisticated Babylonian culture dominated. In 1595 BC, this early Babylonian period came to an end when the city was sacked by the Hittites, a powerful people who had emerged from Anatolia.

The Hittites

The Indo-European Hittites had been based in Hattusa in central Anatolia, a harsh, mountainous region. A warlike people, the Hittites gradually built up an extensive kingdom which dominated the whole of the

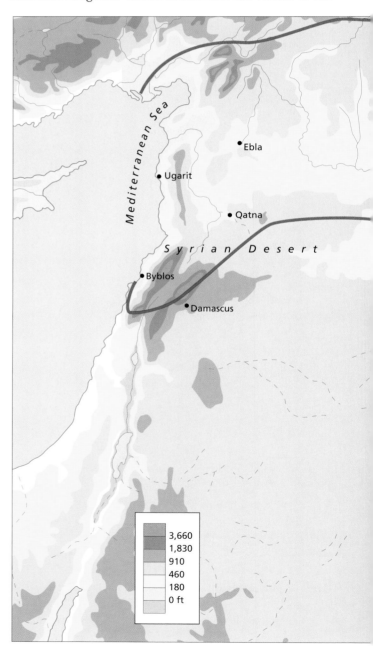

northern Mediterranean region and even threatened Egypt. They created a powerful army and were the first to make effective use of horses, using the horse-drawn chariot as a means of attack. Between 1650 and 1200 BC, the Hittite empire was built around one central ruler or "Great King," who led his troops into battle. As their territory increased, the Hittites developed a system of client kings, leaders who would have been bound to the Great King by loyalty, often cemented by marriage. At times, loyalty would give way to rivalry. A period of instability occurred during the thirteenth century BC, and in 1200 BC the Hittite

kingdom finally collapsed, perhaps as a result of the constant struggles on their main borders—with the Sea Peoples along the coast, the Egyptians in the south-west and the Assyrians to the south.

The Decline of Mesopotamia

Despite their problems with the Hittites, the Assyrians were the most feared people in the region. They conquered territories, sacked towns and massacred their inhabitants; they also built beautiful cities such as Nineveh in the north and their capital Ashur, on the Tigris. In 1224 BC they took control of Babylon away

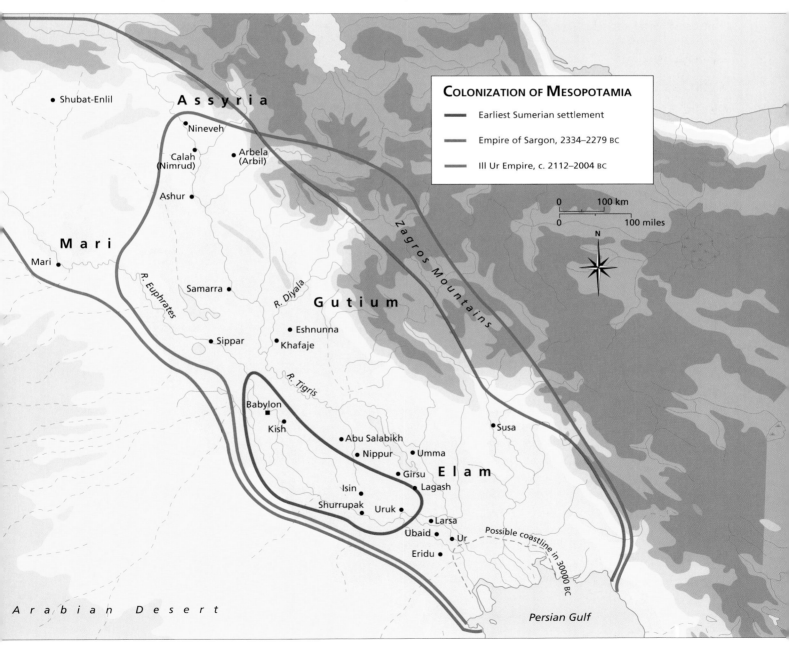

COLONIZATION OF MESOPOTAMIA

— Earliest Sumerian settlement

— Empire of Sargon, 2334–2279 BC

— III Ur Empire, c. 2112–2004 BC

from the Kassites, who had ruled over it since its destruction in 1595 BC. Yet the Assyrian Empire, like the many empires that would follow, became too large to be effectively defended. Despite the might of its army, the constant attacks from nomadic and tribal groups on its borders weakened it and it struggled to maintain control. At its height, the Assyrian Empire stretched from the Mediterranean across to Iran and from the Persian Gulf up to Anatolia. However, in 612 BC, Ashur and Nineveh had been destroyed and the Medians and Babylonians had risen up, claiming independence. In 609 BC the Babylonians, led by Nabopolassar, defeated the Assyrians and destroyed the empire. They reconstructed Babylon and held off the armies of Egypt and Judea to restore Babylonia's

Above: Part of the Ishtar gate in the ancient city of Babylon, 60 miles south of Baghdad. This gate is a reproduction, the original being at the Pergamon Museum in Berlin.
Opposite: Palace ruins at Knossos, Crete. The site is the largest of the preserved Minoan palaces and was excavated and restored by Sir Arthur Evans between 1900 and 1930.

former glory. The Neo-Babylonian Dynasty was led by Nebuchadnezzar (604–562 BC), who was famed for his hanging gardens. In 597 BC, Nebuchadnezzar took the city of Jerusalem by force. In just sixty years, however, the short-lived Babylonian empire had crumbled. It was taken over by the Persians as they began their conquest of Mesopotamia. With the rise of the Persian Empire, the old order had come to a finish.

Early Civilizations

Mesopotamia was the first but not the only civilization to emerge in the ancient world. The northern reaches of the River Nile provided the perfect agricultural conditions for the development of settlements, small towns and eventually cities which would unify in 3100 BC under King Menes of Egypt. Egypt had been colonized by farmers since at least 7000 BC and there is evidence of copperworking from the fourth millennium BC. Its proximity to Mesopotamia ensured regular trade which, combined with the fertility of the soil, resulted in the development of Egyptian civilization.

The River Indus, in modern-day Pakistan, was the setting for the first great cities south of the Himalayan mountain range. In approximately 3500 BC farmers began to settle, and within a thousand years the great cities of Mohenjo-Daro and Harappa had been built. The people of the Indus valley, like the Mesopotamians with whom they traded, had developed a written script and a system of worship. This first Indian civilization was eventually destroyed by the invading Aryan people from the west in 1500 BC.

Civilization in China developed completely independently from the rest of the world, from which it was separated by the impenetrable Himalayas. Various technological developments such as metallurgy and writing were invented by the Shang people without any outside influence, creating a distinctive culture.

The first great European civilization was centered in Greece, where proximity to the Mediter-ranean and the Aegean proved to be important to the growth of a self-sustaining society. On the island of Crete the first culture to develop was the Minoan, whose people had probably arrived by sea from the Greek mainland in around 6000 BC. The Minoans built a huge palace at Knossos which contained a number of religious shrines and statues; their culture was at its strongest during the middle of the second millennium BC. However, the eruption of the volcano on nearby Thera and the invasion of the Mycenaeans marked the end of Minoan civilization.

Like their neighbors the Greeks, the Etruscans in Italy profited from the sea and the richness of their land, not only for agriculture but also for mining. Although Etruscan civilization began much later, in 800 BC, its arrival does show the gradual spread of civilized societies across Europe.

On the American continent, civilization as such developed much later; the Olmecs were the first to build significant cities in Mesoamerica in around 1200 BC. All of these early civilizations and more will be explored at greater length in the following chapters.

Ancient Egypt

Undoubtedly one of the greatest civilizations in the world, Ancient Egypt's complexity and sophistication developed and existed for thousands of years.

The Land of the Nile

Ancient Egypt was the first substantial centrally administered state in the world, something brought about largely by its situation. The River Nile made it possible to achieve high agricultural productivity and hence support a large population. In addition the river's seasonal floods necessitated cooperation in order for communities to benefit from the increased fertility the flood waters brought. Navigating the river was also easy; people could sail along it in both directions with a minimum of effort, facilitating contacts, communication, and trade. From the very earliest period, the Nile was critical to the development of civilization in Egypt.

This civilization lasted for thousands of years, and in order to understand and describe it, a chronology has been developed. One of the main sources of this came from an Egyptian priest, Manetho, who provided a chronicle of Egyptian rulers—the pharaohs—dividing them into thirty-one dynasties. These have since been divided into major historical periods beginning in about 3100 BC, when a king believed to be called Narmer or Menes united the region of the Nile delta (Lower Egypt) and the river valley (Upper Egypt), establishing a capital at Memphis and founding the First Dynasty.

Early Dynastic Egypt and the Old Kingdom

The First and Second Dynasties are collectively known as the Early Dynastic Period and lasted until 2686 BC. The king was established as an absolute ruler, and was associated with the god Horus and the sun god Re. During this time royal tombs were surrounded by subsidiary tombs; these were for sacrificed individuals, so that they could continue to serve the king in the afterlife. However, by the end of the Second Dynasty, this practice had been abandoned and models of servants were used instead.

The Old Kingdom followed from 2686 to 2181 BC, and marked the first of Egypt's great ages; it was a period of great political and social stability, and dynasties changed without conflict. It was during this time that remarkable monuments such as the Great Pyramid at Giza were built. The pharaoh's divine authority increased and officials, who were normally family members, carried out legal and political duties. Taxes and records were kept by the vizier, and massive amounts of labor and resources were used to build the pyramids. Quite apart from workers, specialist craftsmen and artisans were involved in creating the tombs and making the objects to be placed inside. At this time it has been estimated that peasants made up about 80 percent of the population, working the land to provide food for the higher classes through a form of taxation. A religious structure began to emerge as the priesthoods tried to rationalize the multitude of different gods, with cities becoming religious centers for specific gods. The Old Kingdom came to an end after the death of King Pepi II; after acceding to the throne at the age of six, he is believed to have reigned for ninety-four years. As the Sixth Dynasty came to an end with his death, society swiftly began to collapse and the centralized political and economic structure disintegrated.

During the First Intermediate Period that followed, from 2181 to 2055 BC, the government at Memphis was overthrown and a period of anarchy and fighting ensued.

The Middle Kingdom

After a contest between dynasties in the north and south, Mentuhtep II finally emerged as leader to create the Middle Kingdom which lasted from 2055 to 1795 BC, another period of stability. The royal residence was now at Thebes in Upper Egypt, which began to establish itself as one of Egypt's great cities. Amenemes I then seized the throne but as his claim was questionable, he put in place measures to strengthen his position. He began the system of co-regency, putting his son and heir on the throne with him, which meant that his son Sesostris I was able to successfully inherit the title on his death. He also gave greater power to the provincial nobility to ensure their support. A later ruler, Sesostris III, created a new middle class consisting of farmers, craftsmen, and tradesmen and organized the administration so that officials reported to the vizier and the king. A series of

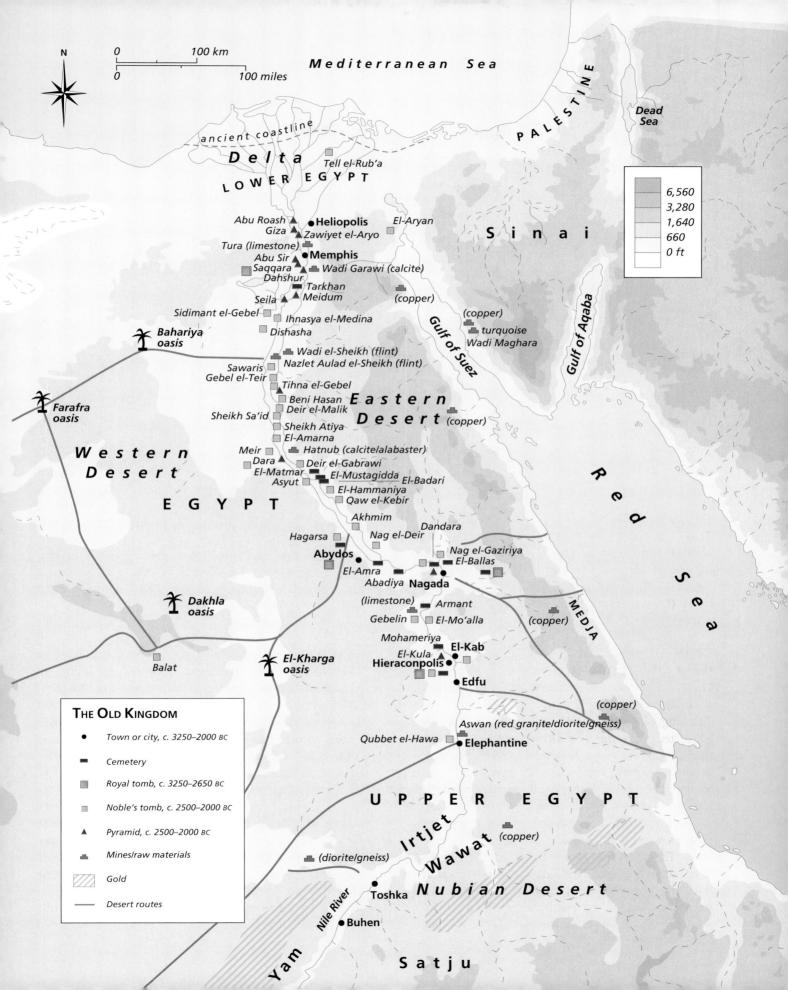

N

0   100 km
0   100 miles

Mediterranean Sea

PALESTINE

Dead Sea

ancient coastline

Delta
LOWER EGYPT

Tell el-Rub'a

	6,560
	3,280
	1,640
	660
	0 ft

S i n a i

Abu Roash   ● **Heliopolis**   *El-Aryan*
Giza   ▲ Zawiyet el-Aryo
Tura (limestone)
Abu Sir   ● **Memphis**
Saqqara   Wadi Garawi (calcite)
Dahshur
               Tarkhan
Seila   ▲ Meidum   (copper)

Gulf of Aqaba

(copper)
turquoise
Wadi Maghara

Gulf of Suez

Sidimant el-Gebel   Ihnasya el-Medina
                         Dishasha
Bahariya oasis

Wadi el-Sheikh (flint)
Nazlet Aulad el-Sheikh (flint)
Sawaris
Gebel el-Teir
Tihna el-Gebel

Farafra oasis

Beni Hasan   *Eastern*
Deir el-Malik   *Desert*
Sheikh Sa'id   (copper)
Sheikh Atiya
El-Amarna

Western Desert

Meir   Hatnub (calcite/alabaster)
Dara
El-Matmar   Deir el-Gabrawi
Asyut   El-Mustagidda
         El-Badari
E G Y P T
         El-Hammaniya
         Qaw el-Kebir

Akhmim

Hagarsa   Nag el-Deir   Dandara
Abydos   Nag el-Gaziriya
         El-Amra   El-Ballas
         Abadiya   **Nagada**

Dakhla oasis

(limestone)   Armant
Gebelin   El-Mo'alla   (copper)

Mohameriya
El-Kula   **El-Kab**
El-Kharga oasis   **Hieraconpolis**
                       ● **Edfu**

R e d   S e a

MEDJA

(copper)

Balat

Aswan (red granite/diorite/gneiss)

Qubbet el-Hawa   ● **Elephantine**

U P P E R   E G Y P T

Irtjet   (copper)

Wawat

THE OLD KINGDOM

● Town or city, c. 3250–2000 BC

▬ Cemetery

▢ Royal tomb, c. 3250–2650 BC

▫ Noble's tomb, c. 2500–2000 BC

▲ Pyramid, c. 2500–2000 BC

⬛ Mines/raw materials

▨ Gold

— Desert routes

(diorite/gneiss)

Nile River
● **Toshka**   *Nubian Desert*

● **Buhen**

Yam   *S a t j u*

Above: Tombs of Old Kingdom pharaohs, the pyramids at Giza were designed to both impress and provide a lasting memorial.
Opposite: Tutankhamun's burial mask is composed of gold, glass, and precious stones.

long reigns helped economic and artistic progress during this era. The religious center remained at Thebes but the political capital was based at It-towy. Hieroglyphics—the Egyptian pictographic writing system—emerged in their classic form during this time and levels of literacy flourished. However, the period was to end in decline.

The Second Intermediate Period, from 1795 to 1550 BC, was again marked by weak rulers and the decentralization of political power. This allowed foreigners known as the Hyksos to enter the country and rule for part of the time, and the capital was moved to the Nile delta. However, technology flourished; new building techniques were developed as were new ways of making weapons, and the horse and chariot were introduced. Relations between the

Egyptians and the Hyksos deteriorated towards the end, and the Hyksos were finally overthrown by Amosis I. This period had made the Egyptians realize that they were vulnerable to invasion and hence would need a professional army; it also gave them the opportunity for trade to develop with other areas.

The New Kingdom

Amosis I was to found the New Kingdom, which lasted from 1550 to 1069 BC. The capital city was now Thebes and Amun-Re became the royal god. During this time the Egyptians were to enjoy military success in Asia, returning with valuable gains and many prisoners of war, who were employed at the temples; the foundations of the Egyptian Empire had been laid. Much is known about the pharaohs of the New

Kingdom, who included Hatshepsut, probably the first female ruler in history. Her reign was peaceful and she was known to have delegated much of her power to her chief minister, Senemut. Her stepson Tuthmosis III succeeded her. He was the pharaoh with the greatest record of conquests; after waging war in the Levant, he seized hundreds of cities and the wealth brought back to Egypt began a century of great prosperity and peace. Later, Amenhotep IV brought many changes. He took a new name—Akhenaten—and founded a new capital, Akhetaten, at Amarna, along the Nile and well away from Thebes. He introduced a new religious belief, swearing allegiance to the god Aten, the disk of the sun, alone and thereby rejecting the previously all-powerful Amun, as well as the whole panoply of Egyptian gods. Rival cults were abolished; the temples of Amun were closed and their great wealth was taken away. Akhenaten is believed to have been the first monotheist, and can be viewed as being excessively fanatical. After his death, the country reverted back to previous traditions and forms of worship, and Akhenaten's capital was abandoned. He was followed soon after by the very young Tutankhamun; his reign was uneventful—he rose to fame posthumously, with the discovery of his intact tomb in 1922. In 1295 BC Ramesses I came to the throne, the first of the Ramessides, generally seen as the mightiest and most authoritative of all pharaohs. However, towards the end of the New Kingdom, weaknesses began to show and the country once again broke into two parts.

The Third Intermediate Period lasted from 1069 to 747 BC, with no single pharaoh actually ruling over the entire country. It appears that dynasties overlapped, both regionally and chronologically. Finally in 747 BC, the Nubian king, Piankhi, united the north and south.

The Late and the Greco-Roman Periods

This began the Late Period, which lasted from 747 to 332 BC. The Nubian pharaohs successfully restored order and a minor religious adjustment allowed the king's daughter to take the position of God's Wife of Amun. The Assyrians, however, threatened stability, repeatedly invading Egypt, and finally sacking Thebes in 664 BC. The country

was then under Assyrian rule until 653 BC, when Psammetichus I gradually reunited it. He used Greek mercenaries to strengthen the army and other foreigners, bringing new commercial and craft skills, were encouraged to settle. Necho came to power in 610 BC; he established the first Egyptian navy and began to cut into the land between the Nile and the Red Sea to make a canal. In 525 BC the Persians invaded and overthrew Psammetichus III. After many revolts and much infighting between dynasties, Egypt was able to regain independence at the end of the fifth century BC. Persia again invaded in 343 BC killing Nectanebo II, the last Egyptian king of Egypt. Persian rule lasted for just over a decade this time.

The Greco-Roman Period began in 332 BC. Philip II of Macedon had been assassinated in 336 BC and his son Alexander had inherited his throne. Between 334 and 332 BC he successfully drove the Persians out of Asia Minor and conquered the eastern

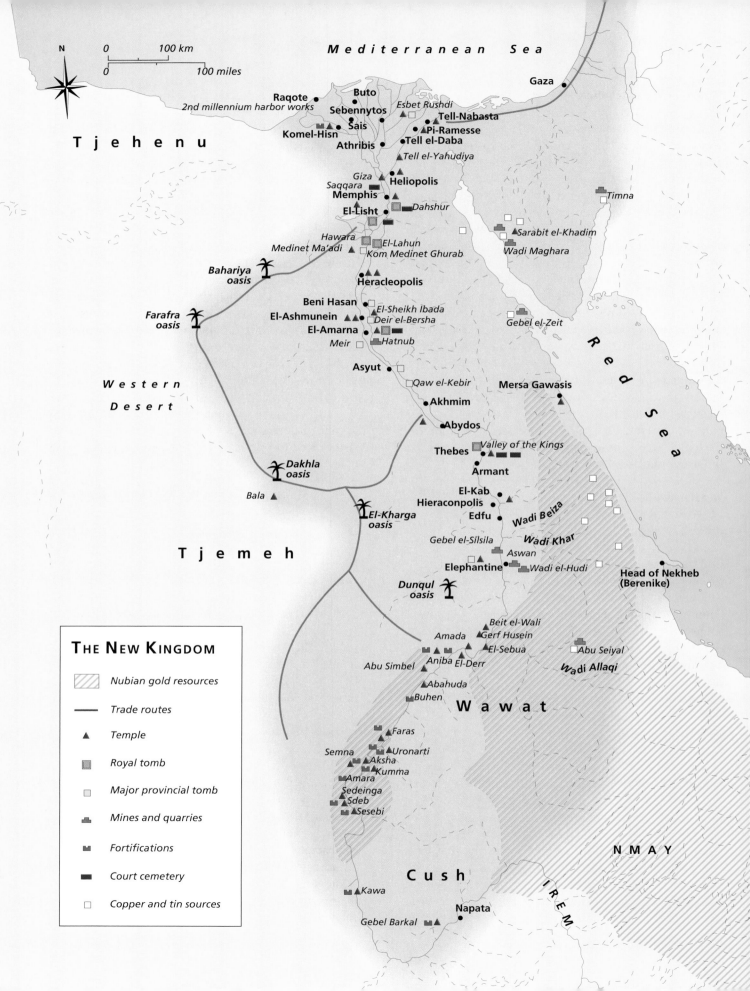

N

0   100 km

0   100 miles

Mediterranean Sea

Gaza

Raqote

2nd millennium harbor works

Buto

Sebennytos   *Esbet Rushdi*

Tell-Nabasta

Sais   **Pi-Ramesse**

Komel-Hisn

Athribis   **Tell el-Daba**

Tell el-Yahudiya

T j e h e n u

Giza

Saqqara   **Heliopolis**

Memphis

El-Lisht   *Dahshur*

Timna

Hawara

Medinet Ma'adi   *El-Lahun*

Kom Medinet Ghurab

Sarabit el-Khadim

Wadi Maghara

Bahariya oasis

Heracleopolis

Beni Hasan   *El-Sheikh Ibada*

El-Ashmunein   *Deir el-Bersha*

Farafra oasis

El-Amarna

Meir   *Hatnub*

Gebel el-Zeit

Asyut

Qaw el-Kebir

Mersa Gawasis

W e s t e r n
D e s e r t

Akhmim

Abydos

Thebes   *Valley of the Kings*

Dakhla oasis

Armant

Bala

El-Kab

Hieraconpolis

Edfu   *Wadi Beiza*

R e d   S e a

El-Kharga oasis

Gebel el-Silsila   *Wadi Khar*

T j e m e h

Aswan

Elephantine   *Wadi el-Hudi*

Head of Nekheb
(Berenike)

Dunqul oasis

Beit el-Wali

Amada   *Gerf Husein*

El-Sebua   *Abu Seiyal*

Abu Simbel   *Aniba*   *El-Derr*

Wadi Allaqi

Abahuda

Buhen   **W a w a t**

Faras

Semna   *Uronarti*

Aksha

Kumma

Amara

Sedeinga

Sdeb

Sesebi

N M A Y

C u s h

Kawa

Napata

Gebel Barkal

I R E M

T H E   N E W   K I N G D O M

Nubian gold resources

Trade routes

▲ *Temple*

▣ *Royal tomb*

▫ *Major provincial tomb*

⬒ *Mines and quarries*

⬓ *Fortifications*

▬ *Court cemetery*

▫ *Copper and tin sources*

Mediterranean. He entered Egypt in 332 BC, where the resident governor quickly surrendered and Alexander was welcomed as a liberator. He was determined to establish his right to rule and traveled to the oracle of Amun in the Libyan desert where he was acknowledged as the son of Amun, and therefore the rightful king. After being crowned at Memphis he put plans into place to repair the temples destroyed by the Persians and founded Alexandria, his twin-harbored capital. He left Egypt after six months and died in Babylon in 323 BC.

After his death his generals held the real power. One of them, Ptolemy, ruled in Egypt and created a culture that welcomed immigrants and encouraged the new Greek-speaking aristocracy; Egypt became integrated into the mainly Greek culture prevalent in both the eastern Mediterranean and the Near East. Alexandria continued to thrive and the first lighthouse was built; gradually cities that were Hellenistic in character began to emerged. In deference to Egyptian culture, the Ptolemies ruled as pharaohs and embraced the culture of brother–sister marriage, continuing to build temples for the gods.

As Roman power grew, Egyptian culture weakened. Cleopatra ruled from 51 to 30 BC and by 36 BC she was openly living with Mark Antony, who ruled the eastern part of the Roman world. Julius Caesar's nephew Octavian ruled the western part and, in 31 BC, had an overwhelming victory in battle against Antony and Cleopatra. Octavian entered Alexandria in the following year and both Antony and Cleopatra committed suicide. In 27 BC Octavian took the title of Augustus and became the first Roman Emperor. Egypt did not become part of the Roman Empire but belonged to Augustus himself, and was bequeathed to his successors. The country continued to prosper but retained the now-dominant Greek culture.

Pyramids and Tombs

A fundamental part of Egyptian life was an absolute belief in the afterlife. As the body was believed to continue to exist on earth, it was vital that an eternal place for its accommodation was created.

Djoser constructed a large funerary monument at Saqqara in 2650 BC, which featured the first stepped pyramid. At nearly 200 ft. high, it was the first large stone building in history, built by his chief minister, Imhotep. Taking eighteen years to build, it had six levels and covered a burial chamber that was lined with red and black granite, situated at the bottom of

a 90-foot shaft. A hundred years later, the first true pyramids were constructed, with huge stone slabs creating straight sides. These were built by the pharaoh Sneferu, the first being at Meidum.

The three most spectacular structures were built by his son Khufu and sited at Giza. The Great Pyramid, his own tomb, was over 640 ft. high and covered in white limestone, designed to shimmer in the sun. It consisted of over two million stone blocks, each weighing 2.5 tons. The entrance was hidden from the outside; inside was a complicated network of corridors and shafts, culminating in the Grand Gallery which led to the King's Chamber where his stone sarcophagus was placed. The other two, slightly smaller, pyramids were built for his son Khafre and his grandson, Menkaure. Each pyramid was surrounded by tombs and temples and had a mortuary temple where daily offerings were made to the dead king. Khafre's tomb was guarded by the Great Sphinx, which was carved from limestone. This was not fully uncovered until 1925; fortunately the sand that covered it helped preserve the structure. It is believed to be a portrait of the king with the body of a lion.

The dead pharaoh's body would be mummified to enable the spirits to recognize it in the afterlife. The brain was removed through the nose and the main organs of the body were taken out and preserved in special jars. Following this, the heart was replaced and the body was then packed with linen and treated with natron—a mineral salt—to dry out completely. It was then cleaned and wrapped in linen strips. The last ritual, the Opening of the Mouth, involved the priests, dressed as gods, touching the dead pharaoh to give him back his powers of speech and allowing him to eat and drink in the afterlife. When the body was placed in the tomb it was judged against forty-two crimes; those that passed went to live in the underworld with the god Osiris. Those weighed down by sin were devoured by monsters; their souls then truly died.

The pharaohs of the New Kingdom chose to be more discreet in their choice of burial chambers and cut into the rock of the place which became known as the Valley of the Kings, partly to avoid the danger of looters. A total of sixty-two tombs were created here for the pharaohs of the Eighteenth to Twentieth Dynasties, and many hundreds more were dug into the surrounding hills for craftsmen and noblemen. Many of the inscriptions found in these tombs have provided historical information on the lives of those placed there.

Above: The Great Sphinx with the pyramids at Giza in the background. Opposite: A statue of the pharaoh Rameses II at the entrance to the Temple of Luxor.

One of the most famous tombs is that built for the young king Tutankhamun. The others had been looted long ago, but his survived intact—the entrance had been hidden by building rubble—until discovered by Howard Carter in 1922. In total about 3,500 items, many in precious metals, were found in the tomb providing an amazing insight into Egyptian life at the time of Tutankhamun's death.

Gods and Goddesses

Huge resources were used to build temples to honor the gods and ensure that peace and harmony prevailed. They were surrounded by vast estates and provided homes for the priests, officials, and workers. The temples were not centers of communal worship but houses for specific gods. It was believed that as long as wealth and attention was lavished on the gods then the country would continue to prosper.

The Egyptians worshiped many different gods and goddesses who were depicted in many different forms, having a variety of different attributes. They were originally associated with specific events, but over the years beliefs changed; a classic example of this is the increased importance of Amun during the Middle and New Kingdoms. The gods were also grouped into specific families: for example, Shu and Tefnut gave birth to Nut, the sky goddess and Geb, the earth god. They in turn gave birth to Osiris, Isis, Seth, and Nepthys. The sun god was to play a central role throughout Egyptian history. As Re, the sun was already a focal point by the Second Dynasty and by the Fifth Dynasty had evolved to be the supreme state god and closely linked to the pharaoh—who took the title "Son of Re." By the time of the New Kingdom, Re was joined to a Theban god called Amun and became Amun-Re.

Some gods had specific roles, such as Osiris—depicted as a mummified man wearing an Egyptian crown—who was king of the dead and judge of the underworld. He was worshiped at Abydos and it was believed that every king would become Osiris after death. The king's successor then embodied Horus, who took the form of a man with the head of a hawk and was worshiped at Edfu. The Egyptians believed that Osiris had been murdered by his brother Seth, and that Horus had fought Seth for the throne of Egypt. In the battle Horus lost an eye, which was eventually restored to him. The eye subsequently became a popular symbol of protection.

There were also many other gods who were worshiped by ordinary Egyptians in their own homes. Images of the gods were believed to have supernatural powers and many people wore amulets for protection. The number of Egyptian gods was vast as they evolved over thousands of years, but belief in their divine power was an essential part of Egyptian life.

Daily Life in Egypt

Most of the information gained about Egyptian social life has come from wall paintings and inscriptions found in tombs. Famous archeological sites such as Akhenaten's city at Amarna have also cast light on the organization and structure of society. Houses in this city tended to have three main rooms and cellars for storage with some of the grander homes having bathrooms. Textiles decorated the rooms and simple oil lamps were used for lighting.

The Egyptians had established a legal system using courts and magistrates, and also had a type of police force. The schools that existed were for training scribes and officials destined for the priesthood or civil administration; ordinary people would be educated at home. It would take a scribe about twelve years to learn the system of hieroglyphs and others would pay for the scribe's services should they need something written down. Skills were handed down within families and an apprenticeship system existed for craftsmen. There were highly skilled sculptors and carpenters, and the Egyptians also specialized in metalwork, jewelry, and glassware. The linen that was produced was of exceptionally high quality and it is estimated that a shawl found in Tutankhamun's tomb must have taken about nine months to weave. Most people worked on the land and were then conscripted to work on irrigation or royal building projects; none were slaves—they all had their own legal rights. In the markets, trade was done by bartering; a monetary system was never established.

The Egyptian family was extremely important, and there were often marriages between cousins; there was no ceremony, just a private legal agreement giving the husband and wife equality with regard to possessions. The staple diet was bread, with fruit and vegetables, often accompanied by beer or wine. Meat tended to be eaten on feast days, as it was so difficult to keep in the hot climate. Simple tunics were woven from linen with jewelry and cosmetics used by both men and women.

The Legacy of Ancient Egypt

Many ideas that existed in Ancient Egypt spread across Europe, were used by the Romans and Greeks, and still exist today. For example, the Ancient Egyptian calendar was used by the Romans and formed the basis of the Gregorian calendar. Its history continues to inspire art and literature and some of the construction methods used still remain a mystery. Whether Ancient Egypt's influence in modern society is obvious or invisible, it was nonetheless one of the greatest civilizations that has ever existed.

The First Chinese Dynasties

The earliest Chinese dynasties presided over a world of growing sophistication, with the full development of a complex writing system and the growth of Confucianism.

The Shang Dynasty

China had been inhabited by humans for thousands of years; however, the first documented dynastic culture is that of the Shang. During the Neolithic Period different groups lived along the vast area of the Yellow River plains under the influence of the Shang kings. Dating from approximately 1523 BC, the Shang was a powerful and politically organized regime whose influence dominated northern China. Although they were probably concentrated in village settlements, the Shang set up some of the first cities in China, in particular their two capitals at Cheng-chou and An-yang. They ruled in city states which were then dominated by a capital city. The capital was never fixed; as power shifted, changing city states became the capital. The king had the same functions as in other cultures: he was a head priest, leader of the military aristocracy, and in charge of the economy. Warfare was very common among the Shang. At times the cities would battle one another, but on the whole aggression was directed at the populations in the north.

The Shang were more civilized than the non-Chinese tribes to the north. They had sophisticated methods of producing bronzework, using clay molds to form elaborate metalwork with molten bronze. Craftsmen also used materials such as jade, clay, and silk to make tools, ornaments and clothing, and trade with other regions in China is evident. They worshiped a god they called Shang-Ti, who ruled over the sun, the moon, the wind, the rain, and other natural forces. Shang-Ti also regulated human affairs. The Shang strongly believed that their ancestors ascended to heaven after death, and ancestor worship became part of their religious ritual. Part of this ritual included human sacrifice, in particular of slaves and prisoners. The most important aspect of Shang culture was the invention of writing, which occurs on oracle bones used for divination.

The Zhou Dynasty

In approximately 1028 BC, the Shang were conquered by the Zhou people from the Wei River valley region in the north-west. The Zhou had originally been vassals of the Shang but, by building allegiances with other disaffected states, they eventually became the stronger power. The Zhou believed in a "mandate from heaven," by which they claimed that any family that was morally worthy might rule; by being defeated the Shang were no longer worthy of the mandate. The Zhou extended the region won by the Shang, reaching down into the middle basin of the Yangtze. Although the Zhou adopted many of the Shang's rituals and administrative systems, they were the first feudal society. The Zhou state was divided into domains, with the royal domains being possessed by the king. The other domains belonged to members of the Zhou aristocracy or were awarded as recognition of service to powerful Zhou families, and the Shang royal family were removed to a domain in the east. Although these domains were originally fiefdoms, over time they grew in power until they were effectively minor kingdoms.

The Zhou kings remained powerful until 770 BC, when they were forced to move eastwards due to attacks from barbarians in the north. The capital was moved to Lo-yang and the central monarchy gradually lost authority to the feudal lords who had come to realize the earthly weakness of the emperor. Between 475 and 221 BC a series of powerful warlords struggled for supremacy in a period known as the Warring States. Despite this instability, Zhou culture continued to flourish and this period is also known as the first Classical Age in Chinese history. Confucianism, Taoism and Legalism were all developed during this period. The Zhou Dynasty which had lasted for 900 years was finally destroyed in 221 BC when the feudal state of Qin triumphed over its enemies and became the first dynasty to unify China.

Confucius and Philosophy

Born around 550 BC, Confucius was a political philosopher and statesman who argued for reform during the insecure period of the Warring States. In 501 BC he was appointed Governor of Chengdu, later becoming the Minister for Justice. His teachings were a guide for a more moral form of statecraft that required a defined social system, and because he stressed social reform he was idolized by the people. He soon became an enemy of many in power and was forced to leave his home, resulting in his traveling across Zhou China followed by a number of disciples. Confucianism taught the importance of obedience within the family and brotherly respect, which was extended into a wider humanist idea. This was in direct opposition to the philosophy of Taoism, which called for a return to primitive social orders and rejecting the material world. Although Legalism, which stressed obedience to the state's ruler, was initially more popular in Zhou China, Confucianism became the dominant philosophy by the second century BC.

Early Chinese Writing

The inscriptions found on the Shang oracle bones are the earliest discovered forms of Chinese writing. The bones themselves tended to be either animal bones or turtle shells which had been highly polished. A diviner would then scrape furrows into the bone and inscribe a question. The bone would then be fired and the diviner would interpret the resulting cracks. The date would then be carved onto the bone, as would the outcome of the original question. The writing itself was pictographic, with words represented by pictures that resembled their meaning. The next stage in Chinese writing came with inscriptions on bronze, which were either carved or cast into bronze vessels. The vessels were used mainly for ritual purposes and were used in both the late Shang period and the Zhou. From the fifth century BC, characters began to be written with brush and ink, usually on wood, bamboo, and silk. As well as being pictographic, the written characters had also become ideological. With the change of the media used for writing came a change in the uses of script, and by the late Zhou period writing was used to record history, philosophy, and literature.

Below: A wine vessel called a gong, dating from the Shang Dynasty, which was found in the tomb of a noblewoman.

The Early Americans

The rich diversity of early cultures in the Americas ranges from the semi-nomadic hunter-gatherers to the sophisticated, complex civilizations developed in Mesoamerica.

Mesoamerican Civilizations— the Olmecs

Early man first entered the Americas before 20,000 BC, and over thousands of years semi-nomadic tribes spread right across the continent. Gradually, with the beginnings of land cultivation, groups began to settle and by the last millennia BC villages became towns and civilizations were built up.

The first "civilization" on the American continent was that of the Olmec people. They were concentrated in the region that is now covered by south central Mexico and their major cities were San Lorenzo, La Venta, and Tres Zapotes. Olmec culture was at its height between 1200 and 600 BC, and many of the features of their civilization contributed to the later Mesoamerican and Andean civilizations that followed. The Olmecs were the first to build large ceremonial mounds and temple complexes from where they could worship their gods. Their religious ceremonies were often focused on human sacrifice, a practice that continued. They also created massive stone heads as monumental sculptures.

In engineering, the Olmecs were particularly successful at cultivating the land for the maize crop that dominated the region. They built large lagoons and reservoirs for agricultural purposes and to drain the swampy regions of the fertile area that they inhabited. Olmec society was clearly divided into hierarchies, with a priesthood, an administrative class, and a manufacturing class who produced many of the fine Olmec crafts and goods. The Olmecs were also the first Mesoamericans to devise a form of writing, based on hieroglyphs, which was adopted by their successors. Their culture died out for unknown reasons in around 600 BC and they were succeeded by

Below: The Pyramid of the Sun at Teotihuacan. Teotihuacan was first settled around the time of Christ and quickly became one of the largest centers of population in the "New World."

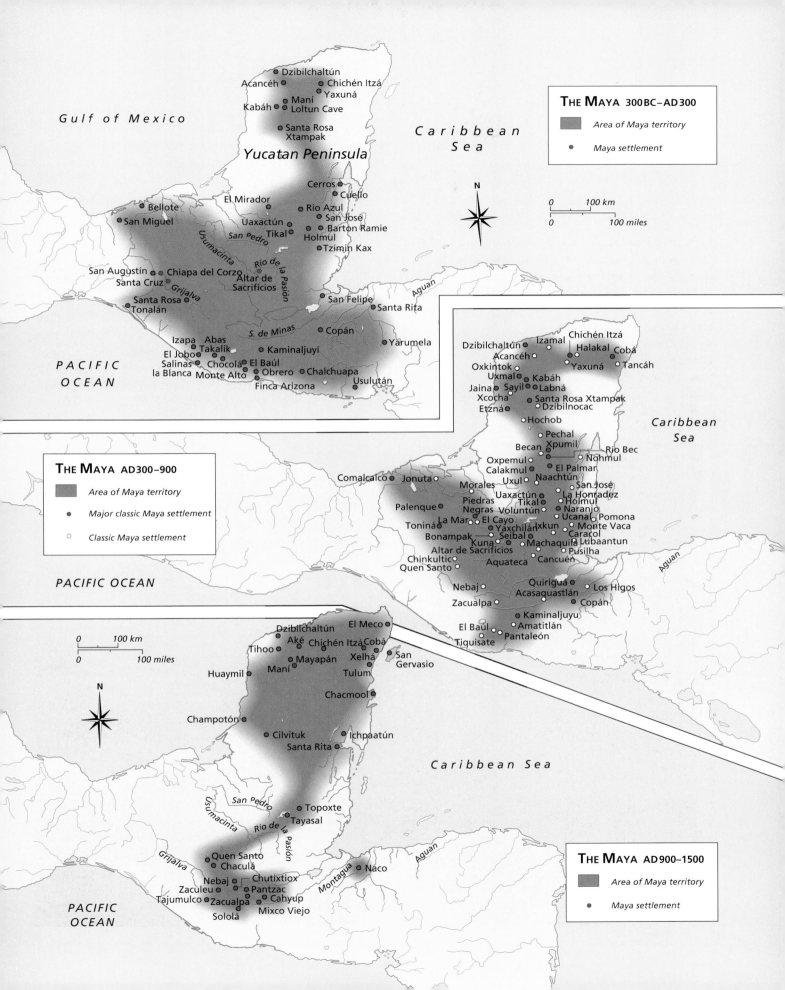

THE MAYA 300 BC–AD 300

- Area of Maya territory
- ● Maya settlement

Gulf of Mexico

Caribbean Sea

0 — 100 km
0 — 100 miles

N

Dzibilchaltún
Acancéh
Chichén Itzá
Maní · Yaxuná
Kabáh · Loltun Cave
Santa Rosa Xtampak

Yucatan Peninsula

Cerros
Cuello
El Mirador
Bellote · Río Azul
San Miguel · San José
Uaxactún · Barton Ramie
San Pedro · Tikal · Holmul
Tzimin Kax

San Augustín · Chiapa del Corzo
Santa Cruz · Usumacinta · Río de la Pasión
Altar de Sacrificios
Grijalva · Aguan
Santa Rosa · San Felipe · Santa Rita
Tonalán · S. de Minas
Copán
Izapa · Abas · Yarumela
El Jobo · Takalik
Salinas · Chocolá · El Baúl · Kaminaljuyí
la Blanca · Monte Alto · Obrero · Chalchuapa
Finca Arizona · Usulután

PACIFIC OCEAN

THE MAYA AD 300–900

- Area of Maya territory
- ● Major classic Maya settlement
- ○ Classic Maya settlement

PACIFIC OCEAN

Dzibilchaltún · Izamal · Chichén Itzá
Acancéh · Halakal · Cobá
Oxkintok · Yaxuná · Tancáh
Uxmal · Kabáh
Jaina · Sayil · Labná
Xcocha · Santa Rosa Xtampak
Etzná · Dzibilnocac
Hochob
Pechal
Becan · Xpumil
Comalcalco · Jonuta · Oxpemul · Nohmul · Río Bec
Calakmul · El Palmar
Morales · Uxul · Naachtún · San José
Palenque · Piedras · Uaxactún · La Honradez
Negras · Tikal · Holmul
Toniná · La Mar · Voluntún · Ucanal · Naranjo
El Cayo · Ixkun · Pomona
Bonampak · Yaxchilán · Monte Vaca
Kuna · Seibal · Caracol
Chinkultic · Altar de Sacrificios · Machaquila · Lubaantun
Quen Santo · Aquateca · Cancuén · Pusilha
Nebaj · Quiriguá · Los Higos
Zacualpa · Acasaguastlán · Copán
Kaminaljuyu
El Baúl · Amatitlán
Tiquisate · Pantaleón

Caribbean Sea

Aguan

N

0 — 100 km
0 — 100 miles

Dzibilchaltún · El Meco
Aké · Chichén Itzá · Cobá
Tihoo · Xelhá
Mayapán · San Gervasio
Huaymil · Maní · Tulum
Champotón · Chacmool
Cilvituk · Ichpaatún
Santa Rita

Usumacinta · San Pedro
Río de la Pasión
Topoxte
Tayasal
Quen Santo · Chaculá
Grijalva · Nebaj · Chutixtiox
Zaculeu · Pantzac · Naco
Tajumulco · Zacualpa · Cahyup
Sololá · Mixco Viejo
Montagua · Aguan

PACIFIC OCEAN

Caribbean Sea

THE MAYA AD 900–1500

- Area of Maya territory
- ● Maya settlement

three major groups, the Teotihuacan, the Zapotecs, and the Mayans.

The Classic Mesoamerican Cultures

The first of the three cultures to succeed the Olmecs were the Teotihuacans, who occupied territory in central Mexico. Although their civilization was based in Teotihuacan itself, their influence spread right across Mesoamerica. At its height, Teotihuacan was home to over 125,000 people, living in a city that was designed in a precise grid. They built two massive pyramids at the heart of the city, the Pyramids of the Sun and of the Moon, demonstrating their religious beliefs. Zapotec culture was situated further south, their major city being Monté Alban in the Oaxaca region, which also contained large ceremonial temples and palaces.

The culture that is most commonly associated with the climax of the classical period in Mesoamerica is that of the Maya. These people were highly influenced by the other Mesoamerican cultures, alongside which they began to grow gradually. Their culture spread across the Yucatan peninsula, reaching into modern day Guatemala, northern Belize and Honduras. They developed an empire consisting of city states which were focused on intensive agriculture and trade; some of the better known Mayan cities include Chichén Itzá, Uxmal, Palenque, and Calakmul. Between around AD 300 and 900, the Maya began producing art of such a high standard that the age became known as a Classic Period. They created sophisticated statues and carved reliefs, many of which were signed by the artist. They developed Olmec hieroglyphs further, and used writing to record events and victories in battle on large decorative stone slabs. Mayan architecture was also sophisticated. They quarried limestone and fired bricks, and important civil buildings were covered with plaster to keep them smooth and to enable decoration. Like their predecessors, the Maya built their temples at the top of huge, stepped pyramids, in order to be close to the gods. They were also keen astronomers and may well have used these structures as observatories. Although Mayan civilization began to die out in the ninth century, post-Mayan cultures continued to exist, their status only being undermined by the arrival of the Spanish in the fifteenth century.

North America—Early Hunters of the Northern Plains

The vast area of land that stretched between the rocky mountains and the Appalachians was abundant in large game such as bison, giant oxen, mastodons, and mammoth. With such food supplies, the inhabitants of the northern reaches of the American continent were able to remain as hunters and pastoralists for thousands of years. Although many of the indigenous animal species were vastly depleted in numbers and even driven to extinction, hunting and gathering remained the more popular way of life for most northern Americans; for many, the extreme weather conditions at the further reaches of the continent meant that a nomadic existence was preferable. In order to supplement their diets, many groups or tribes began to live a more settled existence so they could grow maize, squashes, and beans. Their societies tended to be small, but organized into a hierarchical system. Tribes would often be led by a chieftain, who may also have taken the role of religious leader or shaman.

The Hopewell Culture

Although the majority of Native Americans were semi-nomadic hunter-gatherers, a settled culture did flourish along the rivers in the north-eastern and mid-western regions between AD 200 and AD 400. This, the Hopewell Culture, spread up toward the area now covered by New York, down to Missouri and around the shores of Lake Ontario: however, it was centered on the Ohio valley. The Hopewells were agriculturists who harnessed a range of crops such as sunflowers, squashes, and maize. They also engaged in trade with other peoples across huge areas and certainly made contact with the Maya from whom they were able to introduce Mexican crops such as beans. The Hopewell people also built large burial mounds in which they buried not only their ancestors but also a range of grave goods. These mounds were often very high and built in a variety of geometric shapes. The Hopewell shared many features with the later Mississippian culture that flourished from AD 900 and ended with the arrival of European settlers.

Religious Worship

Polytheism, or the worship of a number of gods and goddesses, was a feature of religious worship across the Americas at this time. The tribes who lived on the northern plains were particularly influenced by the natural elements, and therefore much of their mythology revolved around a belief in natural spirits and gods who controlled the elements. The retelling of sacred myths and stories was central to the worship of the northern Americans and rituals such as dance became a way in which these stories were told. The Mississippian cultures, which developed in Ohio and Illinois, built large burial mounds, many of which contained mass graves of those who might have been

Above: The Cliff Palace of the Anasazi ruins at Mesa Verde, Colorado. These villages date from the twelfth and thirteenth centuries but the Anasazi are thought to have inhabited the region from circa 60,000 BC. Opposite: Statue of Chacmool, the Mayan fertility god, at Quntana Roo, Cancun.

offered as human sacrifices. One of the largest mounds, at Cahokia, held the skeleton of an adult male, lying on a bed of thousands of seashell disks arranged in the shape of a bird.

The Mayans also used large mounds and pyramid structures for worship, with elaborate temples built at the top. They regularly performed ceremonies in order to communicate with their deities, often making minor offerings of maize, fruit, and blood. For more important ceremonies human and animal sacrifices were made, usually on specially constructed altars. Sacrifices to the serpent god, Kalakmul, involved the casting of virgins into snake-filled pits. Unlike the people of North America, the Mayans did not restrict their religion to the forces and elements of nature; their astronomical study was part of a belief in the role of the stars, the moon, and the planets in the destiny of mankind.

Ancient India

Complex civilization developed early in India. Succeeding empires left a legacy that still influences many aspects of life in the subcontinent today.

From Early Inhabitants to Civilization

Modern humans are known to have inhabited the Indian subcontinent for some 30,000 years, probably originally migrating there from Africa into the more easily accessible north-west of the region and dispersing as small bands of hunter-gatherers. It is thought that agricultural practices, coupled with the establishment of small villages, then began around 6000 BC, somewhat later than elsewhere, but the first of the Indian civilizations was amongst the oldest in the world, emerging a few centuries after the great civilizations of Mesopotamia and Egypt. However, it was to survive for only around 750 years, between about 2500 and 1750 BC, and almost nothing is known of its people or their culture.

The Indus River Civilization

As with early civilizations elsewhere, the earliest in India developed around fertile floodplains, in this case those of the Indus River, with at least two major cities forming administrative centers—Harappa in the north and Mohenjo-Daro in the south. These were separated by a distance of almost 400 miles, with the surrounding and connecting lands supporting a series of smaller towns and villages, constituting what has come to be known as the Indus River, Indus Valley or Harappan civilization.

We do not know the names by which these cities, their people, and culture were originally known, though we do know the Harappans to have been literate from pictographs found on seals and pottery fragments. However, their language has never been deciphered, and it is assumed that much must have been recorded on materials such as palm leaves, which would have long since perished. What little else we know comes mainly from the unearthed remnants of the great cities themselves.

They were large, perhaps housing some 20–30,000 inhabitants, were constructed of fired bricks (suggesting the existence of nearby forests for fuel), and reveal an unprecedented degree of planning, with streets constructed on a discernable grid pattern, sophisticated water and sewerage systems, and large buildings for the storage of grain.

The Harappans farmed intensively: they grew barley and wheat for food, cotton for clothing, reared cattle, sheep, goats, pigs, and fowl, and kept domesticated dogs, camels, and elephants. A highly organized and technologically advanced society, they also produced pots and sculptures, and finely crafted jewelry from precious and semi-precious metals and stones, and are known to have traded with other cultures, including the Mesopotamians and Sumerians.

Harappan Religion

Nothing is known of the religious practices of the Harappans, for there appear to be no temples or other sacred buildings associated with their cities, and it has been speculated that the home may have been the principal site for the expression of religious devotion. However, there are perhaps some clues to be found in some of the architecture and artefacts which have been discovered.

Large bath houses and the degree of public sanitation revealed at Harappa, Mohenjo-Daro, and other sites may hint at practices based on ritualized cleansing and purification, a theme which is common in the later religious system of Hinduism. Certain artefacts may also reveal precursors to Hindu deities such as Shiva, seen in seals which depict a horned figure in a yogic sitting positing, whilst others depicting animals and mythical creatures, as well as figurines of apparently pregnant women, may also have had some religious significance.

The Decline of Harappan Society

It seems that the civilization of the Indus River valley disappeared quite suddenly and almost without trace around 1750 BC, and various theories have been put forward to explain this, including climate change, devastation by flooding—a regular occurrence in the area—and over-exploitation of the land, which may well have exacerbated problems brought by the floods. Perhaps the most commonly cited explanation is that the Harappans were conquered by the Aryans, a term applied to nomadic warriors who irrupted into India from Central Asia around 1750 BC. There is certainly some evidence of conflict, particularly at

Herat

Hindu Kush

Kabul

Alexandria
Arachoton
(Kandakar)

Taxila

Nicaea

ARACHOSIA

Bucephala

Sangala

UTTARAPATHA

Hyphasis
(Beas)

Multan

R. Indus

Alexandria

Sind

Thar
Desert

AVANTI

Pattala

BHOTA

Lhasa

Sravasti

NEPALA

Lalia Patan

Mathura Kapilavastu

KAMARUPA

Ayodhya

MAGADHA

Gujerat

Kausambi

R. Ganges

Prayaga

Pataliputra
(Patna)

Bengal

SURASHTRA

Barygaza

Ujjayini

Sanchi

PULINDAS

R. Narmada

SAMATATA

Orissa

Tamralipi

*ancient
coastline*

Arabian
Sea

RASHTRIKAS

BHOJAS

independent trib

KALINGA

Bay of
Bengal

Deccan

KARNATA

Amaravati

SATIYAPUTRAS

CHOLAS

INDIAN   OCEAN

PANDYAS

SINHALESE

Ceylon

VEDAS

MAURYAN EMPIRE, 322–297 BC

🏛 Greek city founded in northeast Asia

Kingdom of Magadha, c. 300 BC

Mauryan Empire, c. 305 BC

Mauryan expansion under Bindusava,
c. 295–268 BC

Mauryan Empire under Emperor
Asoka, 232 BC

◆ Asokan rock edict

▮ Asokan pillar edict

People

→ Saka invasions, c. 170–100 BC

200 km

200 miles

N

Mohenjo-Daro, and the Harappans were indeed eventually succeeded by Indo-European invaders, but it is likely that the decline of early Indian civilization was the result of a combination of factors. It may have been more gradual than previously supposed, and involved at least some degree of assimilation into other cultures.

Aryan Expansion

The Aryan invaders were hardy and warlike people, with no culture as developed as those that they must initially have discovered. In fact, Aryan culture seems centered around conquest and their religion was dominated by the god Indra, a conquering storm-god. They were led by warrior chieftains and entered battle on horse-drawn chariots, migrating into India across the conquered Persian territories (where the word "Aryan" is reflected in the name "Iran") to first establish settlements in the Indus River valley, before expanding eastward across northern India to the floodplains of the Ganges. Here their population was to become concentrated and tribal practices based on cattle herding and warfare would eventually give way to more peaceful settlement and agriculture.

Vedic Civilization

The early history of the Aryans in India, from around 1750 to 1000 BC, is now known as the Rigvedic Period, named after the devotional hymns or poems, the Rig Veda, which survived in oral tradition for thousands of years despite not having been written down until around the fourteenth century AD. Their legacy shapes much of Indian culture to this day. The conquering Aryans regarded themselves as noble or superior, and it was from this belief that the caste system was to develop. Initially, their population was confined to the northern reaches of the Indus and Yamuna Rivers where they maintained the Aryan tribal council systems, with a raja ruling over the group, or janas. These groups also each appear to have had a chief priest, and at this time there seem to have been only two social classes, the Aryan nobility and commoners. In time a third class would be added, that of the people that had been conquered, the Dasas, or "darks". By the end of the Rigvedic Period, four castes or varnas (the caturvarnas, or "four colors"), had been established. The system was headed by the priests, or Brahmans, below which were the warrior nobles, Kshatriya, followed by the peasants—farmers, craftsmen, and merchants known as the Vaishya—and lastly the Shudra, or servants. These castes were to become deeply entrenched and inflexible.

Dominated by the priesthood, the Later Vedic Period of around 1000 to 500 BC is also known as the Brahmanic Period. During this time, early Hinduism began to develop and the Aryans migrated and settled across the densely forested plains of the Doab, between the Yamuna River and the Ganges before settling around the Ganges itself. Here, several kingdoms were to develop, hastened by agriculture, trade, and the abundance of materials such as iron. The period is characterized by a gradual mixing of Aryans with indigenous cultures, rather than by conquest. By the Mauryan Period, around 300 BC, when most of northern India was ruled by Chandragupta Maurya, and Brahmi script seems to appear, it was used to record both the Aryan literary script, and local languages.

The Mauryan Empire

Chandragupta Maurya seized power in the kingdom of Magadha, centered around the city of Pataliputra, soon after Alexander the Great's incursions into the Indus Valley in 326 BC, the shock of which was to provide the impetus for Indian unification, and a centralization of power. Maurya conquered northern India, founding the Maurya Dynasty, which would endure until about 185 BC, when its last emperor was assassinated in what is thought to have been a

Above: Two granite lions, buried under sand for centuries, were unearthed by the force of the 2004 tsunami at the town of Mahabalipuram south of Madras.
Opposite: A relief carving of a Buddha in the Ajanta caves in Maharashtra State, central India, dating from between 200 BC and AD 650.

Brahmin uprising. Chandragupta Maurya's grandson Ashoka further extended the Mauryan Empire, which at its height included almost all of the subcontinent with the exception of the extreme south.

Appalled by the bloodshed of his military campaign, Ashoka converted to Buddhism, which along with Jainism, had been developing since the fifth century. Buddhism was to become the dominant religion in northern India, also spreading throughout much of Central Asia. Following Ashoka's death in 232 BC, the Mauryan Empire began to dissolve. As it disintegrated, India was to be overrun by a series of invaders and was in turmoil for several centuries.

The Guptan Empire

Although the collapse of the Mauryan Empire would engender a return to a number of fractured kingdoms, a universal empire emerged once more, in the form of the Guptas, heralding a resurgence of Hinduism and a new and golden age of Indian culture. In the intervening years, up until the fourth century AD,

dominance was held by the Kushans, or Kueh Shen, descendants of nomadic Mongolian tribes, who propagated a diverse and cosmopolitan culture; trading with Central Asia, China, Persia, Greece, and Rome to vastly enrich Indian civilization.

Following the demise of the Kushans, the Guptas were to assert their authority over most of the subcontinent. Their rule was consciously modeled on the practices of the Mauryan Empire, with a centralized authority, and they re-established a power base at Pataliputra from where trade and industry was regulated, and a set of unified values promoted. However, they also allowed for a level of provincial administration, ultimately providing much of India with over 100 years of peace and stability. During this period, the Indian people were in direct contact with much of the outside world, and trade flourished between Rome and central and south-east Asia particularly, bringing not only material goods but also an exchange of ideas. The Guptan Dynasty is regarded as being amongst the most productive and creative in Indian history. Kalidasa, perhaps India's finest poet, produced poetry and drama, and Sanskrit masterpieces emerged. Impressive achievements were also made in the fields of mathematics, astronomy, medicine, and chemistry. However, the Guptas were eventually conquered in AD 480 by successive waves of invading Huns, or Hunas.

The Greek World

From the Bronze Age Minoans to Alexander, Hellenic cultures—and their arts, philosophy, politics, and science—have had a profound effect on western civilization.

The Early Aegean

The Minoans

Generally considered to be the first of the Greek civilizations, the Bronze Age culture that flourished on the island of Crete was later named after the legendary King Minos. Crete had been inhabited since 7000 BC and its population grew gradually as immigrants from Anatolia and the Aegean islands arrived. Between 1900 and 1700 BC several grand palaces were built on the island. The Minoans had developed a complex society, built around religion and material wealth. The most important of the Cretan palaces was Knossos, which ruled over most of central and western Crete. In later myth Crete was ruled by King Minos, whose wife, according to legend, bore the Minotaur. Minos had the Minotaur shut up in a labyrinth and every ninth year it was fed with sacrificial victims taken from Athens. Although the legend is of later Greek provenance, the labyrinthine structure of the palace and the wall paintings of bulls may well have contributed to the myth. In reality, Minos could have been a priest-king, although there is no evidence of his actual existence.

Religion and ritual were important to the Minoans; they built a large number of sanctuaries around the Cretan countryside, in caves and on peaks. These were certainly linked to the palaces, which may well have organized the animal sacrifices and offerings that took place in them. The Minoan Cretans were also responsible for fine ceramics and jewelry, which they traded with Egypt and Anatolia. They developed their own form of written script, Linear A, which was probably used for administrative records. In 1628 BC, a massive eruption of the volcano on the nearby island of Thera covered Knossos in ash and damaged the palaces and villas on the island. It was not, however, until 1500 BC that the Minoan civilization was completely destroyed. The invasion of the Mycenaeans from mainland Greece brought an end to Minoan rule and marked the beginning of Mycenaean domination in the Aegean.

Mycenae

The Mycenaean civilization was the first Bronze Age culture to develop on mainland Greece. Rather than being one city state, the civilization was formed of large, wealthy groups spread across the southern mainland and Peloponnese. These people were less sophisticated than the Minoans and far more warlike. The main centers of Mycenaean civilization were Pylos, Tiryns, and Mycenae, and their burial sites show that ornate martial objects, such as swords and daggers, were more highly prized as grave goods than the vases and statuettes of the Cretans. Mycenaean society was organized around palaces just as the Minoan civilization was, although the palaces at Mycenae, Tiryns and Pylos are much smaller than those on Crete. They presided over settlements rather than towns and would have been the centers of ceremony, administration, and economics. The palaces were run by groups of officials who answered to a king at the top of the hierarchy. At the bottom was a slave class. Following their conquest of the Minoans, the Mycenaeans continued to use the palace at Knossos as an administrative center until its destruction in 1300 BC. These people were highly influenced by Minoan culture, even adopting their writing system. Examples of the use of Linear B, an adaptation of Linear A, have been found in several sites across the mainland and much of their finely wrought gold and weapons were made by Cretan craftsmen. The tombs that the Mycenaean chieftains and royalty were buried in were modeled on Cretan designs. Built into hillsides, or buried, the beehive-shaped "tholos" chambers were built of brick and contained many grave goods as demonstrations of wealth and power. In around 1200 BC Mycenaean civilization began to decline and most of their palaces were burned down. This may have been as a result of civil war between rival kings or due to invaders from the north, the Dorians.

Homer's Greece

Much of what is believed about the early Aegean Period comes from the literature of the Ionian poet Homer. Whether or not Homer the man actually existed is uncertain; however, two major works are attributed to him, the epic poems the *Iliad* and the *Odyssey*. These focus on the events in the final days of the Trojan War and a period of ten years afterward.

The Trojan War itself was a reality, taking place in around 1260 BC, although many of the events surrounding it, including the reason for it happening, are more mythical. According to Homer and legend, the abduction by the Trojan prince Paris of Helen, wife of the Spartan King Menelaus, resulted in the attack on Troy. Menelaus combined forces with his brother, Agamemnon, the King of Mycenae, who led the attacking army. Although the story of the *Iliad* centers on the role of the Greek hero Achilles, the figure of Agamemnon is crucial. As leader of the Greeks, Agamemnon is depicted as brave but easily discouraged, and his arguments with Achilles cost the Greeks many lives in the war. The Trojan War ended with the sacking of Troy, and in the *Iliad* the Greeks use the apparent gift of a giant wooden horse as a means of getting their men inside the walls. In the *Odyssey* Homer briefly describes Agamemnon's murder on his return to Mycenae while concentrating on the travels of Odysseus as he attempts to return home after the end of the war. Many scholars agree that the subject matter of both works is probably a stitching together of historical events, myths, and folk tales, passed down by traditional bards. The hero of the *Odyssey*, Odysseus, is in fact based upon a traditional Greek character from folklore, known more for his cunning and deceit rather than his heroic principles. However, the Homeric epics reveal a great deal about the traditions of the Mycenaeans, from their fighting techniques to their use of ritual sacrifice before battle.

Below: Knossos was the most important palace on Crete and ruled over most of the central and western parts of the island.

Archaic and Classical Greece

The Beginnings of Classical Greece

The era commonly known as the Classical Period began after the demise of Mycenaean civilization, in around 900 BC. The influx from 1200 BC onward of other groups, such as the Dorians from the north and the Sea Peoples in the south, caused a decline in palace culture and a period known as the Greek Dark Ages set in. During this time, the population of Greece expanded and a process of colonization across the Ionian coast began. The rocky landscape meant that early settlements tended to grow up on the fertile plains between the mountains and near to the coast. By 750 BC many of these settlements had become large city states, operating independently from one another and often at war. This period—between 750 and 500 BC—is referred to as the Archaic. Greece's geographical situation in the Mediterranean meant that it was a natural starting point

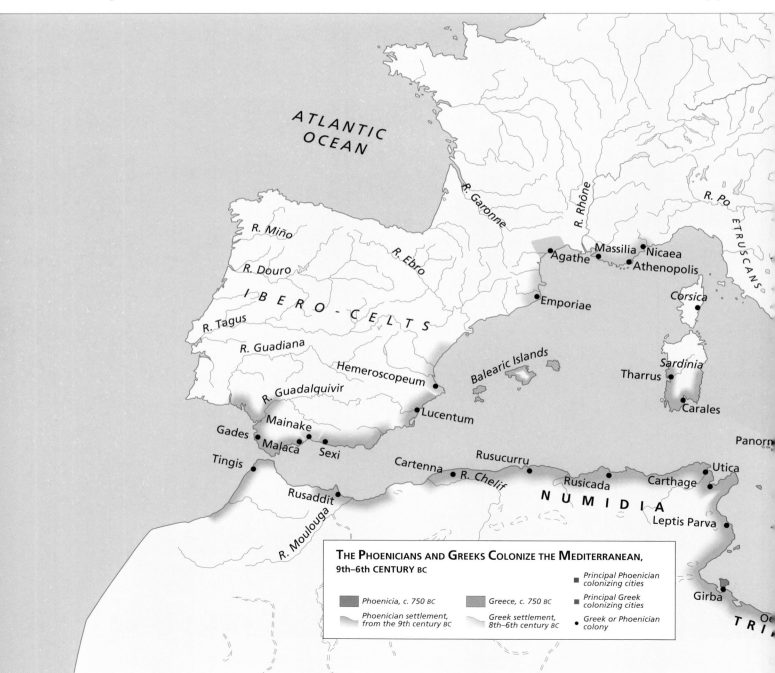

THE PHOENICIANS AND GREEKS COLONIZE THE MEDITERRANEAN, 9th–6th CENTURY BC

- Phoenicia, c. 750 BC
- Greece, c. 750 BC
- Phoenician settlement, from the 9th century BC
- Greek settlement, 8th–6th century BC
- ■ Principal Phoenician colonizing cities
- ■ Principal Greek colonizing cities
- • Greek or Phoenician colony

for travel and exploration across the water. The Greeks were excellent mariners and were able to set up colonies as distant as Emporium in northern Spain and Phasis on the Black Sea. In particular they traded with the Etruscans in Italy and the Phoenicians to the east, building up important outposts in these regions. Trade stimulated both economic growth and political development. An élite class was established, and as their wealth grew, states were able to construct more impressive cities. The richest and largest of these was Athens, which in time became the center of Greek culture, and the period between 500 and 336 BC is known as the Classical Age.

The City States

Greece was rarely one unified country; instead it comprised a number of city states, or "polis." These were often very small communities, clusters of farms and houses surrounding a fortified citadel, or acropolis, in which all the citizens could take refuge during attack. They were separated from other city states by the geography and this independence led to differing styles of functioning. As a result, whenever states were required to unite against an external enemy, coalitions were short-lived, and Ancient Greece was never a single nation. The two greatest city states

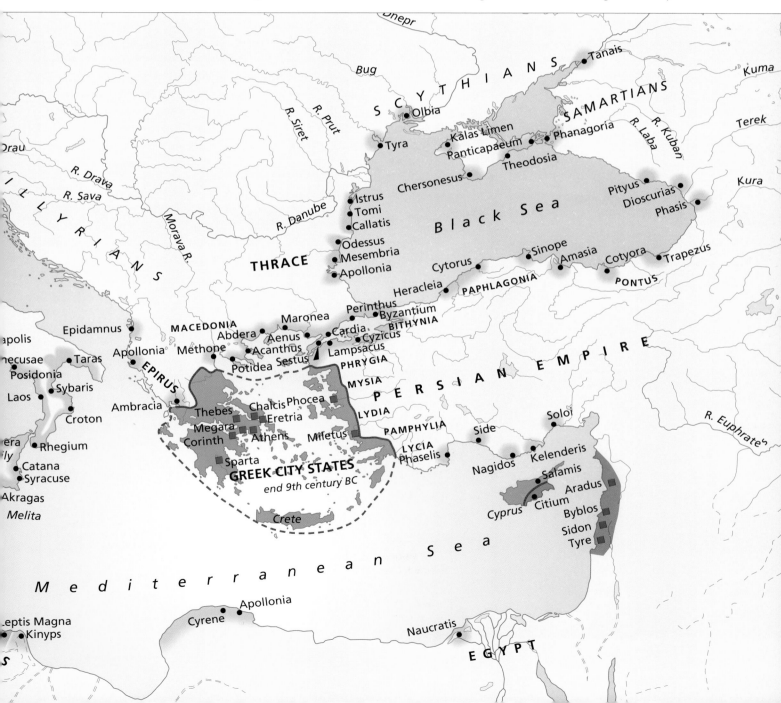

were Athens and Sparta, whose opposing lifestyles resulted in a rivalry that lasted for five centuries. Athens was the largest city state, with a population during its peak of a quarter of a million people. During the Archaic Age many city states, including Athens, came under the control of a series of monarch-like leaders or "tyrants." These were often wealthy individuals who had gained popularity with the people and consequently were able to direct the governance of the city. In Athens a key tyrant was Pisistratus, who ruled for more than thirty years. He boosted Athenian trade abroad and fostered the arts, encouraging religious and cultural festivals. Sparta, however, had established itself as a powerful military state under the leadership of Lycurgus who maintained a more primitive, monarchical form of government. Whereas most city states looked to their acropolis as a means of defense, Sparta relied solely upon its army for protection. City states were spread across the Greek world, including all the islands of the Aegean, and many chose to ally themselves with either Athens or Sparta during the period of conflict called the Peloponnesian War (431–404 BC).

Classical Greece

Politics and Culture

Between 500 and 300 BC Greece, and in particular Athens, entered into an age of enormous economic, political, and cultural growth. With the removal of the Pisistratid Dynasty in 510 BC the Athenians embarked upon a period of democratic rule which lasted for 200 years. To Athenians, democracy was bound up with ideals of liberty and equality; the word itself means "the rule of the people" and the "demos" was the citizen population. This population included not only those who lived in Athens but also the huge coastal plain surrounding the city, Attica; it did not extend, however, to women or slaves. There were three main organs of government: the Areopagus; the Council of Five Hundred, an elected group; and the Assembly, which acted as an arena for debate and gave people a political voice. Perhaps inevitably there was a flowering of political theory and some of the greatest philosophers in history, Socrates, Plato, and Aristotle, all lived during this period. Political and metaphysical philosophy was accompanied by an upsurge in the dramatic arts, with writers such as Aeschylus, Sophocles, and Euripides examining the complexity of human nature in the theatre.

Religion

The inhabitants of Greece shared a belief in the same pantheon of gods and goddesses. Many of their gods originated with the Minoans, but some appear to have been influenced by Asian deities, particularly those found in the Vedas. The supreme god was Zeus who was associated with the heavens, lightning, and kingship. He shared the universe with his brothers: Poseidon, god of the sea, and Hades, lord of the underworld. The home of the gods was believed to be Mount Olympus from where the fortunes and fates of mortal humans were decided by twelve major deities. Of these the more notable include Zeus' sister-wife Hera, goddess of marriage. Apollo was responsible for the passage of the sun across the sky, truth, and healing. Aphrodite was the goddess of love while Demeter was the goddess of fertility and harvest. Dionysus, the god of the vine, was particularly important as, like wine, he could bring both ecstasy and rage. The festival for Dionysus became one of the most important events of the year, with most of the great Greek plays written to be performed at that time. Formal religious activity took place in the acropolis of each city state, which contained temples and shrines. The Acropolis in

Athens held the Parthenon, the huge temple dedicated to the goddess of the city, Athena. Each state had its own deity who protected both state and citizens.

Pan-Hellenism

Several places connected to the gods served to create a sense of Greekness, or Hellenism. One of these was the oracle at Delphi. This pan-Hellenic sanctuary was situated in the mountainous region overshadowed by Mount Parnassos, and Greeks believed it to be the center of the earth. Dedicated to Apollo, the oracle was believed to be a diviner of the truth, and pilgrims would journey to Delphi in order to seek direction in matters as diverse as war, love, and business. Delphic priests were politically powerful and were at the center of an association of city states called the Amphyctionic League, a political organization of central Greek states. With its vital position in the League, Delphi was often the focus of state rivalries.

Olympia in the western Peloponnese was dedicated to Zeus and, as at Delphi, had a large complex of temples, tombs and treasuries to which every polis was given access. It was at Olympia that the first Olympic Games were held in 776 BC. There are two versions of the origin of the Olympics: in one, the games were held to commemorate the victory of the hero Pelops in a chariot race; in the other, the creation of the games was attributed to Heracles. Although the first games are believed to have included only one stadium race, they gradually became a five-day festival of athletics, wrestling, and sacrifice which were greatly valued by the Ancient Greeks.

The Persian and Peloponnesian Wars

The survival of Hellenic culture depended upon the ability of the disunited Greeks to unite to repel a foreign invader, in particular the Persians. In 490 BC, the Persian king Darius I mounted an attack on the cities of Athens and Eretria in retaliation for their support of a revolt by the captured Ionian city states in Asia Minor. Athens had sent twenty ships to aid the Ionians and success had led to their burning of the Persian city of Sardis. The landing of the Persians on the plain of Marathon, only twenty-five miles from Athens, resulted in a famous victory for the outnumbered Athenian force. This first Persian War had a crucial effect on Athens. As a result of the attack, they built up an impressive new fleet

that came to dominate the Aegean. When the Persians attacked again in 480 BC, under the leadership of Darius' son Xerxes, they made their approach to central Greece via the Thermopylae pass. A small Spartan force led by Leonidas was given the task of holding the Persians back, but failed despite heroic efforts. Xerxes sacked Athens and moved his fleet in to destroy that of the Athenians. However, at the Battle of Salamis the new, lighter Athenian fleet was victorious and Xerxes fled. Athens' naval supremacy increased the wealth of the city, and the alliance of Greek states which had formed to repel the Persians gave Athens an imperial position. This position came to be a source of envy for other states, in particular Sparta, and in 431 BC conflict ensued. The struggle between Athens and Sparta was a war of land versus naval power and although Athens seemed impenetrable, the death of Pericles and an expedition to capture Corinthian Sicily led to disaster. With Persian support, Sparta was able to build a fleet to challenge Athens and at the maritime battle of Aegospotami in 405 BC they finally won. Athens became a vassal state of Sparta and, although it gradually restored its independence, it was never as powerful again. Sparta was in turn defeated by Thebes, leading an alliance of discontented states in 371 BC. Continued disputes amongst the Greek states left them vulnerable to external forces and in 338 BC Ancient Greece became part of a new Hellenistic empire.

Below: The Parthenon, built in the fifth century BC, stands on the Acropolis in Athens and is one of the finest examples of Greek Doric architecture.
Opposite: A bust of Alexander who conquered Greece in 336 BC.

Philip of Macedon

Before Philip's accession to its throne, Macedon—to the north of Greece—had been a country weakened by internal strife. Despite being Hellenic, Macedon had always been marginalized by the more cultured Greeks, and towards the north of the country the lack of Greek influence created division. On Philip's accession, Illyrian invaders to the north were threatening the stability of Macedon and he was immediately able to employ his genius for political cunning to repel them. He built up a standing army and trained its soldiers in new techniques, supporting them with an élite cavalry comprised of nobles. The defeat of Illyria brought Northern Macedonia into his kingdom and he then began to move against Athens. Further disputes in the south meant that he was first able to intervene in Thessaly, where his exploitation of gold mines in the region helped to finance Greek mercenaries and bribe politicians. An alliance with several northern states saw Philip given voting rights in the Amphyctiony and, in 346 BC, he led them in a victorious campaign against the Phocians, allies of Athens. Philip's influence in southern Greece grew as he supported minor states in their struggles against the stronger ones, in particular against Sparta. Athens, aware of Philip's intentions, began to respond and in 340 BC open war broke out; with Thebes, they fought Philip at Chaeronea and lost. This victory in 338 BC established Macedonian hegemony in Greece for good. In 336 BC, Philip announced his intentions of waging war on Persia, no doubt to spread his empire, but he was assassinated before operations could begin.

Alexander the Great

Philip's young son, Alexander, inherited the throne in the face of opposition from other nobles, but he quickly established control and demonstrated the same strengths as his father. He had fought with distinction at Chaeronea and, having been taught by Aristotle, was well equipped to lead an expanding empire. In 334 BC he led an expedition across the Hellespont which consisted of the largest army ever to leave Greek soil. Within just three years, he had conquered all of Persia, including the now Persian-controlled Egypt, where he founded the city of Alexandria. He continued to move eastwards, sweeping through Babylon, Susa, and Persepolis in the heart of Persia itself. This large, spreading empire became increasingly martial, with conquered cities under the control of mercenary garrisons and their occupants enslaved. Alexander then set out for India, pressing on into the Hindu Kush; he managed to reach the River Indus before his troops finally rebelled, forcing Alexander to march them back. On his return to Babylon in 323 BC he contracted a fever and died shortly afterwards. Although he was only thirty-three at the time of his death, he had managed to foster an image of himself as invincible and divine. His belief that he was a descendant of Heracles, Perseus, and Zeus encouraged him to demand worship from his subjects, and while the Persians may have recognized this form of loyalty, the Greeks and Macedonians resisted. Despite this, Alexander eventually became a figure of fascination and a model for emulation for numerous successors, including the Roman general Pompey and Napoleon Bonaparte.

Following Alexander's death, his vast empire became the focus of internal struggles between competing generals and politicians. Eventually, three dynastic kingdoms were established: the Antigonids in Macedonia and Greece, the Seleucids in Asia, and in Egypt the Ptolemies. As these kingdoms began to decline, two new powers rose: in Asia, Parthian rule was established and in the Mediterranean, Roman.

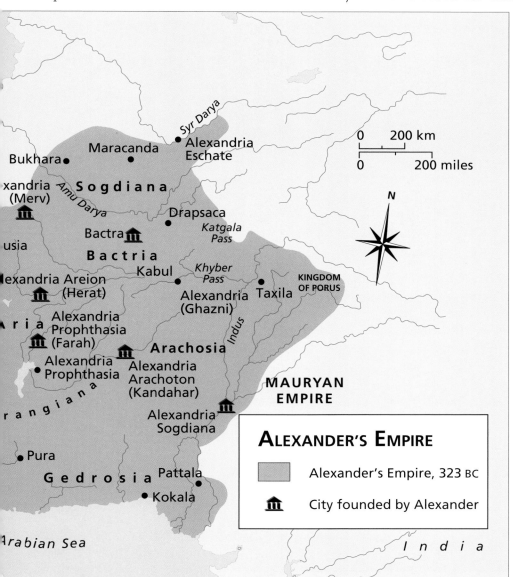

ALEXANDER'S EMPIRE

Alexander's Empire, 323 BC

City founded by Alexander

The Roman Empire

The Roman Empire unified most of Europe for the first time. Its development and institutions still influence today's world.

The Foundation of Rome

Legend states that Rome was founded in 753 BC by the twin sons of Mars, Romulus and Remus. Abandoned as infants, they were reared by a she-wolf before setting off to found their own city. Romulus murdered his brother following a dispute over the site of their new settlement, becoming the first king of what was at the time a fierce and feared tribe. At the end of his life Romulus was said to have been carried off in a thundercloud by Mars, to be deified as Quirinus.

In fact there had been human habitation on the site of Rome for thousands of years. The first Romans were a highly effective and organized people who formed alliances with neighboring Latin tribes in order to gain advantage over the ruling Etruscans; by 265 BC they had subjugated the whole of Italy. Their monarchs were chosen from the nobility, many of whom were themselves Etruscan, and they began to develop sophisticated civic and military systems. The monarchy that had begun with Romulus ended in 509 BC when the tyrannical Tarquinius Superbus was overthrown and a new Roman republic was established.

The Republic

Fearful of being ruled over by a tyrant again, a republican system of government was established by the Romans. The power that had previously belonged to the monarch was to be shared between two annually elected consuls, who were also members of the larger Senate. The senators were themselves high-ranking magistrates, all of whom were elected into office by a democratic process; the US constitution would later be directly modeled on this system. The Republic provided Rome with stability and, eventually, prosperity. When Italian city states were defeated they became allies rather than subjects, earning themselves Roman citizenship whilst providing soldiers for the Roman military machine.

The Punic Wars

As their influence in the Mediterranean grew, the Romans began to prove a threat to the powerful kingdom of Carthage in North Africa. In 264 BC the first of three Punic Wars began, which ended in defeat for the Carthaginians and territorial advancement for the Romans. The Second Punic War began with Hannibal's uprising in Spain leading to his attempt to invade Italy by crossing the Alps with a team of elephants. When the Roman general Cornelius Scipio finally defeated Hannibal and the Carthaginians, Rome was able to add Spain to its growing list of overseas provinces. War in the Mediterranean also resulted in the development of a powerful navy which further enabled foreign conquest and by 31 BC the Romans had annexed the whole Mediterranean area, including Greece, Cyprus, and Asia Minor.

Roman Worship

The worship of religious cults played an important part in Roman life. The basis of Roman religion was Greek mythology, but the Romans renamed the Greek gods and gave them their own titles and characteristics. The sovereign god of Roman worship was Jupiter, and such was his importance that no political action could be accomplished without his judgment. Associated with the power of lightning bolts, Jupiter made the future known to mankind by signs in the sky, such as the weather or the passage of birds. It was also believed that he could alter the course of history and therefore regular rites in his honor were believed to be crucial. Jupiter's wife was Juno, considered the protector of women and of marriage; and the third major deity was Minerva, said to have sprung fully armed from Jupiter's head and representing wisdom and trade. Other notable gods include the god of war, Mars, who was initially associated with fertility and as such lends his name to the spring month of March. Janus, the god of doorways and gates, is often represented as double-headed in order to see in both directions. Associated with beginnings, Janus lends his name to the first month in the calendar, January. Neptune is the Roman version of the Greek god Poseidon, god of water and protector of all water-borne journeys. These and many other deities were regularly worshiped, with specific days being assigned to particular gods. Temples were

ROOTS OF ROME

Roman territory, 298 BC
Samian League, 298 BC
acquired by Rome to 263 BC
Roman colonies, 272 BC
Roman controlled by 270 BC
Carthaginian possessions, c. 260 BC

LIGURIANS

Ligurian Sea

Corsica

Aleria

ardinia

alis

Tyrrhenian Sea

CELTI

ILLYRI

Adriatic Sea

ANS

Pisae
River Rubicon
Ariminum
Arretium
Volaterrae
Sentinum
Ancona
Etruria
Aurinia
Asculum
Volsinii
Hadria
Cosa
Nepet
Volci
Falerii
Caere
Tibur
Alba Fucens
ROME
Praeneste
Ostia
Latium
Arpino
Interamna
Lucera
Tarracina
Camusium
Suessa
Saticula
Venusia
Capua
Beneventum
Cumae
Neapolis
Brundisium
Tarentum
Metapontum
Thurii

Sardinia

Locri
Rhegium
GREEK
Strait of Messina
Panormus
Lilybaeum
Sicily
CITIES
Utica
Syracuse
Carthage
Cossyra

raised in order to facilitate worship and rituals such as sacrifice were regularly performed. The expansion of the Roman world inevitably led to the inclusion of many other forms of worship, and cults such as those devoted to the Egyptian goddess Isis and to the Persian sun god Mithras were accepted parts of Roman culture.

The Empire

In 82 BC the military lieutenant Sulla violently persuaded the Senate to grant him dictatorship over Rome for a period of ten years. The spread of the Romans across the known world had meant that the Republic increasingly relied upon the strength of its armies, and consequently its individual commanders. Political and civil tensions had increased to such an extent during this period that civil unrest had destabilized the Republic and a series of warlords followed Sulla's example, vying for supreme control. The most famous of these was the politician and military genius Julius Caesar, who, along with the generals Pompey and Crassus, initially shared power over the Senate as a triumvirate. However, Caesar used various means to outmaneuver the other two and in 44

BC he seized absolute power for himself. A conspiracy of republican senators put an end to Caesar's reign when, led by Brutus, they assassinated him. Caesar had intended his nephew, Octavian, to inherit his title; however, the Senate replaced him with Mark Antony and further unrest became inevitable. When Antony allied himself too closely with the Egyptian Queen, Cleopatra, Octavian took advantage and defeated the pair at the Battle of Actium in 31 BC. It is this date that is generally considered to be the start of the Roman Empire. Octavian took the name Augustus, which carried historical and religious prestige, and gave himself the title "princeps" —first citizen—suggesting a more democratic status. He was, however, an absolute ruler and reigned as Rome's first true emperor from 27 BC to AD 14.

The Augustan Age was considered to be a golden one. The Empire continued to grow, the Romans could at last enjoy political stability, and culture and the arts flourished. Augustus reputedly claimed that he "found Rome in brick and left it in marble." On his death he was deified and his successor Tiberius maintained the stability that he had inherited.

Because there was no definite law of succession, the position of emperor was insecure; politics at the highest level were tense and often bloody. Of Augustus' immediate successors, Caligula and Claudius were assassinated, whilst the tyrannical and paranoid Nero was eventually banished.

There were a number of notable emperors. Vespasian (AD 69–79) is remembered for his contribution to the architecture of Rome, in particular his construction of the Coliseum. The Emperor Domitian had the floors and walls of his palace lined with highly polished marble in order to detect possible assassins; he was murdered in AD 96. Marcus Aurelius was the philosopher emperor who spent his entire reign dealing with wars in the outer reaches of the Empire, eventually dying of exhaustion. The Empire finally ended in AD 476, when Romulus Augustulus was deposed by the barbarians.

Left: *The obverse of Roman Tetradrachma from the Seleucid Period.*

The Birth of Christianity

During the reign of Augustus, the Empire established a powerful hold over Palestine, particularly due to the ruthless administration of the area by Herod, the client king of Judea. When Jesus of Nazareth, a Jewish carpenter, began preaching to the people and promising them salvation in the kingdom of God, he was initially met with popular support. The message that Jesus and his twelve disciples delivered particularly appealed to the common people who suffered greatly under oppression; many had predicted the arrival of a Messiah. However, the Jewish priests condemned his promises of salvation as blasphemous, whilst the Romans considered him to be seditious. His attacks on the privileged classes and his growing influence made him unpopular and he was eventually arrested. After just three years of teaching, Jesus was crucified by the authorities. Jesus' disciples claimed that he had appeared to them after death, instructing them to continue to spread God's message, and from this point the popularity of Christianity began steadily to grow.

The Coliseum

The Romans particularly enjoyed the spectacle of gladiatorial combat, and most Roman cities were equipped with an arena or amphitheatre. In AD 72, the Emperor Vespasian began the construction of the Coliseum in Nero's private Domus Aurea. Completed eight years later, the building could hold up to 80,000 spectators, whilst its underground complex housed the animals and men that would perform on the central floor. The inaugural games lasted for a hundred days and nights, during which 5,000 animals were killed. Gladiators tended to be prisoners of war or slaves and were usually condemned to fight to the death. The Coliseum was a political arena as well as a sporting one; the exotic animals and foreign peoples that were paraded there demonstrated the power and reach of the Empire in the heart of Rome itself. It was also a place where insurgents, in particular Christians, could be brutally punished.

Above: The Coliseum, so called because it was situated next to a colossal statue of Nero, was originally called the Amphitheatrum Flavium.

The Roman Army

The Roman Empire could not have expanded as it did without its disciplined and organized armies. Although the Roman Army changed and developed over time, the basic pattern of organization remained the same. The standing army was divided into legions which were each made up of around 6,000 men. The smallest unit in a legion was the contubernium, composed of eight men who would share a tent and equipment. Ten of these contubernium were then organized into a century, commanded by a centurion. Six centuries were further organized into a cohort, which was the basic fighting unit. A legion contained ten cohorts and the first cohort in the legion was always made up of élite soldiers, commanded by the legion's finest centurion. The symbol of the legion's honor was the "aquila" or eagle standard, and the man who carried the standard ranked almost as highly as a centurion. The commander of the legion was the legatus who was aided by six military tribunes who would command sections of the legion in battle. Both the legatus and the tribunes were destined for places on the Senate. At the outset of the Second Punic War, Rome possessed the largest army in the Mediterranean. Six legions made up 32,000 men and 1,600 cavalry, together with 30,000 allied infantry and 2,000 allied cavalry. Using a variety of weapons including javelins, archery, and heavy gladius swords, and supported by large numbers of cavalry troops, the legions were highly effective. The organized command structure ensured that the legions could rapidly employ tactical maneuvers to defeat the enemy.

Pompeii

The town of Pompeii on the western coast of Italy had been a Roman colony since 80 BC. Both it and its neighboring town, Herculaneum, were thriving and prosperous ports. In AD 63 Pompeii was struck by an earthquake and over the following years the town spent time and money rebuilding the many temples and villas that had been destroyed. On 24 August AD 79, the volcano Vesuvius, which lay to the north of the town, began to erupt. Pliny the Younger witnessed the eruption and later recorded his observations in

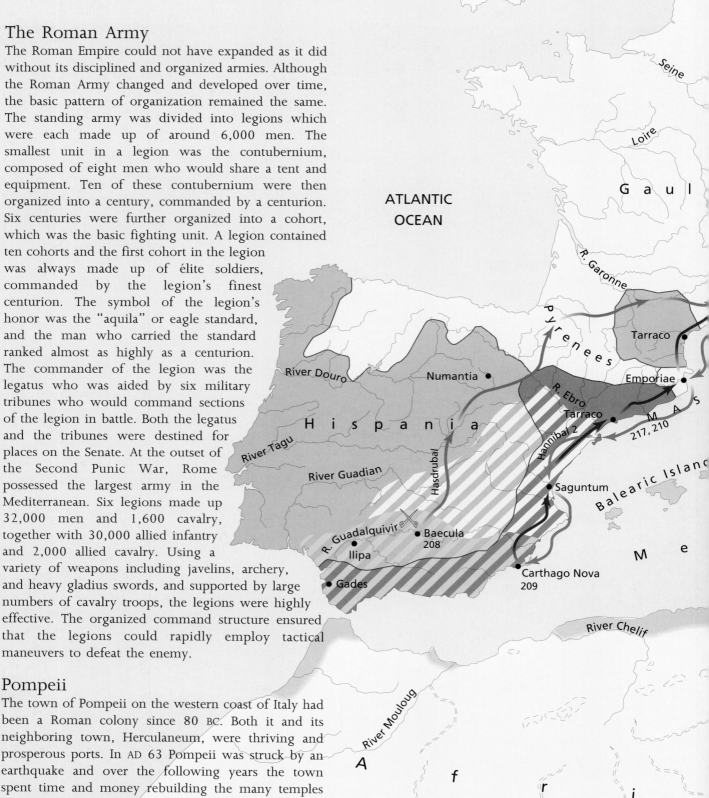

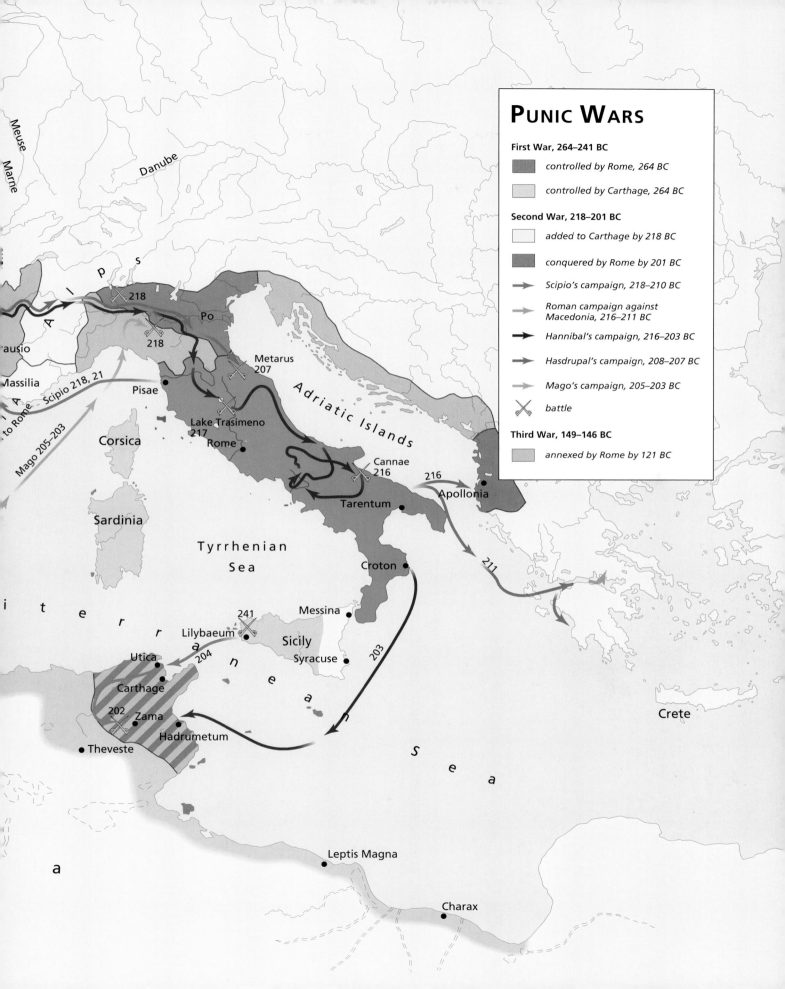

Meuse

Marne

Danube

Alps

p
s
218

ausio

Po

Po

Massilia

Scipio 218, 21

to Rome

Mago 205–203

Pisae

Metarus
207

Corsica

Lake Trasimeno
217
Rome

Adriatic Islands

Sardinia

Tyrrhenian
Sea

Cannae
216

216

Apollonia

Tarentum

211

Croton

Messina

203

Lilybaeum
204

241

Sicily

Syracuse

Crete

Utica

Carthage

202 Zama

Hadrumetum

Theveste

a

Leptis Magna

Charax

letters to the historian Tacitus. He described the earthquakes before the eruption, the twenty-mile-high eruption column, the fall of pyroclastic ash, and the effects of the eruption on the inhabitants. Some 2,000 people were killed as approximately ten ft. of burning hot ash and pumice covered Pompeii. Herculaneum, to the south-east of the volcano, was buried under a river of volcanic mud. Although later emperors considered rebuilding Pompeii it was eventually abandoned and its location forgotten until its rediscovery in the eighteenth century.

The Barbarians

The term "barbarian" is originally Greek and refers to any of the peoples of northern Europe, although in particular to the Teutons, Norsemen, Goths, and Celts. For the Ancient Greeks and then the Romans, barbarians were illiterate, uncultured, and uncivilized. As the Roman Empire spread further away from its center at Rome, many of the northern European tribes

Above: Temple of Apollo, Pompeii. The destroyed city remained buried and undiscovered until excavations began in 1748.

began to place pressure on its furthest frontiers. A particularly difficult border was that of the Rhine–Danube, where the tribes across the rivers mounted relentless attacks on Roman defenses. In some areas, the barbarians were granted Roman citizenship, and by the fourth century AD many were admitted into the army, resulting in a "Germanization" of the Roman Army. By arming the barbarians and attempting to assimilate them into Roman culture, the Romans had effectively allowed hostile peoples to infiltrate the Western Empire on a large scale. As a result of continued contact with the frontiers of the civilized world, these peoples had developed from nomadic peasants to being sophisticated and cultured. They began to establish small kingdoms, as in Gaul, and to assert themselves more and more against the crumbling Roman Empire.

Above: A bust in the Roman bath house at Herculaneum, which was destroyed, along with Pompeii, by the eruption of Vesuvius in AD 79.

The Fall of Rome

The collapse of the Classical Empire occurred over several centuries and for several reasons. One crucial reason was that the Empire had become too large for the Romans to control. In the outer provinces, many soldiers and citizens began to adopt local customs and practices, with many soldiers choosing to abandon military service in favor of the more peaceful option of land ownership. Pressure from invading forces also contributed to the weakening of the Empire. Small barbarian tribes banded together to form more powerful confederations. The Goths united under a single leadership and defeated the army of Valens at the battle of Adrianople in AD 378. The Romans were unable to defeat the Goths again after this.

The vast size of the Empire led to it being divided into two halves, East and West, by Diocletian at the end of the third century. This consequently led to a series of civil wars. Armies were loyal to their generals first and then to Rome, and warring generals used their armies against one another in order to contest for imperial power. Political intrigue led to the frequent rise and fall of emperors, and consequently to unstable leadership. The consequences of this were most felt by the common people, many of whom had begun to turn to Christianity. In AD 313, the joint emperors Constantine and Licinius accepted Christianity as the new religion of the Empire, giving Christian bishops greater privileges. When Constantine defeated Licinius in AD 323, he took sole possession of the Empire and gave himself the new, Christian, title of Pontiff. Seven years later he moved the seat of the Empire from Rome to Byzantium in the East, renaming the city Constantinople. The city of Rome was gradually left vulnerable to attack and eventually, in AD 410, it was sacked by the Visigoths and repeatedly pillaged. The actual end of the Western Roman Empire is marked by the deposition of Romulus Augustulus in AD 476 by the Germanic chieftain Odoacer. The Empire in the East became the Byzantine Empire, and remained in place until 1453.

The Expansion of China

The gradual unification of China, and the increasing strength and power of the emperors, ushered in a period of expansion and the growth of trade.

The Qin

From 403 to 221 BC, China was divided into several "warring states," all competing with each other to achieve dominance. There were seven major contenders throughout the period and between 328 and 308 BC the north-western state of Qin began its rise by extending its territory. It gradually exercised power over its neighbors until, in 221 BC, the Qin were finally victorious in destroying all opposition and became masters of China. The first emperor to enjoy supremacy over a unified China was Zheng, who renamed himself Qin Shi Huangdi, or First Sovereign Emperor of Qin.

His rule was marked by the creation of an authoritarian administration that consolidated his power throughout the vast country that he had annexed. He adopted the rule of Legalism, a school of thought which advocated that the power and authority of the state should be above the well-being of the people. The principle that people should be ruled by a strict system of reward and punishment was imposed by Qin Shi Huangdi in a brutal manner. The old feudal system of government was abolished and a system of prefects was introduced, all rigidly controlled in a centralized bureaucracy. The population was expected to provide the manpower for the massive construction works that took place and to supply the army with soldiers; disobedience was ruthlessly punished. Qin Shi Huangdi was, however, responsible for changes in the infrastructure of China that would aid later emperors and contribute to the development of the country. A system of roads and canals were built to link cities and make the passage of administrators and merchants easier, and national systems of weights, measurements, and writing were established, also facilitating trade.

Below: Over 7,000 terracotta soldiers, horses, chariots, and weapons have been unearthed from the pits in Shaanxi province.

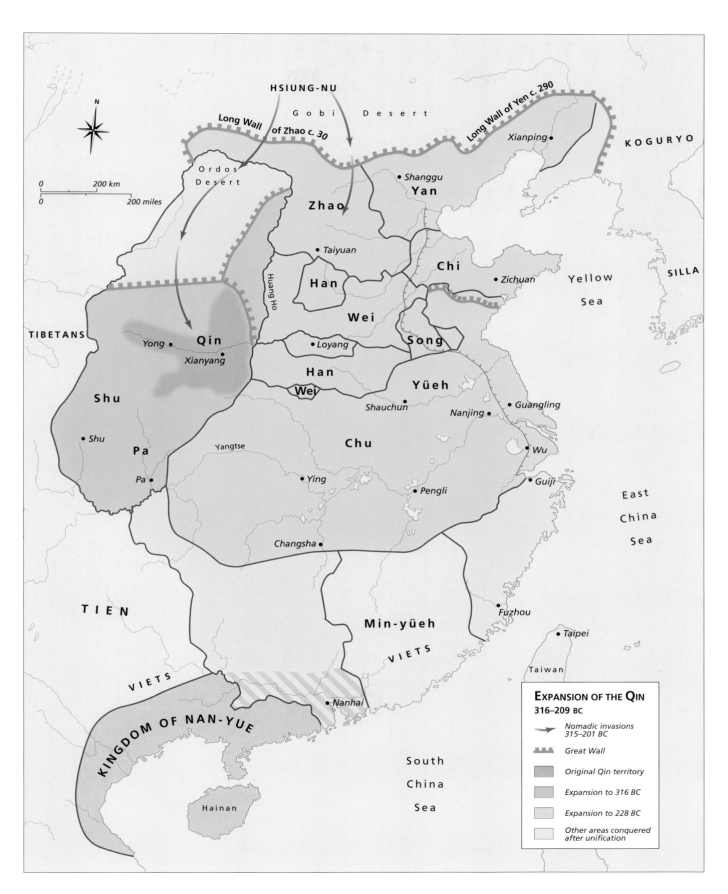

HSIUNG-NU

G o b i   D e s e r t

Long Wall
of Zhao c. 30

Long Wall of Yen c. 290

Xianping •

K O G U R Y O

O r d o s
D e s e r t

• *Shanggu*

Yan

Taiyuan •

Zhao

Chi

SILLA

Han

Zichuan •

Yellow

TIBETANS

Wei

Song

Sea

Yong •

Qin

Loyang •

Xianyang

Huang Ho

H a n

Yüeh

Shu

W e i

Shauchun

Nanjing •

• *Guangling*

• *Wu*

Pa

Chu

• *Ying*

• *Guiji*

East

• *Shu*

Yangtse

Pengli •

China

Pa •

Sea

Changsha •

T I E N

Min-yüeh

Fuzhou •

VIETS

• *Taipei*

Taiwan

VIETS

South

KINGDOM OF NAN-YUE

• *Nanhai*

China

Sea

Hainan

EXPANSION OF THE QIN
316–209 BC

→ *Nomadic invasions
315–201 BC*

Great Wall

Original Qin territory

Expansion to 316 BC

Expansion to 228 BC

Other areas conquered
after unification

The Great Wall

Perhaps one of Qin Shi Huangdi's most impressive achievements was the construction of the Great Wall of China. The construction of lengthy walls was not new and parts of the Great Wall had been built back in the seventh century BC under the Zhou, when the vassal states built their own defense walls to mark their territory. The threat from the nomadic Xiongnu tribes in the north of China encouraged the Qin to join the walls together to hold out the potential invaders. The wall was then extended to more than 10,000 li or 3,000 miles. Constructed entirely by hand, using only local stone, the wall wound its way through both mountain and desert. Garrison stations and signal towers were constructed at intervals along it and the wall became useful not only as a means of defense but also as an aid to communication across the Qin territory. Despite its effectiveness, the Great Wall was costly for the people of the Qin, both in terms of the high taxes which were demanded to finance the enterprise and the loss of life for many of those who built it.

The Terracotta Army

Qin Shi Huangdi had begun work on his mausoleum near to the capital Xi'an before 221 BC. On his death in 210 BC, he was buried in a huge tomb complex at Lintong that also contained a fully armored, life-size army made of terracotta. The army consisted of at least 8,000 warriors and horses, all of which were arranged in various battle formations as a demonstration of Qin Shi Huangdi's power and strength as he entered the afterlife. Each warrior bore a unique expression and pose and it is believed that they were made by an army of craftsmen and artisans using molds of body parts, which were then assembled before individual features were finely carved upon them. The tomb also contained personal items and jewelry. To ensure that no one could rob the tomb after his death, Qin Shi

Despite these changes and the brutality of the regime, hostility and regional tensions still remained and on Qin Shi Huangdi's death, eleven years after his reign began, China was temporarily plunged back into war and the Qin empire broke up.

Huangdi had automatic crossbows placed at the entrance of the tomb to fire on would-be raiders.

The Han Dynasty

The death of Qin Shi Huangdi in 210 BC led to a brief period of civil war in China that ended in 206 BC with the assumption of power by the Han Dynasty. The Han remained in power for the next 400 years, building one of the greatest empires of its day. The Western Han, or earlier dynasty, was founded by Liu Bang who had helped to overthrow the Qin and went on to consolidate the unification process that the Qin had begun. The centralized administration system was maintained by the Han, although initially an element of feudalism temporarily returned as his family and supporters were given control of fiefdoms. These were finally abolished by Han Wu-ti, the first significant Han emperor, who ruled from 140 to 87 BC. During his reign centralized government was reinforced and a civil service was introduced to administer the newly established provincial governments. The state took a more crucial role in the economy, and there were state monopolies of products such as iron, salt, and alcohol. Wu-ti ran a much less brutal regime than the Qin and under him Legalism was gradually replaced with Confucianism as the dominant ideology.

In the latter part of his rule, Wu-ti followed a more expansionist policy and Han China soon spread into the south and south-west. Korea, Vietnam, and Central Asia were colonized, and this expansion led to the opening up of trade routes with the west. The Western Han capital had been based at Xi'an although, after a brief interregnum, the new capital became Luoyang in the east and the dynasty became known as the Eastern Han. This later period, from AD 25, saw the Han gradually weaken as powerful families competed to hold influence over the emperors. Following a series of uprisings and civil war, the Han Empire finally ended in AD 220.

The Silk Routes

The Han had continued to struggle with the Xiongnu tribes in the north, and captured prisoners eventually revealed that it was possible to reach the peoples

Below: A gold cup belonging to a T'ang Dynasty shipment which was found by a German sunken treasure hunter. The entire collection consists of 60,000 pieces.
Opposite: A section of the Great Wall of China which stretches over a distance of approximately 4,000 miles. Sections of the wall had been built under various rulers but not until the Qin Dynasty were the different pieces joined up to make the "great" wall.

known as the Kushan in the area lying just north of India. The Kushan were a tribe of Chinese descent settled in central Asia who had adopted the Buddhist religion; they had also benefited from the Hellenic culture that had existed in the region since Alexander's reign. Wu-ti, keen to link up with these people in his campaign against the Xiongnu, sent out exploratory expeditions under the leadership of Zhang Qian in 138 BC. On their eventual return, Zhang Qian brought back goods from trading ties that he had formed during his journey and, in this way, the Han opened up the Chinese end of the trading routes that had already formed between Central Asia and Europe. The goods and artefacts that Zhang Qian had brought back to Wu-ti were highly desirable, in particular the stronger breed of "heavenly" horse and a new invention, glass.

Caravan traffic across Central Asia became relatively secure and the exchange of goods between China, Asia, and eventually Europe became important. Trading in Chinese goods extended to Rome and gradually western culture was introduced to China and vice versa. The term "silk route" was used because the most common commodity to leave China was silk, a fabric unknown in the west before the opening up of the trading routes. Other Chinese goods soon gained popularity and lacquerware, ivory, jade, furs, and tea were also exported.

The quality of Chinese products was high because of the highly efficient manufacturing processes that were being used. The Chinese had developed a more effective method of ironworking, with furnaces able to fire at much higher temperatures, thereby increasing the quality of the iron. They divided labor, so that artisans became expert in only one aspect of the production process, thus increasing both quality and quantity. They had also developed the manufacture of paper. Material goods were not the only commodities to be passed along the silk route, however; cultural exchanges were also facilitated and Buddhism, in particular, made its way to China.

Religion

The silk route played a crucial role in linking the Asian empires together. Buddhism arrived in China in the first century AD from India and although it was not initially popular, it became the dominant religion by AD 386 under the Wei emperors. Religion in China at the time of the Han was influenced firstly by the ancestor worship that had been a feature of

Chinese religion since the Shang. The adoption of Confucianism added to this the importance of observing ritual, with particular regard to honoring ancestors who would intercede with the spirits of heaven on the behalf of the living. Confucianism also emphasized the symbiotic relationship between the individual and the state through the medium of the family, and it asserted that moral conduct in the family was the basis of society. Buddhism was at odds with Confucianism in that it focused on the search of the individual for enlightenment, or Nirvana, through the suppression of desires. Buddhism taught that until desire was extinguished, individuals would continue to be reborn into suffering and their "karma," or actions in the previous life, would have to be paid for in the next. As Buddhism became the dominant focus of religious worship, Confucianism, rather than being extinguished, became the principle by which the state was administered. The civil service that had been developed under Wu-ti was eventually bound to Confucian ideals, with the development of an examination system that required all prospective civil servants to show scholarly knowledge of the teachings of Confucius. This examination system remained in place for the next 2,000 years.

The T'ang Dynasty

T'ang Emperors

In 581, China was reunified by the Sui Dynasty who ruled for thirty-six years. Eventually the Sui became unpopular because of the level of their spending and the tyrannical means by which taxes were collected. They had begun further works on the Great Wall and the Grand Canal project and these were combined with costly expansion policies in Korea and Vietnam.

Following years of rebellion, the Sui was finally replaced by the T'ang. In 624, Li Shimin persuaded his father Li Yuan to rebel and he himself commanded their victorious army. Li Yuan became the first of the T'ang emperors and eventually abdicated in favor of his son, who was renamed Tang Tai-tsung. Under Tang-Tai and other early emperors of the dynasty, China became a strong and centralized country where the empire relied far less on the aristocracy and more on the civil service. In 690, Wu Zetian became the head of the dynasty, remarkable because she was the only woman to ever become emperor—or empress—

of China. Under the emperor Hsuan-tsung (685–762) China entered a golden age of cultural achievement with the appearance of Chinese opera and with poetry, painting, and sculpture flourishing. The invention of block printing meant that written texts were more readily available and as a result literacy improved. The imperial family also adopted Buddhism as the official religion and it became a permanent part of Chinese culture from this time.

Rebellion

With the development of a powerful military force during the seventh century, the T'ang began to adopt an expansionist policy and the country grew to an extent that would not be matched for a thousand

Below: An extremely rare "Cizhou" peony baluster vase dating from the time of the Northern Song Dynasty.
Opposite: A Cantonese opera star performs on stage. Chinese opera dates back to the T'ang Dynasty with emperor Hsuan-tsung, who founded the Pear Garden, the first known operatic troupe in China. The troupe was located within the confines of the imperial palace of Wu Han. They mostly performed for the emperor's own personal pleasure. To this day operatic professionals are still referred to as "Disciples of the Pear Garden."

years. This huge empire became increasingly difficult to control and in 755 a large-scale rebellion in the north-east seriously weakened the T'ang empire. The leader of the rebellion was An Lu-shan, a military general of northern, and therefore non-Chinese, descent who had amassed a huge fortune. An Lu-shan was successful enough to force Hsuan-tsung to leave the capital Ch'ang-an and to declare himself the emperor of a new dynasty: however, in 757 he was assassinated by his own son. The rebellion resulted in the withdrawal of Chinese occupation from Central Asia, including Turkestan and Tibet. It also reduced the authority of the Imperial leaders, placing power back with the provincial capitals and ultimately with the military generals and warlords who ran these outposts.

Five Dynasties and Ten Kingdoms

During the 870s a series of large-scale peasant revolts reduced the power of the T'ang even further until, in 907, the last of the T'ang emperors was deposed. The period which followed was one of political and social upheaval. A series of five short-lived dynasties ruled in the north while a number of rival warlords set up independent states or kingdoms in the south. China was ultimately split into ten separate regions, and was not reunited until the establishment of the Song Dynasty in 960. This period of constant regional disorder and political dispute led to the decline of the aristocratic class and the increase in importance of the military and merchant élites. The economy suffered as a result of corruption, with a barter economy returning in many parts of the country and famine sweeping across northern China.

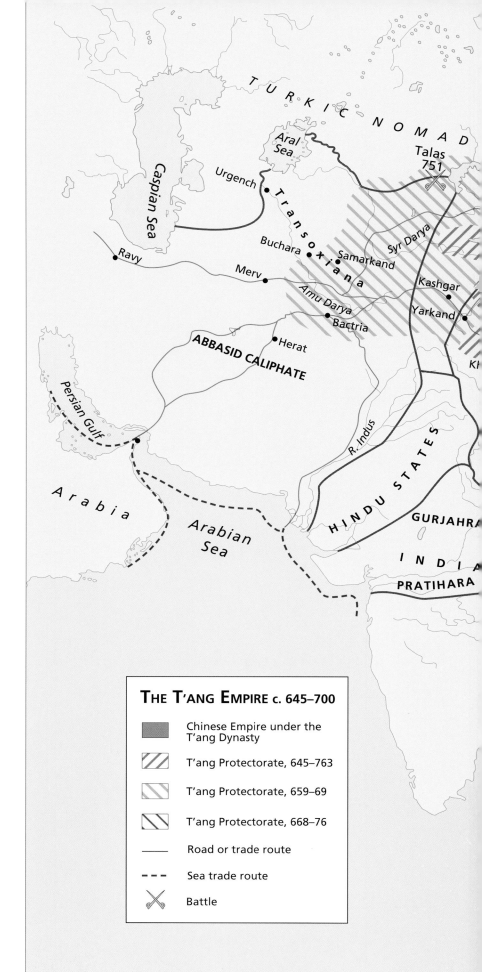

THE T'ANG EMPIRE c. 645–700

Chinese Empire under the T'ang Dynasty

T'ang Protectorate, 645–763

T'ang Protectorate, 659–69

T'ang Protectorate, 668–76

Road or trade route

Sea trade route

Battle

Karakorum

KHITAN

KOGURYO

Sea
of
Japan

J A P A N

V I G H U R S

SILLA

Kaesong

Turfan
Hami

Jojun
(Beijing)

Yellow
Sea

ucha

Sha-chou

Wei-chou Huang Ho

Charkhlik

Lo-yang

East
China
Sea

TIBETAN EMPIRE

Ch'ang-an
(Xian)

Hangchou

Lhasa

Ch'eng-tu

C H I N A

Ganges

Chang Jiang

C

NAN
CHAO

Canton

Tamralipti

Bay of Bengal

P Y U

South
China
Sea

MON

N

DVARAVATI

KHMER

SRIVIJAYA
EMPIRE

0   400 km

0   400 miles

Europe in the Dark Ages

The turbulent period following the collapse of the Roman Empire changed Europe completely. During this time the seeds of the modern continent were sown.

Europe after Rome

Referred to as "the Dark Ages," the period in history following the decline of Rome was considered by some to be a reversal of the cultural advancements made in the previous centuries. The replacing of Roman rule by Germanic tribes such as the Goths and Vandals changed the face of Europe. It was from these people that the major cultural groups of later Europe arose: the French, the Scandinavians, the Germans, and the English. The Germanic tribes had originated from the peoples living along the Baltic coast in the first millennium BC, and by the third century AD they had migrated into the Black Sea area in southern Russia. In 375 invasion by the Huns forced the Germanic tribes to move westwards, deeper into Roman-controlled territories, and the pressure this exerted precipitated the end of the Western Roman Empire.

The Huns had been responsible for many migrations across central and eastern Asia. They were primarily warrior nomads, who may have originated from the Xiongnu tribes in northern China, against whom the Zhou and Qin Dynasties had erected their Great Walls. They had terrorized neighboring tribes with their martial abilities, in particular their use of horses to mount cavalry attacks. As they spread west they collaborated with other tribes, such as the Turkic peoples and the Avars, gaining both territory and power. By the fourth century AD, the Black Huns of Europe had settled in the area north of the Danube in eastern Europe, in the area that would later become Hungary. Under the leadership of Attila (406–453), the Huns regularly raided lands to the west, including Italy, devastating large areas of population. Following Attila's death, the Huns gradually began to decline and disperse. At the same time the Germanic peoples were able to expand and eventually dominate the area.

Germanic tribes

There were three major groups of Germanic tribes inhabiting the lands to the north of the Alps. The tribes to the north inhabited the southern part of Scandinavia; in the east, they lived along the Oder and Vistula Rivers; and in the west they covered the area between the North Sea and the Rivers Rhine and Elbe. Initially, the most important of these groups were the Goths, who had moved south from Scandinavia and into the Vistula region. By the third century, they had divided into two very distinct confederations, the Ostrogoths and the Visigoths. As they migrated south and east, coming into contact with Roman culture, their own societies developed and they formed monarchies and aristocratic classes. The Visigoths were the first to migrate into Italy, and in 410 they captured Rome before continuing westward to settle in

Spain, making their capital in Toledo. In southern Gaul they established an independent kingdom: Toulouse. The Ostrogoths, under the leadership of Theodoric the Great, invaded Italy in 489, where they built up their own brief but civilized kingdom alongside the remaining Romans. The Goths were early Christians and were responsible for the first translation of the Bible into a Germanic language. They were also keen to integrate Roman lifestyles into their own; however, this willingness to assimilate into other cultures was one of the reasons for the short-lived nature of their kingdoms.

The Vandals, a set of tribes that had migrated south through Gaul and Spain, eventually reached North Africa and in 439 conquered Carthage. They established a despotic, monarchical government and ruling class of nobles, removing all traces of the Roman administration. In 534, the Vandals were eventually dismissed by the Byzantine general Belisarius.

The Germanic peoples that had the least success against Rome initially were the Franks. These were originally a set of small tribal groups from the lower Rhine region that had formed a confederacy. The Romans had dealt with the Franks by settling them in agreed territories and they soon changed from mobile, military societies to permanent communities. At first they allied themselves to Rome and assisted them against the Huns and the Visigoths. However, the first significant Frankish king, Clovis, turned against Rome in 486 and won them independence. The Franks became the only Germanic tribe to dominate Europe, creating an empire that lasted until the end of the ninth century.

The Franks

Clovis' first achievement had been to unite the rival chieftains who occupied the valleys of the Rhine. His defeat of the Roman ruler Syagrius in 486 was followed by victories over other Germanic tribes in Gaul, including the Burgundians and the Visigoths in Aquitaine. In 493, Clovis married the Burgundian princess Clotilda and was converted by her to Christianity. This conversion was vital in winning Clovis support from the Romans, Byzantines, and Gauls, which helped to consolidate Frankish hegemony

Above: Clovis I, who extended the Merovingian kingdom to include most of Gaul and south-west Germany.
Opposite: An early illustration of a plowing scene.

in the region. Clovis and his Merovingian Dynasty made their capital at Paris, which became the third most important Christian city after Rome and Constantinople. The Merovingians established their empire by conquest rather than colonization, and there was very little central government administration. In order to maintain control, lands were granted by the king to a variety of nobles who, taking on the Latin word for leader — "dux" — became known as dukes. These duchies became enormously powerful and one family in particular began to dominate the Frankish kingdom. This Carolingian family eventually took the crown from the Merovingians in 751 with the sanction of the Pope, by now an important political force. With his blessing, Pepin III "the Short" became king of the Franks.

The Great Empires of the Dark Ages

New empires grew up at both extremes of the old Roman Empire. Charlemagne established a new unity in the west while Byzantium developed in the east.

Charlemagne

The eldest son of Pepin the Short, Charlemagne or Charles the Great was arguably the most important of the Frankish emperors. He initially shared the kingdom with his brother Carloman, but the latter's death only three years after their accession meant that in 771 Charlemagne became the sole ruler of a reunified kingdom. He embarked upon a career of conquest against the countries which had proved a continual threat against both the Franks and the Church in Rome. He conquered Lombardy in 774 and in 804 was finally victorious over the Saxons, a powerful Germanic tribe

Below: The coronation of Charlemagne as king of Lombardy in 774.

who had remained beyond the reach of Christianity. The battle with Saxony had been long and brutal, but it was concluded with the forced baptism of the Saxon leader, Wittekind. Charlemagne was ruthless against those who refused to convert in new territories, and had taken it upon himself to secure all of Europe as a Christian empire under Rome.

He targeted the Moorish Arabs in Spain, who had occupied the region since 711, and led a crusade across the Pyrenees in 778. Charlemagne's efforts failed to remove the Moors, although he did succeed in creating a buffer zone in the Pyrenees, between Spain and the Frankish lands. The defeat of Charlemagne's paladins at the Pass of Roncesvalles was later immortalized in the medieval epic *The Song of Roland*. Charlemagne had succeeded in establishing a Christian hegemony across central Europe and in 800 he was rewarded by the Church with an imperial coronation in Rome. Charlemagne became the first Western Roman emperor since Romulus Augustulus; however, this was now a position which could only be awarded by the Church. The conferring of the title of emperor by the Pope put a strain on the relationship between the Church and the state that would increase in successive centuries. Charlemagne, unwilling to demonstrate too much deference to the Pope, was initially reluctant to formally use his new title. However, he and his subsequent, if short-lived, Carolingian Dynasty became the first of the Holy Roman emperors—Frederic Barbarossa added the "holy" in the twelfth century—a position that lasted until the beginning of the nineteenth century.

The reinstatement of a Western Roman emperor was resented by the Eastern Empire based in Constantinople, which, although Christian, did not enjoy good relations with Rome. The new emperor was able to establish Europe as an independent state from Byzantium, which Constantinople finally acknowledged in 812. The rule of Charlemagne marked the beginning of a union between German

ICELAND

N

Norwegian Sea

Europe c.1000

EARLDOM OF ORKNEY
TO NORWAY

SCOTLAND

North Sea

NORWAY

SWEDEN

Uppsala
Birka

F I N N I C   P E O P L E S

Ladoga

Novgorod

Baltic Sea

Pskov

B A L T I C   P E O P L E S

KIEVAN RUS

DENMARK
Roskilde   Lund

S L A V S

IRISH
KINGDOMS
Dublin

Cork

WELSH
STATES

York

ENGLAND

London

Hamburg
Bremen

POLAND

Wroclaw

Cracow

Kiev

Rhine

Aachen   Cologne

Frankfurt

**KINGDOM OF
GERMANY**

Lorch

Nitrava

HUNGARY

Mosapurc

PECHENEGS

*ATLANTIC
OCEAN*

Rouen   Paris

Orléans

F R A N C E

Besançon

BURGUNDY

Lyon

Milan

Venice

Danube

Varna

*Bay of
Biscay*

Bordeaux

Avignon

Genoa

Nice

KINGDOM OF ITALY

Adriatic Sea

CROATIA

B U L G A R I A

Nish

Philippopolis

Corunna

Bayonne

NAVARRE

ARAGON

Fraxinetum

Adrianople

LÉON

CASTILE

**MUSLIM
STATES**

Barcelona

Tarragona

Corsica

Rome
**Papal States
Country of Capua**

Pr. of Benevento

Barium

Thessalonica

orto

Toledo

Balansiyah

Balearic Is.

Sardinia

Naples

B Y Z A N T I N E   E M P I R E

*Aegean
Sea*

Smyrr

EMIRATE OF CÓRDOBA

Ishbiliyah

Cartagena

M e d i t e r r a n e a n   S e a

Panormus

Sicily

Chandax

Crete

Sétif

Tunis

Malta

F A T I M I D S

Kairawan

Tripoli

Above: The circus and hippodrome of Christian Constantinople (circa 500).

territories and Rome, bringing northern and southern Europe into harmony and establishing the beginning of a European continent. A further achievement of the Empire was the beginning of a cultural revival. Under Charlemagne, churches and cathedrals were built and manufacture and commerce flourished. Education and the arts were promoted, in particular the institution of Latin as the accepted written and spoken language of government and worship. This Carolingian Renaissance is often seen as the end of the Dark Ages in Europe.

Byzantium

The Europe of the early Middle Ages was essentially divided into two major empires, that of the Franks in the north and the former Eastern Roman Empire, or the Byzantines, in the south. The Eastern half of the Roman Empire had remained subject to the successors of Constantine and remained an empire until the fifteenth century. There were three major influences on Byzantine culture: Roman, Hellenic, and Asian. Initially the Roman influence came from the early successors of Constantine, in particular during the reign of Justinian (527–565), who sought to restore a classic Roman style. A series of successful military campaigns led by the famed general Belisarius resulted in the reconquest of North Africa, Spain and Italy. Justinian also codified Roman law, ensuring that all laws were recorded in published form. His *corpus juris civilis* contributed to the later formation of most European church and civil legal systems.

It was during the reign of Heraclius (610– 641) that the Hellenic influence overpowered the Roman, and Constantinople became the capital of a Greek-speaking, Christian empire. The Greeks had been the dominant peoples in the region of Asia Minor and their language became the official language of government over Latin in the second half of the sixth century. Heraclius had been instrumental in recapturing Jerusalem from the Persians, with whom he had waged war for much of his reign. However, following his death, Byzantium came under threat from the forces of Islam, which had been spreading from the east into Palestine, Syria, and Persia. Although Christian, the influence of its eastern borders resulted in religious disunity. During the eighth and ninth centuries, the period known as Iconoclasm—when various factions fought over the use of religious imagery—resulted in a weakened empire and again territory was lost to the Arabs.

Under the reign of a Macedonian emperor, Basil II, the Empire expanded for the last time, conquering Bulgaria in 1015. During the eleventh century, the Emperor Alexis I was forced to request help from the papacy when Byzantium came under pressure from the Seljuk Turks. The result, in 1096, was the First Crusade. Byzantium and Constantinople were irreparably weakened by the series of holy crusades which followed and when, in 1453, the Ottoman Turks attacked Constantinople the Greeks were unable to resist. Their last emperor, also named Constantine, died fighting the Turks on the walls of his city.

Early European Society

Bubonic Plague

Between 541 and 544 an outbreak of bubonic plague spread across North Africa and southern Europe which is estimated to have killed 25 percent of the population of the Mediterranean by the time it ran its course in 590. Known as Justinian's Plague, it became the first recorded pandemic disease. The offending bacteria were carried by flea-infested rats from Africa into Constantinople and the Mediterranean basin via the Nile trade route which linked the Egyptian port of Alexandria to East Africa. This plague did not spread into northern Europe, due to the lack of any significant European trade with the south. However, the heart of the Byzantine Empire, Constantinople, was severely affected.

According to contemporary historians such as Procopius, the legal advisor to Belisarius, the disease killed as many as 10,000 people a day in Constantinople. Many problems arose there as a result of the disease; the disposal of bodies was particularly difficult, since there was no one who could or would perform this duty. Corpses were burned, discarded in the streets, or remained in houses to rot. As a result the disease quickly spread and famine soon set in, weakening the whole empire.

Feudalism

Society in post-classical Europe was organized into "fiefdoms," where the monarch granted land to his most important barons and bishops in return for their loyalty and the contribution of soldiers for the royal army. These nobles, in turn, divided the fief among the lesser nobility, who became their vassals. At the lower end of the social scale were the peasants, or serfs. Heavy taxes imposed by later Roman emperors such as Diocletian had resulted in an economically depressed class, with many formerly free landowners being forced to serve their wealthier neighbors. The peasants worked the land and produced the goods that the lord and his manor needed. They were heavily taxed and were required to relinquish much of what they harvested as a form of taxation. In exchange for living and working on his land, the vassal-lord offered his peasants protection, although this often extended to exerting justice over them. The construction of fortresses or castles provided both a bureaucratic center for the fief and the means of protection for many of its serfs. The castle also served to assert control over the surrounding area, allowing the resident noble to use the fortified refuge during conflicts with rival lords.

Feudal society depended upon the contracts and oaths established between the nobles and the vassals, who ultimately provided the military support for the nobility in return for their grants of land. This feudal system declined during the fourteenth century when, as a result of the introduction of money, kings were able to hire mercenaries and pay professional soldiers. Having an independent standing army was more effective for rulers than relying upon their often uncooperative nobles.

Below: Penny showing the Coenwulf, King of Mercia (796–821 AD), one of only eight Anglo-Saxon gold pennies ever found.

New World Religions

The great religions of today's world—
Christianity, Hinduism, Islam and
Judaism—began their rise, developing
and extending their horizons.

Islam

The founder of Islam was the preacher Mohammed.
Born into poverty in the Arabian commercial center of
Mecca in around 570, he became a merchant after
marriage to a wealthy widow. At the age of forty,
Mohammed began to preach a new religion which,
although connected, was a revision of both Judaism
and Christianity and had a greater appeal to the Arab
people. Mohammed attacked the superstition and
idolatry that he believed was corrupting the other
major religions. As a basis for his teaching he used the
sacred book the Koran, which he said was the direct
word of God as revealed to him by the Angel Gabriel.
Mohammed exhorted his followers to live a pious,
moral life, respecting an all-powerful, just and
merciful God. God's mercy was to be obtained by
regular prayer, fasting and alms-giving, and the word
"Islam" is a translation of the phrase "submission to
the will of God." Initially, Mohammed's teachings
were disliked by the merchants in Mecca who became
concerned by Islam's increasing popularity. Repeated
persecution forced Mohammed and his followers to
flee to Medina in 622 and this migration, or "hijra,"
marked the beginning of the Islamic era. While in
Medina, Mohammed was able to consolidate his
power, waging a victorious war on Mecca. In 630
Mecca was forced to accept Islam and Mohammed's
final pilgrimage there in 632 resulted in the
confirmation of Mecca as the focal point of the
religion. By the time of his death in 632, Islam had
spread across the whole of central and southern Arabia.

The Spread of Islam

During the next hundred years, Islam spread to
northern India in the east and as far as Spain in the
west. This expansion was facilitated by the work of the
Arabic armies who conquered the lands previously

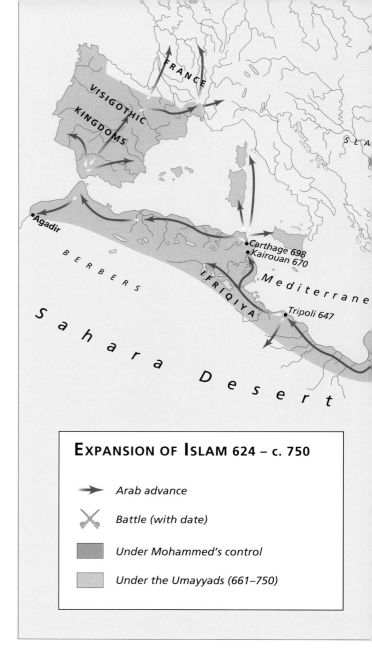

held by the Byzantine and Persian Empires.
Mohammed's successors, otherwise known as the
Caliphate, started with the elected rule of his son-in-
law, Abu Bakr. After crushing any opposition to the
government he moved into Persia, Iraq, and Palestine.
In 636, the second caliph, Omar, defeated the
Byzantines at Damascus and were able to move into
Mesopotamia and Anatolia. From Persia, under the
Umayyad Caliphs, Islam moved further east,
conquering Kabul in 664 and, in 712, northern India.
The march west had begun following the fall of
Damascus in 636, beginning with the conquest of
Alexandria and Egypt in 643, then Carthage in 698. By
711, Arab armies had crossed into Spain from North
Africa and attempted to conquer France. Political
divisions meant that no united Arab empire controlled

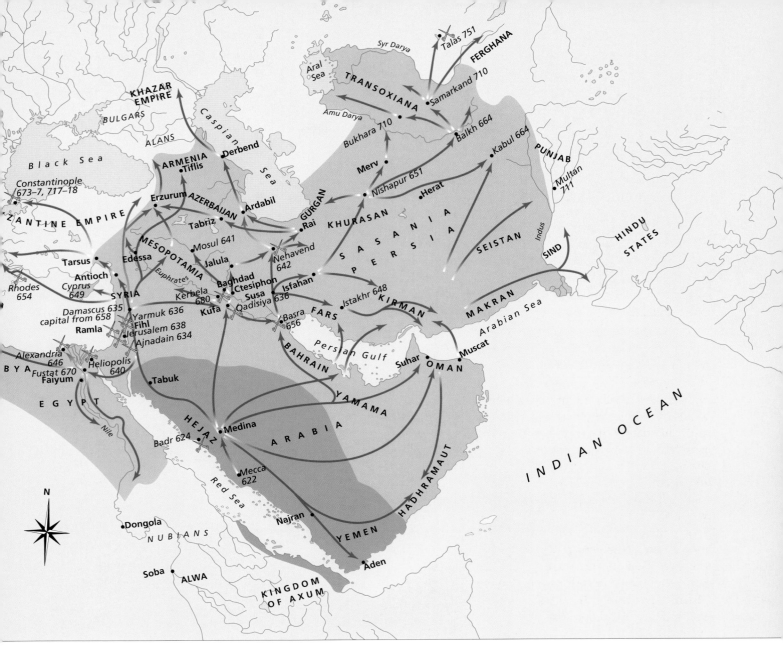

this vast region for long. However, the religion did remain and continued to expand, despite fracturing into two distinct elements: Shiite and Sunni.

The Caliphs

The word "caliphate" means "successors" and applies to the rulers of Islam following the death of Mohammed. The first caliphs were elected, but by 644 political tensions had begun to emerge, caused not only by territorial gains but also by disagreement over the interpretation of the Koran. In 656 a revolt ended in the death of the Caliph Uthman and the election of his rival, Ali. Ali's rule was unpopular with those who had supported Uthman and in particular with the Governor of Syria, Mu'awiya. With the assassination of Ali in 661, Mu'awiya took control of the Caliphate and

moved its capital to Damascus. This Umayyad Dynasty held control of the Islamic empire until 750, when the Abbasid Dynasty replaced it, shifting the capital to Baghdad. The Abbasids traced their descent from the uncle of Mohammed, claiming greater legitimacy to the Caliphate, despite rival caliphates being established in Cordoba and Cairo.

The problem with the succession led to the division of Islam into two factions. Those who recognized the legitimacy of the first caliphs and the traditions of Mohammed represented orthodox Islam and became known as the Sunnis. The other major group of Muslims was the Shiites, who continued to support the claim of Ali and his followers. Although the Shiites are in the minority, they make up the majority of Muslims in present-day Iran and Iraq.

Early Christianity

Following the life and death of Jesus, and his disciples' belief in his resurrection from the dead, the Christian faith spread steadily across the Roman Empire. Conversion to Christianity continued across the Empire despite the threat of persecution, in part because it was rejection of the rule of the emperors. By 313, the emperor Constantine, recognizing the spread of Christianity, converted his Empire and himself to the religion in the Edict of Milan. This act both confirmed and strengthened the authority of the Christian Church, particularly in Rome. The Council of Nicaea, held in 325, served to settle disputes between different forms of Christianity, in particular denouncing the Arian Christians, who denied the divinity of Jesus, as heretics. The Arians had claimed that Jesus was merely human, not God, and capable of right and wrong, whereas the council decided that Jesus was both God and man. This doctrine became central to the later tenets of the Roman, Greek, Anglican, and Protestant churches.

As the Christian religion grew it began to evolve into different sects with varieties of beliefs and practices, and consequently the Church organized itself into bishoprics with centers of ecumenical control in Rome, Constantinople, Alexandria, Antioch, and Jerusalem. The decline of the Western Roman Empire and the rise of Islam initially threatened the Christian Church with disintegration. Alexandria, Jerusalem, and Antioch were lost to Islam, and Constantinople came under attack, whilst Rome was threatened by invading Goths. It was the work of specific Christian missionaries that ensured the religion survived. In Egypt, the Coptic Christians spread their faith up the Nile valley into Nubia and Ethiopia, and in the sixth century Celtic missionaries carried Christianity across northern Europe, converting all but the Saxons. The Persian Nestorians consisted of millions of Christians across Asia, reaching into India where the Church of St Thomas had been founded by the apostle Thomas, and across into western parts of China. The Nestorians

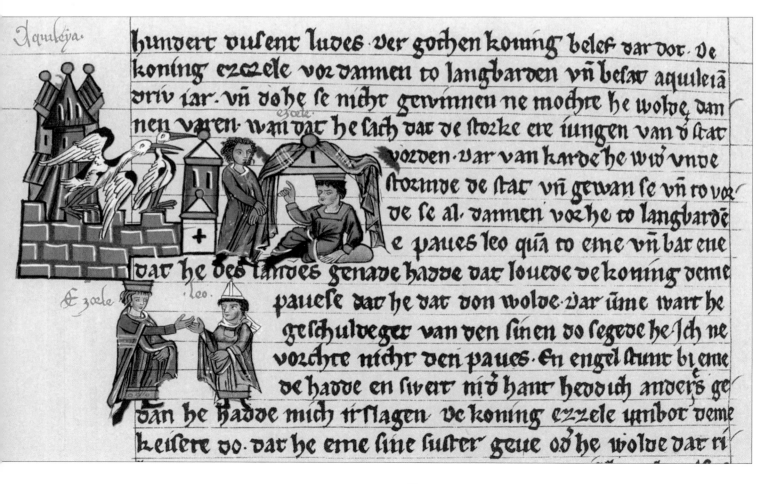

began to decline after the Crusades with the increase in retaliatory persecutions by Muslims; by the fifteenth century, Christianity in Asia had almost completely disappeared.

Popes

The title of Pope was not used until the fourth century; until then the title was "Bishop of Rome." The first papal see was traditionally the Apostle Peter, who had been martyred in Rome in AD 67. It is from this that the popes claimed the authority of representing Christ in the Church, becoming the rulers of all Christendom. For the first five centuries of Christianity the bishops of Rome had shared the leadership of the Church with the other bishoprics in the Eastern Empire, but as these ancient churches were lost to the spread of Islam, Rome found itself at the center of the Christian Church. The first significant pope was Leo I (440–461), who successfully defended Rome from Attila "the Hun" and the Vandals. He was later

Opposite: A reprint of a manuscript page with an illustration depicting Pope Leo I meeting with Attila the Hun, during which the Pope persuaded Attila not to attack Rome.
Above: The golden Dome of the Rock, the Old City walls and a Muslim cemetery as seen from the Mount of Olives in east Jerusalem, Israel.

followed by Gregory I (590–604), who reformed the systems and ritual of the Church and who gave his name to Gregorian chants. The Church, now led by the papacy, became stronger—in part due to churches placing themselves under Rome's protection from either the growing Frankish Empire or the continued threat of Islamic invasion. The other major center of Christianity was at Constantinople, where the practice of worship had begun to differ from that of the western Christians. In 1054 Christianity separated into two distinct forms, Catholic in western Europe and Orthodox in parts of eastern Europe, Russia and Near Asia.

After 1059 the popes were elected by the

College of Cardinals and ruled over vast areas of Italy, known as the Papal States. With this wealth, and as the spiritual sovereigns of Christian Europe, they held considerable political power, which later led to tension with other European rulers.

Judaism

Origins

The Jewish faith began during the Bronze Age in the Mesopotamian region, where certain tribal groups were marked out from others by their monotheistic belief, or worship of a single god. According to Jewish tradition, the first patriarch of the religion was Abraham, with whom God had made a sacred covenant that his were the chosen people, the people whom God had adopted. During the time of Moses, in around 1200 BC, the Jewish people escaped from slavery in Egypt to their promised land, Canaan, later to become Palestine. Canaan had been inhabited by Semitic-speaking peoples since the second millennium BC, and the area eventually came under the control of Hebrew kings such as Saul, Solomon, and David. It was during this time that the great temple at Jerusalem was built that would later be destroyed by both the Babylonians during their invasion of Israel in 586 BC, and by the Romans in AD 70. Although the Jews had built up a powerful kingdom at the turn of the first millennium BC, the invasion by the Babylonians and the Assyrians resulted in their exile from Israel. During this period of exile the temple, which had been the heart of Jewish worship, was replaced by synagogues, and prayers were led by learned holy men called the sofrim, who later became rabbis. The exile encouraged Jewish migration, or the diaspora, across the Mediterranean world, and during the time of the Roman Empire the Jewish faith was tolerated and at

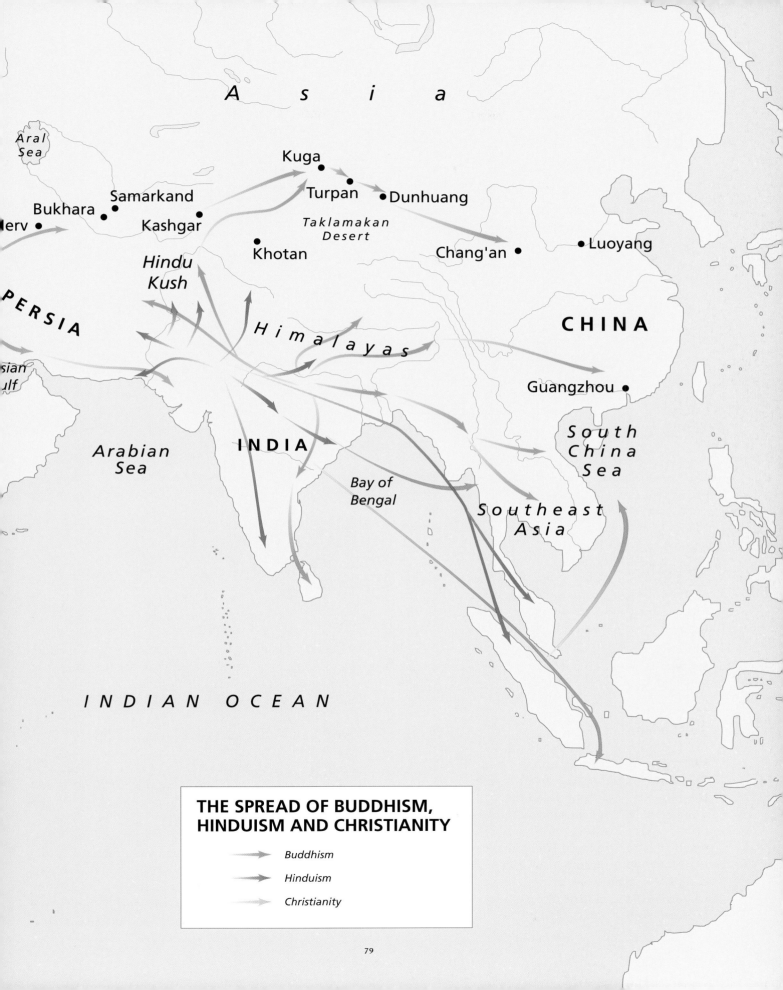

THE SPREAD OF BUDDHISM, HINDUISM AND CHRISTIANITY

→ Buddhism

→ Hinduism

→ Christianity

times favored with legal privileges. In 140 BC, the Jewish state of Judea emerged, ruled over by the high-priest dynasty the Hasmoneans.

However, by AD 6 Judea had been annexed by Rome, becoming a province of the Empire. The Jews in Judea were resistant to Roman rule and in AD 66 the first Jewish revolt ended in a brief period of Jewish control. The revolt was put down by Vespasian in AD 70, with Jerusalem burned and the temple destroyed. Between this period and the conversion of the Empire to Christianity, Jewish communities and culture flourished. In AD 200, the Rabbi Judah codified Jewish law in the Mishnah, which forms part of the Jewish book of instruction, the Talmud.

The Diaspora

The word "diaspora" means "scattering" and refers to the massive migration of Jews out of Israel as a result either of voluntary resettlement or deportation. "Diaspora" has since become used as a phrase to explain the state of being, or of mind, of all Jews who do not live in Israel. During the Roman period large Jewish communities were settled across Asia Minor, in Greece and in Italy. In the Christian era this dispersal continued, with large numbers of Jews settling in Islamic Spain where there was a renowned tolerance. The geographically wide spread of Jewish communities who shared the language, practices, and commercial laws proscribed by the Talmud contributed to their being successful as merchants. Additionally, because of the restrictions placed on Jewish land ownership in Europe, particularly in the feudal societies of northern Europe, many Jewish communities were concentrated in urban centers. Despite their economic contribution to their host countries, most Jewish communities experienced limited tolerance and were regularly expelled by hostile governments and monarchs.

Worship

The primary text of the Jewish faith is the Torah, which is believed to have been revealed to Moses by God on Mount Sinai. The Torah is made up of the first five books of Moses and recounts the history of the Jewish people from Genesis to Deuteronomy, as found in the Hebrew Bible; these five also form the first books of the Christian Old Testament. Considered to be the law of Moses, the Torah is believed to represent the covenant between God and the people and therefore is concerned with humankind. As a faith, Judaism was the background from which Christianity and Islam emerged; however, the Christian doctrine of one God, Father, Son, and Holy Spirit, is heretical to Jews. Likewise the Islamic belief that Mohammed was the last of the line of prophets, which included Jesus, is unacceptable to the Jewish faith since Jews believe in the possibility of future prophets. Jewish, along with Christian and Islamic, monotheism does not allow the worship of lesser intermediaries.

Hinduism

The oldest of the world's religions, Hinduism is a complex religion which has developed from around 3000 BC, absorbing a multitude of faiths and practices. It does not have one unifying founder, prophet, or teacher, nor is it monotheistic; it supports a vast pantheon of gods. However, most Hindus believe in a single universal soul, or Brahman. The foundations of Hinduism are found in the Aryan faith, which had been recorded in 800 BC in the four texts known as the Vedas.

The Hindu pantheon is dominated by Brahma, Vishnu, and Shiva. Brahma is the creator of the universe and the lord of all beings. Vishnu, the preserver, exists in a variety of forms, having nine incarnations, or avatars. These avatars take either

human or animal form, or a mixture of the two, and appear in a number of religious legends. As Vishnu, he is depicted as having four arms, carrying a club, a shell, a discus, and a lotus, and is perceived to be a kindly god. Shiva is the destroyer and is related to both death and restoration. The Hindu faith is rooted in the belief of reincarnation: that man is bound by a cycle of birth, death, and rebirth. A person's destiny in their next existence is determined by their actions in this one; a belief known as karma. The Aryans had developed a class system which has developed to become today's caste system. This dictated that there were several layers to society. In around 600 BC, two major sects were born out of Hinduism. Jainism rejected the class system and developed the concept of "three right ways," including non-violence. Although not a large religious movement, Jainism became very influential at a political level. The other major religion born out of Hinduism was Buddhism.

Buddhism

Buddha, which is the Sanskrit word for "enlightened one," was the name given to Siddhartha Gautama, a Hindu from the warrior class who founded the religious system that became Buddhism. Brought up in extreme luxury, Guatama became aware of the extent of the poverty and suffering around him and the inescapability of death. He gave up his position and family in what became called the Great Renunciation, and set off wandering in search of enlightenment. After six years of study and meditation, he had withstood temptation and received enlightenment at the foot of a bo tree, achieving Nirvana, the obliteration of all desire. Following this he became a teacher of the doctrine of the four noble truths and the path to enlightenment. Unlike other religions, Buddhism does not center on a god or pantheon of deities; instead it emphasizes individuals' deliverance of themselves from eternal suffering. The appeal of Buddhism reached beyond India, where Hinduism remained the central religion despite a brief conversion by the emperor Asoka in the second century BC. It spread via the trade routes to China in around AD 150 and from there to Korea, reaching Japan in 550. The religion also spread south-eastwards into Burma and Siam and across to Sumatra and Java, where the great temple at Borobudur was built circa AD 800.

Below: The temple of Borobudur was the spiritual center of Buddhism in Java. It was lost for many centuries before being rediscovered in the eighteenth century.

Polynesia and Australasia

The early history of Australia and Polynesia is one of migration and feats of navigation, with societies whose beliefs reflect their close relationship with the environment.

Tribes and Peoples

Early humans had migrated into Australasia from Asia across land bridges at least 50,000, maybe 60,000 years ago. These were the ancestors of the native populations of Australia and the Polynesian islands, along with another group of people—the Melanesians—who migrated to islands in the Pacific such as Fiji, Vanuatu, the Solomon Islands, and New Guinea. Australia and the surrounding islands had abundant supplies of food, particularly around the coastal regions, where shellfish and seafood were particularly plentiful. When sea levels rose in the sixth millennium BC, people began to make their way further inland and settlements and tribal territories eventually covered most of the continent. Many also began to make the voyage further east into the South Pacific, journeying as far as Tonga, Samoa, and the Marquess Islands and becoming skilled navigators. It

was from the Marquess Islands that exploratory groups first discovered and inhabited the Hawaiian Islands, Easter Island, and New Zealand. Migrating so far from the dispersal center, these islanders began to develop their own cultures and traditions.

Indigenous Australian tribes had a wide range of traditions and languages. When the Europeans arrived they discovered a number of different tribes, with up to 200 different languages being spoken. The majority of Aboriginal Australians lived in nomadic societies as hunter-gatherers and over time they began to manipulate their environment, developing sophisticated tools and crafts and using fire as a means of hunting and clearing land.

Worship

Aborigine culture was closely tied to their worship of the land, and their reverence of this is demonstrated in

Opposite: Uluru or Ayers Rock. It is the world's largest monolith rising over 1,000 ft. above the desert floor with a circumference of almost 5 miles.
Above: Some of the famous Easter Island statues. The statues range in size from around 6 ft. to over 30 ft. tall.

their belief system, "the dreamtime." The dreamtime is a complex mythology where stories act as myths whilst giving information about the land, such as where waterholes can be found. The connection between the dreamtime and the land meant that many places hold spiritual significance for Aboriginal people, the most famous of these being Uluru, or Ayers Rock. There are a number of animalistic spirits such as the bunyip, the devilish being who lives in swamps, riverbeds, and creeks and is responsible for devouring anyone who enters these places at night.

Worship on the Polynesian islands was different from that of the Native Australians. Despite the geographic distances, many Polynesian islands' religions shared the same mythologies. There is usually a supreme god and a number of subordinate gods who have dealings in human affairs. Creation myths usually focus on the formation of the islands, from either a heavenly fish-hook which pulls the island up from the seabed, or a giant rock thrown down from heaven. Because islanders were influenced by the sea, many of the mythologies deal with sea voyages.

Easter Island

Rapa-Nui, or Easter Island, is probably best known for its giant stone statues. These were carved by the early Polynesian inhabitants of the island, themselves called Rapanui. The Rapanui believed that there was a supreme god and a collection of lesser gods who were made up of their deceased ancestors. It is these ancestors whom the statues of Easter Island are believed to represent. There are almost 900 scattered around the island. About 288 were erected onto stone platforms, whilst the rest remain at the site of the quarry from which they were cut. Nearly all of the statues are carved from very hard volcanic rock and they would then have been dragged by large teams of

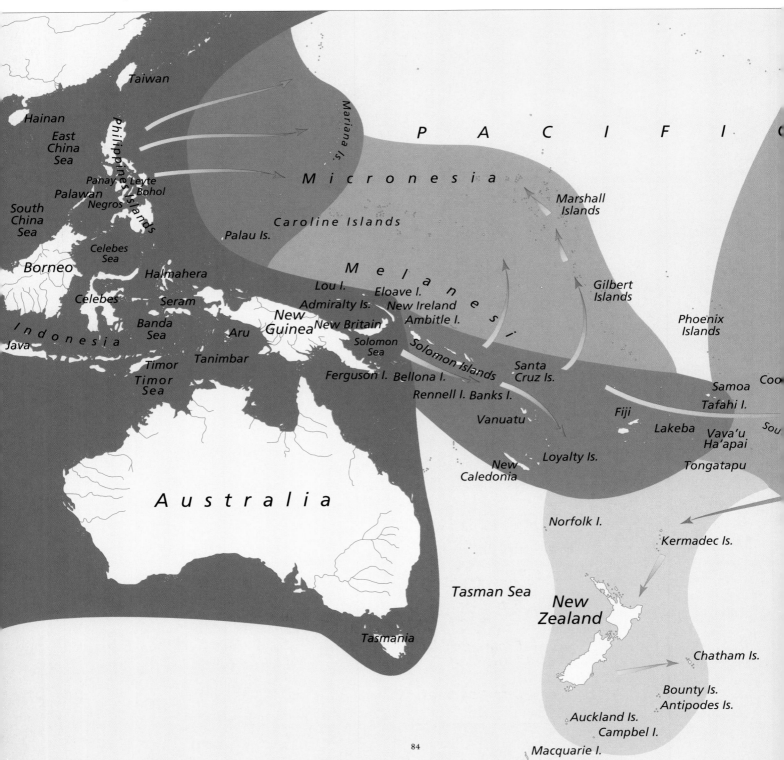

men to their erection site. Although the statues look like giant stone heads, they do have torsos and some have headpieces made of red volcanic rock. The island is now treeless; however it was richly forested when the first Polynesian settlers arrived in approximately AD 300. By 1400, most of the trees on the island had been cut down, for use as fuel, building materials, or possibly logs to roll the statues along the ground. The loss of the forests had a cataclysmic effect on the environment and when the Dutch admiral Roggeveen discovered the island on Easter Sunday, 1722, he found it barren and its inhabitants engaged in intertribal warfare.

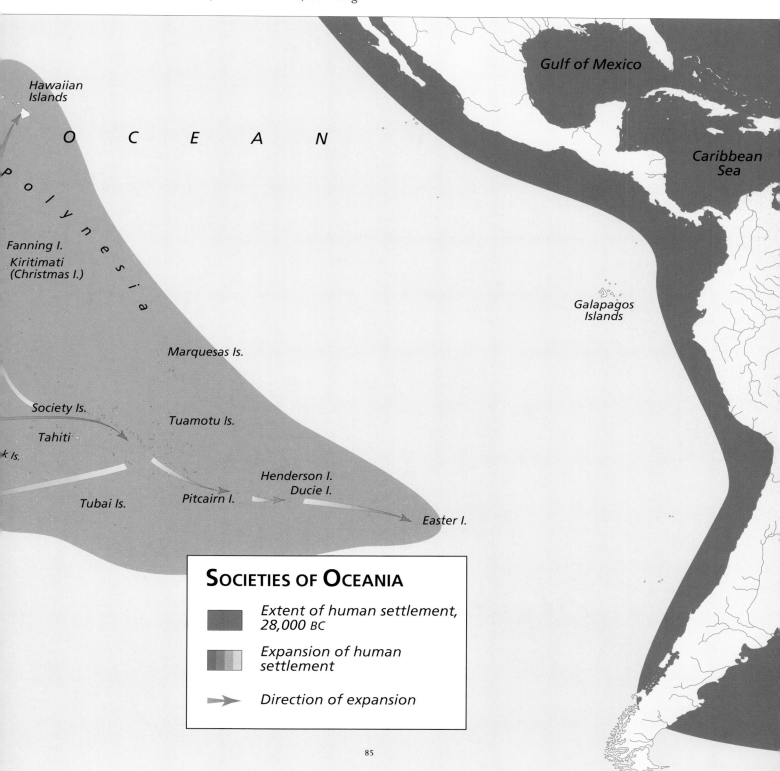

SOCIETIES OF OCEANIA

- Extent of human settlement, 28,000 BC
- Expansion of human settlement
- Direction of expansion

The Vikings

Great seamen and explorers, Viking raiders ranged widely, as did Viking traders—extending their influence to America in the west and Kiev in the east.

Raiders and Traders

In the period from around AD 750 to 1100, the Scandinavians—the people of Denmark, Norway, and Sweden—traveled extensively, with the Danes and Norwegians mainly moving west to Britain and beyond across the north Atlantic, whilst the Swedes ranged eastward to Russia and parts of central Asia. These peoples have come to be referred to collectively as the Vikings or the Norsemen, and are perhaps best known for carrying out brutal raids in western Europe. Indeed, the term "Viking" originally referred only to these raiders and remains almost synonymous with piracy. However, there is some debate as to the origin of the word, which may be derived from either "vik" or "wic," referring respectively to a coastal bay or rivermouth or to a place at which trading took place; and trade routes between Scandinavia, Britain, and the Baltic region are thought to have been established long before the plundering began. In fact, it seems that when Viking hostilities began in Britain at the end of the eighth century, it came as something of a surprise.

Initial Raids and Settlement in Britain

The first historical reference to an attack on Britain concerns an event in 789, when an official went to greet three Viking ships at Portland, only to be killed. This was followed in 793 by the first major recorded raid, which occurred on the island of Lindisfarne off the Northumberland coast, when the monastery there was looted and the monks murdered. Several such raids

were to follow around the British coast, and the practice was to continue for hundreds of years. However, it should be noted that the Vikings were not only pirates, but farmers and craftsmen, most of whom never indulged in raiding. It is certainly true that they employed brutal methods at times, but it was perhaps the fact that these pagans commonly targeted places of Christian reverence that so appalled.

Quite why the Viking raids began as and when they did is not fully understood, but factors include population growth, a need for more land for cultivation and mineral resources, a desire for wealth and power—taking advantage of both eastern and western Europe's growing economy—and exploiting the fact that monasteries were poorly defended and often housed precious objects. The initial raids were fairly small hit-and-run affairs, and larger campaigns were not to be launched for some years to come, but in 825 the Vikings took control of the Faroe Islands, preceding settlement of the Hebrides, Shetland, and the Orkney Islands. By 841 they had established themselves in Ireland at Dublin. Using their impressive longboats,

Opposite: A replica drekar, or dragon-headed Viking longship in full sail. The longship could cross the seas under sail and change to be powered by oars in order to launch a rapid attack on a settlement. Above: Lindholm Hoje, a Viking grave site, near Alborg, Denmark.

which could be used for both long-distance sea crossings and negotiating inland waterways, and aided by favorable wind conditions, the Vikings made several raids between about 842 and 862 in western Europe, which included the sacking of Hamburg and Paris, and raids around the Mediterranean. Further east, Constantinople was attacked and Kiev captured during this same period, and in 860 explorations were launched from the Faroes to Iceland, which was colonized between 870 and 930. In 930 a national assembly known as the Althing was founded in Iceland, which continues to meet to this day.

The Colonization of Britain and Further Expansion

In 865, colonization of Britain began with a major invasion of England by Danish Vikings: the "Danish Great Army". This was a force consisting of several

ICELAND

thousand men which succeeded in securing large amounts of land in England and Scotland. Prior to this, relatively large numbers of Vikings had been landing on British shores, but had been prevented from attacking by large payments of silver, a tax known as Danegeld. York was seized in 867, and by 870 the Vikings controlled the kingdoms of East Anglia, Mercia, and Northumbria. Only Wessex remained in English possession, defended by Alfred the Great. Following a defeat by Alfred in 878, an agreement was reached and the Danelaw was established, providing the Danes with most of the land north of the River Thames, and between 876 and 879 they settled in England in large numbers, although London was to be recaptured in 886. In the year 900, north-west England was colonized by Norwegian Vikings, whilst two years later Dublin was recaptured by the Irish, who would hold it for some fifteen years. Around this time, the Vikings also focused their attention on France, besieging Paris between 885 and 886, and establishing territory in the Seine basin. This was to lead to the foundation of Normandy in 911 and the occupation of Brittany between 914 and 936.

Exploration

In the east, meanwhile, several raids occurred around the Caspian Sea in 912 and 913, but by around 940 it seemed that Viking power was beginning to wane, suggested by a failed siege of Constantinople in 941, and by a series of defeats by the English that would result in the end of Viking York by 954. Exploration continued, however, with Greenland colonized from about 985, around the same time that North America was first sighted from a stray Viking vessel destined for Greenland from Iceland. Initial explorations of the coastline were made, to be followed by further voyages to "Vinland" between 1003 and 1012, and a brief settlement at L'Anse aux Meadows in Newfoundland was probably in existence until around 1020.

Assimilation

In the early part of the eleventh century, Britain was once again subject to Viking raids and large-scale attacks, culminating in 1014 with the conquest of England by the King of Denmark, Svein Forkbeard, who subsequently became King of England, this title then passing to his son, Cnut, just three years later. Cnut's reign was to last until 1035, during which time he also secured power in Norway and Sweden; however, his empire lacked coherence and by 1042 Danish rule in England was over. Although some raids would continue after the Norman invasion of 1066, Scandinavia was gradually becoming more stable and raiding became increasingly unnecessary. By the late eleventh century, the Vikings had been largely assimilated into the populations of the areas in which they had settled, a process that was undoubtedly hastened by their conversion to Christianity, which had begun in the tenth century. By the twelfth century, Viking rule beyond Scandinavia was effectively over. Norway continued to rule over Iceland and Greenland into the 1200s, but returned the Hebrides and Isle of Man to Scotland in 1266. From around 1341, the Inuit began to drive Viking settlers from Greenland, a process which would last until the late fifteenth century, at which time Denmark also ceded Orkney and Shetland back to Scotland.

Norweg Sea

KINGDOM OF ORKNEY

NORTHUMBERLAND

IRISH KINGDOMS

York

Dublin

Dane Law

Cork

WELSH STATES

WESSEX

London

ATLANTIC OCEAN

Normandy • Paris

Orléans •

WEST FRANKISH KINGDOM (FRANCE)

• Bordeaux

Bayonne

Corunna

Avignon

NAVARRE

Fra

ARAGON

LÉON

Barcelon

Oporto

MUSLIM STATES

Tarragona

Toledo

Balansiyah

EMIRATE OF CÓRDOBA

Balearic Is.

Ishbiliyah

Ibn Hafsun (autonomous)

Cartagena M

IDRISIDS

RUSTAMIDS

FINNIC PEOPLES

NORWAY

Hladir

Kaupang

SWEDEN

Uppsala

Birka

Staraya Ladoga
(Aldeigjuborg)
Novgorod
(Holmgard)

DENMARK

Lund

Roskilde

Hedeby

Baltic Sea

BALTIC PEOPLES

KIEVAN
RUS

remen

ine

Cologne

Frankfurt

S L A V S

Cracow

Kiev

AST FRANKISH
KINGDOM
(GERMANY)

Lorch

Nitrava

HUNGARY

Mosapurc

PECHENEGS

R. Danube

Black Sea

nçon

ER
NDY

Milan

Venice

KINGDOM OF

CROATIA

Serbia

Presov

Genoa

Nice

PAPAL STATES

ITALY

Adriatic Sea

BULGARIA

Philippopolis

Nish

Adrianople

Constantinople

Corsica

Rome

Barium

Thessalonica

Naples

Pr. of Benevento

BYZANTINE EMPIRE

Aegean
Sea

Smyrna

Sardinia

Panormus

Sicily

Chandax

Tunis

Malta

Crete

Kairawan

IDS

BIDS)

Tripoli

terranean
Sea

VIKING ATTACKS, TRADE
AND SETTLEMENT c. 910

→ Viking invasions

Everyday Life

Although the Vikings have become notorious for their piracy and raiding of monasteries, ports, and towns, most Scandinavian people of the period in question were peaceful farmers. They lived in small rural villages, where they grew crops such as barley, cabbages, and beans, and reared cattle, goats, sheep, and pigs. Hunting and fishing may have provided much of their food in areas less well suited to agriculture, whilst trade in goods such as hides, walrus ivory, and furs would have provided them with timber for construction and metals like iron in return. Both farmers and raiders are likely to have participated in trade at various times, and raiding itself was often only a seasonal activity. Still others began to extort protection money (Danegeld) rather than continue raiding, and it seems some groups operated as paid mercenaries, protecting kingdoms from other Vikings. The expansion of trading routes in the east, coupled with the movements of Arabs into eastern Europe, also began to introduce large amounts of silver, in the form of both coinage and jewelry. The Vikings were skilled metalworkers in their own right, and silver brooches are amongst the most common of Viking artifacts.

The Viking farmhouse took the form of a long, rectangular structure of stone and timber or turf, with a thatched roof. This was known as the long-house and consisted of a single room in which all domestic activities would have taken place, including cooking, eating, and sleeping. Smaller, semi-sunken outbuildings, meanwhile, would have been used for storage. Large settlements were uncommon in Scandinavia at the start of the Viking age, with no real towns until the late eighth century. However, with increasing wealth, consolidation of power, and the development of ecclesiastical centers as Christianity spread throughout the Viking world, several towns were in existence by 1000 AD. In Britain, settlements initially took the form of simple camps, before agricultural villages were established; following large-scale invasions, existing towns such as York were occupied and developed, typically being fortified with fences and earthworks. Viking buildings in such places took the form of small timber dwellings, and excavations of these sites have revealed such activities as leather- and metalworking, including the minting of coins.

Viking Religion: from Paganism to Christianity

The Vikings were originally pagan, believing in a multitude of gods and demi-gods that related to different aspects of life. Whilst there was no concept of personal spirituality, nor dogmatic theology or priesthood, it seems their religion was based around ritualistic observances, including animal sacrifice. However, little is known about the actual religious practices of the Vikings. Some clues may be gleaned from burial sites, and also from the many stories associated with Viking gods that were preserved in the Eddas— collections of poetic tales believed to have originated in pre-Viking times and which formed the basis of their beliefs. However, these are not thought to have been written down until after widespread Christian conversion, somewhere

between the late twelfth and mid-thirteenth centuries, by which time they were being presented more as mythology than as the founding principles of a religion.

Even so, the Eddas provide an insight into Viking beliefs concerning the relationships between man, the universe, and all its gods, and their creation and destruction. The most important deities were Odin, the creator, and god of war, wisdom, death, and poetry; Thor, the hammer-wielding god of strength and the weather; the brother and sister Freyr and Freyja, god and goddess of fertility; and Loki, god of mischief.

The fact that the Vikings were polytheistic—that they believed in more than one god—enabled them to absorb aspects of Christian doctrine without great difficulty. They probably first came into contact with Christianity in 725 when the first Christian mission traveled to Scandinavia, and then more extensively following their widespread raiding of monasteries. Missions were also established in Scandinavia during the ninth century, but it is thought that these made little impact. It actually seems that Christian conversion occurred most rapidly with the establishment of Viking settlements in Christian lands, such as Britain and Normandy, particularly as more peaceable relations developed and the Vikings were assimilated into the population through marriage. Politically, too, conversion in Christian countries could be advantageous; in 878, Guthrum, a Viking leader, was decreed as ruler of East Anglia following his acceptance of Christianity.

In Scandinavia itself the process was more gradual, but was probably also largely politically motivated, at least on the part of the Viking leaders, in terms of both improving relations with Christian nations and bolstering and consolidating the Scandinavian kingdoms. No doubt both the authority inherent in the ideology of divine ordination, and the more effective administration provided by the bishoprics, were highly influential. Christianity became well-established in Denmark by the mid-eleventh century following the conversion of Harald Bluetooth in 965 and then, perhaps more importantly, following Cnut's ascension to the English throne in 1016. By the early twelfth century the Norwegian king Sigurd was leading crusades to Jerusalem.

In terms of archeological evidence, the transition from pagan to Christian may be witnessed perhaps most strikingly in a change of burial rites. Early Vikings

Above: Burial crosses made from driftwood discovered near a settlement in Greenland, which was colonized by the Vikings about AD 985.
Opposite: Part of a collection of table implements found close to a Viking settlement in Greenland. The Vikings used organic materials such as bone and wood to make everyday items.

tended to cremate their dead along with their belongings, burying their ashes in an urn, and usually marking the spot with a mound of rocks. In some cases the rocks were arranged in the shapes of boats, such as at Lindholm Høje in Denmark, where many graves are marked in this way. Later the Vikings began to bury their dead along with such goods as tools, weapons and jewelry, and even in some cases with their ships and horses. As Christianity spread, however, the Vikings began to adopt the Christian practice of burial without goods. Other evidence may be seen in a number of early Scandinavian churches, which bear pagan motifs.

Early Japan

On the islands of Japan selective external influences and a strong internal identity contributed to the development of a sophisticated court and military culture.

Early Japan

Japan consists of a large group of islands but the country has always been dominated by the largest four: Honshu, Kyushu, Shikoku, and Hokkaido. The first example of organized Japanese culture was found on the low-lying plains of the island of Honshu. The region, Yamato, gave its name to the first period of Japanese history. Because of its island status, Japan was relatively free from outside influences for many thousands of years, and it was only with the arrival of peoples from the Korean peninsula and then from China that Japanese culture really began to flourish.

Below: The Great Buddha of Kamakura is the second largest Buddha statue in Japan. Cast in 1252, it was originally sited inside a large temple. However, the buildings were washed away by a tsunami at the end of the 15th century and now the Buddha stands in the open air.

The Yamato kings had made their capital in Naniwa, now Osaka. Between the fifth and sixth centuries AD, the Yamato were introduced to Buddhism from China, and also to Chinese forms of government. This led to the writing of a constitution based upon Confucian principles. When a rival clan usurped the throne in 645, the new leader, Kotoku Tenna, declared himself emperor and began the Taika Reforms. These declared that the emperor ruled with the authority of heaven and that he should exercise absolute power over all the previously separate states and clans. Japan became a unified empire with a central government.

The Heian Era

With the arrival of the Heian Dynasty in 794, and a period of relative peace and prosperity, Japanese culture was able to flourish independently of Chinese influence. The imperial court was moved to a new capital called Heian-kyo, meaning "city of peace". This city would later become known as Kyoto. Here, the Japanese developed their own style of writing and their own intricate courtly rituals, usually centered on the women at court. Until 1192, the Japanese Empire remained stable and this was mainly due to the influence held by the Fujiwara family. These were a dynasty of close imperial advisors who managed to maintain their influence over the throne by marrying into the imperial line. By ensuring that they were the fathers of empresses and grandfathers of future emperors, they were able to manipulate politics at court. Government below the level of the emperor was organized along Chinese lines, with a council of state run by the most powerful clans in Japan taking care of day-to-day governance. These clans were often in dispute with one another and gradually two became dominant, the Taira and the Minamoto. By the end of the Heian age, these two clans were vying for control of the empire and eventually civil war ensued, marking the end of the first Japanese Empire.

Tsushima
Shimono
Korea
Iki
Dazaifu
Nakadori
Fukae
East China Sea
Amakusa Shima
Koshiki Retto

Yakushima

The Shoguns

When Minamoto no Yoritomo defeated the Taira clan in 1185, he seized power, making use of his powerful military force. This comprised samurai warriors—professional soldiers, initially peasants, who eventually became a caste in their own right.

In establishing a military dictatorship Yoritomo had himself made shogun. A shogun was essentially a military overlord, ruling in the emperor's name—though the emperors were little more than figureheads—and during this period shoguns ruled over all of Japan. The emperor lived on the income from his own estates, and was supported by the shoguns as long as he supported them in return; if he did not, he would be overruled. Under the shoguns, the provinces of Japan regained some of their independence, and their rulers, or daimyo, exercised feudal rights over the people whilst still paying homage to the shogun himself.

Individual shoguns wielded differing levels of control, and different clans rose to—and fell from—prominence; for example, the first shogunate, the Kamakura, declined in 1335 when the Hojo clan was forced from power. Shogunate government remained the main political structure in Japan until the middle of the nineteenth century, though over time the shoguns became less feudal overlords and more hereditary princes, exercising viceregal powers.

THE TAIKA REFORMS IN JAPAN, c. 646–710

- ■ National capital
- ● Provincial capital
- ◌ Administrative centre
- Fortress, with date
- Provincial border
- Road

2,500
1,500
1,000
500
200
100
0 m

0   100 km

0   100 miles

The Crusades

Over two centuries, despite disunity, crusades launched by Christian Europe had the intention of "reclaiming" or "protecting" the Holy Land.

The First Crusades

In 1095 the Byzantine emperor Alexius I Comnenus made a request for assistance to his fellow Christian, Pope Urban II. He asked for mercenary forces to be sent to help the Byzantines defend territory that was under threat from Islam. Byzantium had been fighting off Islamic forces since the sixth century, but a significant defeat at the battle of Manzikert in 1071 had weakened them. Urban II sent far more than a mercenary army, proclaiming at the Council of Clermont that a holy war was needed in order to reclaim Jerusalem for Christendom. Urban's

motives were political as well as spiritual. Launching a massive army overseas would help to combat the internal disputes between the various nobles who ruled over feudal Europe. In addition, sending a crusade into Byzantium would enable the Pope to consolidate his power over the Byzantines.

The fervor that Urban aroused sparked an ill-fated "People's Crusade" that set out in advance

of the main crusade and wreaked havoc as it traveled across Europe; on arrival in Anatolia they were wiped out by the Turks. The main crusader armies marched towards Jerusalem more effectively, ransacking towns and cities along the way. This "Princes' Crusade" was led by some of the most powerful nobles in Western Europe and it took them two years to make their way to the Holy Land. They set up four crusader states at Edessa, Antioch, Tripoli, and finally Jerusalem, which was captured following a long siege in 1099. The first crusade was extremely popular with the people and many left their homes to make the pilgrimage to Jerusalem. Those who returned were seen as heroes and this was the beginning of a new chivalric age.

Defeat of the Muslim forces was possible because of Arabic disunity but following the first crusade they allied in an effort to expel the Christians. In 1144, the capture of Edessa sparked the second Crusade. Pope Eugene III, with the help of the Cistercian Bernard of Clairvaux, had to persuade Louis VII of France and the Holy Roman Emperor, Conrad III, to assist. This second crusade led to a series of defeats, most notably at Damascus, and ended in 1149 with embarrassment for the crusaders.

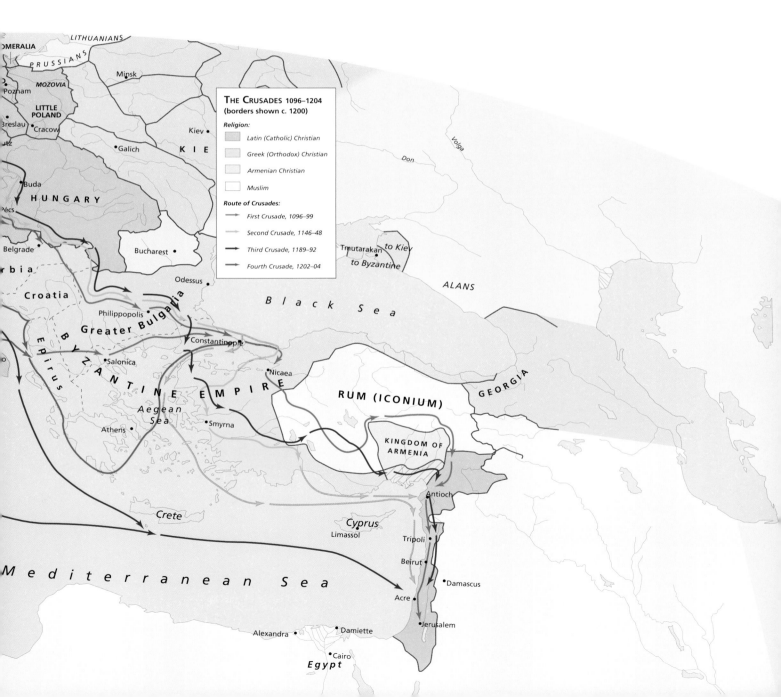

THE CRUSADES 1096–1204
(borders shown c. 1200)

Religion:
- Latin (Catholic) Christian
- Greek (Orthodox) Christian
- Armenian Christian
- Muslim

Route of Crusades:
- First Crusade, 1096–99
- Second Crusade, 1146–48
- Third Crusade, 1189–92
- Fourth Crusade, 1202–04

Conflict in Europe:
The Holy Roman Empire

The position of emperor in the middle ages was first granted by the Pope to Charlemagne in 800. It was a position that was later to become associated with princes from German dynasties. Charlemagne had been king of the Franks, an area that covered both France and Germany, and the Treaty of Verdun in 843 had split this empire into three distinct areas.

Otto I, ruler of the eastern section which included Saxony, Thuringia, and Bavaria, was awarded the title in 962, taking the position from the rulers of the central realm. At the end of the tenth century the emperors of Germany were elected to the position by the leaders of the Germanic people that inhabited the region; these leaders would later become known as the Electors. The elected ruler could only then be crowned by the Pope, implying a role as protector of the church. Despite being an elected position, the title often remained within dynasties, the first significant one being the Hohenstaufens who ruled from 1138 to 1254 and included Frederick I "Barbarossa," who added the word "holy" to the title. The position of Holy Roman Emperor became increasingly powerful through the eleventh and twelfth centuries, often leading to conflict with the Papacy.

Empire versus Papacy

Popes could crown Holy Roman emperors, but it was also the case that the emperors had the power to elect popes. This once harmonious relationship ended in 1059 when the church council in Rome declared that secular rulers should no longer be able to appoint or "invest" any church officials, including the pope. This role would instead be given to the newly created College of Cardinals, which still elects the pope to this day. The church council also demanded the end of the investiture of bishops and archbishops by secular rulers. The ensuing investiture controversy led to Pope Gregory VII excommunicating Henry IV who had himself "dismissed" Gregory as pope. However, Henry had come under attack from his own nobles who had taken advantage of the political situation to revolt. The dispute with the Church over the issue of investiture lasted for five decades and during that time the power of the Emperor was greatly reduced. Compromise was finally reached in 1122 at the Concordat of Worms and investiture was abolished, with the power to elect bishops returning to the Church. Disputes between emperors and popes continued over the following centuries, and the emperor was never again able to fully control the princes and dukes who ruled in his territory.

The Third and Fourth Crusades

In 1187, the great Sultan Saladin attacked and recaptured crusader territory in Syria. His capture of Jerusalem sparked the third of the great crusades. The three great leaders of Christendom—Frederick Barbarossa, the Holy Roman Emperor, Philip II of France, and Richard the Lionheart of England—led the crusade to reclaim the Holy Land. The death of Frederick in Anatolia in 1190 left an unstable alliance between the French and English, hostile nations that had previously been at war. Victory at the siege of Acre in 1191 resulted in a struggle for control between Philip and Richard, with Philip eventually leaving the Holy Land to return to France. Richard then embarked on a series of battles with Saladin in his attempt to recapture Jerusalem and in 1192 resorted to signing a truce which would give passage to Christian pilgrims but keep the city under Muslim control. It was at this time that the order of the Teutonic Knights was established, primarily to provide aid and protection to the Christian pilgrims, although they later developed into a mercenary crusading army with their own territorial ambitions. The third crusade had been a failure, with Richard returning to England in 1192.

Six years later when Pope Innocent III called for another crusade, he was ignored by the leaders of Western Europe who were either in conflict with the church (Germany) or fighting one another (France and England). Financial support came from the wealthy city state, Venice, who agreed to transport the crusaders across the Mediterranean to the object of the crusade, Egypt. The Venetians soon took control and redirected efforts to attacking Constantinople itself with the intention of placing a new emperor on the Byzantine throne. The city was sacked and pillaged and a new Latin Empire established which lasted until 1261. The original intentions of the Crusade were not addressed at all and further attempts at crusading were unpopular and unsupported.

The Fall of the Byzantine Empire

Although the Byzantines had brought about the first crusade, they had quickly distanced themselves from

Above: Krak des Chevaliers (Castle of the Knights) in Syria was taken by the Knights Hospitallers in 1142 and became a crusader stronghold. Opposite: An illuminated miniature from a universal chronicle illustrating the looting of Jerusalem after its capture by the Christians in 1099.

the Church in Rome, which they deeply mistrusted. Attacks on the Byzantines came not only from the Turks but also from the Christian Normans in Sicily and the Venetians, and the events of the fourth crusade permanently weakened the empire. In 1261, the Greeks in Constantinople managed to drive the Venetians out of the city aided by Genoa, a rival city state of Venice. A new dynasty, the Palaeologus, was established in the Byzantine capital, Constantinople, which presided over a less ethnically diverse and rather more Greek population.

The Empire continued to be threatened by invasion from both Venice and the Turks, and in an attempt to protect itself it considered uniting its Orthodox church with Rome, despite the general unpopularity of such a move. However, Rome was reluctant to save the Byzantines, and when the Ottoman Turks began to invade, the Empire received no aid. At the time of its final fall, all that remained of the Empire was Constantinople itself, the southern Peloponnese, and Trebizond on the eastern shores of the Black Sea. The final attack on Constantinople began in April 1453, led by Mehmed II, and the city was taken the following month. Many of the city's occupants fled to Italy, taking with them a number of ancient Greek texts, the discovery of which contributed to the European Renaissance.

Novgorod

Warsaw
POLAND
Minsk

Republic of Novgorod

Russian Principalities

Kiev
Moscow

Bulgar

EMPIRE OF THE GOLDEN HORDE

Odessa

BYZANTINE EMPIRE
Constantinople
Black Sea
New Sarai
R. Volga
Old Sarai

Tiflis

Caspian Sea

Aral Sea

R. Irtysh

R. Yenisey

Damascus

MAMELUKE EMPIRE

Tabriz

IL-KHAN EMPIRE

Urgench

R. Syr Darya

EMPIRE OF CHAGATAI

Bukhara
Tashkent
Samarkand
Khodzhent
Kashgar

R. Euphrates
Baghdad

Merv
R. Amu Darya

Khotan

SHARIFS OF MECCA

Medina
Mecca

A r a b i a

Kerman

Persian Gulf
OMAN

Kabul

TIBET
1294 independent

Hormuz

R. Indus

Mirath
1329

SULTANATE OF DELHI

Sana
YEMEN

Arabian Sea

Delhi

Patna
R. Ganges

Bengal

Gujerat
Somnath

Orissa

N

Bay of Bengal

Hindu States

Goa

0   400 km

0   400 miles

Calicut

Madurai

Ceylon

Kublai Khan's campaigns, 1268–79

Kublai Khan's campaigns, 1274–92

Other Mongol campaign

Mongol Empire

For the first time, most of Asia came under single rule, uniting it in the Mongol Empire, the largest land-based empire yet created.

THE EMPIRE OF THE GREAT KHAN, 1260–c. 1300

- The Great Khanate, 1268
- Conquered by the Great Khan (Kublai Khan), 1268–79
- Western khanates owing nominal allegiance to the Great Khan
- Tributary to Mongol state

Karakorum

EMPIRE OF THE GREAT KHAN

Hsiliang

Khanbalik

Hsian   K'ai-feng   R. Huang Ho.

Nanjing

Hangzhou

R. Chang Jian   R. Yangtze

Dali

Chongqing   Wuchou

Fuchou

Quanchou

Canton (Guangzhou)

1285 Shenglong

Hainan

Vijaya

Angkor

KHMER KINGDOM

ANNAM

CHAMPA

DOM EGU

egu

gan

Yellow Sea

Yangchou

Kao-li

Sea of Japan

JAPAN

1274 and 1281

East China Sea

Taiwan

1281

1281

1292

unsuccessful expedition to Java

The Rise of the Mongols

The Mongols were a group of linguistically related tribes who lived in the further reaches of the Gobi desert of Central Asia. A nomadic people who were ruled over by a number of different chiefs, it wasn't until they were united under one leader that they became the successful warrior force that would conquer most of Asia and parts of Europe. The Mongols were essentially made up of Türks, Kitan, Tatars, Ruruan, and Huns, all of whom had a long history of conflict with China. It was, in fact, a group who were ancestors of the Mongols, the Xiongnu, who had originally necessitated the building of the Great Wall of China. Skilled horsemen and archers, the Mongol tribes were fearsome warriors but their disunity and internal competition prevented them from becoming the serious threat that they would later pose. In geographical terms the Mongol Empire was to become the largest in human history, reaching from the eastern borders of Germany across to Vietnam, and from the Arctic coast of northern Russia down to the Persian Gulf and the Indian Ocean. Their achievement was not simply that of conquering vast tracts of land, however. Mongol armies defeated the most advanced and populated nations of the period, in particular the Chinese, the Persians, and the Abbasid Dynasty of Iraq.

Genghis Khan

It was the influence of one man which enabled the disparate Mongolian tribes to build a powerful empire. Genghis Khan had been born as Temujin during the 1160s, the son of a tribal leader; however, when his father was murdered by neighboring Tatars, he was cast out by his clan. He gradually began to assume a greater status within a new tribe and as a young man showed himself to be a fearless and charismatic leader. On inheriting the leadership of his tribe, he began a long campaign of subjugating neighboring clans until power was ceded to him. He was eventually able, by 1206, to unify the disparate tribes and was named the Genghis Khan or "universal ruler."

Genghis Khan's success lay in his military genius and administrative foresight. He mobilized the Mongols into an effective army of well-trained horsemen who could carry out attacks with speed and precision. This army was organized into units made up of one hundred, one thousand, and ten thousand, each of which could be rapidly redirected during the course of a battle. Brutal in their treatment of conquered peoples, the notoriety of the Mongol troops and their efficiency at dispatching their enemies meant that towns simply surrendered in the face of attack. Many of the people conquered by them were assimilated into their culture and into their

armies, in particular the Turkic people of western Asia. The result of this was that the Mongolian Empire was eventually dominated by Turkish speakers.

Genghis Khan had also established a rule of law in the form of the Yasa, a formal, written set of laws which were intended to keep the Mongol tribes united by removing all opportunities for dispute. This also advocated particularly harsh punishments for the most minor offences. However, in aspects of religion, Genghis Khan did permit tolerance, and under Mongol rule both Islam and Buddhism were able to flourish. Genghis Khan's foreign ambitions were most enthusiastically directed towards China, the country he felt to be Mongolia's greatest enemy. In 1211, he invaded the territory of the northern Jin empire and, although he died before conquest was complete, his actions certainly enabled his successors to finish the task, which they did by 1241. His armies also moved westward across Asia, taking areas around the Caspian Sea and moving into the Caucasus region of southern Russia.

The Yuan Dynasty

On the death of Genghis Khan the vast Mongolian Empire was separated into four Khanates, each ruled over by one of his direct descendants. The Khanate of the Golden Horde ruled over Russia, the Chagatai Khanate controlled the territories of Central Asia, the Ilkhanate ruled over western Asia, in particular Persia and Iraq, while the Great Khanate presided over Mongolia and China.

In 1260, the grandson of Genghis, Kublai Khan, became the Great Khan, and in 1264 he relocated his capital from Mongolia to Beijing. By driving out the southern Song Dynasty and its supporters, Kublai Khan was the first Mongol to rule completely over China, establishing what became known as the Yuan Dynasty. The Mongols were not dynastic rulers and by referring to his rule as a dynastic one, Kublai Khan was acknowledging the cultural importance placed upon the concept by the Chinese. As alien rulers, the Yuan were never popular with the Chinese population, despite their continuing to contribute to the large building projects begun by their predecessors, such as the Grand Canal. The principal reason for this was that rule of the Yuan was essentially an oppressive one. In order to keep the Chinese subjugated trade was restricted and resources were stripped. The Mongols refused to learn the Chinese language and remained aloof from the majority of the population. Government officials, who continued to be members of the Chinese civil service, were unable to communicate effectively with those at the very highest levels of society, which created animosity and conflict.

However, Kublai Khan and his successors gradually began to adopt some aspects of Chinese culture, encouraging the spread of Buddhism and cementing the place of Confucianism in the examinations for the civil service. The gradual "sinicization" of the Yuan emperors ultimately led to their losing influence within the rest of the Mongol Empire, and in 1368 the Yuan were replaced in China by the Ming.

The Golden Horde

When the Great Khan Ogodei, Genghis Khan's son, ordered the invasion of Russia in 1236, that country was not a unified state, but rather a collection of principalities known as Rus. The Mongols mounted a swift and aggressive attack and achieved the only successful invasion of Russian territory ever during the winter months. They had earlier made exploratory raids into the steppes during the 1220s and the final attack in 1236 was more decisive. They used the Russian cold to their advantage, crossing the frozen Volga in order to penetrate deeper into hostile territory. The Mongols destroyed towns and whole populations, including Kiev in 1240, and devastated the regions as far north as Novgorod. The result of this invasion was that the Mongols were able to establish a ruling state, the Khanate of the Golden Horde, under their leader, Ghengis' grandson, Batu.

The majority of the Golden Horde moved back into the steppe region from where they administered their overlordship of Rus territories. They appointed local revenue collectors who oversaw the payment of

Above: An illustration from a Persian literary text showing Genghis Khan in his tent.
Opposite: Portrait of Genghis Khan (1206-27), founder of the imperial dynasty, the Yuan, making China the center of the great Mongol Empire.

tributes from the Russian principalities and who also ensured that subservience to the Mongols continued by encouraging a rule of terror. However, by the late fourteenth century the Golden Horde had begun to collapse, with internal disputes and succession crises leading to irreparable divisions. Gradually the Mongols were pushed back to their territories in Mongolia and northern China, although the Khanate of the Golden Horde continued to exist as the Khanate of the Crimea until its demise in 1783, when it was annexed by the Russian empress Catherine the Great.

The Black Death

The Arrival and Spread of the Plague

No one knows for sure where the plague known as the Black Death originated, but popular myth places the blame on the Mongol armies who carried the disease into Europe from Central Asia. During a siege on the Genoan-controlled city of Kaffa, the Mongols were said to have catapulted infected bodies over the walls and the fleeing citizens took the disease by ship into Italy. From there the plague spread across Europe at an alarming rate, devastating urban and rural communities alike.

Whatever its source, the main carrier of the plague was the black rat which, hosting fleas infected with the *Yersinia pestis* bacteria, was common across Europe. Two other mutated forms of the disease were highly contagious: the pneumonic variant which attacked the respiratory system and was airborne, and the septicemic variant which was carried in the blood. Its spread was facilitated by the general malnutrition of a population used to pestilence and economic depression, a condition the plague served to exacerbate. During the years 1347 to 1350 the disease is estimated to have killed between a third to a half of Europe's population and it continued to recur in brief outbreaks over the next four centuries.

Symptoms

The bubonic variant of the plague was the most widespread and it was identified by large glandular swellings or buboes that could reach the size of an apple. These painful swellings tended to be located at the site of flea bites, most commonly on the neck, armpits, and groin. They would initially be red in color, later turning purple, then black—hence the popular name for this plague. With this form of the illness, death was likely within a week. The pneumonic mutation caused the victim to cough and sneeze, spreading the bacteria, whilst the septicemic variety resulted in near immediate death once the bacteria entered the bloodstream. The speed with which the plague killed its victims terrified the medieval population, who quickly began to lose their faith in the Church and in the alchemy of their healers.

The Consequences of the Black Death

Whilst the disease obviously decimated populations and increased hardship with the disruption to productivity, it also contributed to a fundamental change in the social climate of medieval Europe. The loss of so many peasants greatly affected the position of those who survived the plague, who now found their services in demand; some were able to prosper. With landowners desperate to purchase labor, peasants were able to move from estate to estate and demand higher wages. In order to curtail the increased demands of the serf classes, many countries passed laws to restrict movement, and even sumptuary laws—specifying what different classes could wear—intended to reinforce their lower status. In addition, there were now far fewer people to pay the taxes needed to fund the wars fought by the nobility. Peasants' revolts became more common in Western Europe at this time and anti-establishment—and particularly anti-Church—feelings began to increase.

THE BLACK DEATH
1346–53

—— Major trade routes

1346
1347
1350
1351
1348
1349
1353
Free of Plague

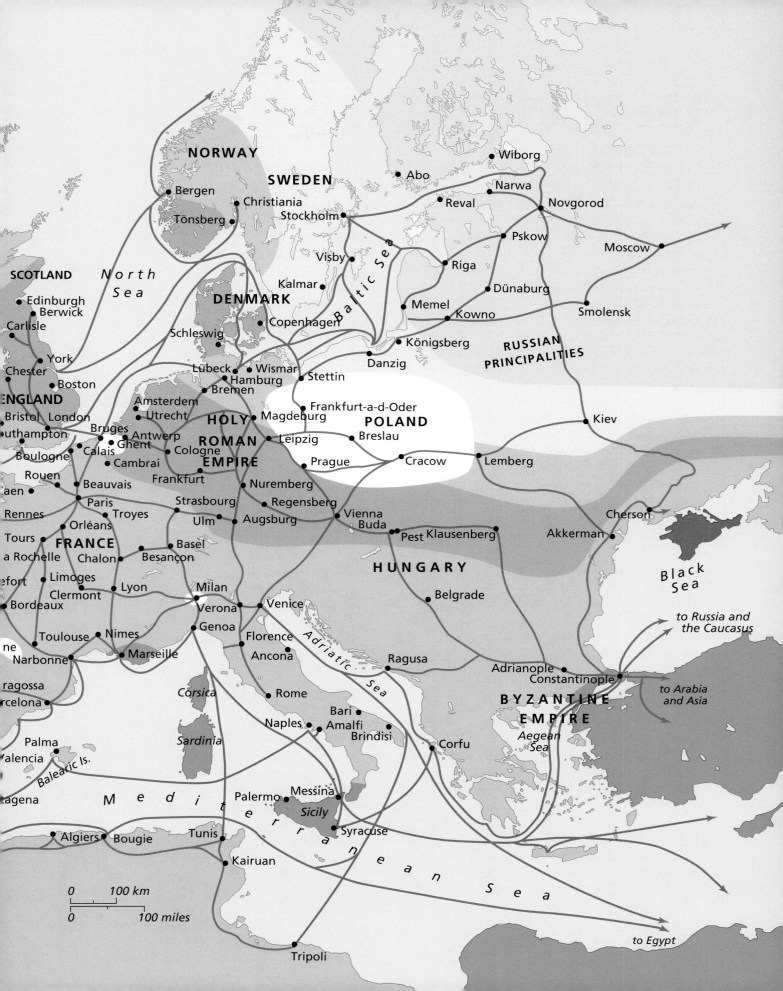

The Rise of Muscovy 1462–1505

Ivan the Great expanded his state of Muscovy, creating a realm covering most of northern Russia, which was able to finally defy the Mongol Golden Horde.

Ivan the Great

Ivan III Vasilevich ruled as Grand Prince of Moscow from 1462 to 1505 and became better known as Ivan the Great. He built upon the work of his predecessors by strengthening the position of Muscovy, uniting the previously autonomous principalities of Russia, and throwing off the yoke of the Mongols. Ivan was the first of the Princes of Moscow who could call himself the sovereign of all Russia.

He began his rule by sharing power with his father, Vasili II, during the prince's final years. On his succession, Ivan determined to continue working to unite Russia, but he approached the task with caution. The first Russian republic to come to Ivan's attention was Novgorod which, growing wary of Muscovy's increasing power, had allied itself with Poland. Using this as a pretext for war, Ivan marched upon Novgorod in 1470 and defeated the state, severing its ties with Poland. Following years of suppression the republic of Novgorod finally accepted Ivan as its autocratic ruler in 1477. Later principalities fell to Ivan through either conquest or diplomatic means and by 1485, with the absorption of Tver, Russia had become a single nation under the control of one leader.

Ivan became the first autocratic leader that Russia was to know. He considered himself to be the heir to the recently fallen empire of Constantinople, since the Russian Orthodox church, like Byzantine Orthodoxy, stood apart from Rome. His marriage to Sophia Palaeologina, niece of the last Byzantine Emperor, also influenced Ivan and he became impressed by Imperial traditions. It was through his wife that he acquired the emblem of the two headed eagle that had previously belonged to the Byzantines. Ivan consequently held himself above all other Russian nobility and the boyars became subservient to his sovereignty, a state of affairs which led to much resentment. On his death, Ivan was succeeded by his son, Vasili III.

The Decline of Mongol Power

Ivan's other great achievement was the rejection of the overlordship of the Mongols, or Tatars. The Mongols had invaded the medieval state of Kievan Rus in 1223 as they swept through from Asia into eastern Europe; one branch of the Mongol force had remained in the Volga River area, becoming known as the Golden Horde. Although this region was principally a Mongol state, it was also made up of Turks, Tatars, Uzbeks, and other central Asian peoples. The Horde was mainly concerned with collecting taxes from the Russian princes who, as vassals to feudal rulers, were required to pay regular tribute to their overlords. Two things, however, weakened the Horde. The Black Death of 1346–7 depleted their numbers and they were also beset by the internal fighting of the heirs to the Khanate. During the 1440s, the Horde was divided by a civil war which resulted in the development of five separate Khanates.

These five separate states were far weaker than the Russian state of Muscovy, which had begun to flourish despite Tatar control. In 1476, Ivan III refused to pay any more tributes to the Khan of the Big Horde, the greater Khanate of the divided Golden Horde. At first the Khan was preoccupied by military struggles in the Crimea, but eventually turned towards punishing Ivan. In 1480 he mobilized his army to march on Moscow. The Muscovites demanded that Ivan take action to defeat the Mongols and so he took his army to meet the Khan. The two forces faced each other across the River Ugra. Battle did not, however, take place, in the main because both armies were waiting for support to arrive. Ivan's reinforcements did reach him but those of the Khan did not, and after several weeks of stand-off in the bitter winter cold, the Khan's troops retired. This act was the first in a series of disasters that led to the disintegration of the Golden Horde. Several months later, the Khan was killed by a rival and Mongol power was further diminished. Ivan's actions meant that the Russians no longer had to pay tribute and were finally independent.

The Kremlin

As a fortress the Kremlin had stood on the Borovitsky Hill in Moscow since the eleventh century; during Ivan III's reign, however, the complex was redesigned and reconstructed as a demonstration of the power and superiority of the Muscovites, who were at the center

Above: A view of the Ivan the Great bell tower sandwiched between the Kremlin cathedrals.

of newly unified Russia. Ivan imported a number of builders and architects from Italy to design the new palaces and cathedrals for his "new" Kremlin, but the buildings they constructed had a uniquely Russian appearance, not an Italian style. The citadel had already been extensively added to by Ivan's predecessors and white, crenelated stone walls had been built around the triangular, 27.5 hectare site in 1368.

In the 1470s, Ivan had the Cathedral of the Assumption built as the seat of the Russian Orthodox Church, where future coronations, assemblies, and state ceremonies would take place. Ivan had employed the Italian architect "Aristotle" Fioravanti to design the cathedral, and he traveled across Russia in order to get an impression of the best of Russian ecclesiastical design. When his work was finished four years later, Ivan was so pleased with the outcome that he had Fioravanti imprisoned to prevent him from leaving

Russia and the architect died in captivity. It was on the steps of the Cathedral of the Assumption that Ivan tore up the charter that bound the Russian princes to the Golden Horde.

Ivan also commissioned the building of the Cathedral of the Archangel Michael, the last resting place of the rulers of Russia for many years, and the Cathedral of the Annunciation, with its golden dome. Ivan's own residence was the Terem Palace; he had the Faceted Palace built in order to hold court audiences in a magnificent throne room and to entertain people with large feasts. Later emperors and empresses would continue to add buildings to the complex, including the enormous gilt bell tower that was dedicated to Ivan the Great.

Europe circa 1400

Division and Disunity: The fourteenth and fifteenth centuries saw disturbances and disagreements in western Europe. Independent city states developed in Italy, and national consolidation began further east.

Social Unrest

The established social order in Europe during the thirteenth century had been feudalism, but with economic decline and the massive reduction in population caused by famine and plague, this began to disintegrate. Rapid inflation and high prices had a profound effect on the poor and the levying of taxes to pay for the wars waged by the nobility made the situation even worse. The devastating effects of the Black Death were not effectively dealt with by the nobility who, in response to increasing demands, simply strove to control the peasants even more tightly.

In France in 1358 a rebellion broke out which soon swept across the country. Peasants rose violently against the nobility, blaming them for the generally dismal circumstances. In many areas the peasants were joined by urban workers, tradesmen, and even parish priests. This "Jacquerie" was eventually suppressed by the aristocracy. In England in the 1380s the Peasants' Revolt was an almost identical reaction to the imposition of a poll tax. The peasants were successful enough to force a meeting with King Richard II who agreed reforms; however, Richard did not keep his promises and the peasants were brutally suppressed.

The increasing amount of corruption and crime was reflected in much of the literature of the age. In England, the legend of Robin Hood, in which a noble outlaw steals from the rich to aid the poor, demonstrated the tendency of landowners such as the Sheriff of Nottingham to steal from the peasants. Chaucer's Canterbury Tales (1387) shows how petty corruption in both the secular and the religious communities was common. In the Low Countries and Germany, the Reynard and Isengrim beast fables were

satires on contemporary society, often focusing on the struggle for power between the church and the aristocracy, and presenting both in a negative light.

The Great Schism

In 1305, in order to get away from the dangerous fighting between the noble families in Rome, the papacy removed itself to Avignon in the south of France. Between 1305 and 1378, seven French popes held office, becoming known as the Avignon popes. Gregory XI returned to Italy but died soon afterward and the Romans insisted upon the election of an Italian as the next pope. Urban VI's difficult and demanding character caused the cardinals to regret their choice and thirteen of them removed themselves to Fondi in Italy in order to elect another Pontiff, Clement VII. Cardinals had elected two official popes, an act which deeply divided the Church, causing what became known as the Great or Western Schism. The leaders of Europe were forced to decide which pope they would acknowledge and political divisions and alliances were apparent in their choices. Followers of the French Pope, Clement, included France, Scotland, Castille, Aragon, Portugal, Savoy, and some parts of Germany. The Roman pope, Urban, was supported by Italy, England, and the majority of the Holy Roman Empire. In 1409, in order to resolve the problem, the Church

Above: The Doge's Palace in Venice was built in the fourteenth century. Venice's position on the Adriatic meant that its fortune was built on trade.
Opposite: A view of Florence, one of the most powerful of the Italian city states, which was dominated by the Medici family during this period.

called a council at Pisa which resulted in the election of a third pope. Finally, in 1417 at the Council of Constance, all three strands of the papacy were ended with the deposition of both the third pope and the Avignon pope, and the resignation of the Roman Gregory XII. With the election of a new Roman pope, it was decreed that the Roman line was the true line and that, furthermore, no one could again have the power to remove a pope, except for the Pope himself.

Italian City States

During this period, the cities of northern Italy developed an independent form of government, becoming city states. The position of most of these states—either on the Mediterranean or on routes from the ports into Europe—meant that cities such as Milan, Bologna, Florence, Amalfi, Venice, Pisa, and Genoa became wealthy commercial centers. With this wealth the cities set themselves up as autonomous powers with communal governments, or Communi, protected by either the Pope or the Emperor. City states favored

Norwegian Sea

N

NORWAY

SWEDEN

Wiborg

Abo

Bergen

Oslo

Narwa

Reval

Novgorod

Tönsberg

Stockholm

Visby

Pskow

Moscow

Riga

Kalmar

Dünaburg

Smolensk

North Sea

SCOTLAND

DENMARK

Memel

Kowno

RUSSIAN PRINCIPALITIES

Falkirk

Edinburgh

Berwick

Schleswig

Copenhagen

Königsberg

Carlisle

IRELAND

York

Lübeck

Wismar

Danzig

Dublin

Chester

Boston

Hamburg

Bremen

Stettin

Kiev

ENGLAND

Amsterdam

Utrecht

HOLY

Magdeburg

Frankfurt-a-d-Oder

POLAND

R. Dnieper

Bristol

London

Bruges

Antwerp

Cologne

ROMAN

Leipzig

Breslau

Southampton

Calais

Ghent

Lille

EMPIRE

Prague

Cracow

Lemberg

Boulogne

Arras

Cambrai

Frankfurt

Nuremberg

Regensberg

Cherson

Rouen

Beauvais

Vienna

Akkerman

Caen

Paris

Strasbourg

Augsburg

Buda

Black Sea

ATLANTIC OCEAN

Rennes

Troyes

Ulm

Pest

Klausenberg

Santiago

Orléans

FRANCE

Basel

Besançon

HUNGARY

to Russia and the Caucasus

Léon

Tours

Chalon

Limoges

Lyon

Milan

Belgrade

R. Danube

Oporto

Vitoria

La Rochelle

Clermont

Verona

Venice

Rochefort

Bordeaux

Genoa

Florence

Ragusa

Adrianople

Bayonne

Toulouse

Nimes

Ancona

Constantinople

Lisbon

Saragossa

Narbonne

Montpellier

Marseille

Corsica

Rome

BYZANTINE EMPIRE

to Arabia and Asia

PORTUGAL

Barcelona

Adriatic Sea

Bari

Corfu

SPAIN

Toledo

Palma

Sardinia

Naples

Amalfi

Brindisi

Aegean Sea

Valencia

Cartagena

Balearic Is.

Cádiz

Seville

Granada

Messina

Palermo

Malaga

Almería

Sicily

Syracuse

Tangier

Oran

Algiers

Bougie

Tunis

Mediterranean Sea

to Arabia

Kairuan

Tripoli

to Egypt

oligarchies, usually controlled by a single family or "signorie" who regularly exercised aggressive policies over rival families and neighbors. Rather than being of noble birth, many of the signorie had belonged to the merchant classes and the establishment of societies loyal to the city rather than to the aristocracy meant the end of feudal society in Italy. Rather than use their own citizens to create armies the signorie bought in mercenary soldiers called condottieri and state rivalries often led to conflict. The strongest of these states became Venice, Florence, and Milan to the north, the central papal states and Naples to the south. Both Venice and its rival Genoa were also powerful naval states, with Genoa holding control over the Tyrrhenian Sea and Venice the Adriatic and the Aegean. Both states colonized a number of overseas islands and ports.

Eastern Europe

Whilst western Europe was suffering from economic depression, famine, plague, and political and social unrest, eastern European kingdoms were beginning to consolidate their power. The German-speaking kingdom of Bohemia was united under King Charles IV (1316–78), later Holy Roman Emperor, who concentrated his energies on the improvement of kingdom over empire. In Poland, political and cultural associations with Lithuania were cemented with the marriage of the Lithuanian noble Wladislaw Jagiello to Queen Jadwiga of Poland in 1386, beginning the Polish Jagiellonion Dynasty. Hungary gradually recovered from the devastation wrought by the nomad armies of the Golden Horde to form a more modern and cultured civilization, led in 1342–82 by Louis the Great.

The migration of German peoples into the Baltic region resulted in the formation of a number of German cities along the coast. Cities such as Lübeck, Wismar, Danzig, and Konigsburg soon formed a trading alliance, becoming known as the Hanseatic League in 1358. During the fourteenth century, the Baltic Sea had become one of the most important trade routes in the world. Although the Hanse cities were independent in nature, they offered allegiance ultimately to the Holy Roman Empire. In Prussia, control was held by the Order of the Teutonic Knights, who had been called in by the Polish dukes to control the Prussian tribes. Granted sovereignty by the Emperor Frederick II in 1226, the Teutonic Knights ran their territory as a military regime. The threat they posed to Lithuania did much to ally that country to Poland and by 1466 the Teutonic Order were forced to acknowledge the sovereignty of the Jagiellonians.

European Trade

Trading networks developed and spread across medieval Europe, extending outside the continent itself. Venice, for example, traded not only with Byzantium, but also with the whole of the Arab Mediterranean. In northern Europe, the German towns of the Hanse provided an outlet for textiles from western areas. Flemish and English woollen cloth was traded to Constantinople and beyond, into the area of the Black Sea, and exotic goods like spices were imported. Thriving trade within Europe also contributed to the development of great commercial centers like Genoa and Antwerp. Trade guilds (or associations) fostered contact across national borders, with merchants working throughout the continent as a whole, and provided the basis for economic growth.

The Hundred Years War

The Struggle for Control of France

In 1337, the English King Edward III declared himself the rightful ruler of France, giving himself the title "King of England and France." He based his claim on his descent from Philip IV of France through his mother. Philip, the last of the Capetian Kings, had no male heir so the vulnerable French enacted a law stating that property could not be passed down through the female line.

Edward invaded France in order to take the crown, which had been given to Philip of Valois. In 1346 the English army, despite being weakened by plague and outnumbered, won an important victory at Crécy. Their weaponry, including longbows and pikes, gave them the advantage. Encouraged, they went on to capture Calais and in 1356 took the French monarch John II prisoner. At Agincourt in 1415, now under the leadership of Henry V, the greatly outnumbered English infantry and archers yet again defeated the French cavalry. Fewer than 500 English soldiers died in battle, compared to over 5,000 French. The English took control of Normandy and Henry declared himself the rightful heir to the French throne. His death in 1422 left his infant son as heir and during the resulting unstable period the French began to unite. In 1428, war began again and the English laid siege to the city of Orleans. Inspired by Joan of Arc, the French

managed to raise the siege the following year. After a series of French victories, the Dauphin, son of Charles VI, was eventually crowned Charles VII. Despite this, Henry VI was crowned at Paris in 1430. However, when the Duke of Burgundy changed allegiance to France in 1435, Paris returned to the French King. The English were gradually removed from French territory until they were left in 1453 with only Calais in their possession and defeat in France contributed to civil war—the War of the Roses—at home. Although hostility between the two countries continued for several centuries to come, this date commonly marks the end of the Hundred Years War.

Joan of Arc

Born around 1412, Joan of Arc was a peasant girl who claimed to have communicated with the Archangel Michael, St Catherine, and St Margaret. In these visions she was told to drive the English out of France and to take the Dauphin to Reims for coronation; she was taken to the Dauphin in 1428 disguised as a boy. She was examined by Charles' theologians for three weeks before receiving permission to lead the army to the besieged city of Orleans.

In her own suit of armor and bearing a white standard, Joan boosted the morale of the troops and encouraged them on to victory. Following the successful passage of Charles to Reims, Joan was then involved in the less impressive attack on Paris where she was captured by the Burgundians, allies of the English. They sold her to the English who put her on trial in 1431 at Rouen under the charge of heresy. Accused of being a witch, of having demonic visions, of merciless killing, and of cross-dressing, Joan was found guilty. Four months later she was burned at the stake where witnesses claimed to have seen a white dove fly out of the flames. In 1456, the Pope authorized an appeal to her sentence and she was officially recognized by the church as a martyr. She was canonized as a saint in 1920.

Left: Joan of Arc, known as "the Maid of Orleans," at Reims Cathedral for the coronation of the Dauphin as King Charles VII. Opposite: Johannes Gutenberg, the inventor of moveable type.

Cultural Revival in Europe

The fourteenth and fifteenth centuries saw a flowering of culture, especially in Italy, and the development of printing and the spread of learning in Europe as a whole.

The Italian Renaissance

"Renaissance" is the term most often used to describe the cultural achievements of the Italians of the fourteenth and fifteenth centuries. There were in fact a series of "revivals" or "rebirths" of classical learning, art, and culture; a twelfth-century renaissance focused in particular on the rediscovery of Aristotle's writings. The Italian Renaissance is perhaps the best known because of the number of artistic, architectural, and cultural achievements of the period.

The wealthy city states were both financially and geographically in a good position to encourage "renaissance." The northern cities were conduits not only for the material goods being brought in from North Africa and Asia, but also for cultural artefacts and learning. From Constantinople, Spain, and the Arab lands came classical texts and scientific and mathematical learning. Their proximity to the remains of ancient Rome also meant that art and architectural styles could be directly examined.

One center of the Italian Renaissance was Florence, ruled over by the powerful Medici family who were patrons to, among others, the artist and sculptor Michelangelo. Other Renaissance artists included Donatello, Botticelli, Raphael, and Leonardo da Vinci. In literature, Petrarch was largely responsible for the development of humanism, a school of thought which saw mankind as intrinsically good, as opposed to the Church's view of mankind as being sinners in need of redemption. Other writers included Dante, who wrote *The Divine Comedy*, and Boccaccio, whose *Decameron* provided a number of stories for Shakespeare. Renaissance architecture was also influenced by the classical, with magnificent new buildings appearing in Florence, Venice, Milan, and Rome. The use of columns, to decorate facades, and domes became a particular feature; some of the most famous Renaissance buildings include the Duomo in Florence and St Peter's in Rome.

Humanism

The development of humanism was partly a response to the growing sense of disillusionment with the Church. It covered literary and scholarly pursuits such as grammar, rhetoric, history, philosophy and poetry, all of which are products of human thought. At its heart was the call for the revival of the classics, in particular for the study of Greek and Latin. It also advocated the view that individuals could use human skills such as reason and logic to improve themselves and gain dignity. As humanism spread northward from Italy it reached other European countries and, with the advent of printing techniques, a wider audience. As humanist approaches were applied to studies of the Bible, there were increased calls for reform in the Church, leading eventually to the events known as the Reformation.

Universities

The development of centers of learning or "universities" in Europe contributed to the end of the "Dark Ages" and the spread of the Renaissance. Academies of learning had existed in Greece and in the Arabic world for many centuries and the first European center of learning had been set up by Charlemagne to train the professionals who would run his empire. Intellectual study, however, had been confined to the monasteries, where the focus had inevitably been on studying the Bible. The first universities to appear in medieval Europe were in Paris and Bologna, where the focus remained on preparing for a career in the Church. In Bologna, the university was a self-regulating institution that was run by the

students, rather than by the teachers, and the main study was law. The university at Paris was run by teachers and as a result attracted some of the finest thinkers of the time, including Pierre Abelard and Thomas Aquinas. In Paris, the focus of study was on theological matters, partly because teachers were paid by the Church. All European Universities were essentially independent organizations which operated their own sets of rules and laws; however, they gradually came under state control.

Johannes Gutenberg

The invention of the movable printing press was vital to the cultural and intellectual development of Europe, since it gave a greater number of people access to the literature of the age, and in particular access to different versions of the Bible. Gutenberg's press was a development from the block printing techniques in use, in that it enabled large numbers of materials to be printed very rapidly. Gutenberg, a metalworker from Mainz, produced his first printed book—known as the Gutenberg Bible—in 1454. He spent three years printing around 180 copies of this Latin Bible, the same amount of time it would previously have taken scholars to produce one single handwritten version. At the 1455 Frankfurt Book Fair, one of the oldest trade fairs in the world, Gutenberg sold his mass-produced copies for a handsome profit. Being a poor businessman, by the time he died in 1468 he was relatively penniless; control of the press had been awarded to his erstwhile partner, Johann Fust. Gutenberg's invention contributed not only to the spread of theological knowledge, but also to the growth in scientific publishing, thereby helping to start the scientific revolution of the next centuries.

Michelangelo and Leonardo da Vinci

Michelangelo Buonarotti was born in 1475 in Florentine territory and in 1488 became an apprentice to an artist in the city. His ability soon recommended him to Lorenzo de Medici and for three years he studied at Medici's academy. After a brief period spent in Rome, Michelangelo returned to Florence in 1500 to complete his statue of David. In 1503 he was summoned back to Rome by the new pope, Julius II, to begin work on his tomb. In 1508 the Pope diverted Michelangelo onto a new project, the painting of the ceiling in the Sistine Chapel. After four years of labor, Michelangelo unveiled his masterpiece which depicted scenes from Genesis, including the Creation. He later painted the Last Judgment on the end wall of the chapel. In 1546 he was appointed the architect of St Peter's, and was responsible for the construction of its dome.

Michelangelo's great rival was Leonardo da Vinci, also a Florentine. Like his contemporary, Leonardo became an apprentice to a painter. In 1482, he moved to Milan where he worked for the Signori, Lodovico Sforza, as an engineer and designer. He produced designs for various inventions, including cannons and machine guns, flying machines, armored tanks, and submarines, although these were never built. His interest in science extended to anatomy, and in 1490 Leonardo produced his famous drawing of Vitruvian man, outlining the mathematical proportions and symmetry of the human body. Leonardo is perhaps best known for two paintings, The Last Supper and La Giaconda, also known as the Mona Lisa.

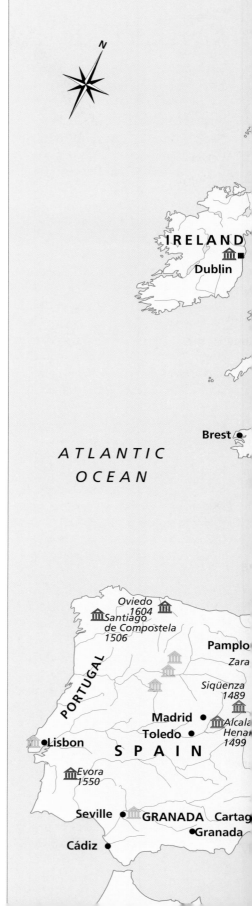

Scale: 0 — 200 km / 0 — 200 miles

North Sea
Baltic Sea
Mediterranean Sea
Adriatic Sea

NORWAY (Danish)

Christiana

S W E D E N

Uppsala 1477

Stockholm

Danish

Danish

OTLAND

Aberdeen 1494

ow *St Andrews 1411*

■ **Edinburgh**

32

York

NGLAND

Lund 1688

Copenhagen 1478

DENMARK

Rostock 1419

Kiel 1655

Greifswald 1456

Lübeck
Hamburg

Königsberg 1544

POLAND

Franeker 1585

Groningen 1614

H O L Y

Harderwijk 1648

Amsterdam

Osnabrück 1630

Frankfurt 1506

istol

Leiden 1574

Utrecht *1636*

Helmstedt 1576

Wittenberg 1502

ondon ■

Antwerp

Pederborn 1614

Halle 1694

Breslau

Brussels

Calais

Cologne 1388

Marburg 1527

Leipzig 1409

Louvain 1426

R O M A N

Giessen 1607

Olomouc 1576

Luxembourg

Mainz *1476*

Bamberg *1648*

Trier 1473

Würzburg 1582

Caen 1432

■ **Paris**

Port-à-Mousson 1572

Ingolstadt 1472

Tyrnau 1635

Orléans

Tübingen 1476

Strasbourg 1621

Dillingen 1549

Linz 1669

Vienna

Pressburg

tes

Dôle 1422

Basel *1456*

Freiburg 1457

Munich

Salzburg 1623

Buda

Bourges 1464

Besançon *1485*

E M P I R E

Graz 1585

KINGDOM OF HUNGARY

Poitiers 1431

F R A N C E

Geneva *1559*

Bordeaux

Valence 1452

Milan

Parma 1502

V E N I C E

Venice

OTTOMAN EMPIRE

Turin 1405

Genoa

Aix-en-Provence 1409

Siena

PAPAL

Urbino 1564

Adriatic Sea

orthez

Toulouse

561

Marseille

STATES

Barcelona *1430*

Corsica

Rome

KINGDOM OF NAPLES

ncia

Palma *1483*

Sardinia

Naples

Cagliari 1626

Palermo *1637*

Messina 1549

Sicily

Catania 1434

EUROPEAN SEATS OF LEARNING 1401 TO 1700

🏛⳨ *Universties and Religious schools founded by 1400*

🏛 University founded 1401–1500

🏛 University founded 1501–1700

The Americas at the End of the 15th Century

Before the arrival of Europeans, the Americas were home to sophisticated cultures, from the civilizations of the Incas and Aztecs to the hunter-gatherers of the north.

The Incas

The Incas, or Tahuantinsuyu, were an imperial civilization based in south America from the early fifteenth century until the arrival of the Spanish in 1533. The word "Inca" means emperor and their society was very much focused upon imperial rule. The Incas had their origins in the area now known as Peru with their capital at Cuzco; however, during the relatively brief period of their existence they came to rule over most of civilized South America. Before their ascendancy, the Incas had been one of a number of small tribal groups based in the southern Andes, but during the reigns of three emperors—Viracocha and his son Pachacuti and grandson Topa—they began a process of expansion and conquest. Their territories reached as far south as modern Chile and Argentina.

In order to rule successfully over this vast empire, the Incas developed a sophisticated hierarchical system. At the very head of government was the Inca, or Emperor, and below him were four provincial governments headed by members of the Inca's family. These nobles then delegated authority to local officials whose responsibilities included ensuring that productivity remained high and that the rule of law was maintained. At the very bottom of society were those who worked on the land or in the mines. Groupings of ten families would be overseen by village officials, to whom they were required to pay tributes for the empire. Ordinary Inca workers were also expected to provide labor for social projects, such as bridge building, and to serve in the army. In return they were guaranteed the support of the community in their old age or during sickness, and in times of crop failure or famine food would be provided from state supplies.

Inca civilization was primarily an agricultural one and the Incas transformed their mountainous landscape with terraces which increased the amount of arable land. They also created intricate art, and were particularly skilled at metalwork, producing fine pieces from both silver and gold, to which they had some access. The Incas are also known for their medical practices, in particular their surgical knowledge which was often applied to cranial surgery.

Religious Beliefs and Practices

The Incas' religious practices were focused mainly on their worship of the sun god Inti. Their creation mythology told of how Inti sent his son, Manco Capac, to earth to found a city and this first emperor of the Incas went on to found Cuzco. Worship of the sun dominated most features of Inca ceremonies. They built a large number of impressive temples dedicated to the sun, always situating them at the highest point in the area so as to be closest to the object of their worship. Their priests lived at the temples where they would carry out acts of divination in order to guide the Incas on all aspects of life. Every day animal sacrifices were carried out in homage to the rising of the sun, and the most commonly used animal was the sacred white llama. The priests would go on to use the dissected lungs of the llamas to divine the future, or to diagnose the source of a particular problem such as an illness.

Inti was not the only god worshiped by the Incas. Their other major gods represented the moon, earth, sea, thunder, and lightning; belief in the power of the natural world was extended to the animal kingdom too. Different animal spirits living on the earth were highly important to the Incas; for instance, the condor represented heaven and the anaconda depicted hell. They also worshiped the spirits who resided in the large numbers of sacred sites that were spread across the Inca world; these spirits could take the form not only of animals but also of boulders, mountains, and streams.

Machu Picchu

Possibly the most famous Inca site is that of the town Machu Picchu, situated approximately 6,800 feet above sea level on a mountain ridge in Peru. The town itself

COLOMBIA

Quito

ECUADOR

Achupallas
Hatun Cañar
Tombebamba

Tumbes

Cusibamba

Chinchasuyu

PERU

Cajamarca

Chiquitoy Viejo
Chan Chan

Huamachuco

Tamborata
Tunsucancha
Huánuco Pampa

Recuay
Paramonga

Pumpu
Tarma Tambo

Pachacamac

Jauja

Lurin

Ollantaytambo

Machu Picchu

Inkawasi

Vilcashuamán

Pisac
Limatambo

BRAZIL

Tambo Colorado

Huari

Cuzco

Ica

Cuntisuyu

Jincamocco

Pikillaqta

BOLIVIA

Nasca

Raqchi

Acan

Pucará

Ayaviri

Antisuyu

Chigna Jota

Hatuncolla

Lake Titicaca

Chucuito

Chuquiabo

Juli

Tiahuanaco

Pomata

Hualla Tampu

Paria

Cochabamba

Tupiza

Collasuyu

Meteorite Tampu

Tilcara

PACIFIC
OCEAN

C
H
I
L
E

La Paya

Pucará de
Andagala

Chilecito

Leoncito

THE INCA EMPIRE 1438–1525 C.E.

Cuzco center

Expansion under Pachacuti,
1438–63

Expansion under Pachacuti
and Topa Inca, 1463–71

Expansion under Topa Inca,
1471–93

Expansion under Huayna
Capac, 1493–1525

Royal Road

Other roads

Modern borders

Ranchillos

Santiago

Potrero de
Payagasta

ARGENTINA

0   200 km

0   200 miles

N

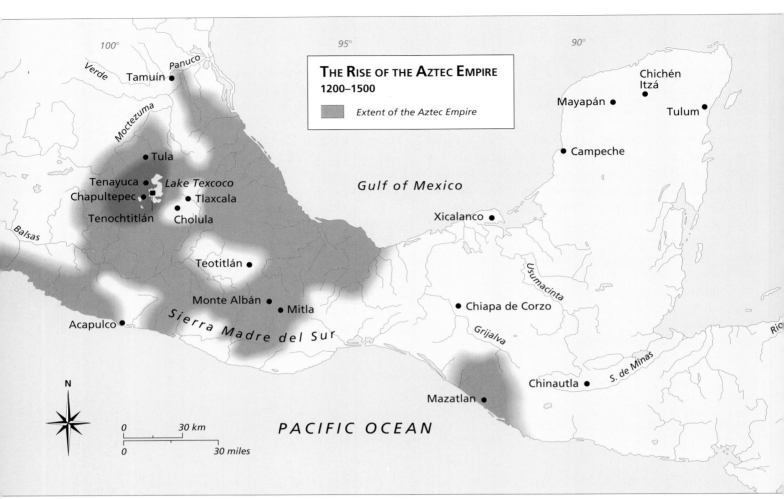

THE RISE OF THE AZTEC EMPIRE
1200–1500

▨ *Extent of the Aztec Empire*

was not fully inhabited throughout the year; instead it acted rather like a religious or country retreat for the Inca nobles. It was built by the Inca Pachacuti in c.1460 and consisted of some 200 buildings, including residences and temples. Rather than cutting away at the rock in the surrounding area, the buildings were built out of loose granite boulders, carved, and then precisely placed together without mortar. Despite the fact that many of the blocks used were multifaceted, the joints between them are so tight that a knife blade cannot be forced between them. The Incas also used their understanding of the difficult landscape to construct buildings in seemingly impossible places such as on steep slopes and precipices. Terraces were built around the site in order to grow vegetables and to prevent the soil from eroding, and in this way Machu Picchu was almost completely self-sufficient. Ceremonies designed to worship the sun included that of intihuafana, in which a priest would enact the hitching of the sun to a large column in order to prevent it from disappearing forever, particularly

important to the Incas during the winter months when the sun was seen for fewer hours in the day. Machu Picchu has also been found to contain a number of mummified bodies. The Incas believed in reincarnation and many of their more important members would be mummified after death, often in a sitting position. Its remote situation meant that on the arrival of the Spanish, Machu Picchu was left undamaged by the conquistadors, who did not know of its existence. However, the town was abandoned by the Incas during the same period, possibly as a result of the smallpox epidemic that had been brought by the Europeans.

The Aztecs

The Aztecs were the most powerful people of Mesoamerica during the fifteenth and sixteenth centuries. They were originally a number of tribal groups who came from the north and were engaged in warfare with the Toltecs. The Aztecs founded a city of refuge on an island in the middle of Lake Texcoco which later became their capital city of Tenochtitlán (now Mexico City). Tenochtitlán became the largest inhabited city in the region as the Aztecs gradually drained the swamps, building up a system of causeways, canals, and artificial islands.

When the Aztecs made the shift from being a collective group of individually led tribes to a single people they began their aggressive expansion policy. They gradually overcame neighboring tribes, initially by making political alliances and then turning on their allies once all the weaker groups had been brought under Aztec control. In this way they were able to quickly subjugate the majority of central Mexico, collecting tributes and raw materials from around 500 smaller states. As overlords, the Aztecs were brutal and despotic. If a state was unable or refused to pay adequate tribute, the imperial army was swift to enact punishment. The Aztecs believed that continuous warfare was crucial in ensuring a continued supply of well trained warriors and needed no excuse to attack either neighboring groups or vassal states. Their approach to battle tactics was, however, unique. Rather than operating armies as combined units with the intention of killing the enemy, Aztec soldiers fought as individuals who were required to capture living prisoners of war. The purpose of this was to supply the Aztec Empire with the large numbers of sacrificial victims it needed. Honor could only be attained by an Aztec warrior if he had taken three or more captives and since Aztec men could not cut their hair until they had achieved this target, it was considered shameful to have long hair.

It was ultimately the aggressive nature of the Aztecs that was to be their downfall. When the Spanish arrived in 1519 with only around 500 troops many of the suppressed peoples of Mesoamerica were only too happy to ally themselves with the Europeans and over 150,000 supported the Spanish in their attack on the Aztecs.

Below: The spectacular site of Machu Picchu.

Society and Religion

Despite their apparent barbarism, the Aztecs were a sophisticated and cultured civilization. Society was divided into three main classes: the nobility, the peasants, and the merchant class. It was from the noble class that the priests, scholars, and leaders were found, while the peasant class supplied the soldiers, artisans, and farmers. They also made use of slaves, although Aztec slaves appeared to enjoy more freedom than their classical European counterparts. Although slaves could be bought and sold, they were not born into slavery and should they manage to escape they could successfully appeal to be freed. All Aztec males began a formal education at the age of fifteen, when they would be taught the religion, rituals, and history of their culture as well as learning a trade or martial skills. Aztec cities not only contained educational institutions but also supported a large number of temples and designated markets where the wide variety of crafts made by the people could be traded. The cities were usually divided into zones and the center of the city was dominated by the temple complex which would also house the schools. Because the Aztecs were skilful enough engineers to drain the swampland around Tenochtitlán, they were also careful enough to have established an effective sewerage system and most dwellings boasted latrines. They also built large aqueducts to supply the city with fresh water.

The Aztecs worshiped a number of deities and, like many other civilizations, developed a number of festivals and ceremonies around the different gods and goddesses. Some of the most prominent of the Aztec gods include Huitzilopochtli, the supreme god and patron of fire, the sun, and war; Itzli, the god of sacrifice, and Quetzalcoatl the feathered-serpent god who created the Aztecs and was patron of the priests.

Sacrifice

The practice of human sacrifice was firmly established in Mesoamerica during the Aztec period. Although the pretext for sacrificing human victims was religious, it was also done for political reasons and served as an

Below: A close-up of the center of the Aztec Sun Stone which has both mythological and astronomical significance.

effective means of civil control. Different gods demanded different types of sacrifice; some received the sacrifice of young girls, others of prisoners, others of the weak and deformed. Victims could die in any number of ways and usually at the hands of one of the temple priests. In Tenochtitlán, the skulls of the sacrificed were displayed upon the Tzompantli, or rack of skulls. Sacrifices were particularly popular on festival days and large numbers of people would be put to death on any one occasion. Although Spanish observers declared that thousands were sacrificed in a brief number of days, these figures were possibly exaggerated for propaganda reasons—but the numbers of those put to death may certainly have been in the hundreds. In general it is thought that up to 10,000 victims were sacrificed each year across the Aztec Empire.

Native American Tribes

Unlike the civilizations in central and south America, the native inhabitants of the north were far less technologically advanced and lived a more nomadic existence. However, these people were organized into definite tribal units, each with their own customs, languages, and social rules. The tribes of the northwest coast, such as the Tlingit, the Chinook, and the Makah, were essentially fishermen, making their living from the sea. Those who lived on the Great Plains, including the Sioux, the Cheyenne, the Pawnee, and the Comanche, were skilled hunter-gatherers, taking advantage of the wealth of buffalo which roamed the area. The tribes in the south, such as the Choctaw, the Natchez, and the Apaches, were gradually introduced to farming methods from the more northerly tribes. To the very north, within the Arctic circle, the Inuit tribes lived a harsh but successful life in unforgiving terrain.

Native American Society

Different tribal units had a wide range of different customs and traditions, though some elements of Native American society were common to most tribes. Most societies were organized in settlements in which family life was important but where the impact of both warfare and religion was deeply felt. Conflict with neighboring tribes over things such as territorial claims led to a need for skilled warriors as well as huntsmen. Many Native American societies initiated their young men into becoming fearless fighters and they also shared a tendency to use tribal dance as a means of summoning up protective spirits and preparing for

war. Although not all tribes were ruled over by a single chief, this was the most common way of organizing the government of tribal societies. Chiefs often held a spiritual position within their society and many tribes, such as those belonging to the Iroquois peoples of the north east, used councils of adult males who would regularly meet to advise the chief. The role of women in most of the tribes tended to be the same; they were expected to tend the crops and livestock as well as caring for the family. In some tribes, such as the Apache, family clans were run by matriarchs, although ultimately all Native American societies were patriarchal.

Dealings with First Settlers

The majority of Native Americans were hospitable to the first Europeans who began to arrive in the sixteenth century. Positive relations with the indigenous Americans were vital to the new settlers, who without their guidance would not have been able to survive in the completely alien environment in which they found themselves. The Europeans were shown where to find the best crops and how to cultivate them, and where was best to hunt and fish. In return the settlers brought with them horses which were reintroduced to the northern plains, having been extinct for several centuries. The arrival of horses greatly improved the possibilities for trade and travel for the Native Americans.

However, the colonists also brought diseases such as measles and smallpox to which the native people had no immunity; thousands died. The initially successful relationship between the settlers and the natives was ultimately to fail, as gradually the native peoples found themselves being displaced and often abused by the incomers. As the colonists themselves began to struggle for supremacy in their new world, many Native Americans found themselves becoming allies to one or another colonial nationality. In the case of the Mohawks, the tribe itself was divided as some allied themselves to the British, whilst others, who had been converted by Catholic missionaries, supported the French in the conflict between the European powers.

Resistance to the encroachment of white settlers resulted in the Indian Wars, which lasted from 1622 until 1890 and as early as the mid-eighteenth century, Native Americans were finding themselves removed from their land and forcibly relocated into reservations, or sent further west beyond the frontier.

The Ming Dynasty

Under the Ming emperors, China experienced a period of cultural renewal—and of expansion, trade, and exploration—which, though it declined, lasted for three centuries.

Zhu Yuan-Chang

With the decline of the Mongol Yuan Dynasty, China was again forced into a period of political instability, competing warlords and divided provinces. During the first half of the fourteenth century a series of rebellions took place which resulted in the establishment of a number of kingdoms run by individuals who had been members of the merchant or peasant classes. One of these rebel rulers was Zhu Yuan-Chang, the son of peasants and a leader of a sect known as the Red Turbans. In 1356, Yuan-Chang captured Nanjing

and from there gradually set about conquering neighboring territories. By 1369, he had succeeded in conquering all of China and in expelling the Yuan, and it is from this date that the Ming Dynasty is recognized; Yuan-Chang adopted the name Ming which means "brilliant" and titled himself Ming Hongwu.

His reign was marked by the need to consolidate the absolute rule of the imperial power. He built a capital city at Nanjing and established a number of complex rituals associated with the imperial role that served to give him a divine air. He abolished the office of chief minister, giving himself absolute control over the administration of the empire, a demanding and time-consuming duty. He also removed the threat of dangerous court intrigue by curtailing the powers of court eunuchs, concubines, and court ladies. In addition, he dealt ruthlessly with any dissenters and was particularly brutal with scholars whom he felt had insulted him, a reflection, perhaps, of his low birth.

Considered by many to be the greatest of the Chinese emperors, Hongwu set about the task of undoing much of the damage done by the Mongols, in particular focusing upon reconstructing China's ruined agricultural economy. He was responsible for low levels of land taxation and reforestation as well as the resettlement of abandoned land. Hongwu's administrative reforms were designed to strengthen the bureaucracy of the civil service and also to control the enormous population. He brought back the civil service examination system that had declined under the Yuan and made the examinations themselves far more

Left: The Forbidden City, home to two dynasties of emperor, Ming and Qing, was inaccessible to the majority of the Chinese population for 500 years.

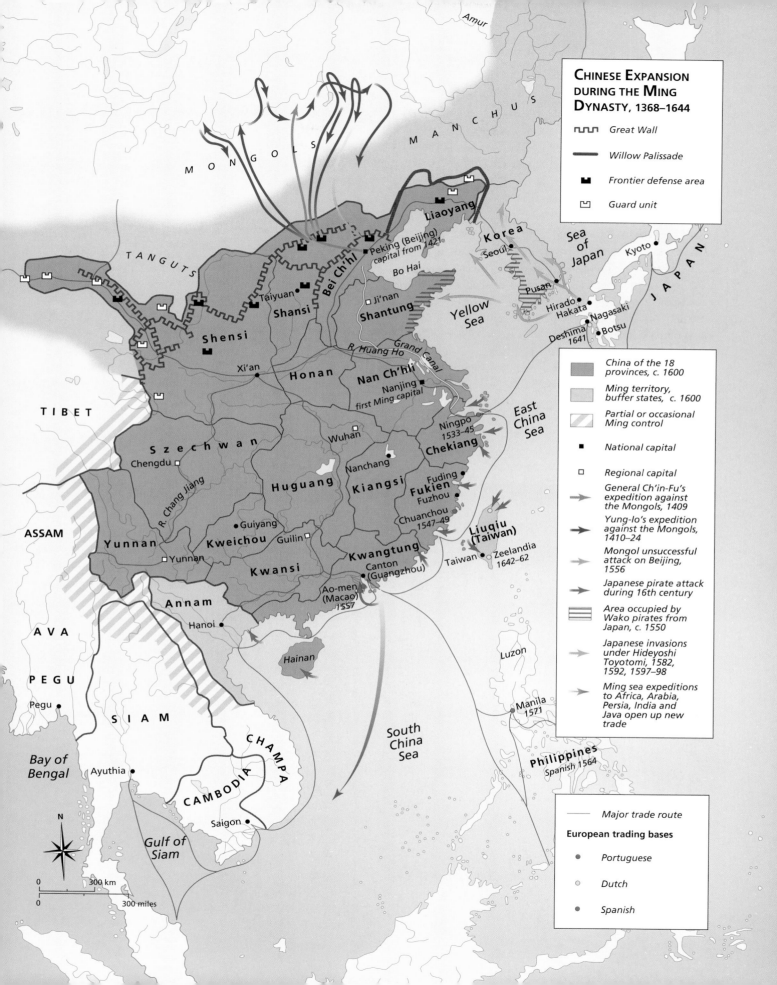

MONGOLS

MANCHUS

Amur

TANGUTS

Liaoyang

Peking (Beijing) capital from 1421

Korea

Seoul

Sea of Japan

Kyoto

JAPAN

Bo Hai

Pusan

Taiyuan

Shansi

Bei Ch'hli

Shantung

Ji'nan

Yellow Sea

Hirado
Hakata

Nagasaki

Deshima 1641

Botsu

Shensi

Xi'an

R. Huang Ho

Grand Canal

Honan

Nan Ch'hli

Nanjing first Ming capital

TIBET

Szechwan

Chengdu

Wuhan

Ningpo 1533–45

Chekiang

East China Sea

Huguang

Nanchang

Kiangsi

Fukien

Fuding

Fuzhou

Chuanchou 1547–49

Liuqiu (Taiwan)

Taiwan

Zeelandia 1642–62

ASSAM

R. Chang Jiang

Guiyang

Kweichou

Guilin

Yunnan

Yunnan

Kwangtung

Canton (Guangzhou)

Kwansi

Ao-men (Macao) 1557

AVA

Annam

Hanoi

PEGU

Pegu

SIAM

Ayuthia

Hainan

South China Sea

Luzon

Manila 1571

Philippines Spanish 1564

CHAMPA

CAMBODIA

Saigon

Bay of Bengal

Gulf of Siam

N

0   300 km

0   300 miles

rigorous, creating an institution that remained in place until 1905. He also had a census of the population taken and, understanding from first-hand experience the dangers of social mobility, decreed that occupations were to become hereditary, thus reducing the risk of lower-class uprisings. Chinese society was grouped into three classes: peasants, craftspeople, and soldiers. Hongwu died in 1398 and was succeeded by his grandson Zhu Yunwen, the Jianwen emperor.

Exploration and Trade

Jianwen's reign as emperor was short lived; in 1402 his uncle, Hongwu's fourth son, took the throne for himself. He named himself Ming Yongle and ruled for twenty-two years. It was during Yongle's reign that China began a policy of naval expansion. In 1405 Yongle financed a number of maritime expeditions that were designed not only to discover new territories, but also to expand trade. The reforestation programme that Hongwu had begun supplied the lumber for China's new navy and expeditions were organized and led by the court eunuch and imperial aide, Cheng Ho. Between 1405 and 1433, Cheng Ho took the Chinese fleet on seven voyages of

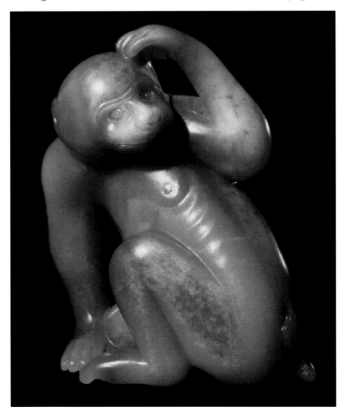

Above: A carving of a monkey made from jade dating from the Ming Period.
Opposite: A dragon sculpture on a tiled wall in the Forbidden City.

discovery, crossing the Indian Ocean and reaching as far as Jeddah in Arabia and Mogadishu on the east coast of Africa. They also traveled south to the islands of Sumatra and Java, and the Malay archipelago. The Chinese were able to trade their silk, paper, and perfumes for spices, tea, and cotton. At this point the navy was the largest in the world and commercially more powerful than that of the Portuguese. However, the Chinese people were unenthusiastic about the cost of maintaining the navy and with the death of Chung-Ho in 1433, spending was reduced and the navy allowed to decline. The resulting lack of sea power meant that in later years China's coastline was regularly raided by pirates, many of whom were Japanese. Although the early part of Yongle's reign had included the successful invasion of both Annan (Vietnam) and Korea, the failed attempt to annex Mongolia in 1449 resulted in the Ming taking a more defensive attitude. The empire gradually became more isolationist.

The Forbidden City

In 1421, Yongle moved the capital from Nanjing to Beijing, where it has remained ever since. The heart of the new capital was the palace complex built by Yongle, called the Forbidden City. It took fourteen years and an estimated 200,000 men to build the complex, which consisted of seventeen palaces containing a total of 9,999 and a half rooms covering 72 hectares of land. The complex could not contain 10,000 rooms as this was the divine number of infinity which could only exist in heaven, and the half room is in fact a staircase. The emperor's ceremonies and public affairs of state were conducted in the three main halls of the palace: the Hall of Supreme Harmony, the Hall of Middle Harmony, and the Hall of Preserving Harmony. Routine business was carried out in the private apartments of the inner court, such as the Palace of Heavenly Purity or the Hall of Mental Cultivation. Palace life was organized into strict routines and rituals which all served to maintain the divine aura of the emperor. Women and eunuchs lived in restricted areas and those permitted to enter the palace to speak with the emperor were required to prostrate themselves before him. Many of those who entered the palace complex as servants, concubines, or eunuchs were destined never to leave it again.

Population Explosion

From the start of the Ming Dynasty the population of China began to grow. Hongwu's agricultural policies had resulted in a steady increase in available food and, alongside the trade policies of later emperors, the general surplus of goods served to increase the standard of living. In addition to this, the period covered by the Ming was a relatively stable one; previous dynasties had been affected by rebellions which generally caused huge loss of life. A succession of plagues in the sixteenth and seventeenth centuries did slow down the population growth for a while, but by the time the dynasty came to an end in 1644, the total population of the empire had doubled to around 130 million people. This increase necessitated an improvement in agricultural techniques, and goods from the north, such as cotton, began to

be transported south via the Grand Canal network. Trade with Europe had slowed down mainly due to the Chinese belief that their culture required nothing from any other; however, some trade with Europe still existed and in this way crops brought to Europe from the New World—such as potatoes, tobacco, and maize—were quickly established in China.

Porcelain

With a prosperous economy the demand for art and luxury goods increased and, combined with improvements in the manufacturing processes, commodities such as textiles and ceramics flourished. The Ming Period is particularly associated with the production of fine porcelain decorated with distinctive blue on white hand-painted scenes. Decorative motifs included dragons, the phoenix as well as other animals and plants and garden scenes. Later Ming porcelain became much more colorful, with the use of red, yellow, and green glazes. Trade with the Portuguese in the sixteenth century led to an increase in demand for Ming porcelain, which was highly sought after in Europe. The production of porcelain had been held under state control and was concentrated at factories in the Jiangxi province, but they were unable to cope with production demands and control was passed into local hands.

Decline

There are a number of reasons for the decline of the Ming empire. Despite its economic success, the administration was still plagued by aggressors on its borders, in particular the Japanese along the coast and the Mongols to the north. A series of military expeditions against the Mongols in the north and the Manchus in the north-east proved costly and the government levied increasingly high taxes that were extremely unpopular. Eventually a series of rebellions broke out in the north and north-west in the early seventeenth century and these coincided with crop failure and a subsequent famine in Shanxi province. Under these conditions, the ambitious Manchus took advantage and invaded Beijing in 1644, taking the capital and forcing the suicide of the final Ming emperor, Chung-Chen. The defeat of the Ming was exacerbated by the failure of the administration that had been established by Hongwu. The absolute rule of the emperor had initially been successful, but later, more-indulged rulers were no longer prepared to work at governing. The lack of a first minister resulted in a lack of continuity in government and the empire suffered from both neglect and, eventually, corruption with the effective domination of the eunuchs at administrative levels.

Mughal India

Their Delhi base allowed the Muslim Mughals to expand their rule over northern India. The arts and trade flourished—European trading posts were established for the first time.

Post-Guptan and Mughal India

As the Guptan Empire collapsed in the wake of the Huns between AD 400 and 500 and centralized control weakened, power became dispersed amongst local, feudal leaders, who established a number of smaller kingdoms. A succession of dynasties would henceforth vie for power until the emergence of three major imperial formations between about AD 550 and 750: the Pushyabhutis, Chalukyas, and Pallavas. In turn, these were succeeded by the Rashtrakutas, Pratiharas, and Palas, before the Cholas came to dominate during the tenth century and power shifted to the south. However, the fragmented north, weakened both by wars between its kingdoms and by raids from the south, became increasingly vulnerable to attacks from the Turkic Muslim armies gathering in the north-west. These first established a sultanate at Delhi in 1206, from where Muslim rule would ultimately be extended throughout much of India by five successive Islamic dynasties of Turkish and Afghan origin. However, it was not until the arrival of a sixth, and the foundation of the Mughal Dynasty, that power was to be completely consolidated.

Babur

The Mughal Dynasty was founded in the 1520s by Zahiruddin Muhammad Babur, "The Lion," a prince descended from two ferocious warriors—on his father's side from Timur known in the West as Tamerlane, who had himself sacked Delhi in 1398, and on his mother's side from Chingiz Khan, perhaps more familiar as Genghis Khan, the Mongol conqueror. In fact "Mughal" is essentially the Persian version of the word "Mongol." Despite his lineage, or perhaps because of it, Babur was to rise from fairly inauspicious beginnings to become a great conqueror. Born in 1483, he inherited the relatively small kingdom of Ferghana or Turkestan from his father at the age of eleven and spent many years attempting to recapture the Timurid capital, Samarkand, a project which was to prove ultimately unsuccessful. However, in 1504 he was to enlarge his kingdom with the capture of Kabul in Afghanistan, from where he set his sights on Delhi. In 1526, he crossed into Hindustan and attacked the forces of the Delhi Sultanate at Panipat, to overthrow the Afghan sultan Ibrahim Lodi. Babur's army was small, consisting of perhaps just 12,000 men, but he was aided in his conquest by the employment of superior technology, for his forces were equipped with primitive artillery and muskets. Following his victory, Babur seized Agra and Delhi and established himself as the new sultan, but it was not until he had successfully repelled attacks from a confederation of Rajput forces in 1527 that his position was secured. Over the course of the next three years, up until his death in 1530, Babur expanded his territories eastwards across the Ganges to the edge of Bengal, controlling an empire that extended from Turkestan southwards to the Deccan. In his short reign over the region, Babur had little time to establish a consolidated administration, and the empire inherited by his son, Humayun, was essentially under occupation rather than governance.

Humayun

The kingdom inherited by Humayun was still in its infancy, and with it he inherited numerous difficulties, including rebellions by Rajput kings, Afghan generals, and even the treacherous actions of his own brothers who coveted his power. In fact, between 1530 and 1540, Humayun gradually lost control over the region and in 1540 was deposed by the Afghan general Sher Shah Sur, or Sher Kahn, who had served under Babur as ruler of Bengal. Humayun retreated to Persia as an exile where, over the course of fifteen years, he regrouped his forces, putting together an army with which to regain his lost territory. Aided by the king of Persia, Humayun recaptured Kabul and Kandahar, and by 1555, having defeated the armies of Sher Shah Sur's son, Islam Shah, he re-ascended the throne at Delhi. Humayun then began to look towards governmental, social, and cultural improvements, mainly founded on Persian models, but just a year after securing the future of the Mughal Dynasty, he was to die in an accident, breaking his neck as he fell down a flight of stairs. Although the dynasty had been precariously balanced during Humayun's rule, by the time of his death the

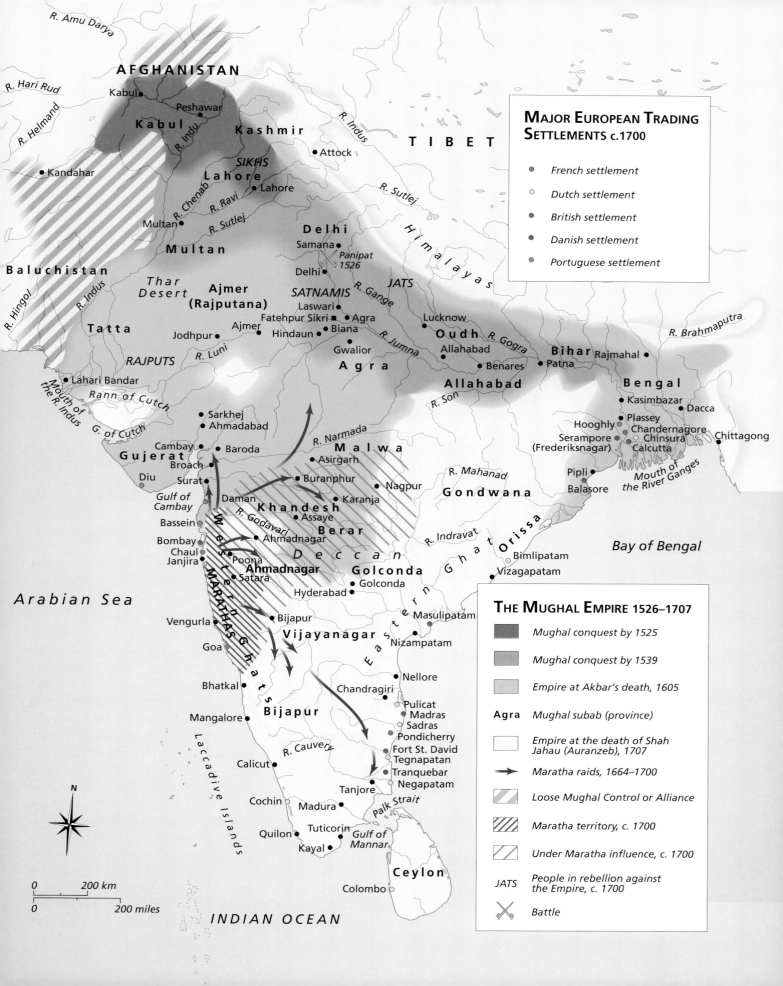

R. Amu Darya

R. Hari Rud

R. Helmand

AFGHANISTAN

Kabul

Peshawar

R. Indu

Kashmir

Kabul

R. Hari Rud

R. Helmand

Kandahar

SIKHS

Lahore

Attock

TIBET

R. Chenab

R. Ravi

Lahore

R. Sutlej

Himalayas

Multan

R. Sutlej

Multan

Baluchistan

R. Hingol

R. Indus

Thar Desert

Ajmer (Rajputana)

D e l h i

Samana

Panipat 1526

Delhi

JATS

R. Gange

Tatta

SATNAMIS

Laswari

Fatehpur Sikri

Agra

Lucknow

Oudh

R. Gogra

R. Brahmaputra

Bihar

Rajmahal

RAJPUTS

Jodhpur

Ajmer

Hindaun

Biana

Gwalior

Allahabad

Benares

Patna

Bengal

R. Luni

R. Jumna

Agra

R. Son

Allahabad

Kasimbazar

Dacca

Lahari Bandar

Rann of Cutch

Mouth of the R. Indus

G. of Cutch

Sarkhej

Ahmadabad

R. Narmada

Malwa

Asirgarh

Nagpur

R. Mahanad

Gondwana

Hooghly

Plassey

Chandernagore

Chinsura

Chittagong

Serampore (Frederiksnagar)

Calcutta

Cambay

Baroda

Buranphur

Karanja

Pipli

Balasore

Mouth of the River Ganges

Gujerat

Broach

Diu

Surat

Daman

Gulf of Cambay

Khandesh

R. Godavari

Assaye

Berar

R. Indravat

Orissa

Bassein

Ahmadnagar

D e c c a n

Bimlipatam

Bombay

Chaul

Janjira

Poona

Satara

Ahmadnagar

Golconda

Golconda

Hyderabad

Vizagapatam

Arabian Sea

Western Ghats

MARATHAS

Bijapur

Vijayanagar

Masulipatam

Eastern Ghats

Bay of Bengal

Vengurla

Goa

Nizampatam

Bhatkal

Nellore

Chandragiri

Pulicat

Madras

Sadras

Pondicherry

Fort St. David

Tegnapatan

Tranquebar

Negapatam

Mangalore

Bijapur

R. Cauvery

Calicut

Tanjore

Palk Strait

Cochin

Madura

Gulf of Mannar

Laccadive Islands

Quilon

Tuticorin

Kayal

Ceylon

N

Colombo

200 km

200 miles

INDIAN OCEAN

Above: The sixteenth century Mughal emperor Akbar is depicted astride an elephant.
Opposite: Shah Jahan ordered work to begin on the Taj Mahal in 1630 upon the death of his wife who died in childbirth.

Mughals were once more poised to consolidate northern India, and the task was entrusted to his son and successor, Akbar.

Akbar the Great

Akbar, meaning "great," was aptly named, for it was under his reign that perhaps the greatest achievements of the Mughal Dynasty were made. The empire was not only massively expanded in terms of its wealth and territory, but unified by the institution of radical political and social reform. Akbar realized that for the empire to remain stable it was necessary to forge alliances with Rajput kings, and he did so by appointing them to high civil and military positions, allowing them to preserve state borders and providing a degree of autonomous rule, establishing provinces of the empire in place of disparate feudal kingdoms. Akbar also won favour with the Rajputs by marrying a Rajput princess. He further won loyalty amongst his Hindu subjects by abolishing a tax on non-Muslims, having Hindu literature translated, and taking part in Hindu festivals. Hindus could also be counted amongst his ministers, and he demonstrated a high level of religious tolerance.

Although he was illiterate, Akbar was highly intellectual and had a particular interest in both philosophy and theology; he assembled representatives of all faiths to debate religious matters. The outcome of these debates was a religious theory of his own devising called Din Ilahi, which brought together ideas from various sources and proposed the idea of universal tolerance. Akbar was also interested in music, art, architecture, and literature, all of which flourished during his reign. He established a vast library and hundreds of workshops, drawing artisans and scholars of diverse origins, and built walled cities. In the capital of Agra, Akbar built an impressive red sandstone fort to house his court, consisting of hundreds of pavilions, lavishly adorned with carvings and wall paintings.

Despite his great accomplishments, towards the end of his reign Akbar's life was tainted with sadness, marred by conflict with his son, Prince Salim, who in 1600 and again in 1602 attempted to seize power, declaring himself emperor whilst his father was away. Whilst there was eventual reconciliation, when Akbar died in 1605 the experience had somewhat broken him.

The Mughal Dynasty after Akbar

Following Akbar's death, Salim assumed power and adopted the name Jahangir, meaning "world conqueror." However, despite several military campaigns led by his son and successor Prince Khurram, or Shah Jahan, "king of the world," whose victories he claimed as his own, very little territorial expansion actually occurred during either of their reigns, and the fact that they ruled over a great empire with relative stability could really be attributed to the actions of Akbar. Furthermore, seriously addicted to alcohol, Jahangir was content to delegate much of his responsibility, particularly to his wife Nur Jahan, her father Itimad-ud-Daula and brother Asaf Khan, and whilst they governed over a highly productive economy, Jahangir was free to indulge his passions for nature, art, and architecture, leaving behind opulent tombs and other monuments in Agra, Sikandra, Lahore, and Allahabad after his alcohol-induced death in 1627.

Shah Jahan inherited probably the richest kingdom in the world at that time, and during his reign Mughal architecture was to reach its peak, most notably with the Taj Mahal in Agra, constructed as a tomb for his beloved wife, Mumtaz Mahal, and which would also become his final resting place after his death in 1666. Although Shah Jahan's successor Aurangzeb, "conqueror of the universe," who had become emperor in 1658 after imprisoning his father, managed to sustain and expand the empire throughout his long reign, the roots of its decline can also be traced to the period of his rule, and the essential character of the Mughal Dynasty founded by Babur and developed by Akbar was to alter radically.

Aurangzeb showed none of the religious tolerance of Akbar and was determined to convert all of India to Islam, bringing him into continuous and ultimately irreconcilable conflicts which served to overstretch his resources and disaffect huge sections of the population. The tax on non-Muslims was re-introduced, temples were desecrated and mosques built in their place, and much of the art, music, and dance that had defined Mughal India was outlawed. Simultaneously, with the establishment of numerous Portuguese and French trading posts in the coastal provinces, the Hindu Marathas, whom Aurangzeb was determined to conquer, were increasing in wealth and power. When Aurangzeb died in 1707, he left behind him some seventeen potential claimants to the throne, ensuring a power struggle that would lead to seven years of bloodshed and ultimately a more fractured empire. As the Mughal Dynasty collapsed, its obvious weakness both encouraged further rebellion from within and attracted the attentions of foreign powers eager to expand their own empires.

Age of Exploration

Initial European curiosity about the world led to systematic exploration in search of trading opportunities and material resources, but developed into the establishment of colonial empires.

The Beginnings

European exploration and discovery of the wider world accelerated during the fifteenth century. There had been earlier travelers, bringing back reports that were regarded as imaginary or wildly exaggerated, but from the middle of the 1400s exploration became more systematic and deliberate—and was often driven by economic reasons rather than simple curiosity.

Beginning in the twelfth century, there had been something of a "renaissance" in technology in Europe, and crusading activity had further expanded the European view of the world, bringing Europeans into contact with Arab knowledge and technology. Meanwhile, the growing prosperity and strength of the Yuan (Mongol) Dynasty in China led to them trading and sharing knowledge with the Arabs and, through them, with Europeans. New maritime trading routes grew up alongside the overland route—the so-called Silk Route—enabling increased exports into Europe from the east. Luxury goods were not the only things imported; there were also new technologies which would eventually enable the Europeans to become the great explorers of the world. These, including the stern-post rudder, the magnetic compass, and gunpowder, would prove vital.

Trade—both in goods and ideas—was a strong motivating factor; the drive to find new trade routes and safe passages to new lands carried a significant financial reward. But Europeans were also engaged in an attempt to spread Christianity, and this formed a significant part of their expansion.

Marco Polo

One of the first individuals definitely known to have set out in search of new opportunities was Marco Polo. There were reports of others, such as Prester John, an alleged Christian "priest-king" in the east, but they seem to have been fictional. When Marco Polo died in 1324 he had seen more of the world than any European then alive. A Venetian, he had traveled from his native city to China, across India and through the Indian Ocean to the Arab world.

His father and uncle were merchants who, noting the opportunities to trade with the east, had embarked on a journey into the Mongol Empire and through it to China. This first expedition lasted nine years and included their introduction to the first Mongol emperor of China, Kublai Khan. The return

journey took them three years, and two years later, in 1271, they went back, taking with them the 17-year-old Marco.

It took them three and a half years to reach the Khan and Marco remained in his court as his loyal servant for a further seventeen years. During this time he traveled the length of Asia, recording local customs for the Great Khan. He eventually returned to Venice in 1295. Three years afterwards he was captured in a sea battle and held prisoner in Genoa with a writer called Rustichello who persuaded him to let him ghostwrite his story. It is generally believed that Rustichello embellished the tale; however, in his dying years, Marco Polo is said to have remarked that he had only told half of everything he had seen and that had he reported it all, nobody would have believed him.

Above: Christopher Columbus comes ashore on the island he named El Salvador.

Opposite: When Marco Polo died in 1324, he had seen more of the world than any European then alive.

The Portuguese

The Portuguese led the way in European maritime exploration with a series of expeditions to explore the coast of Africa beginning in 1415. These were, at least in part, a response to changing economic conditions and the need to find a direct route to the east without any of the disruptions and dangers of inland travel.

Prince Henry of Portugal, also known as Henry the Navigator, set up a naval base at Sagres. This became a center of excellence, attracting the most eminent people in many fields including navigation

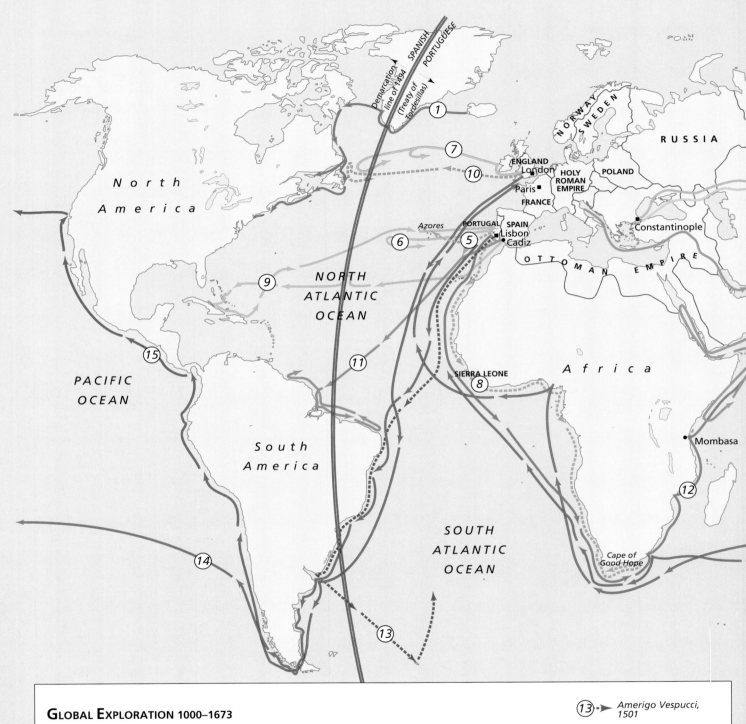

GLOBAL EXPLORATION 1000–1673

① Norwegians, Icelanders, c.1000

② Friar Rubruck, 1253–55

③ Nicolo and Maffeo Polo, 1262

④ Marco Polo, 1272–95

⑤ Portugese discover Madeira c.1419, Azores c.1427

⑥ King Manuel of Portugal sends expedition west to locate Antillia, unsuccessful

⑦ Bristol Merchants attempt to find "Isles of Brazil", 1480–81

⑧ Bartholomew Diaz, 1496–88

⑨ Christopher Columbus, 1492–93 (1st voyage)

⑩ John Cabot, 1497 (1st voyage)

⑪ Amerigo Vespucci, 1499 (2nd voyage)

⑫ Vasco de Gama, 1427–98

⑬ Amerigo Vespucci, 1501

⑭ Magellan (del Cano after Magellan's death), 1521–22

⑮ Drake, 1577–80

⑯ Abel Tasman, 1642–43

⑰ Chinese explorations under Zheng He 1415–17

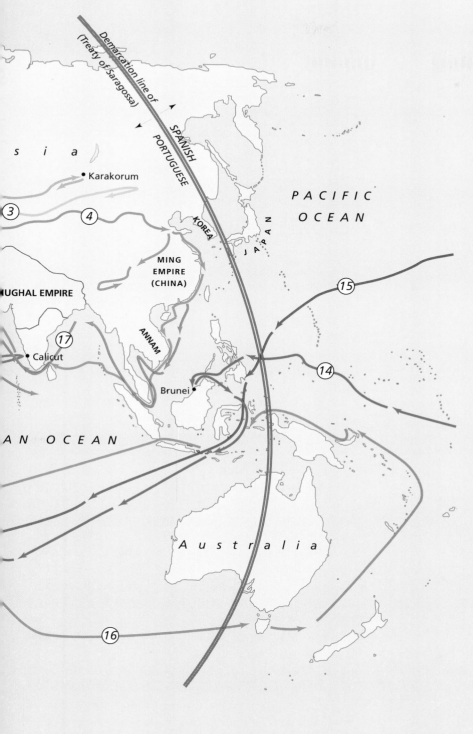

and shipbuilding, and Portuguese caravels—vessels which combined European hulls with Arab sail technology—could now cope with the rough seas around Africa.

The Portuguese developed a systematic approach to exploration, instilled by Henry's professionalism. They gradually worked their way around the coasts of Africa, expanding their knowledge with each journey. The breakthrough came when Gil Eannes managed to sail round the Cape of Bojador, on the coast of what is now Western Sahara. No ship had managed to pass this seemingly impossible stretch of water before, and some believed it to be the edge of the world. The psychological achievement was almost as important as the naval one and Portuguese sailors began to view the sea as a challenge, rather than as an impossible obstacle. By 1460, they had traveled as far as Sierra Leone, ominously bringing back slaves as well as gold and spices. By 1474, they had crossed the Equator and in 1488 Bartholomew Dias reached the Cape of Good Hope.

Originally the superintendent of the Royal Warehouse in Lisbon, Dias had been commissioned by his sovereign, King John II, to find the mythical priest-king, Prester John. He was given command of three ships and told to sail around Africa. On their journey the Portuguese took six Africans dressed in European clothing. They were left at various points along the coast, tasked with showing the inhabitants the goods which the Portuguese could sell them. As they deposited the last of these, the fleet was caught in a tremendous gale which finally subsided, but left them far out to sea. Swinging their vessels east, they sailed for several days without any sight of land before altering their course to the north. Eventually distant mountains were

sighted and the explorers headed for the coast, traveling along it until they reached the tip of Africa—the Cape of Good Hope. Dias wanted to continue, but on this occasion the crew refused and they returned to Lisbon.

The Portuguese sailor Vasco da Gama finally managed to sail around Africa in 1497. Once this had happened, the east was open to the Portuguese; there were new trading routes to dominate and lands to conquer. They encountered the Arab merchants who traded between Africa and Asia and were involved in a vicious battle to claim supremacy of the waters; a stronghold at Goa on the Indian coast was established after the defeat of the Arabs there in 1510. Goa became the major Portuguese city in India and was their central trading point for eastern exports—most importantly, spices and gold. The Portuguese in Goa also built churches and monasteries, leaving an indelible mark on the area.

Christopher Columbus

Christopher Columbus was born in 1451 in Italy, the son of a weaver. Little is known about his early years, but in 1476 he arrived in Portugal. Already a competent sailor, he increased his knowledge of the sea with voyages as far-flung as Britain in the north and the Gulf of Guinea in the south. He believed it was possible to reach the Indies (which at that time meant China and Japan) by sailing westwards. By Columbus's time, most educated people believed that the world was round, but there was no agreement on its size, and no knowledge of what lay to the west of the Canary Islands. Columbus himself thought that Japan could be reached by sailing west from there. The Portuguese monarchy refused to fund Columbus's expedition, believing his figures to be wrong, and he turned his attention to Spain. Here King Ferdinand and Queen Isabella also initially refused his proposal.

Columbus was not easily put off. Not only was he ambitious and single-minded, he also believed that God was urging him on. His religious fervor—and the unique business opportunity of a new trade route—impressed several important Spaniards, and they renewed his case with Isabella. Columbus was eventually given royal permission, though he was actually funded by independent merchants, and on September 6, 1492 he set sail from the Canary Islands.

Columbus's ship, the *Santa Maria*, was accompanied by two smaller ships, the *Pinta* and the *Niña*, captained by two Spanish brothers. The voyage was difficult due to growing tensions between Columbus and the brothers, and the sailors' fears that they would reach the edge of the world. There was talk of mutiny but, fortunately for Columbus, land was sighted on October 12. Columbus always believed that he had reached the Indies, though in reality the island he landed on, and which he named El Salvador, was just off the coast of what came to be called America.

Columbus's first assessment of the native people was that they would make "good slaves" and he set about claiming the land for Spain and exploring it for signs of gold. He found enough evidence to justify leaving a colony of men behind. He returned to Spain a hero, but despite making several other valuable discoveries in later expeditions to the region, his popularity steadily declined as tales of his bad behavior towards both the native people and his own men were reported. Today his reputation is no less ambiguous, with some calling him the father of America while others see him as a symbol of the death and destruction that was to come to the original inhabitants of the continent.

Other Europeans after Columbus

Portugal discovered Brazil in 1500. The opportunities to expand into this virgin land were extremely valuable, not only because of the material resources. Slaving stations were established along the coast, which they used to run their Brazilian plantations and slaves were shipped over from Portuguese strongholds in Africa, where the gold supply had been exhausted.

Thanks to their early dedication to maritime exploration, the Portuguese had the advantage in world trade by the start of the seventeenth century. Their domination was short-lived, however, as European nations refused to allow them to continue their monopoly.

The first serious rival to Portuguese overseas interests was the Dutch, who were emerging as a separate nation, throwing off Spanish rule. The Dutch had a tough commercial fleet—the so-called "sea beggars"—whose interests were in trade. The Dutch East India Company was set up in 1601, initially to fund their wars of independence, and it became one of the most powerful trading forces in the world. In 1619 it established a base at Batavia (now Jakarta) south-east of the Portuguese colonies at Goa and Malacca. This gave the Dutch an advantage and, through strategic strongholds and close relationships with local leaders, they developed a monopoly in precious goods coming from South-East Asia. The Dutch were able to lay claim to many important trading locations, establishing further colonies in Borneo, Indonesia, and India, which they maintained with often harsh discipline.

The French founded colonies on the Canadian coast early, at the end of the fifteenth century. At first these colonies acted as bases for preserving the fish caught off the coast of Newfoundland but trade with the native inhabitants in fur, initially in beaver fur, proved lucrative. Other colonies were established in Canada, gaining access to the interior through the exploration of the Saint Lawrence River.

The English discovered scarcely any of the world's coastlines; their success, rather, lay in colonizing the new lands found by others. It was Sir Francis Drake who launched England toward a future of imperial success. In 1577 he was charged by Queen Elizabeth I with circumnavigating the world. Unofficially, he was also instructed to plunder as many Spanish vessels as he could. He returned with enough treasure to pay off all of England's foreign debts and leave some over to begin the foundations of what would become the East India Company.

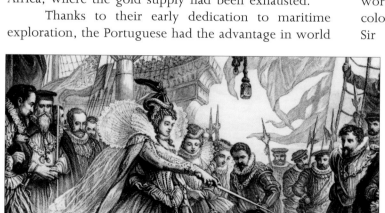

Left: April 4 1581, Queen Elizabeth I of England knights the explorer Francis Drake on board his ship, the Golden Hind at Deptford. Drake returned in September 1580 from his successful circumnavigation of the globe, bringing a shipload of spices. Opposite: Portuguese explorer and navigator Vasco da Gama being greeted by the Samorin in Calicut on the Malabar Coast of India.

The Americas— Conquest and Colonialization

From small beginnings in the islands of the Caribbean, the Spanish eventually came to control huge areas of the Americas, destroying empires in the process.

The Beginnings

Christopher Columbus had landed in the Americas in 1492; over the next twelve years he discovered a number of Caribbean islands, including Cuba and Hispaniola, and even landed on the mainland, in what is now Venezuela. His discoveries, together with those of the Portuguese—who had landed in Brazil in 1500—inspired many others to try their fortunes in the new lands.

Until 1518, Spanish exploration was confined to the Caribbean and the Gulf of Mexico. Their attempts to establish trading posts in the region were unsuccessful; the local economy operated at too basic a level to support them. The Spanish therefore developed an exploitation economy instead, with the use of forced local labor in both mining and farming. However, dreadful working conditions and the arrival of "new" diseases took their toll on the indigenous workforce, and the Spanish were left without enough workers to sustain their new colonies. Their interest then turned to the mainland.

The Conquistadors

The conquistadors, essentially military adventurers, were groups of Spanish explorers who, from the early sixteenth century, set out across Central and South America in search of land and riches in the name of Spain. They operated as individual armies, often recruiting indigenous people, and tended to preach the superiority of Christianity. Many were inspired by Columbus's success.

One of the earliest and most famous conquistadors was Hernán Cortés, born in 1485. In 1518 the governor of Cuba sent him to explore the Yucatan peninsula, but once ashore he acted completely independently, and acknowledged only the authority of the Spanish king. He founded the city of Veracruz and burned his ships in a symbolic act, then marched his small force inland. Here he was able to form an alliance with the Tlaxcalans, who were one of the Aztec Empire's subject peoples.

He and his allies entered the Aztec capital Tenochtitlán in 1519, but he himself had to return to the coast, in order to explain his actions to a force sent from Cuba. During his absence the Spanish who remained in the city became so unpopular that they were expelled by the Aztecs when Cortés returned. However, the emperor Montezuma was killed during the confusion of his return, and Aztec resistance was additionally hampered by the possibility that Cortés might be an incarnation of one of their deities. The resentment of the peoples they had subjugated was also critical. When Cortés and his allies launched their attack on the city in 1521, it fell—and the collapse of the Aztec Empire brought all their subject territories under Spanish control.

The position of Cortés in the eyes of the Spanish government is indicative of the political position of the conquistadors. For, while they respected him, they were deeply suspicious of his desire for power and refused to confirm him as governor of "New Spain." The conquest of the Inca Empire was an act of remarkable daring and deceit on the part of the conquistadors and, in particular, Francisco Pizarro. Pizarro, born in Spain in 1476, had been with the expedition that first looked on the Pacific when Panama was crossed in 1513, and this became a base for further exploration, and for exploratory journeys along the Peruvian coast.

Pizarro landed in Peru with a very small force of 177 men, and between 1531 and 1533 he managed to conquer the main cities of the Inca Empire, largely by subterfuge. The Inca Emperor, Atahualpa, was taken hostage and eventually put to death, and a puppet ruler was installed in his place. However, the situation in Peru became more confused than the apparently comparable circumstances in Mexico. Civil wars broke out, both among the conquistadors themselves and among the Incas, who rebelled against the puppet emperor Manco. Pizarro himself was a victim of one of these fierce vendettas: the son of one of his men, who

NORTH
ATLANTIC
OCEAN

VICEROYALTY OF NEW SPAIN

Audiencia of Nueva Galicia

Monterrey
Saltillo
Durango
San Luis Potosí
Guadalajara
Guanajuato
Tampico
Mexico
Veracruz
Mérida
Campeche

Gulf of Mexico

St. Augustine

Havana

Audiencia of Santo Domingo

Santiago

Santo Domingo

Audiencia of Mexico

Oaxaca

Audiencia of Guatemala

Guatemala

Granada

Caribbean Sea

Maracaibo

Santa Marta
Cartagena

Coro
Caracas
Cumaná
Mérida

Panamá

Audiencia of Santa Fé

Bogotá

Audiencia of Panamá

Cali
Popayán
Pasto

Quito
Guayaquil
Tumbes
Moyobamba

Audiencia of Quito

unexplored Spanish territory

Amazon

VICEROYALTY

unexplored Spanish territory

OF PERU

Cajamarca
Trujillo

PACIFIC OCEAN

Audiencia of Lima

Lima
Cuzco

Arequipa
Arica

La Paz
La Plata
Potosí

Audiencia of Charcas

Salta
Tucumán

Asunción
Corrientes

Mendoza
Valparaiso
Santiago
Concepción

Audiencia of Chile

Córdoba

Buenos Aires

SOUTH ATLANTIC OCEAN

THE STAMP OF SPAIN, AFTER 1550

- *Spanish territory*
- —— *Boundary of viceroyalty*
- - - - *Boundary of audiencia*
- ■ *Audiencia capital*
- ● *Major provincial center*
- *Under English control or influence*
- *Under French control*
- *Under Dutch control*

N

0   500 km
0   500 miles

had been killed by Pizarro's brother, murdered him in Lima in 1541.

The Myth of El Dorado

Christopher Columbus is said to have been the first person to have heard of El Dorado. However, the myth became popular from the 1530s onwards, when explorers inspired by the success of Cortés and Pizarro began to press further into South America, specifically into the area now known as Colombia.

As the conquistadors came into contact with local tribes they began to hear the story of a golden or "gilded" man: El Dorado. There was a tribe which, for the initiation of a new ruler, allegedly covered him in gold dust and floated him on a raft of reeds across the surface of Lake Guatavita. With him on the raft went the tribe's chiefs and a large amount of gold. The prince then, according to legend, threw the treasure into the lake and dived into the water, washing the gold off his skin. Golden artefacts found on the shore of the lake gave credibility to the story. (Later attempts to drain the lake all failed.)

Shortly after the myth first surfaced it began to change, until El Dorado became a huge city, made entirely of gold, somewhere in South America. The idea of a vast golden city was extremely exciting to the Spanish, who were already impressed by the treasure found by the early explorers. The city of El Dorado was, unsurprisingly, never located, though many believed it to be somewhere along the Orinoco River. It was not a uniquely Spanish myth, either: the English adventurer, Sir Walter Raleigh, made two journeys up the Orinoco in search of El Dorado, the first in 1595 and the second in 1617.

Goods from the New World

Quite apart from the precious metals they so craved, the Spanish brought many products to Europe from the Americas which we take for granted today. There were new types of timber, new kinds of dyes for fabrics and other materials—and foodstuffs, arguably the most important in the long term. Perhaps most notable among these was the potato. Potatoes were discovered in the Andes, and were in cultivation in Europe by 1570. They were also used to feed slaves in Spanish colonies, as well as hospital inmates.

Another food now in widespread use is chocolate, the name of which comes from the Mayan word "xocoatl." The cocoa plant, from which chocolate is made, was thought to be holy by the

Aztecs and the early chocolate drink which they created from it was believed to bring knowledge and wisdom. Cortés brought chocolate to Europe in 1528 and until 1606 only the Spanish knew how to make it, which gave them a trade advantage. The cocoa plant also provided the materials for making cocaine which, apart from being used for pleasure, was seen as a medicine and used to dull pain.

Perhaps the most widely used "medicine" which the Spanish brought back from the Americas was tobacco. It is believed that tobacco cultivation began in the Americas in around 6000 BC; it was completely unknown in the west. The native peoples had many uses for it; they believed that the plant came from a goddess and smoking was a communal, ritualistic activity. On his arrival in the Americas, the indigenous people offered Columbus dry tobacco leaves as a friendly gesture.

Over the next fifty years tobacco use grew throughout Europe; the Spanish were the first to export it commercially. By the early 1570s Spanish doctors were prescribing it as a cure for over thirty medical problems and by 1577 it was being recommended in England as a cure for, amongst other things, cancer.

Colonial Consequences for Spain and Portugal

The Iberian peninsula became the center of European trade during the relatively brief period that Spain and Portugal dominated world exploration. Unbelievable hauls of gold and silver came from the New World, making Spain and Portugal mighty economic powers. The influx of wealth from the new colonies was not without its problems, however, as before long the Iberian economies were suffering from inflation.

Wildly inflated prices changed the economic landscape. Those who already had wealth and power found that their fortunes were diminishing in value daily, making it less desirable to be a landowner and much more desirable to be in—previously despised— commerce. The old feudal economic system, in which ownership of land was so crucial, was collapsing and being replaced by a modern system based on trade.

Right: Francisco Pizzaro managed to conquer Peru in just a few years but was assassinated in Lima, which he had founded and called Ciudad de los Reyes, in 1541.
Opposite: A detail of a manuscript showing the Tlaxcalan suing for peace with Hernán Cortés.

European Empires Between the 16th and 18th Centuries

Between the sixteenth and the eighteenth centuries, Europe was dominated by the growth of large nation states. France, England, and Spain had all developed monarchies and national identities that had become distinct from both the Church and the Holy Roman Empire. At the end of the Hundred Years War, France had begun to increase in prosperity and security, despite conflict with the Holy Roman Empire. Internal religious divisions resulting from the Reformation weakened France, but the accession of Henry of Navarre, the first Bourbon king, ended this. The Bourbon Dynasty ruled France until the Revolution in the eighteenth century, and Bourbon monarchs were temporarily reinstalled on the throne in 1814. Of the Bourbons, the most well known are Louis XIV, the "Sun King," and Louis XVI, husband to Marie Antoinette and victim of the guillotine.

In England the internal struggle of the houses of Lancaster and York in the Wars of the Roses came to an end with the accession of the Tudors. The two most notable monarchs in this dynasty were Henry VIII and his daughter Elizabeth I. They were followed by the Stuarts, whose dynasty was interrupted in 1649 with the execution of Charles I following the civil war between the monarch and parliament. In 1660, following the death of the parliamentary leader Oliver Cromwell, Charles' son and heir was returned to the throne as Charles II, but with much-curtailed powers.

In Spain, the Kingdoms of Castille and Aragon were united under Isabella and Ferdinand, whose first success was to expel the Moors and establish a Catholic state. Revenue from the New World ensured that Spain was wealthy and when Charles I inherited the throne of Spain in 1516 and the Holy Roman Empire in 1519 he extended Spanish influence. Charles was succeeded by his son, Philip II, who championed Catholicism in the wake of the Reformation. Under Philip, Spanish territory overseas was increased and the power of the Inquisition reached new heights. However, Philip was the last successful Hapsburg king in Spain and the country gradually declined under the leadership of genetically disadvantaged monarchs.

Further east the rise in power of the Muscovy princes and the decline of the Golden Horde saw the beginnings of a Russian Empire. The ruler to unite all Russia was Ivan III, but it was Ivan IV—better known as Ivan the Terrible—who became the first official tsar in 1547. During the later reign of Peter the Great, Russia was modernized and became a more forceful European power, adopting a policy of aggressive expansion into China, Persia and Sweden.

Sweden itself had greatly expanded during the seventeenth century following successful conflicts with its neighbors Norway, Denmark and Poland. The successful outcome of the Thirty Years War also saw Sweden receive territory east and south of the Baltic, resulting in its domination of the region. The Netherlands also benefited from the treaties signed to end the Thirty Years War, gaining their independence from Spain and growing to become a major naval and economic power.

Left: King Ferdinand and Queen Isabella of Spain who supported Christopher Columbus's voyage to discover America.

Arctic Circle

Norwegian Sea

THE EMPIRE IN HAPSBURG EUROPE c. 1600

— Holy Roman Empire boundary 1618

Spanish-Hapsburg land

Austrian-Hapsburg land

Hapsburgs' traditional allies

Hapsburgs' enemies

Church lands

"Spanish Road", main supply routes to Hapsburg possessions

0   200 km

0   200 miles

SWEDISH EMPIRE

NORWAY (Danish)

Danish

Baltic Sea

Danish

Lithuania

D. of Prussia

POLAND

SCOTLAND
• Edinburgh

DENMARK

• Lübeck   • Stettin

IRELAND
■ Dublin

• York

ENGLAND

• Bristol

■ London

• Calais

North Sea

1566
Dutch revolt   Hamburg •

Amsterdam
The Hague •
Utrecht •
UNITED PROVINCES
Antwerp •
Brussels •
SOUTH NETHERLANDS

Münster
Munster •
Cleves •
Berg
West Phalia
Paderborn **Anhalt**
Mainz •
Hessen Kassel
Bamberg •

Brandenburg
Berlin •

• Breslau

Silesia

Bohemia

Moravia

KINGDOM OF HUNGARY

ATLANTIC OCEAN

• Brest

■ Paris

• Orléans

• Nantes

FRANCE

Luxembourg •
Rhine Palatinate
Württemberg
Lorraine
Upper Palatinate
Bavaria
Augsburg •
Munich •

Pressburg •

Vienna •

Archd. of Austria

• Buda

R. Danube

• Mohács

Sundgau
Besançon •
Charolais
Bugey
Franche Comté
Geneva •
D. of Savo

Basel
Swiss Confederation
Vorarlber
Trent
Tirol
Salzburg •
Carniola

REP. OF VENICE
Milan •
D. of Milan
Venice •
Mantua •

OTTOMAN EMPIRE

• Bordeaux

Adriatic Sea

Genoa •
Modena
REP. OF FLORENCE
Lucca

• Toulouse

San Sebastián •

• León

NAVARRA

Pamplona •

• Burgos

CASTILLA

ARAGON

Saragossa •

• Marseille
Roussillon
REP. OF GENOA
REP. OF SIENA
Siena
Papal States
• Rome

Corsica

KINGDOM OF NAPLES

Naples •

Madrid •
Toledo •

CATALUÑA
• Barcelona

Valencia •

Palma •
KINGDOM OF MAJORCA (1521–24)

Sardinia

PORTUGAL

• Lisbon

Córdoba •
Seville •
Jaén •
Murcia •
Granada •
GRANADA
Cádiz •
Cartagena •

• Palermo

Sicily

Mediterranean Sea

Algiers •   Bugia •

Tunis •

The Age of Scientific Discovery

The growing nation states of Europe provided a setting for a period of extraordinary discoveries in mathematics, the sciences—especially astronomy and medicine—and philosophy.

Above: Justin Susterman's portrait of Galileo, astronomer, mathematician, and physicist.

Astronomy

In 1543, Nicholas Copernicus published his essay *On the Revolution of Celestial Bodies*. Copernicus had written his treatise in 1530, but its contentious content meant that he did not publish it until the year of his death. In it, Copernicus explained that then known planets in the solar system all revolved around the sun, each moving in its own orbit. Not only this, but he asserted that each planet, including the Earth, spun on its own axis. Copernicus' ideas would have seemed ridiculous to many of his peers. Since the time of Ptolemy, it had been generally accepted that the celestial bodies revolved around the Earth, which remained static at the center of the universe; it was not generally assumed that the ancients could be wrong. However, astrological predictions based upon ancient theory were beginning to result in errors when compared to actual observations. Copernicus, who had been educated in theology at Bologna and Padua Universities, had begun to experiment mathematically with the possibility that the sun was at the center of the universe. His findings explained the astrological discrepancies.

In 1598, the Italian astronomer Galileo stood up against the Church and the Inquisition to support Copernicus' theory. The suggestion that man was not the center of the universe was heretical and Galileo was tried in Rome then kept under house arrest until his death in 1642. He himself had been responsible for a number of scientific discoveries including the satellites of Jupiter and the spots on the sun. Galileo had built his own telescope, perfecting a design that had first been invented in 1609 by Hans Lipperhay of Holland. Galileo communicated his Copernican ideas with the German astronomer and mathematician, Johannes Kepler. Kepler also believed in Copernicus' theory and used mathematics and geometry to prove it. In addition he discovered that all planets move in orbit, with the sun as the focus, and that the speed of a planet's orbit is related to its distance from the sun.

Medicine

Much of the medical theory practiced in Europe during the sixteenth and seventeenth centuries still rested on the ideas of Galen, the Greek physician to the Romans who had died in 201 AD. The main beliefs were that medical science was based upon the four classical elements: fire, earth, water, and air, and that health could be restored in someone if these elements were brought back into balance in the humors of the body. There also persisted the belief that illness could be brought about by spiritual means such as witchcraft, sin, or astral forces. As a result medical study in Europe was often hampered by the control of the Church.

In contrast, medical knowledge was far more advanced in the Muslim world and physicians such as Al-Razi (860–930) and Avicenna (980–1038) had already made important anatomical and chemical discoveries. During the Renaissance, many significant Arabic texts made their way to Europe and, combined with a later interest in anatomical experimentation, progress was slowly made. Realdo Colombo (1516–59) made important anatomical discoveries such as the structure of the eye and the relationship of the lungs to the heart. The surgeon William Harvey, influenced by both Islamic learning and René Descartes, correctly described the circulation of the blood through the body. The advances made in anatomy across Europe were helped by the establishment of a number of learned societies such as the Royal Society in London (1662) and the Academy of Sciences in Paris (1666).

Discoveries

Key discoveries in the sciences, mathematics, and philosophy all contributed to the rapid development of European society at this time. Important scientific

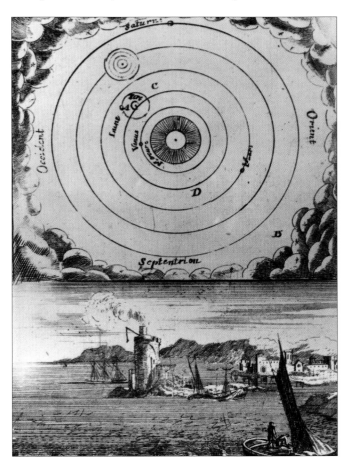

Left: 1685: A diagram of the solar system by French philosopher René Descartes.
Above: Nicolaus Copernicus whose theory of the solar system was published in 1543.

inventions included the construction of the microscope during the sixteenth century. Although the actual inventor is unknown, it is the Dutchman Anton van Leeuwenhoek who is credited with improving the final version. In 1643, Torricelli invented the barometer, which measured atmospheric pressure. The vacuum pump, first constructed by Otto von Guericke in 1645, was an invention that would later prove vital in industrial innovation and the development of the motor engine. The first steam engine was patented in 1698 by Thomas Savery, who had been encouraged to build a device that would pump water out of mine shafts. In 1714, Daniel Gabriel Fahrenheit developed the first accurate mercury thermometer and in 1731 the sextant was invented by John Hadley, which greatly enhanced nautical navigation. René Descartes lived from 1596 to 1650 and made vital contributions to mathematical methods. Descartes is widely believed to be the father of modern mathematics and his methods were also closely linked to philosophical thought. Isaac Newton (1642–1727) was the English mathematician and philosopher who made three crucial discoveries: the method of calculus, the composition of light and, most famously, the law of gravity. These, and other discoveries, all contributed to a general sense of understanding and ushered in an age which has since been called the Age of Reason.

The Ottoman Empire

From a small state in Western Anatolia to a major world power – the Ottoman rulers created an empire of great strength, complexity and artistic sophistication.

The Origins of the Ottomans

The origins of the Ottoman Empire lay in Western Anatolia. During the fourteenth century the small state surrounding Sogut began to take advantage of the decline of the Seljuk Turks and expanded at the expense of their neighbors. The collapse of the Seljuks precipitated a general struggle for power in the region and the Muslim Ottomans were driven in part by a desire to convert new territory to Islam. Under the leadership of Osman I (1259–1326), after whom the empire was named, they took control of Bursa, making the city their capital. In 1345, Osman's successor, Orhan I, took Karasi. In 1361, the Ottomans took the city of Edirne (Adrianople) and made this their new capital. From here the Ottomans made their threat to Constantinople obvious and they began a series of lengthy and unsuccessful sieges. Although most of their conquests before the turn of the century had been in the Balkans, Constantinople was the great prize.

By 1403 the Ottomans had subdued Bulgaria, Macedonia, Serbia, and much of Greece; however, in 1402 an attack by the Mongol leader Timur brought campaigns in the region to an end. When the Mongol conqueror of Persia and central Asia moved into Anatolia, Bayezid I (1360–1403) was forced to respond. At the Battle of Ankara in 1402 Timur defeated Bayezid, taking him captive. Timur's death in 1405 meant that further Mongol advances ended but the death of Bayezid had left the Ottomans with a succession crisis which lasted for eleven years. During this hiatus, the Balkans and the Anatolian states slipped out of Ottoman control. When Mehmet I finally became sultan in 1413 he began the restoration of the empire.

The Political Structure of the Empire

The head of the Ottoman Empire was the sultan, who enjoyed absolute power. Initially, the rulers of the Ottomans had titled themselves "gazis", or holy warriors, but during the reign of Murad (1360–89) the title sultan, or monarch, was used instead. In later centuries caliph, or religious leader, was also adopted. Although the sultan had complete control, he was aided in the administration of the empire by a bureaucracy of officials who were led by the grand council, the Divan. The Divan consisted of just three vizirs in the fourteenth century; by the seventeenth there were eleven. The head of this group was known as the grand vizir, who directly consulted the sultan.

The other powerful institution at the heart of the Ottoman government was the harem. The harem was ruled over by the "valide

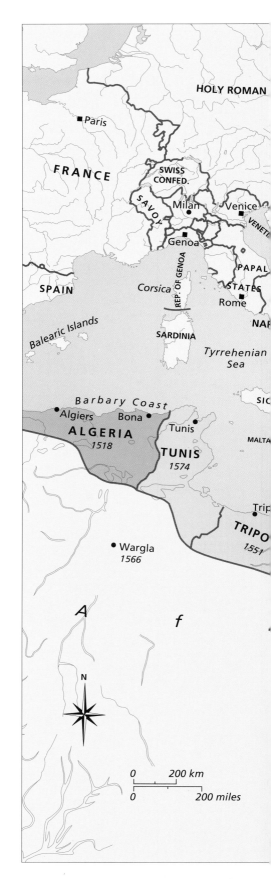

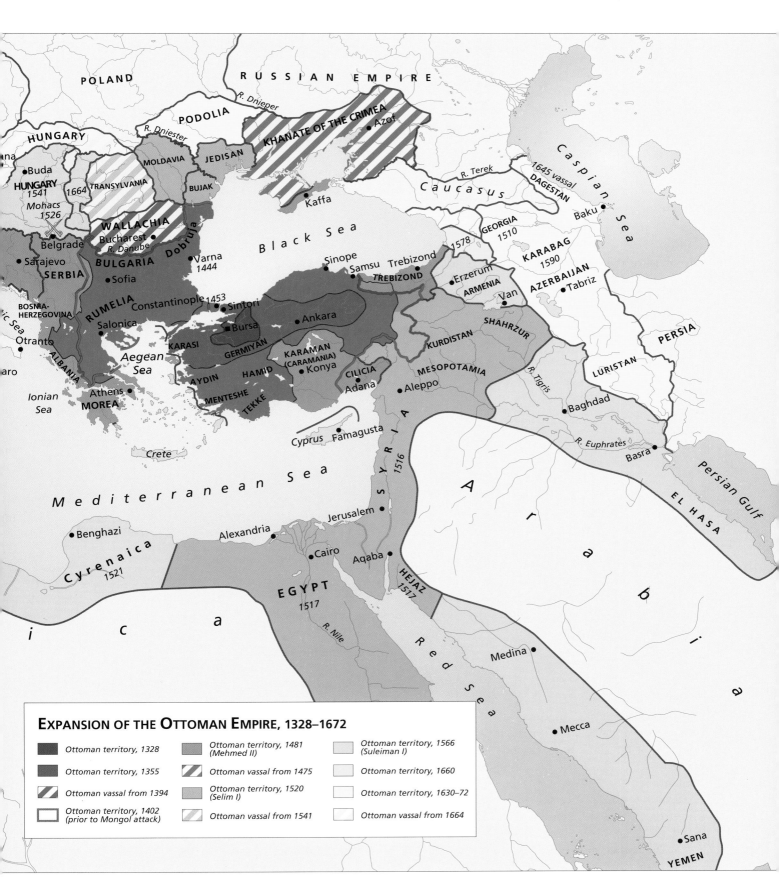

POLAND

RUSSIAN EMPIRE

R. Dnieper

PODOLIA

R. Dniester

KHANATE OF THE CRIMEA

Azof

HUNGARY

•Buda

HUNGARY
1541

MOLDAVIA

JEDISAN

Caucasus

R. Terek

1645 vassal

DAGESTAN

Caspian Sea

Baku•

1664 TRANSYLVANIA

BUJAK

*Mohacs
1526*

•Kaffa

WALLACHIA

GEORGIA
1510

•Belgrade

Bucharest•

Dobruja

•Sarajevo

R. Danube

BULGARIA

•Varna
1444

1578

KARABAG
1590

SERBIA

•Sofia

•Sinope

Samsu Trebizond

•Erzerum

AZERBAIJAN

•Tabriz

BOSNIA-
HERZEGOVINA

RUMELIA

Constantinople *1453*

TREBIZOND

ARMENIA

•Van

PERSIA

Otranto•

Salonica

•Sintori

SHAHRZUR

ic Sea

ALBANIA

KARASI

•Bursa

•Ankara

KURDISTAN

LURISTAN

Aegean
Sea

GERMIYAN

MESOPOTAMIA

R. Tigris

Athens•

AYDIN

HAMID

KARAMAN
(CARAMANIA)

•Aleppo

•Baghdad

*Ionian
Sea*

MOREA

MENTESHE

•Konya

CILICIA

•Adana

R. Euphrates

•Basra

aro

TEKKE

Cyprus Famagusta

SYRIA
1516

Persian
Gulf

Mediterranean Sea

Crete

EL HASA

A

•Benghazi

Alexandria

•Jerusalem

r

Cyrenaica
1521

•Cairo

Aqaba

EGYPT
1517

HEJAZ
1517

a

b

i

c

a

R. Nile

Red Sea

•Medina

i

•Mecca

YEMEN

•Sana

EXPANSION OF THE OTTOMAN EMPIRE, 1328–1672

- Ottoman territory, 1328
- Ottoman territory, 1355
- Ottoman vassal from 1394
- Ottoman territory, 1402 (prior to Mongol attack)
- Ottoman territory, 1481 (Mehmed II)
- Ottoman vassal from 1475
- Ottoman territory, 1520 (Selim I)
- Ottoman vassal from 1541
- Ottoman territory, 1566 (Suleiman I)
- Ottoman territory, 1660
- Ottoman territory, 1630–72
- Ottoman vassal from 1664

sultana," the mother of the sultan, who often got involved in state politics. Second in importance was the sultan's first wife or mother of his firstborn son, and after her were the four other official wives. The harem also contained a number of concubines, both of the sultan and his most important officials, plus young women about to be used in political marriages. Serving the harem were two levels of eunuchs, the black eunuchs and the white. The black eunuchs were African slaves who served the women and were run by the chief black eunuch, a particularly powerful member of the court. The white eunuchs were mainly Balkan slaves and served the palace school where selected boys who would later become either officials or Janizaries were educated. The Janizaries were the sultan's elite cavalry and bodyguards. They were usually Christian slaves, carefully selected from conquered lands and trained under strict, monastic conditions. Although not forced to convert to Islam, most of them did.

Conquests

With the reconstruction of the Ottoman state during the reigns of Mehmed I (1413–21) and his son Murad II (1421–51), the empire was soon ready to expand again. In 1444 they defeated the Polish crusaders at the battle of Varna on the western coast of the Black Sea. Murad then went on to suppress Balkan resistance,

bringing the eastern and southern Balkan states back under Ottoman control. It was under Mehmed II, "The Conqueror," that the Ottomans became a world power.

In 1453, Mehmed finally managed to take Constantinople, making this former center of the Byzantine world the new and permanent Ottoman capital. Constantinople's position as both the gateway from the Mediterranean to the Black Sea and a vital point at which Europe met Asia made it a crucial victory. Not only were they now the heirs of the Byzantines, they also controlled the major trade routes. Mehmed also saw the complete absorption of Bosnia, Serbia and Herzegovina into the empire, as well as the final suppression of all other rival Anatolian states. Under Selim I (1512–20) the empire was preoccupied with the aggression of the Safavid Empire of Iran, who as Shiite Muslims were in religious opposition to the Ottomans. In 1514, the Ottomans managed to defeat the Safavids and consequently their influence spread further east. Selim also began to attack the Mameluke Empire of Egypt and Syria and by 1517 had conquered Cairo. Ottoman success at conquest was partly due to the disorganization and declining powers of many of their adversaries. They were also willing to engage with the cultures that they met, being quick to absorb ideas from the Hellenic and Egyptian societies they encountered. Their general lack of brutality toward the conquered meant that they were often welcomed.

The Capture of Constantinople

Mehmed was determined to defeat Constantinople, which had always successfully resisted attack from the Ottomans. He prepared for his final assault on the city with great care, establishing a number of strategically positioned fortresses along the Bosporus. These would act both as a means of preventing supplies from entering the city and as a defense against any possible assistance that might come from the Church and the Holy Roman Empire. He had prepared his army in the use of the latest military technologies, in particular making use of Hungarian-designed cannons. On 2 April 1453, Mehmed's army began its siege of Constantinople. Despite the use of cannon fire, the Turks were unable to breach the city's outer walls and for several weeks Constantinople held out. Eventually, however, one of the main gates was breached and the city soon fell to the Ottomans. The last Byzantine Emperor, Constantine XI, died in the battle to save the city. Despite calls for aid to the Pope, no assistance had been offered. Although the city was sacked by its conquerors, Mehmet ensured that his troops were restrained in order to ease his conquest of the city and many of its citizens welcomed their new leaders.

Hagia Sofia

The Hagia Sofia was the largest church in the Christian world when the Ottomans invaded. It had been built during the sixth century by the Emperor Justinian following the destruction of a predecessor on the same site during riots. Justinian commissioned architects who would design an unrivaled structure. The huge dome of the church measured a hundred feet in diameter and rather than being supported by pillars it was engineered to hang above the central space supported by four arches. The church was richly decorated with Byzantine mosaics made of glass and gold, and marble pillars in greens, white, and purple. When Mehmet II captured the city, the church remained undamaged; it was converted into a mosque, however. This conversion resulted in the covering up of the mosaic images of Christ and other saints, in the main because Islam forbids the depiction of the human form. A wooden minaret, added to the building by Mehmet, was later replaced by Süleyman with four grander structures. Hagia Sofia represented the pinnacle of Byzantine design and influenced the future design of mosques both in the city and across the Empire. The failure of the architect Atik Sinan to improve upon the geometric dimensions of the dome resulted in his execution by the disappointed Mehmet II.

Süleyman the Magnificent

It was under the Sultan Süleyman (1494–1566) that the Ottoman Empire reached its peak. During his forty-six-year reign the empire increased its territory in Europe, taking Hungary in 1526 and threatening Austria. Süleyman took a particular interest in destabilizing Europe, seeing it as the Ottomans' greatest threat; he built a fleet which dominated the Mediterranean, capturing Greece and major islands such as Rhodes and Cyprus which had previously been held by the Venetians. He also captured huge territories in North Africa, extending from Morocco across to Egypt. Süleyman styled himself Caliph, or ruler of Islam, which justified his annexation of other Islamic countries such as Azerbaijan, Iraq, and Arabia. The enormous wealth that Süleyman obtained from the control of the Mediterranean and specifically Egypt gave him the resources to build a powerful and spectacular empire, and he focused on Constantinople.

Above: Süleyman, known as "Kanuni" the Lawgiver, in his homeland, has always been called "Süleyman the Magnificent" by the Europeans. Opposite: Hagia Sophia was converted from a Christian church to a mosque by Mehmet II after the Turkish conquest of Istanbul in 1453.

As a keen patron of the arts, Süleyman promoted the construction of a number of impressive architectural buildings in Constantinople (Istanbul). He also organized the administration of the empire, making it more efficient, and rewrote the Ottoman legal system which existed alongside the Shari'a laws found in the Koran.

In his personal life, he was less impressive. Influenced by his former concubine and later wife, Roxelana, Süleyman had two of his more able sons executed in order to promote Roxelana's eldest son. During Süleyman's reign, the Ottomans were generally feared by the Europeans, with only the French monarch Francis I having the foresight to engage in diplomatic relations with Süleyman. However, following the Sultan's death in 1566 and the succession of his ineffectual son Selim II, the Empire began its slow decline.

Religious Divisions in Europe

Increasing knowledge, interest and involvement in religion, together with dissatisfaction with the established Church, led to major upheavals in Christianity that affected all of Europe.

The Origins of the Reformation

"Reformation" refers to the religious revolution that occurred during the sixteenth century. There were a number of causes of reformation in Europe. A general sense of dissatisfaction with the Roman Catholic Church had been growing since the Renaissance. Many, particularly those in northern Europe, felt that the Church had become complacent as the guardian of Christianity; too many members of the clergy were seen as lazy and corrupt and their intellectual and moral qualifications for the role were often questioned. This dissatisfaction was combined with a growth in devotion to the Bible and scriptures which had been fed by the invention of the printing press in 1445. A number of new translations of the Bible had made it accessible to a wider readership, and this resulted in

challenges to the authority of the Church. The Renaissance had been characterized by the development of humanism and this spread to northern Europe where it was taken up by theologians such as Desiderius Erasmus.

Erasmus (1466–1536) was a devout Christian and a humanist who felt that the rituals and practises of the Church were at odds with the teachings of Christ. His writings called for the reform of the Church from within; however, they influenced those who would choose to reform the Church by any means. The prominent English humanist, Thomas More (1478–1535) was also a devout Catholic who would later be executed by Henry VIII for refusing to renounce Rome. More, like Erasmus, felt that reform was needed, and he too wrote essays which criticized the abuses of the papacy and the Church. The writings of these and other prominent humanists were highly influential and were read in particular by the German Augustinian monk whose actions would spark the reformation itself, Martin Luther.

Martin Luther

Born in 1483, Martin Luther had spent three years at an Augustinian monastery before his ordination in 1507. In 1510 he visited Rome, where he saw at first hand the selling of indulgences to finance the building of St Peter's Basilica. The sale of indulgences was one of the most controversial practices of the Church, which many reformers found offensive. Part of religious doctrine centered on the belief that only through repentance of sin was mankind guaranteed entry into heaven. Repentance itself was a personal, internal state and in order to prove to the outer world that a person was repentant, they were required to do good, charitable works. The concept of indulgence was devised to give people the opportunity to buy the good works and charity performed by the clergy in order to show their repentance. As a result the Church was able to garner a large amount of money with which it could finance itself and its functions; sinners could, in turn, sin and then purchase forgiveness.

When Luther returned to Wittenberg he began

to develop his theological argument against indulgences and the completed "ninety-five theses" was dramatically nailed to the door of Wittenberg church in 1517. This blasphemous action resulted in violent dispute and Luther was called to Rome to answer for his actions but refused to go. When he was excommunicated by the Pope in 1521 he burned the papal bull that had been issued against him. Charles V called Luther to the Diet of Worms, where he took a stand upon his views and, despite being banned by the Empire, he found protection from the Elector of Saxony. In the latter years of his life Luther produced a new German translation of the Bible. He died in 1546.

Protestant Division

Luther's actions had resulted in violent religious outbursts and eventually a form of civil war. His principles were adopted by a number of leaders who were keen to break free from their relationship with the Roman Catholic Church. The outcome of the reformation was not therefore the reform of the Catholic Church but the splintering of Western Christianity into two distinct forms, Catholicism and Protestantism. Furthermore, Protestantism was made up of a large number of different interpretations, sects, and, churches. In the Swiss city states, or cantons, the ruler of Zurich was Ulrich Zwingli who, influenced by Luther, developed his own ecclesiastical reforms. He decreed that unless something were specifically and literally permitted by the Old or New Testament then it was unchristian. Zwingli's radically fundamental Christianity was eventually adopted across the Swiss region.

Other states followed the Swiss example and Protestantism spread across the Holy Roman Empire, to the Baltic countries and west into France. The ideas of John Calvin, a Frenchman forced to flee to Geneva, became particularly popular during the second half of the sixteenth century. Calvin had published his most important theories in 1541, and by 1562 Calvinist churches had sprung up in France, Germany, the Netherlands, and Scotland. Calvinism was the foundation of Presbyterianism and Puritanism; it acknowledged the supreme power of God, the idea of

Above: Portrait of John Calvin (1509–64), French theologian and reformer who adopted Protestantism in 1534 and established religious government in Geneva.
Opposite: Martin Luther, leader of the Protestant Reformation who was excommunicated by the Catholic Church in 1521.

an elect few being predestined to be saved, and the repression of pleasure and frivolity.

Other minority groups and sects were established in this period. The Anabaptists were particularly notable for practising adult baptism, as had appeared in the Bible. Their belief in strict church discipline as opposed to the law of the state meant that they were persecuted by both Catholics and

N

0   200 km
0   200 miles

NORWAY

*North
Sea*

SWEDEN

Baltic Sea

DENMARK

FINLAN

ES

LI

COURLA

⌂ *Northern mission
1673, 1678, 1688*

⌂ Königs
TEUTON
ORDER
PRUSS

Schleswig

Holstein

Lübeck   Pomerania   • Danzig

Emden   Mecklenburg   • Stettin

⌂ *Scottish mission
1653–94*

• St. Andrews

• Glasgow

Bremen   Hamburg   **Brandenburg**

Groningen   **Brunswick**   • Berlin

**KINGDOM
OF
POLAND**

W
15

③
IRELAND

• York

• Dublin

Netherlands   Münster   Magdeburg   • Wittenberg

Amsterdam   **Saxony**   **Silesia**

Leiden   Utrecht   Dortmund   Dresden Breslau

⌂ *English mission
1623–88*

• Norwich

ENGLAND

Middleburg   Ghent   Breda   Cologne   Hessen-   Mühlhausen   Leipzig   • Breslau

①   Antwerp   Kassel

Lille   ②   Wetzlar   Zwickau   **Prague**
1576, 1612

• Canterbury   *1594, 1597*   Maastricht

Tournai   Frankfurt   Bamberg   Upper   **BOHEMIA**

Rhine   Wurzburg   Palatinate

Palatinate   Ansbach   Nuremberg   **Moravia**   **KINGDOM
OF
HUNGARY**

• Rouen   Worms   *1538*

• Meaux   Heilbronn   Regensburg

1500   Würt-   Hall   Donauwörth   **Vienna**
1524

• Alençon   • Troyes   temberg   *1573,1583*

Strasbourg   Ulm   **Bavaria**   ②

**ATLANTIC
OCEAN**

Paris   Munster   Augsburg *1573,1583*

②   ⌂ Munich   **Graz**
1573, 1583   *1581, 1621*

FRANCE   Basel   Zürich   Innsbruck

②⑥   *1529*

Marmoutiers   Bourges   Lucerne   **R. of
Venice**

French congregation, 1580   Freiburg   Bern

1528   Trent   **OTTOMAN EMP**

• Limoges   Geneva   Brescia   • Venice

La Rochelle   *1536*   Milan   *Ursulines, 1535*   *1500*

• Lyon   **Savoy**   Verona

Bordeaux   • Périgueux   Turin   Ferrara   ①

• Bergerac   *Barnabites,*   Mantua   Ravenna

1530   Bologna   *Fathers of the
Good Jesus, 1526*   • Dalmatian congregatio

Rodez   • Orange   Genoa

Montauban   Albi Millau   **Papal States**   *Adriatic
Sea*

Gaillac   Nimes   Florence

Toulouse   Avignon   *1560*   ⑱⑦   Camerino

Montpellier   *Pères doctrinaires, 1592–97*   *Capucins,
1525–1528*

• Pamplona

NAVARRE   *Corsica*   Rome   **Naples**
Theatines, 1524

CASTILLE   • Mannesa   *Jesuits, 1540*

③①   Naples
1511

⌂ Madrid   **CATALONIA**

1505

• Toledo

Sardinia

Balearic Is.   Messina

M e d i t e r r a n e a n   S e a   *Sicily*   Gr
Isl

other Protestants. These most radical of Protestant groups were centered in Moravia, Friesland, and Germany, and were particularly popular with the peasant class. In 1521 a peasant revolt was incited with the intention of beginning a Christian revolution against all forms of authority. Despite the brief establishment of an Anabaptist state at Münster, the revolt was brutally suppressed.

Henry VIII

The arrival of the Reformation in England was of more political than religious importance. Henry VIII had been married to the Spanish princess Catherine of Aragon for twenty-four years when he decided to annul the marriage. His motives were divided; he and Catherine had been unable to produce a male heir to the throne but he was also captivated by Anne Boleyn who was pressuring him into marriage. Henry's request for a divorce from the Pope was denied and in response he broke with the Church, divorced Catherine, and married Anne. After severing all ties with Rome, Henry made himself the head of the Church of England, calling himself "Defender of the Faith." Anyone who refused to acknowledge Henry's supreme ecclesiastical power was accused of treason and from 1534 onward many people were executed. Henry went on to have Anne executed for witchcraft in 1536 and married four more times, producing his only male heir, Edward, in 1537.

Above: Henry VIII of England who broke from the church of Rome giving himself the title "Defender of the Faith".

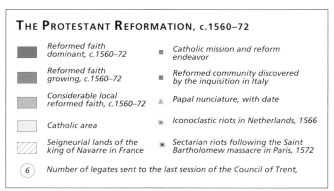

THE PROTESTANT REFORMATION, c.1560–72

▮	Reformed faith dominant, c.1560–72	▪	Catholic mission and reform endeavor
▮	Reformed faith growing, c.1560–72	▪	Reformed community discovered by the inquisition in Italy
▮	Considerable local reformed faith, c.1560–72	⚑	Papal nunciature, with date
▢	Catholic area	✳	Iconoclastic riots in Netherlands, 1566
▨	Seigneurial lands of the king of Navarre in France	✳	Sectarian riots following the Saint Bartholomew massacre in Paris, 1572
⑥	Number of legates sent to the last session of the Council of Trent,		

Tensions between Anglicans and Catholics would continue to plague English politics until the eighteenth century. The Protestant boy-king Edward VI reigned for only six years and he was followed by his elder sister Mary, daughter of Catherine of Aragon and a devout Catholic. "Bloody" Mary was responsible for the mass executions of heretics in an attempt to overturn the Protestant reforms. She was succeeded in 1558 by her Protestant younger sister, Elizabeth, the daughter of Henry and Anne Boleyn. Like her father, Elizabeth was to become one of the most famous of the English monarchs and although she had to deal with religious turmoil, her reign—which lasted for forty-five years—saw the Church of England fully established.

Above: Portrait of Gaspard de Coligny II (1519-1572), French Huguenot admiral and convert to Protestantism who supported Henry of Navarre. He was murdered on St. Bartholomew's Day.
Opposite: Oliver Cromwell, a Puritan, led the parliamentary forces against King Charles I during the English Civil War.

Catholic Counter-Reformation

The Roman Catholic Church did respond to the threat posed by the Protestant Reformation. Although many reformers had eventually rejected the authority of the pope, others remained loyal and continued to press for internal reforms. In 1545, Pope Paul III commissioned a number of specially appointed cardinals to look into the abuses of indulgences and the appointments of corrupt clerics and bishops. This first meeting of the Council of Trent was the basis of the Catholic response to the Reformation. Although the council upheld the basic structure of the Church and supported most of the practices that the Protestants had criticized, it did produce some administrative reforms. Under Pope Paul IV, more aggressive means of countering the Protestant movement were undertaken, including increasing the powers of the Inquisition and the burning of heretics. A number of monastic orders were revived during the period including the Capuchins, whose work included the giving of charity to the poor, and the Oratorians. The establishment of the Jesuit order by Ignatius Loyola also served the purposes of the counter-reformation. The aims of the Jesuits were to educate obedience to the scripture and to preach obedience to the Church, and their missionary work across Europe and the New World won many back to the Catholic fold. Although the counter-reformation had some success in re-establishing the Catholic Church, it had been permanently damaged by the process of the Reformation.

The French Wars of Religion

A series of wars in France between the Catholics and the Calvinist Huguenots broke out in 1562. When the weak, fifteen-year-old Francis II came to the throne in 1559, three of France's noble families vied for control, the Guises, the Bourbons, and the Montmorencies. Of these, the Guise family was the most powerful and the most Catholic and they controlled the monarch, to the displeasure of French Huguenots. When Francis died, his equally weak successor Charles IX was controlled by his mother, Catherine de Medici, who was a powerful and political regent. Catherine sought the support of the Huguenots against the Guise family and granted them increased tolerance, but ultimately she was a Catholic and wanted France to remain a Catholic country. The Guises attacked a congregation of Huguenots in 1562 beginning the wars, but the most reviled act of the wars was the St Bartholomew's Day massacre in 1572. Catherine, fearing the increased power of the Huguenots, had persuaded Charles that he was endangered by an assassination plot and, convinced, he ordered the massacre in Paris. During three days, over 20,000 people were murdered by the Catholic League, led by the Guises.

The instability of France was encouraged by the support of Spain's Philip II for the Catholic League and England's Elizabeth I for the Huguenots. The new French king, Henry III, was more moderate, and struck up an alliance with the Huguenot Henry of Navarre, making him his heir. As Henry IV, he converted to Catholicism and ended the wars with the Edict of Nantes which granted Huguenots rights of worship.

The Thirty Years War

The Thirty Years War was a complex religious and political conflict that lasted from 1618 to 1648. In essence it was a power struggle between the kings of France and the Hapsburg rulers of the Holy Roman Empire. The Empire was now a collection of self-governing states, half of which were Catholic and half Protestant, the majority of which would later unite to become Germany. These religious differences led to rivalries such as that between the Calvinist state of the Palatine and Catholic Bavaria. When Frederick IV of the Palatine formed an alliance with England, France, and the Netherlands against Spain, Maximillian of Bavaria formed a Catholic League and war eventually broke out between the two. The Thirty Years War was the first full European war, drawing in most of the major powers including Sweden, Denmark, and Transylvania, and involving numerous alliances and conflicts. The eventual collapse of Spain led to the threat of defeat for the Empire and in the Treaty of Westphalia of 1648, the Thirty Years War was concluded in favor of the French.

The English Civil War

The last great war of religion in Europe was the civil war fought in England from 1642 to 1648. In this case the rival factions were the monarch, Charles I, together with his supporters, and the English Parliament. Although the monarch was the divine head of state, Parliament played a vital role in the administration of England. Growing concern over both the king's increasing power and the influence of his Catholic queen motivated Parliament, led by Puritan Protestants, to restrict royal authority. After a gradual growth in hostility, including Charles' removal from London, open war broke out. Initially the Royalists were successful and threatened to take London from the Parliamentarians. However, Parliament allied with their Protestant neighbor to the north, Scotland, and threatened Charles on two fronts. The creation of a highly disciplined and motivated army under the leadership of Cromwell enabled the Parliamentarians to defeat Charles at the Battle of Naseby. In 1647 Charles handed himself over to the Scots, who immediately sent him to London and into Parliamentary custody. In order to prevent further bloodshed when Charles failed to compromise, Parliament authorized his execution. The public beheading of the monarch in 1649 had important repercussions across Europe. It was generally accepted that monarchs held their position by the divine right of God and that they were all-powerful. The English, by establishing a Commonwealth led by Oliver Cromwell, had greatly reduced the power of the sovereign and had proved that revolution was possible.

France 1643–1715

During a long reign, Louis XIV rebuilt France and extended it, turning it into a dominant power expressed in his lasting legacy—the Palace of Versailles.

Louis XIV

During the reign of Louis XIV (1638–1715), who was known as the Sun King, France became the most influential and feared state in Europe. Louis was only four when he inherited the throne in 1643 and power was held by his mother Anne of Austria, aided by the unpopular Cardinal Mazarin. Mazarin's imposition of heavy taxes caused intense opposition and Anne ordered the arrest of leading dissenters in 1648; Parisians took to the streets and the royal family was forced to flee. For the next five years the situation was chaotic, but this ended with a general amnesty in 1653.

On the death of Mazarin in 1661, Louis took responsibility and began to rebuild France, which had been negatively affected by the years of war and civil disruption. Louis was concerned with turning France into a force able to compete with its European neighbors, in particular the Spanish Habsburg Empire which pressed in on two of his borders. He built up the army and improved the navy, then entered into a series of aggressive foreign policies designed to extend and reinforce France's borders. He also set about improving France's road network and waterways, all of which helped to facilitate the country's increasing trade. Louis had abolished the position of chief minister at the start of his rule and he governed the realm by himself as an absolute ruler, successfully removing the influence of other noble families. However, he was an extravagant monarch and despite France's outward dominance, its people lived with oppressive taxes which were required to finance wars and building projects. Both the clergy and the nobility were exempt from paying tax, so the burden fell most heavily on the peasants and workers, encouraging resentment that would finally erupt in 1789. Louis died in 1715; his reign had lasted for 72 years, the longest ever achieved by a major European monarch.

Expansion and Aggression

Louis XIV's intense desire for military glory led to a series of wars; by 1670 France was the greatest power in Europe. He attacked Holland in 1672, beginning a war that lasted seven years, and which alerted the rest of Europe to his ambitions. Within the next decade most neighboring countries had united against him. Striking first, he marched eastward with great brutality; in the Palatinate atrocities were carried out under his direct orders. However, after nine years of war he was forced to renounce almost all his gains.

In yet another war Louis was finally defeated badly, losing 30,000 of his 50,000 troops at the Battle of Blenheim in 1704, and suffering more heavy losses at the Battle of Malplaquet a few years later. Territory was regained before his reign ended, but the economy of France was ruined.

Religious Persecution

Louis was determined that France should be an entirely Catholic country and in 1685 he revoked the law which had granted French Protestants—the Huguenots—freedom of worship and other rights. Armed raids, torture, a scorched-earth policy, and the confiscation of goods and property ensured that even within a few months France's Huguenot population decreased substantially. Many converted, many were caught trying to escape—but many succeeded and fled to Protestant countries. They possessed valuable economic skills and often joined the armies of Louis' enemies. Louis also acted against the Jansenists, a sect that sought to return to the discipline and simplicity of the early Church. His actions were to have wide-ranging consequences.

Versailles

When Louis came to power, he decided to find a site for his new court near to Paris, but beyond the disorder of the city. He chose a hunting lodge that had been built for his father and employed a team of architects and decorators who would convert a relatively simple structure into a grand palace. Louis moved into Versailles in 1682, although the construction of the palace itself continued until 1688. Versailles was a statement of Louis' power and position. It served as the center of his government and his own chambers were at the literal heart of the building complex. Louis demanded court attendance at Versailles which helped to keep the notoriously difficult nobles "imprisoned" in the palace. Keeping the nobles away from the city and somewhere they could do less plotting enabled Louis to centralize his government and hold on to his absolute power. Following his death Versailles was temporarily abandoned, but it was later occupied by Louis XVI and Marie Antoinette, who made significant additions to the palace complex.

The Man in the Iron Mask

The legend of the man in the iron mask is based upon a true story. In 1703 an unidentified prisoner in the Bastille died and was buried with his iron mask still fixed in place. This person had been kept in the Pignerol prison for over forty years before being moved. A number of stories circulated as to the true identity of the mysterious prisoner and one of these was that he had been the twin brother of Louis, incarcerated in the tower as a boy in order to protect the King's position. This rumor was eventually turned into a number of plays and stories, the most well known being that written by Alexandre Dumas, who also wrote the novel *The Three Musketeers*. In Dumas' version of the masked prisoner story, the musketeers replace the man in the iron mask with the spoilt young monarch and the more responsible ex-prisoner grows up to become the Sun King. In truth, the royal prisoner is believed to have been a treacherous minister called Count Girolamo Mattioli.

Below: The Palace of Versailles could accommodate some 20,000 people, including servants, by the time it was complete.
Opposite: Louis XIV established an absolute monarchy in France famously quoted as saying "L'état, c'est moi" ("I am the State").

Colonial North America

The dominance of Spanish colonies in the Caribbean and North America was challenged by other European nations, and a period of intensive settlement and competition began.

Spanish Expansion

Following their conquests over the Aztecs and Incas in the early sixteenth century, and the subsequent discovery of large quantities of silver, Spanish settlement in the Americas increased rapidly, driven by the prospect of accumulating great wealth and an abundance of fertile land for farming. The Christian missionaries that followed took it as their duty to spread God's word to the "pagan natives." As more territory was secured and exports of silver increased, there was also a need for the establishment of defensive positions, particularly around the Caribbean and Gulf of Mexico, where piracy by the English, French and Dutch was rife. By the middle of the sixteenth century, the Spanish dominated much of Central and South America, and were beginning to expand their possessions northward beyond Mexico, into North America.

Simultaneously, other European arrivals, notably the English, French, Russians, and Dutch, were beginning to challenge Spanish supremacy in the Americas. Ultimately this prompted the Spanish to extend their claims, establishing fortifications in Texas, moving westward to California and north along the Pacific coast towards Alaska in an attempt to check the progress of new settlers.

Early French and English Settlement

The first major gains were made by the French in the northeast. The French had been fishing for cod in the waters around Newfoundland from the early sixteenth century, and small numbers were soon trading with the local inhabitants. By the early 1600s, following further exploration inland from the Gulf of St Lawrence, numerous settlements were founded, beginning with Quebec in 1608 and Ville-Marie in 1642. These were to form the basis of a lucrative fur trade, and provide bases for further expansion westward along the Ottawa to the Great Lakes. In the latter part of the century the French moved south along the Mississippi valley to the Gulf of Mexico, but although several more towns were set up and the region claimed by

Left: An etching of the Mayflower that carried the Pilgrim Fathers from Plymouth to America.
Opposite: Jamestown was founded by the settlers in 1607.

the French and named Louisiana, it would take until around 1750 for the French to consolidate their possessions; most settlers remained concentrated in the north.

The English, meanwhile, who had embarked on voyages of exploration in the wake of the discovery of the New World, and had taken to looting Spanish shipping throughout the sixteenth century, also turned their attentions to the possibility of colonization. In 1584 a reconnaissance mission organized by Walter Raleigh discovered Roanoke Island off the coast of what is now North Carolina. Raleigh named this land Virginia, and although a colony was established there the following year, the island was deserted in 1590 when a relief mission arrived—the colonists were never found. In 1606, James I granted charters to two companies, one of which was based in London, and the other in Plymouth, and both made attempts to colonize the mainland of North America. The first permanent settlement, Jamestown, was founded by the London Company on the James River in Virginia in 1607.

Captain John Smith and Jamestown

Initially, Jamestown and its settlers struggled to survive. Leadership was lacking, many of the colonists refused to work and were instead obsessed with searching for gold, several succumbed to disease and famine, and raids by the indigenous people claimed further lives. However, in 1608, Captain John Smith became president of the Jamestown council, and improved relations with the local Powhatan people, who began to provide the settlers with supplies of corn—Smith had in fact been captured by them the previous year and was spared from execution by the intervention of the chief's daughter, Pocahontas. Smith also enforced a stricter work regime, increased supplies and ultimately ensured Jamestown's survival. In 1609, however, the London Company, now renamed the Virginia Company, assumed responsibility for the colony. It replaced Smith and his council with a governor and government of its own, and Smith went back to England. During the

next ten years or so over 8,000 new settlers were to arrive at the colony, but despite attempted reforms, land provision and the wide-scale production of tobacco for export to England, Jamestown continued to be beset with problems. Attacks by the local tribes were renewed and disease and famine persisted for several years. Smith returned to explore the New World in 1614, sailing north of Virginia between Penobscot Bay and Cape Cod, a region he named New England.

The Arrival of the Pilgrim Fathers

The Protestant Reformation in England, which followed the accession to the throne of Elizabeth I in 1558, produced numerous dissenters, amongst them a group of Puritans who by 1606 had formed a separatist church. Faced with religious oppression, members of this group began to emigrate to Holland in 1607 and 1608, settling for ten years at Leyden. However, these immigrants found life in Holland difficult. Stricken by poverty, fearing the influence of the Dutch on their English ways and religious practices, and with the renewed prospect of war between the Netherlands and Spain, they began to look toward the New World for a potential refuge. In 1617, arrangements were made with the Virginia Company to organize passage, first back to England and then across the Atlantic. However, it was not until 1620 that thirty-five Pilgrims, along

Further Settlement

Shortly after the founding of the Plymouth colony, several settlements began to develop in New England; firstly at Naumkaeg in around 1626, which would later become Salem, followed in 1630 with the founding of Boston by the Massachusetts Bay Company. This had been organized the previous year by a group of Puritans wishing to escape the continued religious upheaval in England, and was granted a royal charter for trade and settlement, the king apparently unaware of their religious views. Before leaving England, company members signed an agreement which also provided them with the authority to govern the colony, effectively creating a Puritan theocracy in Massachusetts. Between 1630 and 1642, in what has come to be known as the "Great Migration," over 20,000 immigrants arrived in New England. They largely prospered, establishing several villages around Massachusetts Bay, and dividing land allotted by the company quite evenly, although village leaders, usually well-educated or skilled heads of families, tended to receive slightly more land, which they passed on to their children.

However, as successive generations divided family land, the towns became overcrowded and others felt that they held

with around seventy others, referred to as "Strangers," set sail in the *Mayflower* for America. Although supposedly bound for Virginia, the *Mayflower* instead reached Cape Cod in New England, resulting in conflict between the Pilgrims and the Strangers.

In an attempt to avoid mutiny, and out of a necessity to establish and ensure the rights of all concerned, the Mayflower Compact was drawn up, and in December the *Mayflower* landed in Plymouth, where a settlement was immediately founded. Although exhaustion, disease, and the harsh winter claimed the lives of around half the Plymouth colonists, the rest were saved by the friendly local people, who taught them to hunt, trap, and raise crops. The following fall the colonists gave thanks for their first successful harvest, a celebration which later developed into Thanksgiving.

little sway in government affairs. Families increasingly spread out to found new communities in western Massachusetts, Maine, and New Hampshire, often engendering conflicts as town councils were reluctant to lose their tax contribution. Although most of the New England settlers regarded themselves as Puritans, there were also religious conflicts, and with increased immigration came increasing religious diversity, which in turn led to settlers breaking away to establish colonies such as those at Rhode Island and Connecticut.

In 1633, the first English Catholic immigrants founded Maryland in northern Virginia, but they welcomed Protestants and the settlers practised religious tolerance, even during the English Civil War of the 1640s, by which time the Catholic population in Maryland had become a minority. In 1664, England also claimed several territories from the Dutch, including Delaware, New Jersey, and New Amsterdam, which was renamed New York. By the early eighteenth century, the English had possession of most of the eastern coast of North America, as well as control of Hudson Bay and large claims in the Caribbean.

The Colonization of the Caribbean

The first European settlement in the Caribbean was begun inadvertently, when the Santa Maria was wrecked off the north coast of Hispaniola on Christopher Columbus's first voyage. However, the settlement did not survive its first year, and thoughts of establishing a trading post were quickly abandoned in the face of a lack of commodities. The first proper colony was established by the Spanish in eastern Hispaniola in 1502, with the founding by around 2,500 colonists of Santo Domingo, from where the Spanish quickly moved out throughout the Caribbean, settling Jamaica in 1509 and Trinidad the following year. After the conquest of Mexico and the discovery of gold there, interest in working gold on the islands

decreased, compounded by the problem of dwindling native populations. However, due to the labor shortage this produced, the first African slaves were brought to the Caribbean around this time.

By the early 1600s, as other Europeans were beginning to establish themselves in the Americas, they also looked at the Caribbean, and in 1621 the Dutch began to move against Spanish territories, to be joined by the English settling in St. Croix in 1625. Barbados was settled by the English that same year, and in 1628 they took possession of Nevis, followed by Antigua and Montserrat in 1632. A colony was also planted on St. Lucia in 1638, but by 1642 it had been destroyed by the native Caribs.

The French, meanwhile, successfully colonized Martinique and Guadeloupe, later expanding their possessions to St Bartholomé, St Martin, Grenada, St Lucia, and western Hispaniola. In 1655 England seized Jamaica from the Spanish. At that time it had a population of about 3,000 Spaniards and their slaves—the Indian population had been eradicated—and it rapidly became England's most important acquisition

Below: Harvard University in the town of Cambridge, established by Puritan leaders of the Massachusetts Bay Colony.
Opposite: An illustration depicting the Native American Squanto from the Pawtuxet tribe who served as guide and interpreter for the pilgrim colonists at Plymouth Colony and Massasoit. He died after contracting smallpox while guiding William Bradford's expedition around Cape Cod, Massachusetts.

British North America

New York

UNITED STATES

Viceroyalty of New Spain

claimed by
Britain,
Spain
and
Russia

**Government of
New California**

Louisiana

Arizpe

Durango

Monterrey

Florida

Havana

Valladolid

Mérida

Mexico

Santiago

Oaxaca

Chiapas

Santo
Domingo

León

Cartagena

Caracas

Cumaná

**Captaincy-General
of
Venezuela**

Bogotá

PACIFIC OCEAN

NORTH ATLANTIC OCEAN

Popayán

**Viceroyalty
of New
Granada**

Quito

Manaus

Guayaquil

Río Negro

Belém

**Rio Grande
do Norte**

São Luis

Fortaleza

Ceará

Natal

Grão-Pára

Olinda

Piauí

Recife

Trujillo

**Viceroyalty
of Peru**

Paraíba

Cuzco

Salvador

Mato Grosso

Bahia

Lima

Cuiabá

Arequipa

La Paz

**Minas
Gerais**

Espiritu Santo

Rio de Janeiro

Rio de Janeiro

São Paulo

Santos

Salta

Asunción

**Sao
Paulo**

Viceroyalty of Río de la Pla

Tucumán

**Intendency
of
Cordoba**

Santiago

Porto Alegre

Rio Grande do Sul

1777 ceded by Spain

Buenos
Aires

Montevideo

Concepción

**Intendency
of Buenos
Aires**

*SOUTH
ATLANTIC
OCEAN*

HISPANIC AMERICA, c. 1780

Spanish territory

Portuguese territory

British territory

French territory

Dutch territory

N

0   600 km

0   600 miles

in the region. Much like the early colonists of the North American mainland, the first British settlers in the Caribbean attempted to recreate a microcosm of European society, importing English law, political institutions, and the Church. Though these institutions were to endure, time and circumstance altered the social context, and a series of plantation societies developed, on which African slave labor was used to produce vast quantities of exports such as sugar and rum for the North American and European markets.

French and British Rivalry

During the seventeenth and eighteenth centuries, England and France were engaged in a worldwide struggle for dominance that resulted in a series of wars, both in Europe and throughout their colonies. As both nations extended their claims in North America, bitter rivalries developed that would ultimately end in conflict. Part of this growing hostility was based on territorial expansion, but initially much of it centered around the fur trade. The French had established trade with the Algonquian and with the Huron peoples in the early seventeenth century and had allied with them against the Iroquoian Confederacy, who were the main suppliers of furs to Dutch and English settlers. Encouraged by the English, the Iroquois made frequent raids to intercept furs bound for Montreal and Quebec, and almost completely wiped out the Hurons in 1649,

severely threatening the future of the French fur trade. The situation was made worse in 1670 by the establishment of the Hudson's Bay Company by the English, which took control of the entire drainage basin of the Hudson Bay. The French were thus caught between the Hudson's Bay Company and the English colonies to the south, whilst the English colonies along the Atlantic coast were contained by New France and Acadia in the north, and by French expansion along the Mississippi Valley. Conflict broke out from around 1686 when the French seized several of the Hudson's Bay Company's posts, and fighting continued until the signing of the Treaty of Utrecht in 1713.

There then followed a period of around thirty years of peace, during which time France strengthened its position, building forts in the Ohio Valley, and arranging new Native American alliances. However, when Anglo-French competition in the Ohio Valley sparked conflict in 1754, marking the beginning of the French and Indian War, the French and their allies were unable to hold up against an English colonial population of over a million, backed as they were by the expanding military and naval might of Britain. The war was effectively over by 1759 with the surrender of Quebec, and the result, assured by the 1763 Treaty of Paris, was that New France came under British control.

Africa and the Slave Trade

The extensive use of slavery was critical to colonial success, and the development and consequences of the trade in people continue to affect today's world.

Early African Civilizations

Africa has an ancient history of civilization. One of the oldest of these civilisations arose in Nubia, in modern-day Sudan. It grew up alongside Ancient Egypt and though the two cultures benefited from contact, in terms of both trade and the spread of ideas, their relationship was fraught with conflict. At one stage Egypt occupied Nubia—for 500 years, from approximately 2800 BC—and the Nubian Kush Empire occupied Egypt from 770 BC. The Kush Empire had united the disparate parts of Nubia some seventy or so years earlier and thrived until the fourth century AD. The coming of Christianity and the rise of the Ethiopian Axumite Kingdom forced it into decline.

In West Africa there was an equally strong tradition of great civilizations. In the fourth century the King of Ghana ruled over a complex society, with a road system and a code of law, that was supported by in excess of 200,000 soldiers. This was replaced by the Mali Empire from 1200 onward, and the city of Timbuktu became a center for trade and learning.

Further south, on the plateau of Zimbabwe, a powerful culture developed, drawing its wealth from trading with the coastal states of East Africa. Its capital, Great Zimbabwe, where construction began about 1250, was a substantial city. The buildings included a massive stone enclosure containing a conical tower, and the city may have had as many as 18,000 inhabitants.

The Beginnings of the Slave Trade

There had long been trade between Mediterranean Africa and Europe. The Ancient Greeks had begun to establish a relationship with some African cultures, and the Romans had strong links with the continent, particularly with the Egyptians. However, by the fifteenth century European knowledge of Africa had become a mixture of the remnants of classical learning, contemporary myths and stories, and what could be gleaned from a scattering of biblical references.

Gradually, European expeditions were mounted and in 1482 the Portuguese established a trading port at Elmina on the coast of modern Ghana. Vasco da Gama sailed around the continent in 1497 and from

Above: A group of Abyssinian slaves in iron collars and chains.
Opposite: An illustration dating from circa 1835 showing slaves aboard a slave ship being shackled before being put in the hold.

this time on the Europeans became increasingly involved in Africa, exporting raw materials for building as well as gold and ivory.

However, by far the most lucrative trade was in slaves. "Factories" were set up along the west coast, from Senegal to Angola; even at this early stage, the exceptional brutality of the trade was much in evidence, as was the involvement of other Africans. European involvement was new, but slaves had long been traded within Africa—between East African rulers, for example, and between them and their Arab neighbors. The Portuguese in their turn came to rely on local rulers, who would gather up captives and trade them with the Europeans. Initially African slaves were put to work on the colonized islands off the coast of the continent; some were used in Europe. The very first shipment to the Americas, which became the focus of the slave trade, left Lisbon in 1518.

The Development of Slavery

In the middle of the sixteenth century there was a major change, as slaves began to be shipped across the Atlantic in considerable numbers to the islands of the Caribbean, to Brazil and the mainland of North America. The slave trade grew massively from this point, and the consequences of this—in political, economic and demographic terms—continue to affect the world today.

For their traders, slaves were a commodity like any other and their journey across the Atlantic was called the "middle passage". They were the central component of what became known as the "triangular trade" – trade goods were shipped to Africa and exchanged for slaves, who were then shipped on to the Americas, and exports from there were returned to Europe. For some traders, carrying slaves was simply a way of filling their empty holds between Europe and the Americas, and making money while doing so. Commercially, the trade became very significant; huge profits could sometimes be made. This, together with the fact that slaves were seen as cargo and not as human beings, encouraged appalling conditions, especially during transport. The disgusting state of many slaving ships led to the spread of disease and a mortality rate of 10 percent was the norm; on many voyages this was much greater. In addition, were a slaver to get into any serious difficulty, the "cargo" would be dumped overboard.

The value of the slave trade led to diplomatic disputes, occasional outbreaks of war, and a struggle for supremacy as various nations sought to control it. The prosperity of many colonies, and even their continued existence, rested upon a supply of slave labor. Between 1518 and 1650 the Spanish and Portuguese colonies imported about half a million slaves, and the trade

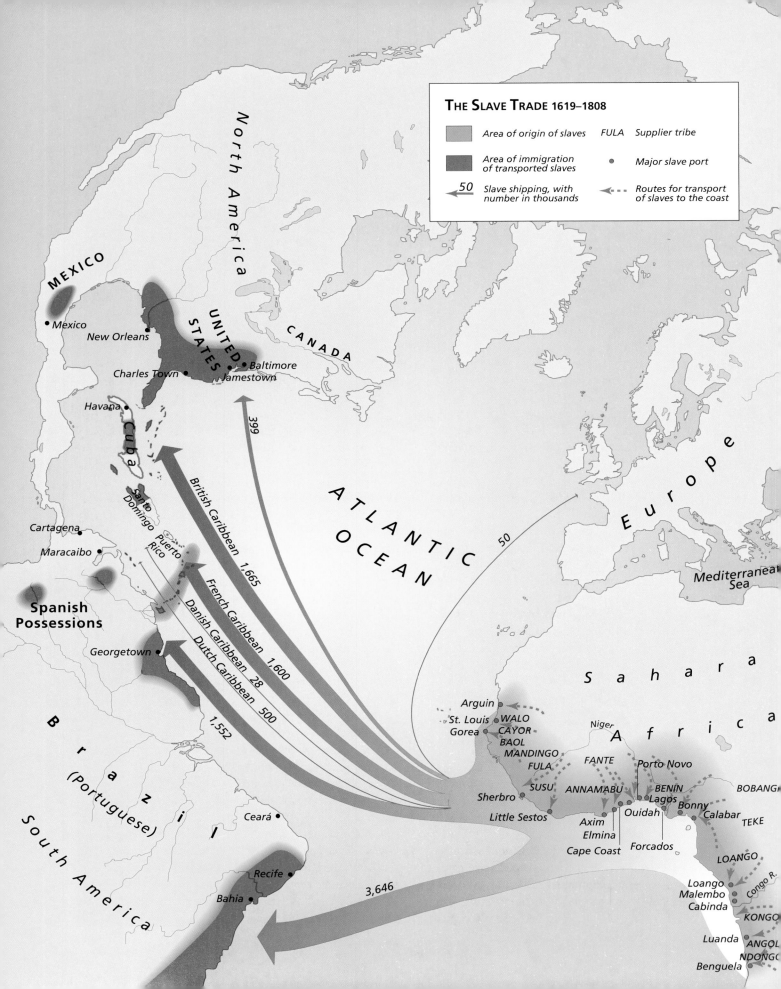

THE SLAVE TRADE 1619–1808

Area of origin of slaves

Area of immigration of transported slaves

FULA   Supplier tribe

Major slave port

Slave shipping, with number in thousands

Routes for transport of slaves to the coast

North America

MEXICO

Mexico

New Orleans

Charles Town

Baltimore

Jamestown

UNITED STATES

CANADA

Havana

Cuba

Santo Domingo

Puerto Rico

Cartagena

Maracaibo

Spanish Possessions

Georgetown

B r a z i l (Portuguese)

South America

Ceará

Recife

Bahia

ATLANTIC OCEAN

Europe

Mediterranean Sea

S a h a r a

A f r i c a

Niger

Arguin

St. Louis

Gorea

WALO

CAYOR

BAOL

MANDINGO

FULA

SUSU

Sherbro

Little Sestos

Axim

Elmina

Cape Coast

FANTE

ANNAMABU

Ouidah

Forcados

Porto Novo

BENIN

Lagos

Bonny

Calabar

BOBANG

TEKE

LOANGO

Loango

Malembo

Cabinda

Congo R.

KONGO

Luanda

ANGOL

NDONGO

Benguela

399

British Caribbean 1,665

French Caribbean 1,600

Danish Caribbean 28

Dutch Caribbean 500

1,552

50

3,646

mushroomed wildly after 1650. They often used their slaves on sugar plantations, though Spanish slaves were also to be found in Mexican silver mines; most, however, worked in Colombia, Venezuela, and Cuba, and these places became critical to the Spanish economy. The Portuguese expanded their plantations in Brazil and imported many more slaves from 1700, in order to fully exploit the silver mines of Minas Gerais. Dutch, British, and French slaves worked in their Caribbean and Guyanese colonies and also on the North American mainland, where smaller numbers of people were often employed, for instance on tobacco plantations in Virginia and Maryland.

Slaves were a resource, and it was important not just that they worked, but that they had children – to provide the next generation of slaves. However, fertility was low; they were frequently overworked, underfed and abused, and also succumbed to a range of "new" diseases. Mortality was high, and any expansion consequently demanded the import of fresh slaves from Africa. The number of people traded is often debated, but it is thought that in the eighteenth century alone, more than six million were shipped to the Americas from Africa. Only a few areas, like Virginia and Maryland, experienced a natural increase in the slave population. Here the environment was better: tropical diseases did not take their toll and overall conditions were slightly better than on the plantations further south. But the fact remains that, wherever they were, slaves had the legal status of property and were traded and guarded as such.

There was some resistance from the slaves in the colonies. Slave revolts increased in the late eighteenth and early nineteenth centuries, but none succeeded except that which arose in 1791 under Toussaint L'Ouverture in the French colony of St Domingue. This became the independent state of Haiti in 1804.

Abolition

There had always been voices of dissent in Europe, people who protested against the trade in human beings, but the movement against slavery didn't really gather momentum until the 1770s. The seeds of abolitionism in Britain were sown when Granville Sharpe successfully petitioned the Lord Chief Justice to grant freedom to James Somerset, an escaped slave from America who had been recaptured in Britain. Although this was successful, little changed as a direct result, and in the 1780s a group of evangelical Christians began

to campaign for the complete abolition of slavery. This campaign grew and a nationwide abolitionist movement set about collecting evidence, generating publicity, and lobbying Parliament. William Wilberforce was a leading and vocal member who campaigned tirelessly, raised awareness and influenced public opinion. In addition, in the face of the Industrial Revolution's ideals of free trade and the French Revolution's ideals of human equality, slavery began to seem much more of a barbaric anachronism.

In 1807 the British Parliament declared that it was illegal to buy, sell, and transport slaves; in 1834 it was declared illegal to own them. That year all children under six in the West Indies were declared free and the slaves there were transferred to six-year, unpaid apprenticeships. These apprenticeships were just as exploitative as slavery itself, if less permanent, and were outlawed in their turn in 1838. British abolitionists had begun to campaign for an end to slavery in America. Here the abolitionist cause had been growing, especially in the North, developing into a fierce and effective anti-slavery movement. Escaped or freed slaves like Frederick Douglass lectured widely, and many writers supported abolition; Harriet Beecher Stowe's *Uncle Tom's Cabin* was particularly influential. The end of slavery in America finally came about in 1865, with the close of the American Civil War.

In the end the abolition of slavery was brought about by a combination of factors, partly by abolitionist campaigns, partly by economic decline, and partly by political events. However, traditional slavery in Africa continued in many places until the late nineteenth century and was only outlawed in Nigeria in 1936. There are still some remote places on the continent where it continues, and abolitionists continue to campaign.

Consequences

In Africa one of the most serious results of the slave trade was depopulation: in the Niger basin, for example, entire communities were devastated by slaving raids which brought famine and disease in their wake.

Ultimately, perhaps, the most damaging legacy of the slave trade was that it encouraged violence as the norm and created a climate in which white people were somehow thought to be superior to black people. The pernicious influence of this continues to this day.

The Expansion of Russia 1547-1796

The reigns of Tsars Ivan the Terrible, Peter the Great and Catherine the Great were marked by territorial expansion and modernization, but also by repression and savagery.

Ivan the Terrible

Ivan IV, the grandson of Ivan the Great, inherited the throne of Russia at just three years old. He actually came to power thirteen years later in 1547, and the early years of his reign brought peace, stability and prosperity. However, Ivan's rule gradually became less humane. He was responsible for the laws that kept the peasants tied to the land, creating a class of serfs. He also formed the first security force, the oprichniks, a private army which Ivan could use against the Russian nobility, the boyars.

In 1558, Ivan embarked upon a costly and futile war against Livonia which eventually included Poland, Lithuania, and Sweden. The war lasted for twenty-two years and resulted in no territorial gains whatsoever.

Below: A portrait of Ivan the Terrible.
Opposite: The Catherine Palace is situated some fifteen miles outside St Petersburg. It was originally commissioned by Peter the Great and named in honor of his wife, the empress Catherine I.

During this period, his wife Anastasia died and Ivan believed, possibly correctly, that she had been murdered by the boyars. He gradually became more paranoid and less stable, and his oprichniks found themselves given greater powers, which they were quick to abuse. Ivan began a reign of terror in which thousands of Russians found themselves either banished to distant and remote corners of his Empire or brutally put to death. His religious fanaticism encouraged him to devise means of execution based on biblical descriptions of hell and he was even responsible for the death of his eldest son. Remorse led to him being re-christened as a monk, and on his death he was buried in his monk's habit. Russia's wealth was soon depleted and by his death in 1584 the country was almost in ruins.

However, Ivan was not only renowned for his appalling crimes. He did succeed in adding to the territorial gains of Russia with the annexation of Kazan and Astrakhan—the latter giving him control of the entire course of the River Volga—and much of Siberia. Ivan was also the first ruler of Russia to take the title "Tsar," which is a translation of the Latin word, Caesar.

Russian Society

Several factors shaped Russia's identity between the period 1547 to 1680, but the legacy left by the departed Mongol overlords was crucial. The Mongols had brought with them their distinctly eastern way of life which would leave a mark on Russian culture. With the rise of Muscovy and the beginning of a Russian empire, territories in the east which were previously Mongol were quickly won and the empire spread to a huge size.

However, Russia was surrounded on all borders by hostile nations: to the west, Sweden, Finland, Poland, and the Holy Roman Empire; to the south the Ottomans and in the east the Chinese. This added a distinctly isolationist element to Russian culture. As the rest of Europe was experiencing enlightenment and reformation, isolated Russia was left behind. Following the loss of Constantinople, it saw itself as the last bastion of Orthodox Christianity and as a result became ruthlessly intolerant of other religions, in particular Islam and Judaism. Russian society was itself deeply divided, with a feudal system that encouraged great wealth for the ruling princes and boyars and extreme poverty for its peasants. Russian peasants found themselves tied to the land, becoming serfs, essentially slaves who could be bought or sold along with the land on which they worked.

Peter the Great

Peter came to the Russian throne following the death of his oldest brother Feodor in 1682. He initially shared the throne with another half-brother, Ivan, who was mentally disabled, and since Peter was only ten years old at his accession, Russia was effectively run by his half-sister, Sophia. The young Peter was uninterested in governing, instead pursuing his hobbies of seamanship and shipbuilding, which took him to Europe to study western methods. His interests in military tactics enabled him to overthrow his sister in 1689, and when his brother Ivan died in 1696 Peter became sole ruler.

Peter I is perhaps best known as the tsar who westernized Russia. He built up Russia's first navy and was able to take the port of Azov from the Ottomans. In his war against the Ottomans Peter looked to western Europe for allies, and he traveled to Brandenburg, Holland, the Holy Roman Empire, and England. Although he failed to gain support, he did learn much from his tour and on his return built up a western-style army. He also established an education system for all males, funded an Academy of Sciences and changed the calendar from the Russian system to the Julian calendar. He even insisted that courtly dress codes followed European styles rather than Russian tradition.

Peter's reign may have been one of incredible expansion and progression, but he was not a humane ruler. He levied high taxes in order to finance his military expeditions which fell on everyone except the nobility and the Church. Peter taxed essential items such as salt and alcohol—and even beards. At his most ruthless he was responsible for the mass torture and deaths of those rebellious nobles who had sought to return his sister to the throne in 1698; Peter himself acted as one of the executioners and had the bodies hung from the walls of the Kremlin. In 1718 he had his son and heir, Alexei, tortured and executed for disagreeing with his policies. In 1721, Peter gave himself the title Emperor instead of Tsar and on his death, in 1725, left Russia as a leading European state rather than the backward nation he had inherited.

Peter's Territorial Gains

In line with his cultural aims for Russia, Peter's focus for expansion was aimed at the country's western borders. In particular, he intended to take territory bordering the Baltic Sea to give Russia unopposed access to western Europe. In 1700 he began the Great Northern War against Sweden, which at the time controlled Ingria, Estonia, and Livonia and dominated the Baltic. Although the first major battle ended in defeat for the Russian forces, Peter learned from their errors and set about building a superior fleet with which to combat the Swedes. By 1703, he had taken Ingria and set about building his new capital, St Petersburg, on the shores of the Baltic. Six years later, the Russians achieved a resounding victory over the Swedes at Poltava, which effectively reduced Swedish control of the Baltic and increased that of the Russians. By the time peace was agreed in 1721, Peter had gained vast areas of land around the southern and eastern shores of the Baltic and had also taken lands to the south including Lithuania and the Ukraine.

St Petersburg

During the course of the Great Northern War, Peter needed a fortress to defend the newly conquered lands on the Baltic, and in 1703 he built the Peter and Paul Fortress. A small town grew up around it, and by 1712 it was large enough for Peter to declare it the new capital, St Petersburg. Although much of the accommodation was made of wooden houses, Peter forced his nobles to move from the luxury of Moscow to his new city. Despite being built upon wet, swampy

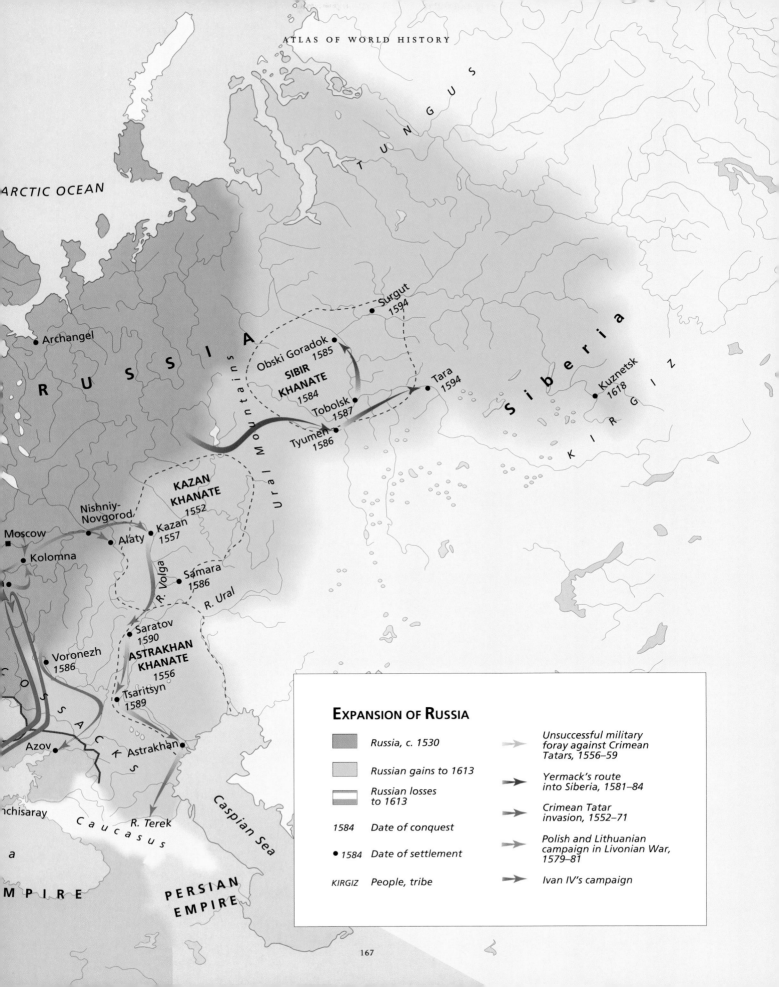

ARCTIC OCEAN

Archangel

R U S S I A

T U N G U S

Surgut
1594

Obski Goradok 1585

SIBIR
KHANATE
1584

Tobolsk
1587

Tara
1594

Siberia

Kuznetsk
1618

K I R G I Z

Tyumen
1586

Ural Mountains

KAZAN
KHANATE
1552

Nishniy-
Novgorod

Kazan
1557

Moscow

Alaty

Kolomna

Samara
1586

R. Volga

R. Ural

Saratov
1590

ASTRAKHAN
KHANATE
1556

Voronezh
1586

C O S S A C K S

Tsaritsyn
1589

Azov

Astrakhan

Caspian Sea

a

hisaray

Caucasus

R. Terek

PERSIAN
EMPIRE

MPIRE

EXPANSION OF RUSSIA

Russia, c. 1530

Russian gains to 1613

Russian losses
to 1613

1584   Date of conquest

● 1584   Date of settlement

KIRGIZ   People, tribe

Unsuccessful military
foray against Crimean
Tatars, 1556–59

Yermack's route
into Siberia, 1581–84

Crimean Tatar
invasion, 1552–71

Polish and Lithuanian
campaign in Livonian War,
1579–81

Ivan IV's campaign

Above: Catherine the Great was an enthusiastic patron of the arts. She built the Hermitage Museum and commissioned buildings all over Russia as well as founding academies and libraries.
Opposite: Russian officials cutting off boyars' beards and sleeves under the new reign of Peter the Great.

construction of any stone buildings beyond the city, and all stone masons were required to work in the capital. In 1714, Peter had a summer palace built and later on he commissioned the building of the Winter Palace further along the River Neva. Because of its strategic position as a port, much of the city was taken up with buildings devoted to shipbuilding and the navy, the center of which was the huge Admiralty complex. By 1725, the year of Peter's death, the city saw 90 percent of Russia's trade pass through it. After Peter's death, building in the city continued, and a number of baroque palaces and churches were erected.

Catherine the Great

The next great period of Russian expansion took place under the empress Catherine II, known as Catherine the Great. Catherine was actually a German princess who had been married to the Russian heir, later Peter III. She was not interested in her weak and ineffectual husband, instead taking a series of lovers at court, many of whom exercised political influence. Six months after becoming tsar, the unpopular Peter was deposed and later murdered by a faction led by Catherine's lover at the time, Grigori Orlov. Catherine became the Empress of Russia in June, 1762 and her reign lasted for thirty-four years.

land, St Petersburg quickly grew; Peter had a system of canals built which drained the water from the land and which earned the city the title of the "Venice of the North."

He also drafted in large numbers of peasants to work on the grand building projects which had been designed by teams of European architects and engineers. In order to ensure that work on St Petersburg was completed quickly, Peter prohibited the

She instituted a number of reforms in Russian society that favored the nobles, giving them back the hereditary rights they had lost under Peter the Great and granting them land and serfs. She also attempted to bring about some reforms in agriculture, establishing a free economy and encouraging foreign investment in underdeveloped areas. However, little changed for the majority of the Russian people and her rule was marred by a number of revolts and rebellions. Like her

predecessor, Peter the Great, Catherine was keen to westernize Russia and most of her territorial expansions were either westward or southward. In 1768 she embarked upon the first of several wars with the Ottoman Empire when a troop of Cossacks entered Ottoman territory and slaughtered the inhabitants of Balta. War followed and Catherine eventually won the former Ottoman state of Crimea on the Black Sea. The Russians now had access to a number of vital ports in the south, which strengthened them further. Her westward expansion involved the commonwealth of Poland and Lithuania, which had been weakened by a series of wars against the Russians, Swedes, and Prussians during the seventeenth century. The decline of the Polish Government enabled the Russians to take control and in 1764 Catherine was able to place another of her lovers on the Polish throne. The partitions of Poland, which took place in the second half of the eighteenth century, resulted in the division of Polish Lithuanian territory between Russia, Prussia, and Austria, with Russia gaining the largest part. Not only did Catherine seek to make territorial gains, she also attempted to inject some of the elements of the European Enlightenment into Russian culture, and became a great patron of the arts. Catherine died in 1796 and was succeeded by her son Paul I.

The Cossacks

The steppes of South Russia and the Ukraine were inhabited by a number of independent communities of warrior peasants called Cossacks. Their existence on the borders between the weaker Muscovy and the Ottoman Empire had served to protect the Russians from Turkish aggression, although this was not something the Cossacks had necessarily hoped to achieve. They were aggressive and regularly attacked neighboring lands, not only those belonging to the Turks and the Tatars, but also Russian and Polish–Lithuanian territories. Cossack warmongering increased tensions between the eastern Europeans, Russians, and the Ottomans in the fifteenth and sixteenth century and although nobody admitted to responsibility for any Cossack attacks, they were in fact often employed as mercenaries by both the Russians and the Poles. The Cossacks provided military expertise in exchange for autonomy, and gradually became servants of the Russian Empire which granted them the freedom they prized. In 1670 a band of Don River Cossacks revolted against the harsh laws in place against the Russian peasants. Although the Cossacks were eventually defeated, the support they had from the peasants was an example of the relationship the Cossacks had with Russia's working poor. During Catherine the Great's reign, the Cossack uprising led by Emelyan Pugachev led to the death of almost 30,000 people and further demonstrated the power of peasant revolt.

The American Revolution

The American War of Independence, or the American Revolution, saw the creation of a powerful new nation, the United States of America.

The Beginnings of Colonial Unrest

Prior to the conclusion of the French and Indian War in 1763, colonial Americans had enjoyed at least a hundred years of "salutary neglect." Despite being subjects of the British Empire, and typically having crown-appointed governors, in practice the settlers in North America had long-established traditions of self-government. Additionally, many English laws and regulations which would have otherwise hampered prosperity in the colonies were not strongly enforced. After 1763, however, with an expanded territory to manage and a huge budget deficit, Britain sought to gain greater control of the colonies, seeing them as a potential source of revenue with which to pay off its war debts. In 1763, Britain imposed a Proclamation Order, demarking the westward extent of its territory and forbidding settlement beyond the Appalachians. Although this line proved impossible to police effectively, the move antagonized many settlers who had expected that victory in the French and Indian War would have assured the opening up of the west.

Over the next ten years or so, this initial affront was to be followed by the introduction of a series of measures that would foster a growing resentment toward Britain, such as the tighter regulation of existing trade laws and taxation, and the introduction of several new duties.

The Revenue and Stamp Acts

The first revision of taxation was heralded by the 1764 Revenue Act, also known as the Sugar Act, which attempted to improve on the regulation of the Molasses Act of 1733 in order to compete with French traders and try to prevent smuggling. However, other goods covered by the legislation included coffee, some wines and printed textiles—and it also further regulated timber and iron exports, severely disrupting the colonial economy. The colonists objected strongly to the enforcement of these duties, particularly as they

Below: The "Boston Tea Party" took place on 16 December 1773.

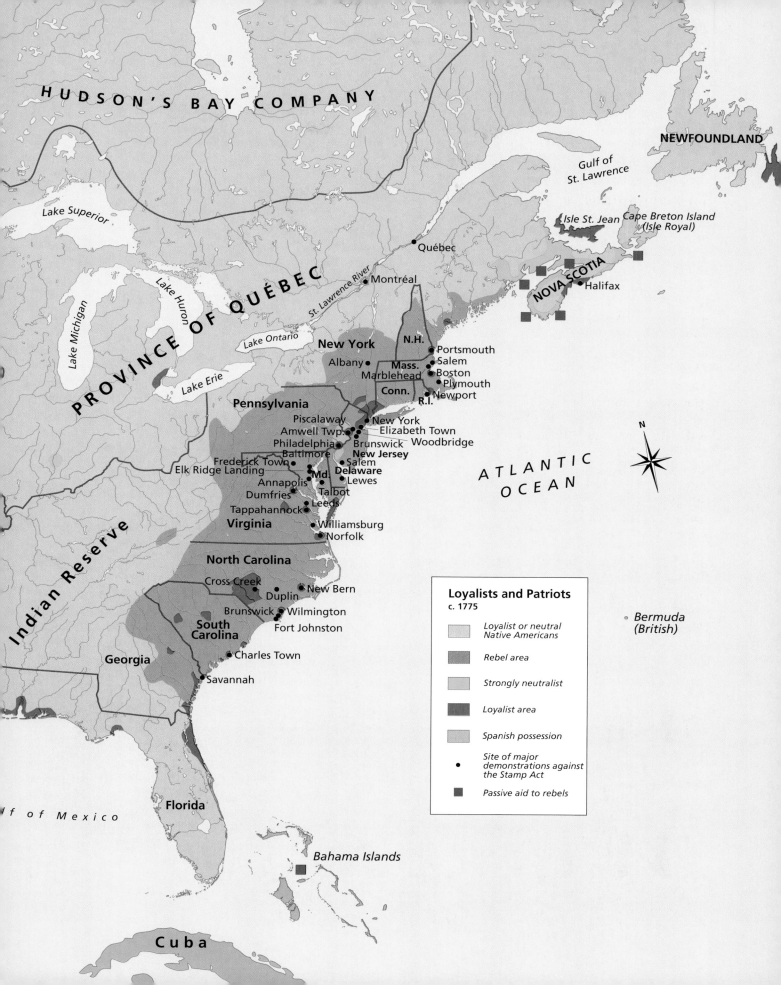

HUDSON'S BAY COMPANY

NEWFOUNDLAND

Lake Superior

Gulf of
St. Lawrence

Isle St. Jean   Cape Breton Island
                 (Isle Royal)

NOVA SCOTIA
• Halifax

Lake Huron

Lake Michigan

St. Lawrence River

• Québec

• Montréal

P R O V I N C E   O F   Q U É B E C

Lake Ontario

Lake Erie

N.H.

New York
Albany •

Portsmouth
Salem
Mass.
Boston
Marblehead Plymouth
Conn.   Newport
R.I.

Pennsylvania

Piscalaway
Amwell Twp.   New York
Philadelphia   Elizabeth Town
Baltimore Brunswick   Woodbridge
Frederick Town   **New Jersey**
Elk Ridge Landing Salem
        Md. **Delaware**
Annapolis   Lewes
Dumfries   Talbot
Tappahannock Leeds

Virginia   Williamsburg
               Norfolk

North Carolina

Cross Creek   New Bern
Duplin
Brunswick   Wilmington
South   Fort Johnston
Carolina

Georgia   Charles Town

              Savannah

Indian Reserve

**ATLANTIC
OCEAN**

N

• *Bermuda
(British)*

Florida

f of Mexico

Bahama Islands

C u b a

Loyalists and Patriots
c. 1775

- *Loyalist or neutral
  Native Americans*
- *Rebel area*
- *Strongly neutralist*
- *Loyalist area*
- *Spanish possession*
- • *Site of major
  demonstrations against
  the Stamp Act*
- ■ *Passive aid to rebels*

were not represented at all in the British Parliament, and there were also concerns that the British government would attempt to extend their powers of taxation.

This they promptly did the following year with the introduction of the Stamp Act, under the terms of which almost any formally written or printed material, including legal documents, advertisements, newspapers, pamphlets, and even playing cards, had to be produced on stamped paper upon which a tax was levied. In an attempt to avoid colonial dissent, the revenue generated was to be allocated to defense in the colonies. Further to this, the Quartering Act, which was passed just days later, required colonists to provide British troops with barracks and supplies. However, the Americans attested that they had committed money, manpower, and supplies toward their own defense during the French and Indian War, and were no longer at great risk from attack. Thus the continued British military presence became increasingly unwelcome, and suspicion grew that the troops were being stationed in the colonies to enforce the Stamp Act, and to suppress the rights and freedoms of colonists rather than to defend them.

Opposition

Almost immediately, the constitutional assemblies condemned the Stamp Act, declaring that there should be "no taxation without representation," but the British government was unmoved by such arguments, and refused to capitulate to their demands. However, the situation became more problematic on the streets of New York and Boston when the people began to make their protests felt with acts of violent disorder. The circumstances in Boston, which was gripped by post-war recession, and where people had historically defended local interests by means of demonstrations (which had more than once erupted into rioting), were particularly volatile; confronted by this unprecedented tax, it was not long before anger spilled over into acts of aggression. During the summer, angry mobs destroyed the homes of tax collectors and senior colonial officials, including that of the lieutenant governor, and demonstrations, violence, and intimidation rapidly spread throughout the colonies, ensuring that even before the law came into effect in November, there would be no one willing to collect the tax. In October, nine of the thirteen colonies were represented at a Stamp Act Congress in New York, where resolutions condemning the act were passed and

proposals made to pressure the British Parliament by means of a commercial boycott. Opponents of the Stamp Act refused to import British goods, ultimately prompting British merchants to petition for its repeal. This proved successful, and the Stamp Act was repealed in March 1766.

However, Britain simultaneously introduced the Declaratory Act, which confirmed its right of governance over America, and there still remained the problem of attempting to raise revenue. A solution was attempted in 1767, with the introduction of the Townshend Acts, which included new duties on everyday commodities such as paper, paint, glass, and, tea, saw the direct payment of colonial governors by the crown, and extended the scope of the Quartering Act, all of which prompted renewed calls for boycotts of British imports. Unsurprisingly, much of this dissent emanated from Boston, where a patriotic group, the Sons of Liberty, which had been active in organizing protests against the Stamp Act, was threatening the authority of the governor. The following year, in response to pleas from its governor, Boston was occupied by British troops, and an uneasy standoff ensued. In March 1770, however, violence flared once more, when British soldiers fired upon an angry mob which had gathered outside the Custom House, killing five people; an event that quickly became known as the "Boston Massacre."

The Boston Tea Party and the Intolerable Acts

That same year, most of the duties imposed by the Townshend Acts were repealed, but the duty on tea remained in place, and in principle continued to be a source of consternation for colonists. In practice, the duty was almost entirely avoided as large quantities of tea continued to be smuggled into the colonies by Dutch merchants. Parliament responded in 1773 with the Tea Act, which provided the East India Company with a monopoly on the tea trade and forced down prices by permitting tea to be shipped directly to the colonies. Again, the colonists were moved to protest; dockworkers refused to unload tea, many governors feared possible uprisings, and as a result many of the East India Company's ships were turned back, or their cargoes left to rot on the docksides. In Boston however, the authorities were more insistent, demanding that tea be unloaded and taxes duly paid on it, leading to the act of sabotage that became known as the "Boston Tea Party." On December 16, 1773, a group of men disguised as Mohawk Indians boarded the *Eleanor*, the *Beaver* and the *Dartmouth* in Boston Harbor and dumped their cargoes of over forty tons of tea into the sea. The British reacted by increasing the number of troops in Boston and with further legislation in May and June of 1774, once more revising the Quartering Act, and introducing four new acts: the Boston Port Bill, which closed the port of Boston to all colonists until the damages from the Boston Tea Party were paid for; the Administration of Justice Act, which stated that British officials could not be tried for capital crimes in colonial courts, but would be extradited and tried in Britain; the Massachusetts Government Act, which effectively annulled self-rule in the colony; and the Quebec Act, which extended the borders of the British Canadian territory of Quebec south into the upper Ohio Valley, west of the Proclamation Line, but absorbing land that contained pioneer settlements.

These Acts were collectively and formally known as the Coercive Acts, but the colonists referred to them as the "Intolerable Acts," and were spurred to call an inter-colonial congress in order to discuss a unified response to British actions. In September 1774, the First Continental Congress was held in Philadelphia, and was attended by representatives from all of the colonies except Georgia. A declaration was drawn up that claimed that the Coercive or Intolerable Acts were unconstitutional, and that refused to recognize British authority in domestic matters. It was also agreed that the boycott of all British imports should be resumed; that if Massachusetts was attacked, the other colonies would unite to defend it, and that if reconciliation had not been achieved by May 1775, a Second Continental Congress would be held.

The Battle of Lexington and Concord

Just one month before the Congress was due to reconvene, however, the first shots of the American War of Independence were fired at Lexington, Massachusetts. The British general, Thomas Gage, had sent some 700 soldiers to seize and destroy guns and

Below: *A depiction of the burning of Charles Town which took place during the Battle of Bunker Hill in 1775.*

Above: George Washington became the first president of the United States in 1789.

Opposite: 4th July 1776: The signatures on the Declaration of Independence, the document in which the American colonists proclaimed their political separation from British rule.

the Minutemen were beginning to swell. Having found and destroyed a small part of the colonists' supplies, the soldiers headed back toward Boston, but as they returned, they were attacked by a militia of Minutemen, farmers, and townspeople. By the time the troops reached Boston, over seventy British solders had been killed, a further 174 wounded, and the British garrison rapidly found itself besieged.

Therefore, when the Second Continental Congress assembled in Philadelphia in June, it had to confront the fact that wide-scale conflict was a distinct possibility. There was also much discussion of compromise, but it was ultimately agreed that provision must be made for a military defense in the event of war. George Washington was appointed commander in chief of the Continental Army and made immediate plans to travel to Boston.

The Battle of Bunker Hill

Before Washington had the chance to leave Philadelphia, the British, planning to secure the high ground surrounding Boston, attempted to seize the Dorchester Heights and Charlestown peninsula. The Americans, however, heard of the British plan and decided to seize and fortify the Charlestown peninsula first, establishing defensive positions on Bunker's Hill although, for reasons that remain unclear, they instead fortified Breed's Hill nearby. The following morning, the somewhat shocked British set out to reclaim the peninsula. General Howe, commanding the main British assault force, led two frontal charges against the American position, which proved costly to his troops—and also ineffectual, failing to inflict significant casualties amongst the colonial militia. However, after obtaining reinforcements and a resupply of ammunition, Howe ordered a third charge with fixed bayonets, and the British overran the Americans, who were exhausted and themselves now low on ammunition, forcing them back toward the mainland. The British won the battle, but also sustained huge numbers of casualties in relation to the militia. This battle served to strengthen

ammunition that the colonists had collected in the town of Concord, outside Boston, and also planned to arrest important colonial leaders. However, word of British intentions had reached the colonists and as troops marched into Lexington, they were to find themselves confronted by a militia of around seventy-five "Minutemen," so called as they had to be ready to fight on a minute's notice. The British soldiers fired on them, inflicting at least eight fatalities, before continuing on their way to Concord. Meanwhile, the people of Concord were busy hiding their arms and ammunition in surrounding towns, and the ranks of the colonial alliance, and the number of casualties sustained by the British proved that the British Army was not completely invincible.

The Declaration of Independence

As conflict continued over the winter of 1775–76, any thoughts of a political negotiation faded, and in January 1776 an anonymous, anti-monarchist pamphlet entitled Common Sense was published by Thomas Paine, which sold in vast numbers. By June, a Virginian, Richard Henry Lee, put forward a resolution for independence from Britain, and Congress assembled a group of five men to draft a written declaration. They were John Adams, Benjamin Franklin, Thomas Jefferson, Robert Livingston, and Roger Sherman. All contributed to its contents, but the youngest member of the committee, Thomas Jefferson, was largely responsible for its final form. It set out to describe the position of the Continental Congress, which now acted as a provisional American government, rejecting the authority of an oppressive British parliament and monarchy, which did not have the support of the people it attempted to govern. Drawing on European political philosophies and Enlightenment thought, the Declaration of Independence attempted to gain foreign support and aid for the American cause. It marked the official separation of the thirteen independent—but united—colonies (now referred to as states) from Britain, formally established the revolutionary government and officially declared war against Britain.

The War of Independence

Following the battle for the Charlestown peninsula in 1775, the Americans continued to lay siege to Boston, preventing essential supplies from getting through to the British, and in April 1776 Howe and his troops evacuated the city, to regroup on Staten Island, New York, in June. From here they outmaneuvered George Washington's army to enter the city and force an American retreat across the River Delaware, following which Washington defeated a force of German mercenaries at Trenton in December, and British troops at Princetown in early January 1777. The British then mounted two offensives. Howe advanced on Philadelphia, defeating Washington's forces at Brandywine Creek and Germantown, but General Burgoyne's attempt to

isolate American troops in New England failed, and he sustained heavy losses in battles at Bennington, Bemis Heights, and Freeman's Farm, eventually surrendering at Saratoga on 17 October.

The French, now recognizing American Independence, and the possibility of American victory, decided to enter the war on the side of the Americans in 1778, and around 5,000 French soldiers joined forces with Washington's army as action shifted to the south. Spain and Holland followed suit, declaring war against Britain in 1779 and 1780 respectively. In spite of the disaster at Saratoga, Britain fought on, deciding to concentrate northern forces at New York in an attempt to hold the city, whilst General Cornwallis invaded the southern colonies. In 1780, Savannah and Charleston were captured and Cornwallis advanced into Virginia; however, short of supplies and confronted by large American forces, he was forced to retire to the port of Yorktown, where he hoped that the Royal Navy would arrive in support. Instead, a French fleet sailed

Fac similes of the Signatures to the Declaration of Independence July 4. 1776. from Binns' Celebrated Engraving.

Above: 1776: Benjamin Franklin (left), American politician, writer, and inventor, drafting the Declaration of Independence. The drafting committee included future presidents of the United States Thomas Jefferson, John Adams, Roger Sherman, and Robert R. Livingstone.

into Chesapeake Bay, effectively sealing Cornwallis's fate. He now came under attack from both land and sea, and with no immediate prospect of relief, was forced to surrender in October 1781.

The British had hoped that loyalists would join them in the towns and cities that they occupied, and although their presence sometimes subdued the colonists, little lasting support was gained in this way, with townspeople frequently employing guerrilla tactics and turning on the British as they moved between the different colonies. Finally convinced that the war was unwinnable, Parliament began negotiations for peace in 1782, which were formally concluded in September 1783, by the signing of the Treaty of Paris, which recognized the independence of the United States.

Birth of the United States

Following the events of the American Revolutionary War, during which the thirteen separate colonies had united on a temporary basis against the common threat of the British, a weak central government was formed. This was based on the Articles of Confederation that had been drawn up in 1777 to formally create the United States of America and deal with the immediate challenges presented by the war.

However, after the conflict had finally ended, it rapidly became clear that there was more to producing a strong nation than simply raising, funding, and directing an army. A government had to be able to raise adequate funds through taxation, act on behalf of trade and industry, bolster national pride, and foster a strong national identity which would be respected beyond its own borders. In short, it had to be protected from division within and depredation from without. Congress, however, had no authority over taxation, no means to enforce its own rulings, and no ability to increase its powers if necessary. Therefore, in 1787, the Constitutional Convention met in Philadelphia in order to revise the Articles of Confederation. Delegates agreed on the need for a stronger central government, but also knew that many people still feared such institutions, and so the task was to work out exactly what form a new government would take. In doing so, many divisions were highlighted, but out of these conflicts of ideas came compromises that ultimately improved the Constitution, imbuing the document with a degree of flexibility that would allow for continual debate, revision, and future compromise. The omission of a bill of rights, intended to guarantee individual freedoms in the face of the newly strengthened government, caused much debate and opposition to the Constitution during the period of its ratification, almost threatening to halt the process. However, a promise was made that the first amendments to the Constitution would create a formal Bill of Rights, following which the required nine of the thirteen states complied—and the US Constitution was officially adopted in 1789.

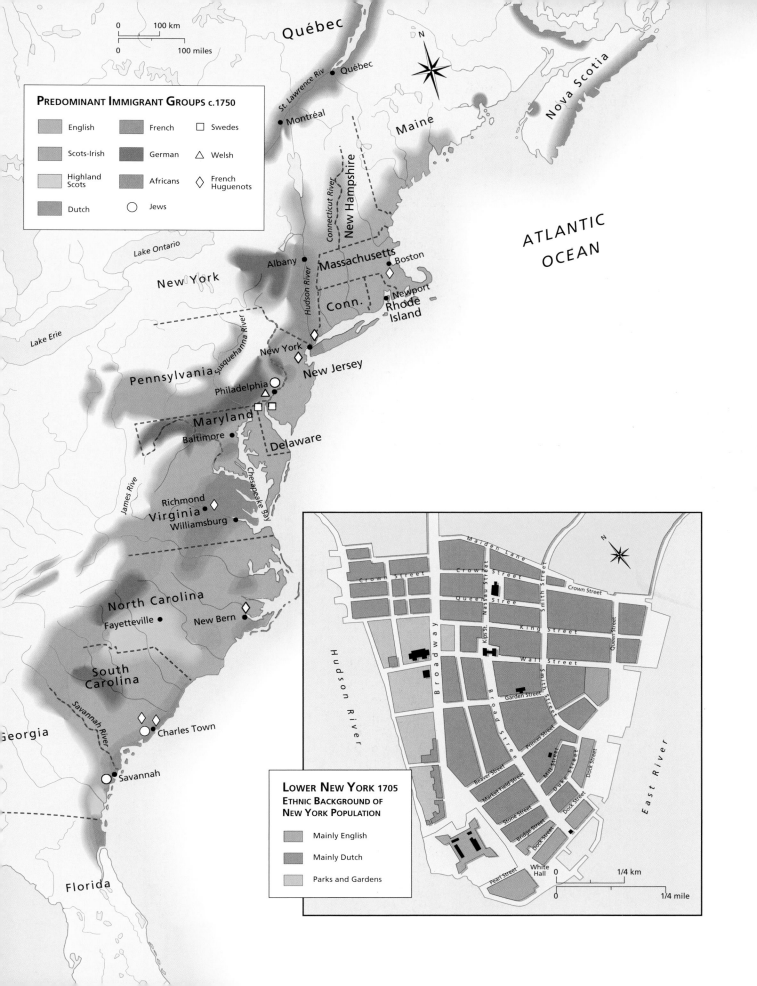

QUÉBEC

0   100 km
0   100 miles

N

PREDOMINANT IMMIGRANT GROUPS c.1750

English
Scots-Irish
Highland Scots
Dutch

French
German
Africans

Swedes
Welsh
French Huguenots

Jews

St. Lawrence Riv

Québec

Montréal

Maine

Nova Scotia

Lake Ontario

New York

Albany

Connecticut River

New Hampshire

Massachusetts

Boston

ATLANTIC OCEAN

Lake Erie

Pennsylvania

Susquehanna River

Hudson River

New York

Philadelphia

New Jersey

Conn.

Newport

Rhode Island

Maryland

Baltimore

Delaware

James Rive

Richmond

Williamsburg

Virginia

Chesapeake Bay

North Carolina

Fayetteville

New Bern

South Carolina

Savannah River

Charles Town

Georgia

Savannah

Florida

LOWER NEW YORK 1705
ETHNIC BACKGROUND OF NEW YORK POPULATION

Mainly English
Mainly Dutch
Parks and Gardens

N

Maiden Lane

Crown Street

Crown Street

Crown Street

Queen Street

Kips St.

Hudson Street

Smith Street

Queen Street

King Street

Broadway

Wall Street

Broad Street

Garden Street

Smith Street

Princes Street

Mill Street

Dirk Street

Dock Street

Beaver Street

Market Field Street

Stone Street

Bridge Street

Dock Street

Dock Street

Dock Street

Pearl Street

White Hall

Hudson River

East River

0   1/4 km
0   1/4 mile

The French Revolution

A time of extraordinary upheaval, the French Revolution marked the beginning of the end for absolute rule in Europe, and ushered in a more modern age.

Life in Eighteenth-century France

French society before 1789 was dominated by the absolute power of the monarch. Like most European nation states, there was a general belief in the concept of the divine right of kings—that justification to rule came from God, not from any democratic process or election. Countries were therefore subject to the changing attitudes and whims of their monarchs, many of whom were not well suited to running a country. In France there was also a history of tension between the ruling monarch and the nobles who surrounded the throne. The nobles were able to exert influence through the system of provincial "parlements" which acted as judicial and administrative centers throughout the country. Without the approval of these parlements a Royal decree could not become law.

In order to counter the power of the nobles, Louis XIV had built up a wealthy middle class known as the bourgeoisie, who had gradually become more ambitious. At the bottom of society was the peasant population, the majority of whom lived and worked on the land. French involvement in the American War of Independence provoked a financial crisis, and resulted in increased taxation. The burden of this taxation fell on the peasants. In addition, immediately before the Revolution poor harvests and food shortages had worsened their situation, increasing their resentment. The urban working class, the rural peasants, and the bourgeoisie all resented the privileges enjoyed by the nobility and the clergy, neither of whom felt the pressure of taxation nor the increasing food prices. Encouraged by the ideas of the Enlightenment and the American Revolution, there was a growing desire for change. Many soldiers in the French army had fought alongside the Americans in their revolution and they returned to encourage the spread of revolutionary ideas. Crop failures eventually led to high prices and a shortage of bread, which ultimately motivated the Paris mob into taking action.

Louis XVI and Marie Antoinette

When he ascended to the throne in 1774, Louis XVI was initially popular. In 1770, he had married the daughter of Francis I of Austria, Marie Antoinette, who at the time was aged only fifteen. Although affectionate, the King and

Queen did not produce a child for seven years, something which made Marie Antoinette unpopular. Adding to her unpopularity was her Austrian connection, her tendency to elevate favorites and her financial frivolity. The Queen openly enjoyed the privileges of her position and sought the company of unruly courtiers, and soon became the target of insulting pamphlets and court scandals. Her lack of understanding of the situation of those beyond the court made her seem even more irresponsible. Marie Antoinette is accused of responding to the news of the peasants' inability to afford bread with "let them eat cake;" however, this rumor was put about simply to undermine her reputation even further. Louis, meanwhile, appeared to be attempting to improve the dire financial system of France. Under the advice of his chief minister for finance, Robert Turgot, he initiated reforms which would have redirected taxation onto landowners. However, the parlements, run by the landowning nobility, rejected the decree and the reforms were never passed. Louis' reign was eventually beset by one financial crisis after another and he was increasingly seen as indecisive and weak and, like his wife, he became a target for criticism. Once the

revolution got underway, Louis' indecision and apathy led to a series of poor decisions. Although he had claimed to be supportive of the reforms demanded by the French people, the decision of the King and Queen to escape from Paris in 1791 to raise support was considered a treasonable action. It was this act, plus suggestions of Louis' attempted negotiations with foreign powers, that led to his imprisonment, and ultimately to his execution in January 1793. Marie Antoinette, who during the years of their virtual imprisonment had demonstrated a more decisive and headstrong character, was not executed until October of that year.

Establishment of the National Constituent Assembly

The French Revolution began on June 17, 1789 when the Third Estate, which consisted of representatives of the bourgeoisie and the common people, declared itself the National Assembly. The events leading up to

Opposite: Portrait of Marie Antoinette, wife of Louis XVI.
Below: The storming of the Bastille prison in Paris by a mob helped by royal troops.

this moment are complex. In short, representatives of the three main sections of society made up the First Estate (the clergy), the Second Estate (the nobility), and the Third Estate (everyone else). In May 1789, the King had reluctantly called together these Estates in order to try to solve the problem of France's crippled economy, but the Estates General failed to reach any satisfactory decisions.

The Third Estate's proclamation of a National Assembly was intended to be revolutionary; they claimed to be an assembly of the people, not of an "estate." However, the constitution drawn up in 1791 still limited the right to vote. The Assembly took control of the financial situation, declaring past forms of taxation illegal and attempting to deal with food shortages for the poor. Although they claimed they were working with the authority of the King, Louis was well aware that his position as the absolute ruler had been undermined. His actions in attempting to resist the National Assembly persuaded the people of Paris—referred to as the Paris mob—that Louis was about to stage a coup. They reacted by storming the Bastille prison. On August 4, the Assembly abolished the feudal rights of the nobility, a critical moment in the Revolution. Throughout France, nobles and clergy, towns and cities lost all privileges and all the Church-owned lands were nationalized.

Once the revolution had begun its course, the Assembly itself started to show signs of fracture. Different factions began to appear; some wanted to negotiate with the nobility, others wanted to establish a constitutional monarchy, some leaned toward the right, others to the left. Eventually, led by Honoré Mirabeau, the more middle-class faction to the center and left of the political spectrum held the majority. The National Assembly became the National Constituent Assembly and set about writing a constitution for France, beginning with the Declaration of the Rights of Man, a statement of principles modelled upon the American Declaration of Independence. The Ancien Regime was discarded in favor of "liberté, egalité, fraternité."

The Storming of the Bastille

The Bastille prison in Paris was first built as a royal chateau in 1370 and had been turned into a state prison by Louis XI. It became an unpopular symbol of the authority of the monarchy and as a result a target for the anger of the Paris mob. The people of Paris had been kept continually informed of the actions of the

N

0   60 km

0   60 miles

ATLANTIC OCEAN

REVOLUTION IN FRANCE, 1789–93

Area of 'Great Fear' agrarian revolt

Major town in which a revolutionary committee replaced the town council, 1789

Major town in which a revolutionary committee shared power with the town council, 1789

Center of counter revolution, 1792–93

Sustained Federalist resistance, 1793

Federalist and other civil unrest, 1793

Advance of French revolutionary armies

Advance of European anti-revolutionary armies

French victory   *European victory*

Naval blockade   *Occupied by France, 1792–93*

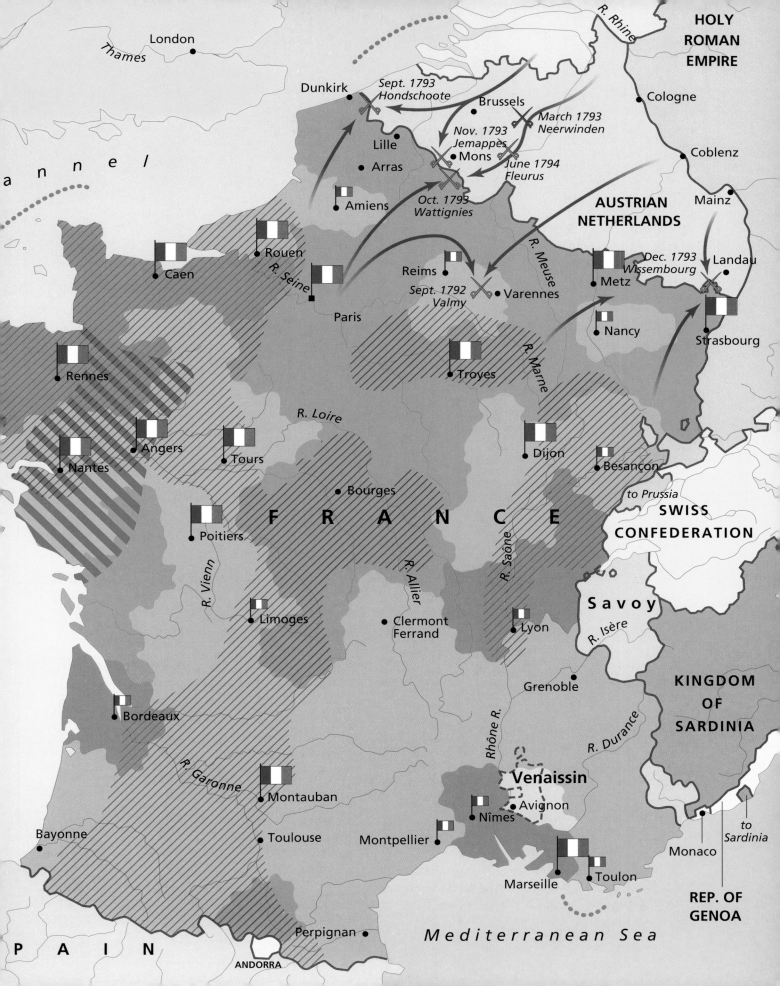

Above: A depiction of the execution of Louis XVI on January 21 1793. His queen, Marie Antoinette, shared his fate and was beheaded on October 16, 1793.

National Assembly through the distribution of pamphlets and the grounds of the Palais Royal had become a meeting place for large crowds of excited Parisians. When news of Louis' dismissal of his sympathetic finance minister Jacques Necker reached the people, they turned on the Bastille in their anger. The crowd marched through the city and although the Bastille held only seven prisoners at the time, headed for the prison which also housed a large quantity of armaments. The governor of the prison was murdered and his severed head paraded through the streets; several guards were also killed and all seven prisoners—four forgers, two lunatics and one sexual deviant—were released. The mob marched on to the Hotel de Ville, where they seized the mayor and assassinated him. Similar insurrections occurred across the country as peasants attacked chateaux and other symbols of oppression. France still celebrates July 14 as Bastille Day, similar to Independence Day in the US in its importance.

Robespierre

The King and Queen had been imprisoned following their thwarted attempt to flee Paris. In 1792 France was declared a Republic. The Paris crowds, becoming more violent, engaged in the September massacres in which thousands of people were killed. The King and Queen were executed in 1793. Following their execution, the Revolution entered a more dramatic phase known as the Reign of Terror. The leader of this "reign" was Maximillian Robespierre.

Robespierre was a lawyer who had been elected to the Estates General in 1789. His views were extreme and radical and he became known as the "Incorruptible." His gift for oratory and general rabble-rousing made him popular and with the death of Mirabeau in 1791 his position in the Constituent Assembly increased. Robespierre's extreme left-wing views were at odds with many on the Assembly and he found a position within a club called the Jacobins, which consisted of revolutionary-minded bourgeois gentlemen across France. Under the leadership of Robespierre, the club became associated with more extreme attitudes. Most infamously, Robespierre was instrumental in the ruthless rule of terror for which the French Revolution is so often remembered. He advocated the systematic execution of anyone who opposed the Jacobins and who appeared to support counter-revolution and almost 40,000 people were executed in Paris and the surrounding provinces. Robespierre himself became a victim of the guillotine in 1794. His own comrades, concerned by his dictatorial behaviour and the dramatic fall in his popularity, turned on him.

The Guillotine

The guillotine was the invention which enabled the Jacobins to successfully dispose of so many people in so short a time. In 1789, a member of the Constitutional Assembly, Joseph Guillotin, proposed that a more effective method of executing nobles be adopted. The Guillotine was intended to swiftly decapitate victims in a more efficient manner than a headsman or executioner. It was designed by a member of the French College of Surgeons, Dr Antoine Louis. Having been released by a spring, the single blade dropped down onto the victim's neck and could then be hoisted back up ready for the next subject. The guillotine was first used in April 1792, and both Louis XVI and his Queen were executed in this manner. The use of the guillotine provided a great spectacle for the Paris mob, who initially proved to be a willing audience, cheering on each fall of the blade. Popular legend has it that older women would sit watching the executions whilst knitting and that the sound of their needles would be the last thing the doomed would hear. As a method of execution, the guillotine remained legal in France until 1981.

From Terror to Dictatorship

With the death of Robespierre, the Jacobins lost their position in the Assembly, now called the National Convention. Instead, the more conservative members of the Convention, the middle-class doctors and lawyers who had initiated the revolution in 1789, were in the majority. The reign of terror came to an end as the people, sickened by the bloodshed, called for peace. With the government now back under the control of the middle classes, the poor and working class were again subject to high prices and in 1795 the common people of Paris attempted to revolt again. This time the troops supported the government and put the revolt down.

The new Convention set about establishing a democratic constitution known as the Directory. In this they elevated five members of the convention to become executive directors. The revolution had been deeply unpopular with other rulers in Europe and war with foreign troops had kept the French army occupied since 1792. In 1798, the commander of the Revolutionary armies in Italy and Egypt returned to France a hero, having won a series of battles. When members of the directory staged a *coup d'état*, they called in this military hero, Napoleon Bonaparte, to protect their new government. Napoleon went on to overthrow the Directory himself and established a military dictatorship that would last until 1815. The Revolution had ended.

Effects of the Revolution

Although the original revolutionary principle of "equality" appeared to have failed in 1799, and the emergence of a dictatorship undermined the principles of "liberty" and "fraternity," the revolution did change France. Feudalism was a thing of the past and the middle classes were the new dominant power. France itself was unified as a country and the previous era of kings, conflicting duchies and warring nobles—the Ancien Régime—would never return. The revolution also created a sense of democratic change, as the French had attempted to institute various means of electing their leaders. The French had shown the rest of Europe what the power of the people could do, particularly when their liberty was at stake. In this way, although the revolution itself appeared to have failed, it did succeed in ushering in a more modern age in France, and eventually in Europe.

Napoleonic Europe

A superb general, Napoleon pushed French control across most of Europe.
Opposition and resentment spread and united, however, and his empire was short-lived.

Napoleon Bonaparte

Born on the island of Corsica in 1769, Napoleon Bonaparte was the son of an Italian lawyer who served Louis XVI. As a young boy, he was sent to France for his education, later joining the prestigious École Militaire in Paris. In 1785, he earned his first military commission as a second lieutenant, aged only sixteen. When the French Revolution began in 1789 he returned to Corsica, but by 1793 he was clearly on the side of the republicans, changing his name from Napoleone Buonaparte to sound more French. Napoleon quickly rose through the ranks of the army, earning himself an impressive reputation and popularity.

In 1796 he took command of the demoralized troops on the Italian border and led them to a clear victory against the Austrians at Lodi, Napoleon's first victory over foreign troops. Despite his troops being poorly equipped, Napoleon's skilful use of tactics meant that his forces were able to repeatedly defeat the Austrians, eventually forcing them to sign a treaty. In 1798, Napoleon moved on to attack British-held Egypt. Although the occupation was eventually ended by Lord Nelson in the Battle of the Nile, Napoleon's time in Egypt did lead to the discovery of the Rosetta stone, the famous key to Ancient Egyptian hieroglyphs. His troops are also credited with having shot off the nose of the sphinx as target practice, although this may be a myth. In 1799, Napoleon left Egypt to return to Paris, where it was feared that Royalists were taking control of the government. Napoleon supported a *coup d'état* and then seized power for himself, becoming First Consul of France. Under his leadership, France's government was finally centralized, the Bank of France was established and Roman Catholicism was declared the country's official religion. He also reformed the French legal system, implementing the Napoleonic Code and, in 1802, changing the constitution so that he could remain First Consul for life. With war with Britain looming, Napoleon sold off French lands in America, in particular Louisiana, in order to finance the army. In December 1804, he was crowned Emperor of France in the cathedral of Notre Dame and his wife Josephine was made Empress.

Napoleonic Europe

A brilliant general, Napoleon developed a modern technique of warfare that dispensed with many of the siege tactics employed in the past. His troops outmaneuvered the enemy and Napoleon was soon able to exert his domination over his European rivals. Territories such as Switzerland, Spain, Italy, Naples, and Westphalia were annexed and ruled over from Paris or by members of the Bonaparte family. The princes of western Germany submitted to Napoleon's rule, becoming dependent states, and in 1806 the Holy Roman Empire was abolished. With his influence reaching across western Europe, Napoleon contributed to the development of modern Europe.

The Napoleonic Code was a collection of laws dealing with civil matters and it consolidated the principles of the French revolution: that all men are equal in law and all have the right to property. Because the code was implemented across Napoleonic Europe, feudalism was effectively abolished. The Napoleonic Code became the origin of a number of European and Latin American legal systems and would eventually contribute to the legal documentation of the European Union.

Napoleon's Europe was a place where merit and wealth became the sources of power, not birthright and privilege. Because many of Napoleon's social and legal reforms were of a secular nature, they were also adopted by some Islamic rulers, in particular the Ottomans. His annexation of German territories and the Italian states also had a lasting effect on these countries. Neither country had a sense of nationalism, having been divided into smaller states for so long; being led by one administration helped to contribute to a rising sense of "being German" and "being Italian."

The Napoleonic Wars

Napoleon was keen to emulate the Roman emperors and build a huge empire with Paris, instead of Rome, at the center. However, the British were equally as keen to curtail his ambitions. The British feared the shift in the balance of power towards their regular enemy France, particularly for economic reasons. In

1805, Britain declared war on France and formed an alliance with Russia, Prussia, and Austria. Later that year Admiral Nelson defeated the combined French and Spanish navies in the Battle of Trafalgar. However, at the battle of Austerlitz the Austrians were defeated and Napoleon was able to negotiate the possession of all of northern Italy, crowning himself King of Italy. Prussia was defeated in 1806 and then Russia in 1807, and in the Treaty of Tilsit Napoleon demanded that both countries should ally with France and partake in the boycott of British goods. Napoleon's intention was to ruin the British economy. However, the boycott served to weaken that of the Russians, who relied upon exporting timber and grain in return for British manufactured goods. Tsar Alexander I was soon forced into abandoning the boycott and partly as a result of this insubordination, and partly due to his territorial ambitions, Napoleon took an army of 500,000 to Russia in 1812. He was forced to march all the way to Moscow, which was easily taken by the French. However, the supply lines were far too long and Napoleon was forced to retreat. During the march back to France the Russian winter took its toll on Napoleon's troops and over 300,000 fell victim to hunger and cold. With his army weakened and French morale at a low, the British, Austrians, Prussians and Russians attacked again. At Liepzig, the Battle of Nations saw a French defeat and the allied forces were eventually able to invade France. Napoleon abdicated in 1814 and was forced to retreat to Elba.

Josephine

Born on a plantation on the West Indian island of Martinique, Marie Joseph Rose de Tascher de la Pagerie was to become famous as the first Empress of France and Napoleon's first wife. In 1779 she arrived in France to marry the aristocrat, Alexander, Viscount of Beauharnais, with whom she had two children, Eugene and Hortense, the latter of whom would later marry Napoleon's brother. During the revolution,

THE NAPOLEONIC EMPIRE, c. 1812

- Ruled directly by Napoleon
- Ruled by members of Napoleon's family
- Dependent state

Iceland

Faeroe Is.
to Denmark

Shetland Is.

ATLANTIC
OCEAN

*North
Sea*

Scotland
• Edinburgh

Ireland
Dublin •

UNITED KINGDOM
OF GREAT BRITAIN
AND IRELAND

Wales

England

London ■

Channel Is.

N

0   200 km
0   200 miles

DENMARK - NORWAY
United until 1814

Bergen •

Christiana •

Gothenburg •

Copenhagen •

Helgoland
1807–14 to Br.   Hamburg
Bremen •
1807–10
to Fr.

Amsterdam •
1810 to Fr.
Antwerp •

Brussels •   Cologne •

WESTPHALIA

Hannover ■
Brandenburg
Berlin •

Erfurt •

Frankfurt •

CONFEDERATION
OF THE RHINE

Munich •

• Paris

FRANCE

• Orléans

• Tours

Bern •
HELVETIA

Lyon •   • Geneva
1798–1814 to Fr.   Milan •

Turin •   **ITALY**

Bordeaux •

• Toulouse   Marseille •   LUCCA
Florence •
Tuscany
Papal
States
Rome •

Cataloña
1808–13 to Fr.
Barcelona •

SPAIN

Madrid •

Balearic Is.

Minorca
1798–1802 to Br.

Corsica

SARDINIA

Palermo •

SICILY

S W E D E N

Stockholm •

Åland Is.

Gotland

*Baltic
Sea*

to Sweden

REP. OF
DANZIG

Königsberg •
East
Prussia
P R U S S I A

Silesia

GRAND DUCHY
OF WARSAW

Warsaw ■

Cracow •

Finland
1809 to Russia

Helsingfors •   ■ St. Petersburg

Revel •   Novgorod •

Riga •

Smolensk •

Vilna •

Bialystok •
1807 to Russia

R U S S I A N

E M P I R E

Ternopol •
1809 to Russia

Galicia

A U S T R I A N

E M P I R E

Bohemia
Prague •

Vienna ■

Styria   Buda
(Ofen)   ■ Pest

Carinthia   **H u n g a r y**

Illyrian Provinces

Venice •

Transylvania

Banat

Belgrade •

O T T O M A N

Moldavia

Bessarabia
1812 to Russia

occupied by
Bucharest •

Wallachia

Bulgaria

Sofia •

E M P I R E

MONTENEGRO

Macedonia

NAPLES

Naples •

*Adriatic
Sea*

Corfu
1807–14 to Fr.

*Aegean
Sea*

Thessaly

Athens •

Ionian Is.
Occupied by Br.

Crete

Constantinople ■

Gibraltar •
Ceuta
to Spain

Oran •

Algiers •

MOROCCO   **ALGERIA**

Mediterranean   Sea

Bona •

Tunis •

Tunisia

Malta
1798 to Fr.
1800 to Br.

Oporto

PORTUGAL

Beauharnais was executed and Josephine was imprisoned for a year. She escaped the guillotine mainly thanks to the death of Robespierre, after which she was soon released.

Josephine quickly became a Parisian socialite and embarked on a number of affairs, one of which was with the young General Bonaparte who was six years her junior. In 1796 Josephine and Napoleon were married in what was to be a relatively happy love match. Josephine accompanied her husband on his military tour of Italy, but returned to Paris before he left for Egypt. As a popular socialite, she was able to influence his career in Paris, smoothing the way for his triumphant arrival in 1799. Possibly as a result of an injury when falling from a balcony, Josephine was unable to provide Napoleon with an heir and in 1809 she consented to an annulment of their marriage; theirs became the first divorce under the Napoleonic Code. Napoleon went on to marry the niece of Marie Antoinette, Marie-Louise of Austria, who produced the future Napoleon II in 1811. However, he remained attached to his first wife, continuing to write to her at Malmaison, her home, and is believed to have uttered her name as his final words on his deathbed. Josephine herself had retired on a comfortable pension and spent her time breeding roses. She died in 1814, one month after Napoleon's exile to Elba.

The Final Defeat of Napoleon

With Napoleon removed to Elba, the coalition forces, determined to remove any threat of further French aggression, decided to restore the Bourbon Dynasty to the French throne and Louis XVIII became king. Louis' reign was generally unpopular; the French feared a return to the days before the revolution and did not want to lose their hard-won liberty. Napoleon, who may well have been aware of this, escaped from captivity. Although he had been sent to Elba with the task of governing the island, he had been carefully watched over by Austrian and French guards. On his arrival in France in 1815, the forces which had been sent to arrest him kneeled before him and welcomed his return and Napoleon returned to Paris in triumph.

One hundred days of rule followed. Declared an outlaw by his enemies, Napoleon decided to attack before the troops could be amassed to attack him. He mobilized his army to attack Belgium where the British and Prussian armies were camped, fighting the Prussians first at Ligny. Then, at Waterloo, Napoleon attacked the British forces, who were led by Arthur Wellesley, the Duke of Wellington. It was here that Napoleon was defeated for the last time. He surrendered to the British hoping for leniency, but was instead banished to the remote island of Saint Helena in the South Pacific. While there he was constantly accompanied by an English officer and his boring existence soon led to depression. Having lost all will to live, Napoleon died in 1821. He requested that his ashes be cast into the Seine.

Below: Josephine was born on plantation in Martinique as Marie Joseph Rose de Tascher de la Pagerie. She was married to Napoleon in 1796, her first husband having been executed during the "Terror".
Previous pages: More Italian than French by birth, Napoleon seized power in France in 1799 and had himself crowned Emperor five years later.

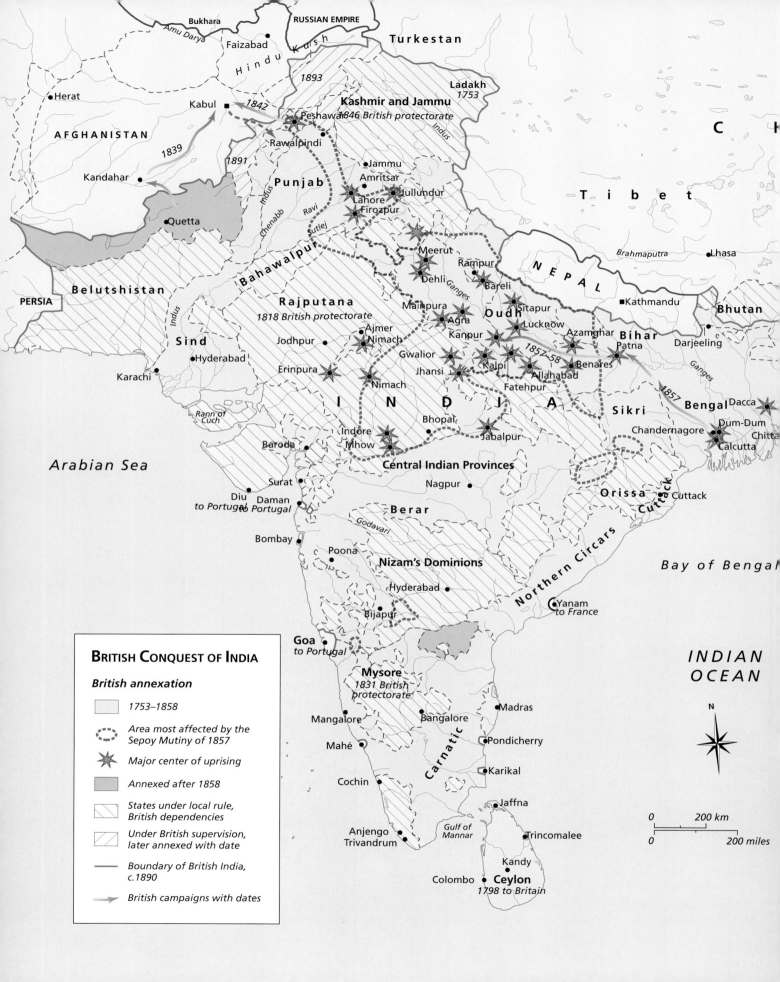

RUSSIAN EMPIRE

Bukhara
Amu Darya

Faizabad

TURKESTAN

Hindu Kush

Herat

1893

Kabul
1842

Peshawar
1846 British protectorate

Ladakh
1753

Kashmir and Jammu

AFGHANISTAN

1839

Rawalpindi

Indus

Jammu

1891

Kandahar

Punjab

Amritsar
Jullundur

Quetta

Lahore
Firozpur

Indus

Ravi

Chenabb

Sutlej

Meerut

Rampur

N E P A L

Brahmaputra

Lhasa

T i b e t

Belutshistan

PERSIA

Bahawalpur

Dehli
Ganges

Bareli

Sitapur

Kathmandu

Bhutan

Sind

Indus

Rajputana
1818 British protectorate

Mainpura
Agra

Oudh
Lucknow

Azamgarh

Bihar

Darjeeling

Hyderabad

Ajmer
Nimach

Jodhpur

Kanpur

1857–58

Patna

Benares

Ganges

Karachi

Erinpura

Gwalior

Kalpi

Allahabad

Sikri

1857

Bengal

Dacca

Rann of Cuch

Nimach

Jhansi
Fatehpur

Chandernagore

Dum-Dum

Chitta

I N D I A

Bhopal

Jabalpur

Calcutta

Arabian Sea

Indore
Mhow

Central Indian Provinces

O r i s s a

C u t t a c k

Cuttack

Baroda

Surat

Diu
to Portugal

Daman
to Portugal

B e r a r

Nagpur

N o r t h e r n   C i r c a r s

Bay of Bengal

Godavari

Bombay

Poona

Nizam's Dominions

Hyderabad

Bijapur

Goa
to Portugal

Yanam
to France

Mysore
1831 British protectorate

Madras

BRITISH CONQUEST OF INDIA

British annexation

1753–1858

Area most affected by the
Sepoy Mutiny of 1857

Major center of uprising

Annexed after 1858

States under local rule,
British dependencies

Under British supervision,
later annexed with date

Boundary of British India,
c.1890

British campaigns with dates

Mangalore

Bangalore

Pondicherry

C a r n a t i c

Mahé

Karikal

Cochin

Jaffna

Gulf of Mannar

Trincomalee

Anjengo
Trivandrum

Kandy

Colombo

Ceylon
1798 to Britain

**INDIAN
OCEAN**

N

0   200 km

0   200 miles

N   A

●Mandalay

B U R M A

S I A M

Rangoon
●

India
Under British Rule

The British interest in India began with small
trading posts and culminated in complete control
of the subcontinent, control which could not
be sustained.

British Footholds in India

Following the lead of the Portuguese and Dutch, a group of British
merchants formed an East India Company in 1599 and the following year,
with the authority of Queen Elizabeth I, it was granted a monopoly on
British trade with the East Indies. Several voyages were made to the region
in the early seventeenth century with the aim of establishing a British
presence and the first successes came in 1619, with the foundation of a
trading post, or "factory" at Surat, and then between 1634 and 1639, with
Fort St George at Madras.

By 1647, almost thirty trading posts had been established, and despite
conflicts with the Dutch, Portuguese, and native Mughal powers—notably
becoming involved in a near disastrous campaign against Emperor
Aurangzeb between 1688 and 1691—by the end of the century the British
East India Company had vastly expanded its operations in India. Numerous
small trading posts were established along both coastlines of the
subcontinent, and larger settlements were developing at Madras, Bombay,
and Fort William in Calcutta.

The Rise of British Power

Despite the growth of trade and settlement in India throughout the
seventeenth century, the British wielded no real power, either commercially
or politically, but as the Mughal Empire began to collapse following the
death of emperor Aurangzeb in 1712, the British were poised to fill the
vacuum that was created. However, from its foundation in 1664, the French
East India Company, the Compagnie des Indes, had been steadily gaining
wealth and territory and increasing the size of its armies. By the early
eighteenth century the conflicts in Europe, which had seen Britain fighting
with various alliances against France, had spilled over into overseas
possessions. Here rivalries were already increasing and it was guaranteed
that a struggle for power would ensue. Initially, the French appeared to have
the upper hand and captured Madras in 1744, but in 1751 their fortunes
were to change at nearby Arcot, where Robert Clive, previously a clerk with
the East India Company, successfully captured and then defended the French
stronghold with a small force of British and Indian soldiers. In 1756,
conflict shifted north, as the ruler of Bengal, Nawab Siraj-ud-Daulah,
launched an attack on Fort William, capturing it and imprisoning people,
many of whom subsequently died in a holding cell—an incident that has
become known as the "Black Hole of Calcutta."

Above: The central offices of the Dutch East India Company at Hugli in Bengal, c.1665.

By this time Clive was a lieutenant colonel, and governor of Fort St David. He recaptured Fort William in 1757, before going on to capture the main French settlement in India, Chandernagore, effectively removing the French threat. He defeated Siraj-ud-Daulah's extensive forces at the Battle of Plassey, a feat achieved by a political conspiracy that involved the defection of one of the nawab's generals, Mir Jafar. Jafar was installed as nawab, paying Clive a large salary for the privilege. The East India Company, now effectively in charge of Bengal, began to tax Mughal lands and command their troops. Henceforth, the Company would no longer be an organization purely dedicated to trade, but an authority with real political power. Having traveled to England to be knighted, Clive returned to India in 1765 to take his position as Governor and Commander in Chief of Bengal, establishing the first seat of power in what would become the British Indian empire.

British Conquest

Whilst the British East India Company had by 1757 laid the foundations of empire and secured a degree of control, its agents were not used to governing, and from around 1767 the first calls came from Britain that Indian possessions should be brought under the sovereignty of the Crown. Following a severe famine in Bengal from 1769–70 which almost devastated the Company, the state intervened, but at a price: that the Company should begin to relinquish its power to the British Government. The India Bill, or Regulating Act of 1773, and the India Act of 1784, established greater parliamentary control over the Company. The government would supervise, and to an extent, regulate policy, placing India under the rule of a succession of governor-generals, and thereby introducing a system of dual control which would last until 1858.

The period was characterized by the pursuit of British expansion, either by the formation of "subsidiary alliances" or by conquest. The policy of subsidiary alliances saw the creation of "Native States," in which local princes retained their titles, and ostensibly their rule, but passed much of their power to the Company, particularly in matters of defence and foreign affairs. "British India" proper consisted of those territories that had been directly annexed by the British, typically as a result of military conquest. Under such governor-generals as Warren Hastings, Lord Cornwallis, Lord Wellesley, and William Bentick, the British sought to pacify, "civilize" and "improve" their subjects through social reforms, which included attempts to reform taxation, education, the rule of law, and the justice system. Persian was replaced by English as the language of the courts, and there were Christianizing attempts that saw some Indian social and religious practices outlawed.

Following successful military campaigns against the Sultan of Mysore in 1799, the Marathas in 1818, the Sikhs in a series of conflicts between 1845 and 1848 and the continued annexation of land under the governors-general Dalhousie and Canning, the British occupation of India was essentially complete by 1849, with almost all of India either dependent upon or under direct rule of the Company. From 1851 India's infrastructure began to develop, with the construction of telegraph and rail systems, and improved irrigation, which provided employment for Indians and Anglo-Indians. Whilst many Indians were loyal to the British, or at least tolerated their rule, for many more the annexation of land, severe taxation and westernizing attempts which impinged on their customs contributed to increasing resentment.

The Indian Mutiny of 1857

The growing resentment against the British spilled over on May 10, 1857, when sepoys, Indian soldiers of the British Indian Army, mutinied near Delhi, marking the beginning of a year-long insurrection against the British. The uprising was sparked by the issue of ammunition rumored to have been greased with pig and cow fat, offending the religious beliefs of both Muslim and Hindu soldiers. More generally it could be seen as a reaction to the rapid social changes and modernization put into effect by the British, and also as an abortive attempt on the part of Muslims to resurrect the dying Mughal dynasty. The uprising was quashed by the British with large numbers of loyal Indian troops by mid-1858, when the last of the mutinous units surrendered. Following this the last of the Mughals, Emperor Bahadur Shah, was tried for sedition, convicted and exiled to Burma, formally marking the end of the Mughal empire. As a direct consequence of the revolt, which had represented the first serious threat to British rule in India, the British dissolved the East India Company and assumed direct

rule. India was to be governed by the Crown, and the governors-general were replaced by viceroys, marking the beginning of the British Raj under Queen Victoria.

The British Raj and the Rise of Indian Nationalism

Queen Victoria was proclaimed Empress of India in 1877, and as such promised to ensure the welfare of her subjects and provide them with equal treatment under British law. However, mistrust of British rule had become a legacy of the 1857 rebellion and British attitudes toward Indians had also shifted, towards insularity and even xenophobia. Victorian India was therefore somewhat divided. On the one hand, there was a renewed distance between Indians and the British, and on the other, a desire for greater cooperation and inclusion. Several reforms took place from the late 1800s into the early twentieth century which would provide Indians with greater participation in the political process. This ultimately gave rise to—and provided an outlet for—the expression of a renewed national identity, which fostered hopes of self-government. In 1885 the Indian National Congress was founded in order that Indians might have a voice in the governance of their country, and the Government of India Act, or the Morley–Minto Reforms of 1909, provided Indians with limited roles in the legislative councils.

However, nationalist sentiments were not confined to the Congress, and in Bengal and elsewhere, armed revolutionaries began to launch terrorist campaigns against British officials and institutions. Around this time, strategies of mass non-violent resistance and non-cooperation also began to emerge as effective forms of protest, tactics that would continue to be employed for the duration of British rule. During and immediately after World War I, in which many Indians had served, it seemed that further concessions—and constitutional reforms of 1917 and 1919—were pointing the way towards eventual self-rule. However, 1919 was also to see the violent enforcement of draconian law, intended to suppress opposition to British rule: in disturbances in April, nearly 400 unarmed Indians were massacred in Amritsar. This further spurred political leaders, such as Mohandas Gandhi and Jawaharlal Nehru and their supporters, to demand greater action, heralding the emergence of a widespread movement against British rule.

The European Discovery of Australia

The "discovery" of Australia by European explorers, notably the British, was swiftly followed by the development of settlements, initially for use as a penal colony.

European Exploration

Several European adventurers and explorers reached Australia in the seventeenth century, but it was the arrival of the Englishman James Cook that was the most significant. Cook was an accomplished seaman who had fought in the British navy at Quebec during the American wars against France. He was also an excellent mapmaker, and as such was sent by the Royal Society to explore the Southern Ocean. Cook arrived first at New Zealand in 1769, only the second European to do so, and made a map of its coastline. He then sailed across to unexplored Australia, landing on August 22, 1770. He had landed in the south-east—at a place which became Botany Bay—and decided this would be the best location for an English settlement. When the first full English fleet arrived in 1788, they decided to find a more suitable settlement site, moving further north to Port Jackson, later to become Sydney. The land around both Botany Bay and Sydney was mountainous and not particularly attractive for settlers. Gradually explorers began to move inland, displacing the Aborigine inhabitants, and in 1829 Britain annexed the whole continent.

British sovereignty wasn't claimed over New Zealand until 1840, by which time the indigenous population, the Maoris, were becoming aware that theirs was not an equal relationship. A series of Land Wars between the Europeans and the Maoris led to the significant loss of Maori territory.

British Settlement

The British were not the only Europeans to take an interest in colonizing Australia; the French were also keen to take advantage of the possibilities of new territories. In order to protect their interests against the French, the British established a number of fortified settlements in colonies across New South Wales and Victoria and on Van Diemen's Land, now Tasmania.

In 1786, George III's government decided to use Australia as a base for its penal colonies. Before this, the English had made use of their colonies in North America as a place to send convicted prisoners, but with American Independence they had been forced to withdraw. The first shipload of convicts arrived in 1788 at Port Jackson carrying 586 male and 192 female prisoners, many of whom had been

Left: Caged prisoners below deck on a transport ship bound for Australia.

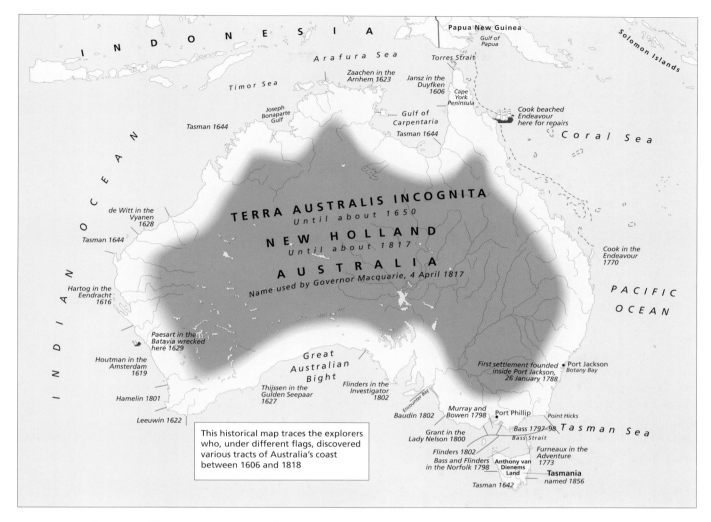

Papua New Guinea
Gulf of Papua
Torres Strait
Arafura Sea
INDONESIA
Solomon Islands
Timor Sea
Zaachen in the Arnhem 1623
Jansz in the Duyfken 1606
Cape York Peninsula
Cook beached Endeavour here for repairs
Coral Sea
Joseph Bonaparte Gulf
Gulf of Carpentaria
Tasman 1644
Tasman 1644

TERRA AUSTRALIS INCOGNITA
Until about 1650
NEW HOLLAND
Until about 1817
AUSTRALIA
Name used by Governor Macquarie, 4 April 1817

de Witt in the Vyanen 1628
Tasman 1644
Cook in the Endeavour 1770
PACIFIC OCEAN
Hartog in the Eendracht 1616
Paesart in the Batavia wrecked here 1629
Houtman in the Amsterdam 1619
Great Australian Bight
First settlement founded inside Port Jackson, 26 January 1788
Port Jackson
Botany Bay
Hamelin 1801
Thijssen in the Gulden Seepaar 1627
Flinders in the Investigator 1802
Leeuwin 1622
Encounter Bay
Baudin 1802
Murray and Bowen 1798
Port Phillip
Point Hicks
Bass 1797-98
Tasman Sea
Bass Strait
Grant in the Lady Nelson 1800
Flinders 1802
Bass and Flinders in the Norfolk 1798
Anthony van Diemens Land
Furneaux in the Adventure 1773
Tasmania named 1856
Tasman 1642

INDIAN OCEAN

This historical map traces the explorers who, under different flags, discovered various tracts of Australia's coast between 1606 and 1818

convicted of petty offences such as theft. Between 1788 and 1867 when the practice was ended, over 160,000 people were transported to the penal colonies. Although the conditions were harsh, many convicts remained in Australia at the end of their sentences and some were joined by their families from Britain and Ireland. It was not only the convicts who began to settle in Australia: many of the soldiers and administrators who worked for the penal system also elected to stay despite being so isolated from their homeland.

The Pace of Change

Soon free settlers began arriving in Australia, taking up sheep farming on a large scale in the 1820s, when exploitation of the plains inland from the original settlement became possible; the wool exported to Britain became the basis for Australia's economy. More territory was opened up in the 1830s and the rate of immigration increased; wheat also became a significant export. Gold strikes in the 1850s led to another acceleration in immigration, and the population rose from just over 400,000 in 1850 to 4 million by 1900. Wool and gold were also central to the New Zealand economy and the export of meat became important from the 1870s, after the development of refrigerated shipping. New Zealand was the first country to offer workers' pensions and also the first, in 1893, to give the vote to women.

The effect of European settlement on the indigenous population was severe in both countries. Increasing demands for pasture land and mineral resources brought settlers into conflict with the original inhabitants; imported diseases took their toll and both Aborigine and Maori populations declined until the 1930s. Campaigns for better treatment began in the first part of the twentieth century, meeting with varying success.

The Industrial Revolution

Industrialization radically changed the whole world. New sources of power led to mechanization, and new forms of communication and transport were developed.

The Causes of Industrialization

Several factors led to the increase in industrialization in the nineteenth century. In Europe the growth of large empires, in particular that of the British, meant huge trade opportunities. Increasing export markets encouraged productivity and as a result large modern factories began to appear. In Britain the pace of industrial development had begun to speed up during the eighteenth century, as the empire reached its largest extent. Towards the end of this century and the beginning of the nineteenth, other European countries, such as Belgium and Germany, also began to build up their own manufacturing economies. The industrialization that began in Britain gradually began to radiate out into northern and western Europe and then across the Atlantic to the eastern seaboard of the United States.

The growth in scientific knowledge also contributed to the industrial "revolutions." Possibly the most crucial invention was that of steam power, which would drive the engines of factory machinery. In order to create steam, coal was needed and some of the most industrialized parts of Europe were also those situated on huge coalfields. Britain benefited from the coal mines of South Wales, the Midlands, and the North of England; in Germany the Ruhr valley was the heart of the coal industry with deeper seams being found further north. The French coal seams were mainly situated in the south, with access to the Mediterranean port of Marseilles being vital.

Industrialized areas benefited further from access to major communication and trade routes, most often provided by rivers, canals, and the sea. The British had the advantage of being a small island with no town any great distance from the sea; they also had a network of major rivers and canals to ensure raw materials and manufactured goods could be transported easily. Likewise, the river valleys of northern Germany and Belgium were also crucial. Not only was geographical location important, but so was the location of the

workforce that was needed to work in the factories. Land enclosure in Britain during the centuries preceding the nineteenth had meant a large number of the rural peasant population had moved into the towns in order to find work. On mainland Europe, peasants had remained tied to the land for longer, although eventually they too would find themselves migrating to the larger towns and cities. Large ports, such as Liverpool, Hamburg, Marseilles, and Rotterdam, were also industrialized urban centers.

The Effects of Industrialization

The development of industrial economies dramatically changed the face of the world. Industrialized economies would eventually become the economic world leaders of the early twentieth century. The superpowers of Germany, France, Britain, Japan, and the USA all benefited from their superior economies. Industrialization made the capitalist economy the most successful and productive means of supporting and financing a nation. Capitalist democracies would become the richer nations in the globalism of the later twentieth century.

During the nineteenth century, however, the immediate effects of the industrial revolution may not

Opposite: An engraving depicting female workers (and a male foreman) at an English cotton mill in 1833.
Above: The beginnings of what was to become Salt Lake City pictured in c. 1850. The railways were important in the development of North America.

have seemed so positive. The urbanization of the poor led to a decrease in living standards for many across Europe, with starvation and disease just as rife as they had been in preceding eras. The relationship between the manufacturers, who aimed to keep costs down to increase profits, and the poorly paid and exploited workers led to class conflict. Poor living conditions in nineteenth century Europe influenced thinkers such as Karl Marx, who in 1848 published the *Communist Manifesto*. Industrialization, therefore, had influenced not only social but also political change. The emergence of Communism in opposition to capitalism was vital to the changes undergone in a number of countries, most spectacularly in the events which took place in Russia during the early twentieth century.

The Steam Engine

Steam engines were vital to industrialization in that they powered pumps, trains, and steamships. At its most simple, a steam engine works by boiling water to

Above: English physicist Michael Faraday.
Opposite: Interior of the Krupp steelworks in Essen, the chief arms supplier of the German Empire.

produce steam under pressure. This pressurized steam then pushes against a turbine or piston forcing it into motion, and it is this motion which drives the wheels of the engine. Although first invented in 1698, steam power was to go through a number of refinements before being used to power the first ship in 1802. The most influential adaptations to the steam engine were made by the Scotsman James Watt. Born in 1732, Watt devoted his life to improving the steam engine and, without the changes he implemented, the steam engine as it was would not have been able to power the industrial revolution. He was responsible for the separate chamber which condensed the steam and made the engine more efficient, and he also invented the pressure gauge, and the crank and flywheel which provided rotary motion. It was a Watt engine that drove the experimental steam boat *Clermont* up the Hudson in 1807.

Railways

The arrival of the railways was crucial to the success of industrialization. A rudimentary form of railway had been operating in Britain before the nineteenth century, where simple tracks made of stone and iron carried wagons pulled by horses from coal pitheads and quarries. The development of the steam engine was the catalyst for change. In 1804 a Cornish tin miner, Richard Trevithick, harnessed a steam engine to a mine wagon. Inspired by this George Stevenson created his *Rocket*, the first working steam locomotive that was capable of pulling carriages. The first railway was opened between Liverpool and Manchester in 1830 and this sparked a boom in railway construction. After 1850 the British state had to intervene in order to standardize the gauge of the tracks, which up until then had been made to a number of widths. By doing this, Britain became the first country to have a fully working, truly national rail transport system. Railways spread across Europe, linking more isolated regions and communities and contributing to economic integration.

Textiles

Machine-filled factories became the heart of industrialized nations. The development of processes which would vastly increase productivity meant that huge factories filled with machines driven by large labor forces became a familiar sight across Europe. In the production of textiles, the development first of the water-powered spinning frame by Arkwright in 1769, and then Cartwright's invention of the steam-powered weaving loom in 1792, revolutionized the industry. In America, Eli Whitney invented the cotton gin, the automated machine that separated the cotton seed from the short staple fiber in 1793. The consequent increase in the supply of raw cotton meant that the demand for cotton cloth was greater. By the mid-nineteenth century, America was producing three-quarters of the world's cotton, with much of this shipped from the Southern States to New England and on to England for the weaving process. Factories now produced not only cheaper cloth, but pottery, glassware, clocks—in fact anything for which there was a keen market.

Telegraphic Communication

Communication was also vital to a healthy economic climate and during the nineteenth century postal services across Europe had steadily grown. By 1875, the Universal Postal Union had been established to link foreign countries by mail. However, the advent of telegraphic communication meant that communication across vast distances could be instantaneous, if somewhat simplified. In 1837 the first electric telegraph messaging was used in London and the following year Samuel Morse patented his electric telegraph in the United States. In 1866, transatlantic communication occurred for the very first time following the successful laying of the first transatlantic telegraph cable from North America to Europe.

Electricity

In 1821, Michael Faraday demonstrated how electrical power could be used for mechanical purposes. His discovery of electromagnetism led to the invention of the electric dynamo, and eventually to the development of electric generators. In 1873 a dynamo that provided more prolonged electrical output was developed and although its power was often limited and more expensive it gradually became popular. Until the beginning of the twentieth century, cheaper electricity could only be produced by generators that used falling water: hydroelectrics. The factories of mountainous Northern Italy, where coal was not an available raw material, were commonly powered by electricity. In 1890 Florence boasted the first electric tram. By the 1930s, however, most of Europe had become electrified, leading to the rapid rate of industrialization in countries such as Russia, which had been slower to industrialize in the nineteenth century.

Weapons

The development of firearms from the sixteenth century onward had become increasingly important. With the technological innovation of the nineteenth century it was inevitable that the instruments of warfare would also undergo rapid change as well. The advent of the machine gun was a key development in weapons manufacture. Guns which could fire bullets in rapid succession and which were also machine loaded were introduced in 1862 with the Gatling gun. This was first used in the US Civil war and was later adopted by the US navy. The French-designed Mitrailleuse consisted of thirty-seven rifle barrels mounted like a cannon. In 1883, the Maxim gun, another US design, employed a more effective method of reloading by using the recoil energy of the fired bullet to load the next, improving both the speed of firing and the gun's efficiency. One of the greatest armaments manufacturers was Alfred Krupp, whose family steel business in Essen was turned into one of the largest and most successful factories in Europe. When Krupp inherited the family firm it had five employees; by his death in 1887 there were 20,000, a testament to the demand for manufactured weapons during the nineteenth century.

Russia's Last Tsars

The rule of the last tsars of Russia was marked by increasing repression—and by increasing errors and determined opposition from many sectors of society.

The Decline of the Romanov Dynasty

The tsars of the nineteenth century all sought to reinforce their positions as autocratic rulers, despite the growing discontent of the Russian people. The reign of Nicholas I (1825–55) began with the suppression of the Decembrist Conspiracy, a group of army generals and boyars who sought to reduce the powers of the new tsar. The majority of Nicholas I's domestic policies were designed to prevent any form of subversion and to strengthen his own position. In 1826 he created his own secret police force, called the "Third Section," a force that relied upon a network of informers spread throughout the empire. In 1830 he brutally suppressed a rising in Russian Poland, abolishing the Polish constitution and reducing the country to a Russian state. His response to the "Eastern Question"—how to deal with the rapidly declining Ottoman Empire—roused the suspicions of the British and French and sparked the Crimean War.

Nicholas was followed by his son, Alexander II who, having inherited a disastrous war and a huge population in economic crisis, knew that he would have to modernize Russia if it were to compete with the other industrialized nations of Europe. His main achievement was the 1861 emancipation of the serfs, which gave Russia's twenty million serfs limited freedom and their own strips of land. Alexander was, however, a conservative and his motivation was not to institute liberal reforms but rather to boost the economy. The serfs were required to make payments to the state in return for the land they received, which was often of poor agricultural quality; they were also expected to provide crops for export. The emancipation reforms led to much resentment, by both the peasants who were crippled by the so-called redemption debts and their former owners, who now found themselves without a workforce. Much of Alexander's reign was taken up with dealing with assassination plots and revolutionary terrorists. In 1866 he survived an assassination attempt made by Polish reactionaries; however, in 1881 the terrorist group the People's Will succeeded in blowing him up in St Petersburg.

Alexander's son, Alexander III, was even more repressive than his father. Both he and his advisors were intolerant of non-orthodox religions and in particular persecuted the Russian Jews. They also sought to intimidate and alienate non-Russian members of the population, such as Ukrainians, Poles, Finns and Lithuanians. As a result the period was one in which a large number of secret underground organizations were formed, including a Russian Marxist group. In response, Alexander strengthened the security police force, giving it greater powers. Alexander's successor was his son, the weak and easily influenced Nicholas II, who was destined to become the last of the Russian tsars.

The Crimean War

The origins of the Crimean War lay mainly in the issue of who would dominate the territories owned by the Ottomans after that empire's seemingly inevitable collapse. Russia, hoping to annex lands in eastern Europe which were vassal states of the Ottoman Empire, had occupied Moldavia and Wallachia (later Romania) in 1853. The Russians and the Turks had long been involved in conflict, but tensions had been increased by disputes over the control of holy sites in Jerusalem and these tensions had spilled over to involve France as well. The British were particularly suspicious about Russian motivation and feared their gaining an opportunity to dominate the Black Sea and thus also overland trade routes into Asia. When the Turks declared war in September 1853, combat was centered mainly in Moldavia and Wallachia. The Russians were eventually expeled and the Austrians moved into the region in order to keep the Russians out. The French and the British had joined the war on the side of the Turks in March 1854 and during that year a number of key battles were fought in the Crimea, the most important being those of Balaclava and Inkerman. The Russian port of Sevastopol, which had been besieged by allied troops since early in 1854, finally fell in September 1855 and the new tsar, keen to end the war, agreed to sign the Treaty of Paris in 1856. The Russians were forced to return Bessarabia to Moldavia and to accept the neutralization of the Black Sea.

Chaos and incompetence dogged both sides of

the conflict and the famously doomed charge of the Light Brigade during the Battle of Balaclava was just one example of the military and logistical problems that were experienced. Outbreaks of cholera simply added to the woes experienced by the soldiers, and this was the first war to involve newspaper journalists who could report the poor treatment of the wounded. The reports that reached Britain prompted Florence Nightingale to set up the first nursing hospital in Scutari, and Mary Seacole to establish the British Hotel near Balaclava.

Rasputin

The Russian monk Rasputin played a small but crucial role in the downfall of the Romanov dynasty. The influence he held over Tsar Nicholas II and his wife Tsarina Alexandra was vital in contributing to their unpopularity and the serious errors they each made in events leading up to their deaths during the Russian Revolution. Rasputin himself was a wandering peasant pilgrim who had been born in Siberia in 1871. He had made himself indispensable to the Tsar and Tsarina by easing the symptoms of their eldest son's hemophilia. However, to the rest of Russian society, Rasputin was a more controversial figure. Rumors persisted that he was a member of a religious sect that encouraged sinful practices, that he enjoyed the company of a number of women from St Petersburg's higher society and that he was a heavy drinker. During World War I, his unpopularity increased and he was erroneously accused by many of being a German spy. By 1916, the Russian parliament, the Duma, and the boyars had decided that Rasputin needed to be removed and an assassination plot was conceived. The manner of his death became as infamous as his life. Three members of Russia's élite tricked him into visiting a house in order to carry out a healing. Whilst there, he was plied with wine and cakes which were laced with cyanide. Despite this Rasputin did not die, and so his assailants shot him three times: in the chest, back, and head. This did not kill him either and so the desperate men beat him around the head. They then tied him up in a sheet and threw him in the River Neva, where he finally drowned after apparently struggling to free himself from his bonds.

Below: An illustration of the charge of the Light Brigade at Balaclava during the Crimean War.

Manchu China and the Qing Dynasty

Manchu rule brought change to China, from early expansion to the upheavals of the nineteenth century, culminating in the end of imperial rule.

The Manchus

The area of Manchuria, north east of central China, was mountainous and had been sparsely populated by pastoral nomad tribes called the Jurchen. In 1616, the Manchu leader Nurhaci organized Manchu society, uniting the separate tribes of the Jurchen. In 1636, his son, Abahai, changed the name Jurchen to Manchu and also changed his dynastic name, Jin, into Qing. Nurhaci had claimed the "Mandate of Heaven" before his death, effectively declaring his intention to take the imperial throne, and his son continued this aim. During the late 1630s Abahai invaded northern China. When the rebellion of 1644 resulted in the suicide of the Ming Emperor, Abahai's successor Dorgan marched on Beijing, suppressed the rebellion and put Abahai's son Fu-lin on the throne, beginning the Qing Empire.

Although the Manchus were of non-Chinese descent they integrated elements of Chinese culture into their way of governing. Despite this, as foreign rulers, they were bitterly resented by many Chinese; loyalty to the Ming continued until the end of the seventeenth century. Fu-lin was a child on his accession and so power rested with Dorgan, an unpopular first ruler. He allocated Chinese land to Manchu princes and made the Manchu custom of wearing pigtails mandatory. He did, however, retain many Chinese institutions, including the practice of Confucian rituals in the court, the temples and the civil service. Rather than suppress Han Chinese culture, the Qing assimilated themselves into it, becoming Manchu Chinese.

China Under the Qing

The two most notable Qing emperors were Kangxi (1661–1722) and his grandson, Chien-lung (1736–96). Kangxi

Left: Henry Pu-Yi was only three years old when he became emperor in 1908. China was already politically unstable at this time but by 1911 his father, who had been acting as regent, was forced to resign and in 1912 Pu-Yi formally renounced the throne, although he continued to live in the Forbidden City.
Opposite: A Chinese Boxer, in full regalia, during the Boxer Rebellion.

Chien-lung was twenty-five when he ascended to the throne in 1736 and was well-prepared for his imperial role. During the early part of his reign, the empire enjoyed security, peace, and prosperity. Tibet and Taiwan were incorporated and Korea, Vietnam, and Burma all paid tribute to the emperor; the Qing had created the largest Chinese Empire in history. This accumulation of territory was not enough, however, to support the rapidly increasing population. Also, as Chien-lung aged he lost much of his control and corruption began to seep into imperial government; the Qing Empire began its steady decline.

Pressure from beyond the empire came in particular from the British who by the middle of the eighteenth century controlled trade with India. The Anglo–Chinese Wars, or Opium Wars, during the nineteenth century resulted in the victorious British gaining commercial rights in China too.

The Boxer Rebellion

By the end of the nineteenth century, China had been forced to accept what was in effect a free-trade policy, and foreign influence grew. In addition, attempts at internal reform failed, becoming tangled up in the politics of the imperial court. Resentment at the situation culminated in the growth of the Boxer movement, a xenophobic, anti-Christian popular upheaval, which was given official encouragement. Foreigners and Christian converts were murdered and the foreign legations in Beijing were besieged. The Boxers were eventually suppressed by military intervention from a combined international force, with troops from all the Great Powers operating under a single commander. The outcome was yet more humiliation for China, and the rebellion left the country even more unstable.

came to the throne in 1661 aged only eight; by the time he was thirteen he had expelled his regents and was ruling alone. He returned land to the Chinese, suppressed corruption, and reduced taxation. He believed in the importance of being learned, both for himself and his officials, and was a great sponsor of the arts and sciences. Militarily, Kangxi successfully ended the long-running rebellion of the Chinese states or "Three Feudatories" that had initially aided the Manchu rise to power. In response to the threat posed by the Russians, the Chinese under Kangxi expanded into Turkestan and Outer Mongolia. The Treaty of Nerschink in 1689 saw the Chinese and Russians define their border.

As China strove to modernize itself in order to compete with the west, the tradition of imperial government was destined to come to an end. Pu Yi, the last Qing and the final Chinese Emperor, was deposed in 1911.

The Development of the United States

From early beginnings as a new nation, and despite internal conflicts and wars with neighboring states, the United States developed into a major world power.

The Early Years of the Union

When George Washington was elected as the first president of the United States in 1789, the same year that the US Constitution came into effect, he had already proven himself a capable leader, both militarily and politically—after all he had succeeded in uniting the often disparate colonies, albeit with difficulty. However, by the beginning of Washington's second term, divisions within what had essentially been an inclusive coalition government resulted in the formation of oppositional political parties.

Thomas Jefferson, the secretary of state, and the treasury secretary, Alexander Hamilton, left their offices to form the Republican and Federalist parties respectively. Although this can be seen as a reaction to

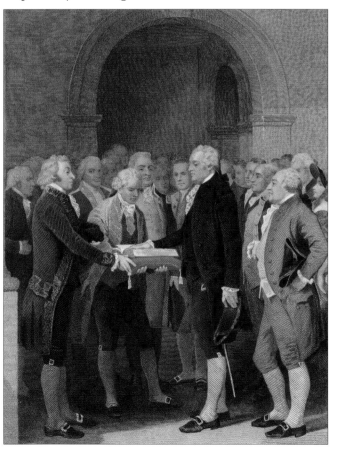

growing internal disputes—Jefferson envisaging a rather more agrarian society, which protected the rights of the individual, as opposed to Hamilton's vision of a strong Federal government supported by industry—it was a combination of these internal differences, political upheaval elsewhere in the world, and the foreign policy Washington adopted in relation to it, that was to prove decisive. Washington advocated neutrality with regard to external conflicts, but also attempted to maintain good relations with foreign powers in order to support essential trade.

When war broke out between France and Britain (then a member of an anti-French coalition) in 1793, American loyalties were divided. In 1778, America had formed the alliance with France that had seen French troops enter the War of Independence against the British but by 1793 trade with Britain had become of prime economic importance once more. Fearful of incurring the wrath of either nation, America officially adopted a position of neutrality. Regardless of this, Britain began to interfere with American and French trade, searching and even seizing American vessels and thus prompting the Americans to agree to a settlement, which became known as Jay's Treaty. Already sympathetic to the French cause, the Republicans were angered by both Britain's actions and the American government's capitulation to their demands, whilst the Federalists viewed Republican sympathies as unpatriotic at best, and at worst as an attempt to undermine the state. Meanwhile, the French also reacted angrily to the treaty, seeing it as breaching the alliance of 1778.

When Washington, having decided not to stand for a third term, delivered his farewell address in 1796, his warnings concerning the dangers of both partisan

Left: April 30, 1789: The inauguration of George Washington as the first president of the United States at the Federal Hall in New York City. Robert Livingston (left), Chancellor of New York State administers the oath of office. Also present (from left to right) are Arthur St Clair, Samuel A Otis, General Henry Knox, Roger Sherman, (Washington), Baron Friedrich von Steuben, and John Adams.

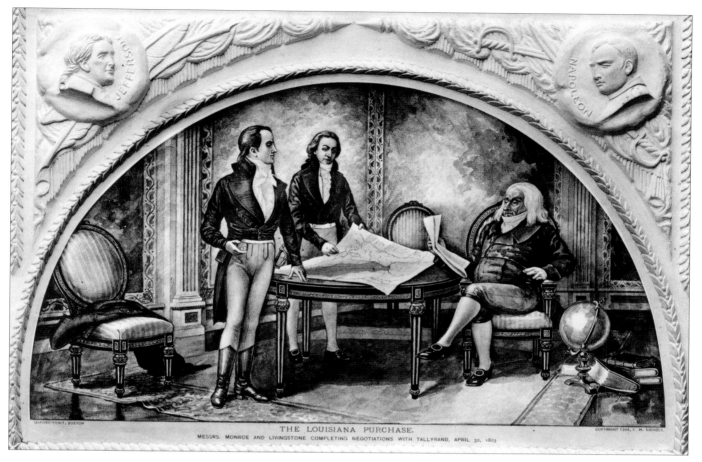

THE LOUISIANA PURCHASE.
MESSRS. MONROE AND LIVINGSTONE COMPLETING NEGOTIATIONS WITH TALLYRAND, APRIL 30, 1803

politics and involvement in foreign affairs were particularly poignant. America itself was becoming increasingly divided, and the possibility of conflict with both Britain and France loomed. Washington was succeeded by John Adams, a Federalist, with Jefferson as his vice-president, and soon after France began to act as Britain had previously done, intercepting merchant shipping. In response, Adams armed commercial vessels, and an unofficial naval war between America and France—known as the Quasi-War—broke out. Adams refused to declare open war and in fact tried to negotiate a settlement, despite growing anti-French sentiment amongst much of his cabinet and the public as a whole. Instead he attempted to consolidate Federalist power by introducing a series of laws under the Alien and Sedition Acts that were supposedly designed to protect America from foreign threats, but in practice served to suppress opposition to his policies and support for France. These acts, or at least the abuse of them, proved hugely unpopular. They inadvertently served to bolster support for the Republicans, and when Thomas Jefferson was elected president in 1800 he began to work to diminish Federalist influence.

Above: April 30, 1803: Statesmen, James Monroe who became fifth president of the USA, and Robert R Livingstone completing negotiations with Comte Talleyrand for the Louisiana Purchase.

The Louisiana Purchase

Although some westward expansion had occurred by this time, its reach did not extend much beyond the Ohio valley, and despite Jefferson's own long-held fascination with the largely uncharted west, it seems that he did not intend to seek to acquire more territory for the nation when he came to office. However, in 1803 Jefferson was presented with an offer that he could not refuse. In 1800, Spain had ceded the territory of Louisiana—an area at the time roughly equivalent to the entire United States—to Napoleon Bonaparte's France. However, faced with the prospect of a return to war with Britain and an uprising in the French Caribbean colony of Santo Domingo, the French had failed to take control of the region by 1802, and it remained in Spanish hands.

Prompted by a dispute with the Spanish over the shipping of American crops from New Orleans, and fearing that French control of Louisiana would eventually herald even greater threats to trade and necessitate a reconciliation with Britain, Jefferson sent James Monroe to Paris. He was to join Jefferson's minister to France, Robert Livingston, in order to negotiate the purchase of New Orleans, and as much of Florida as possible. However, to great surprise, and even before Monroe's arrival, Napoleon proposed the sale of the whole Louisiana Territory to Livingston. Following negotiations, the price was agreed at $15 million, and although Jefferson was concerned that the purchase was unconstitutional—indeed, the Constitution contained no provision for such a purchase—he was also acutely aware that time was of the essence. Initially Jefferson drafted a new amendment, but fearing that Napoleon might revoke the offer, the proposed purchase was instead submitted to the Senate, which quickly approved it.

At the time of the Louisiana Purchase, Meriwether Lewis and George Rogers Clark were already preparing to lead what would become their famous expedition to the Pacific, and the acquisition of Louisiana immediately opened up the possibility of further exploration and settlement. For Jefferson, Louisiana represented the land in which his dream of a pastoral society would be realized, but again foreign relations would quickly come to dominate domestic matters.

The Embargo Act and the War of 1812

Parts of the Louisiana Territories bordered, and even included, Spanish and British claims and disputes were quick to surface, prompting Jefferson to enter into further negotiations with Napoleon. This in turn prompted a breakaway movement within the Republican Party, known as the Tertium Quids, which feared that Napoleon was attempting to gain influence in America. A failed attempt by former vice-president Aaron Burr to seize Texas also highlighted domestic disputes at this time, but Jefferson's main problem would prove to be the increasing hostility of France, and to a much greater extent, of Britain. When conflict was resumed between the two nations in 1803, America again attempted to maintain its neutrality, but both Britain and France returned to seizing American shipping—the British even adopting the practice of impressment, whereby captured American sailors were forced into service in the Royal Navy. In response, the Embargo Act was passed in 1807 halting trade with both Britain and France: an attempt to pressurize them into a cessation of hostilities against American

commercial vessels. Ultimately the US was badly affected by the ban and Jefferson was forced to lift it in 1809, just days before the end of his presidency. His successor, James Madison, initially continued to pursue a peaceful settlement with Britain, but numerous young Republican "War Hawks" within the Congress began to demand a military response, and in 1812 war was declared. To begin with American forces did not fare well, and their attacks on Canada were repelled, but some naval successes prevented a full-scale British invasion and led to victories such as the Battle of the Thames in 1813. However, the following year, Napoleon having been defeated, British forces were redirected from Europe and managed to seize the city of Washington, where they burnt the White House to the ground. The British troops marched on to Baltimore, which the Americans successfully defended (inspiring Francis Scott Key to write "The Star Spangled Banner"). They also repulsed a British attack from Canada, by which time Britain was beginning to seek a way out of the conflict. Negotiations began in the Belgian city of Ghent and the war was officially ended with the signing of the Treaty of Ghent in December 1814. However, this news took some time to reach America, and from late December into January, a group of Federalists convened at Hartford and discussed secession from the Union; meanwhile fighting also continued, notably at the Battle of New Orleans, where the British were badly defeated. When peace was finally restored, the Hartford Convention appeared to many to be treasonous, and effectively heralded the end for the Federalist Party.

The Era of Good Feeling

The period following the War of 1812—from 1815 to around 1824—was to become known as the "Era of Good Feeling," a term coined by a Boston newspaper after a visit there by President James Monroe, who had been elected in 1817. During this time, attention returned largely to domestic affairs and was characterized by relative national unity. Federalist influence had now waned, ending the disunity engendered by partisan politics, as had the threat of foreign intervention and conflict.

The war had also produced other, rather more unexpected benefits. As a result of the British naval blockades and America's retaliatory trade sanctions, domestic industry had actually begun to flourish, particularly in the north-east, whilst simultaneously agriculture in the south and west became more

Above: circa 1885: A wagon train of American homesteaders moves across the open plains, migrating to the west.

intensive in order to meet the growing demand for raw materials. As the domestic economy grew, so did the Union, with six new states—Indiana, Illinois, Maine, Mississippi, Alabama, and Missouri—admitted between 1816 and 1821, mainly as a result of settlers moving into the Louisiana Territory.

However, the Era of Good Feeling was not untouched by hardship, and the economic boom created problems of its own, which were most widely experienced in "The Panic of 1819," America's first major financial collapse. As a result of extravagant speculation in the west and the unconventional practices of many state banks, and in an attempt to control soaring inflation, the recently established Second National Bank tightened its credit policy and recalled its loans, immediately ruining state banks and bankrupting many individuals. The crisis was exacerbated by a renewed influx of foreign goods, a downturn in exports, and a fall in the price of cotton, leaving domestic industry and agriculture unable to compete, in turn causing widespread unemployment and homelessness. Despite the panic, Monroe was re-elected in 1820 without opposition, but was to face another, more divisive, issue that same year.

The importation of slaves had been abolished some twelve years earlier in 1808, and slavery had been ended, at least officially, in almost all of the northern states by 1790. However, its importance in the southern states had intensified in relation to the increased productivity of cotton, sugar cane, and tobacco plantations, particularly during the War of 1812. When Missouri, a state with a slave economy, applied to be admitted to the Union in 1820, a bitter row ensued, although this was less to do with the morality of slavery than with the balance of power in the Senate. As it stood, power in the Senate was divided equally between eleven "free" and eleven "slave" states. In order to maintain that balance, the Missouri Compromise was arranged, whereby Maine joined the Union as a free state, and slavery was permitted in Missouri and south into the territory of Arkansas, but would be banned to its north and west. If the end of the Era of Good Feeling had been signalled as early as 1819 or 1820, it was certainly over for many by 1824, which witnessed a return to partisan politics with the founding of the Democratic party, led by Andrew Jackson, and his claims of corruption over the election of John Quincy Adams that year. He and his supporters immediately began to prepare for the next election, and in 1829, Jackson became the seventh president of the United States.

The Removal of Native Americans

By around 1820, the American frontier reached as far as the Mississippi, with the effect that many Native American tribes had been pushed westwards and displaced from their lands. By the time Andrew Jackson came to office, that frontier had been extended still further, at the cost of more Native American territory and lives, and Jackson, a forceful proponent of "Indian removal," had himself already proven instrumental in that process. In 1814 and 1818, he had commanded military campaigns against the Creeks and Seminoles respectively, acquiring millions of acres of land in Georgia, Alabama, and Florida. In negotiations between 1814 and 1824, he had been influential in securing several treaties which had removed land from the southern tribes in exchange for land west of the Mississippi, providing the United States with yet more territory in Georgia, Alabama, Florida, North Carolina, Kentucky, Tennessee, and Mississippi.

However, relatively small numbers of Native Americans undertook such voluntary migrations, and large numbers remained in the US. In 1823, the Supreme Court gave them a right of occupancy, but they had no rights of ownership and adopted several strategies in an attempt to safeguard their land, including peaceful assimilation. In 1827 the Cherokee declared themselves to be a sovereign nation, even adopting a written constitution—based on the fact that the US had previously declared them to be such, so that they might legally cede their lands. However, a year after taking office, Jackson introduced the Indian Removal Act, and for years to come, native peoples would be encouraged, coerced, duped and forced to give up more and more of their land in the face of American westward expansion. This ultimately led to a policy of eradication that would result in the brutal Indian Wars between 1860 and 1890, and which would culminate in the massacre of the Sioux at Wounded Knee. However, up until around 1840, military clashes were more infrequent, and the government made some provision for the protection of those Native Americans who chose to remain in the US; however this protection was typically lax and hostilities often erupted, providing Jackson with the excuse for militarily enforced removal.

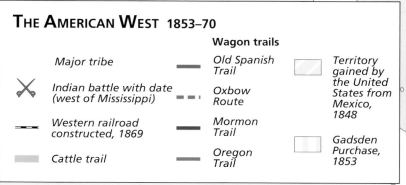

THE AMERICAN WEST 1853–70

Wagon trails

- *Major tribe*
- ✗ *Indian battle with date (west of Mississippi)*
- ▬ *Western railroad constructed, 1869*
- *Cattle trail*

- ▬ Old Spanish Trail
- ▬ ▬ Oxbow Route
- ▬ Mormon Trail
- ▬ Oregon Trail

- Territory gained by the United States from Mexico, 1848
- Gadsden Purchase, 1853

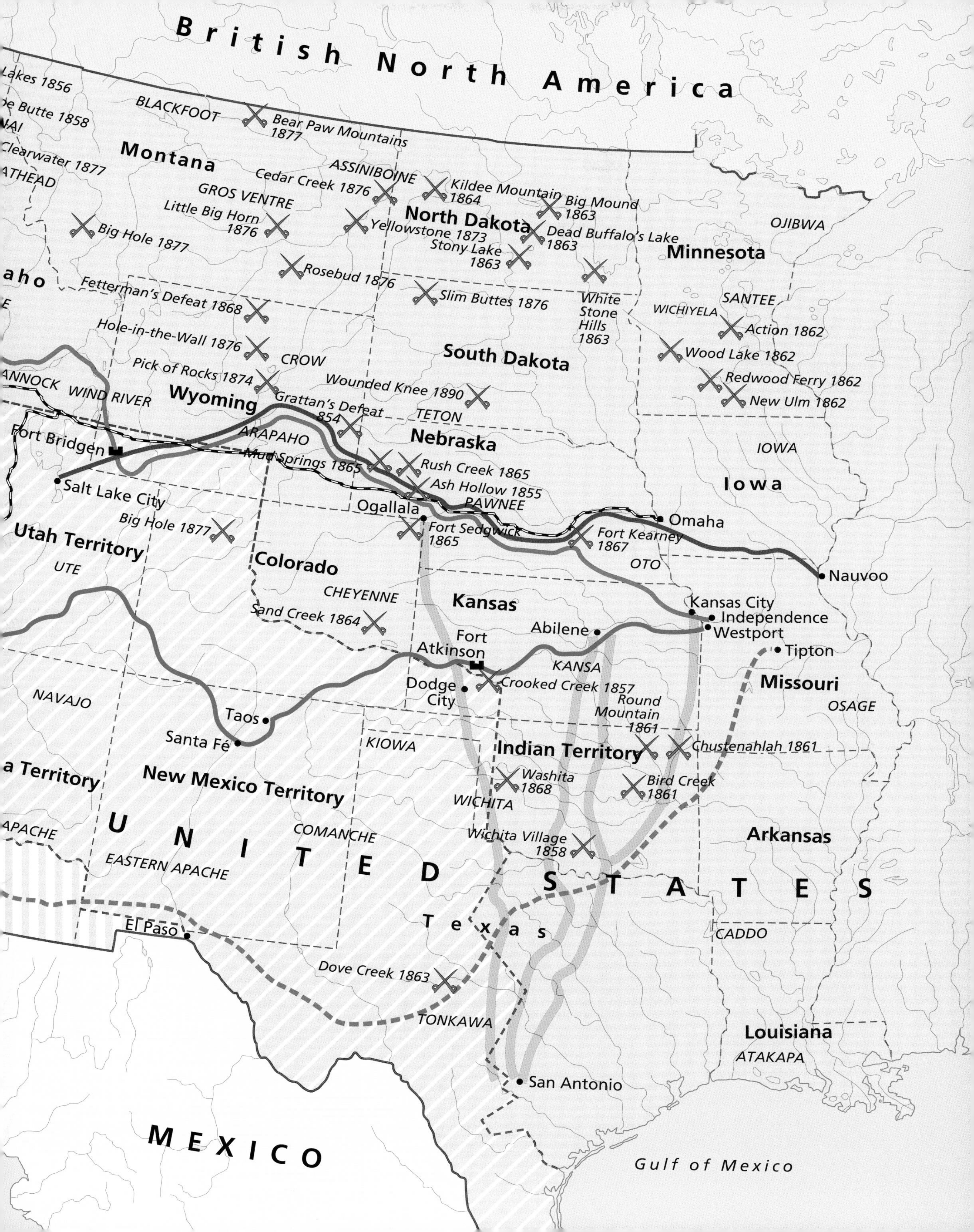

British North America

Lakes 1856
de Butte 1858
WAI
Clearwater 1877
ATHEAD

BLACKFOOT
Bear Paw Mountains 1877

Montana
Cedar Creek 1876
ASSINIBOINE
Kildee Mountain 1864
Big Mound 1863

GROS VENTRE
Little Big Horn 1876
North Dakota
Yellowstone 1873
Dead Buffalo's Lake 1863

OJIBWA

Big Hole 1877
Stony Lake 1863

Minnesota

aho
Fetterman's Defeat 1868
Rosebud 1876
Slim Buttes 1876
White Stone Hills 1863

SANTEE
WICHIYELA
Action 1862

Hole-in-the-Wall 1876
CROW
South Dakota
Wood Lake 1862

Pick of Rocks 1874
Wounded Knee 1890
Redwood Ferry 1862

ANNOCK
WIND RIVER
Wyoming
Grattan's Defeat 854
TETON
New Ulm 1862

Fort Bridger
ARAPAHO
Nebraska
IOWA

Salt Lake City
Mud Springs 1865
Rush Creek 1865
Iowa

Utah Territory
Big Hole 1877
Ash Hollow 1855
PAWNEE
Omaha

UTE
Ogallala
Fort Sedgwick 1865
Fort Kearney 1867
OTO
Nauvoo

Colorado
CHEYENNE
Kansas
Kansas City
Independence

Sand Creek 1864
Abilene
Westport

Fort Atkinson
Tipton

NAVAJO
Dodge City
KANSA
Round Mountain 1861
Missouri

Taos
Crooked Creek 1857
Chustenahlah 1861
OSAGE

Santa Fé
KIOWA
Indian Territory

a Territory
New Mexico Territory
Washita 1868
Bird Creek 1861

APACHE
U N I T E D
COMANCHE
WICHITA
Arkansas

EASTERN APACHE
S T A T E S
Wichita Village 1858

El Paso
CADDO

T e x a s

Dove Creek 1863

TONKAWA
Louisiana
ATAKAPA

M E X I C O
San Antonio

Gulf of Mexico

Other tribes, such as the Cherokee, were tricked with illegitimate treaties. In 1833, a small group agreed to voluntary migration but by 1838, when the vast majority remained on their land, thousands of troops were sent to move them. So began the "Trail of Tears," during which around 4,000 Cherokee died of disease, starvation, and exposure as they were forced west. By 1837, some 46,000 Native Americans had been removed from the land east of the Mississippi, and treaties had been secured that would lead to the removal of even larger numbers.

Vast amounts of land were now open to American settlement and the establishment of further plantations in the south. From the 1840s, cattle and wagon trails such as the Mormon, Oregon, and California trails were established westward across the Great Plains. In turn this quickly led to the development of canal and rail systems, facilitating larger volumes of trade between the north, the south and the west, and speeding the continued development and expansion of the United States.

The Mexican War
In 1821, having overthrown the Spanish, the Mexicans acquired Texas. They had begun to trade there with

Americans, who rapidly also started to settle in the region. In fact, the pace of that settlement was so fast that the American settlers soon outnumbered the Mexican population, and some began to call for its inclusion as a US state. Led by Sam Houston, the American civilians launched a successful revolution in 1835 and the following year declared their independence from Mexico. Initially reluctant to annex Texas, a slave state, America finally did so in 1845, increasing tensions both within and between the two nations.

Simultaneously tension was mounting with Britain over claims to Oregon, but this was resolved in 1846 when Britain decided to move the headquarters of the Hudson Bay Company further north to Fort Victoria, and a division was agreed along latitude 49° North. War broke out with Mexico that same year, and for a year and a half the conflict raged throughout Texas, New Mexico, and California, American settlers there having also staged an uprising. Mexico resisted

Below: The main street of Dawson City, a gold mining town in Canada, during the Klondike gold rush.
Opposite: A Union infantryman in uniform carrying a large rifle and bayonet.

stubbornly, but its unstable government and America's superior military might ensured a relatively easy victory for the United States. In 1848 Mexico surrendered, ceding land north of the Rio Grande and the Gila Rivers which now includes the modern states of California, Arizona, Nevada, Utah, New Mexico, the western parts of Colorado, Texas, and even the south western quarter of Kansas. The United States now held a vast swath of land from coast to coast across the continent. In 1853, further territory was acquired from Mexico, with the Gadsden Purchase, initiated by James Gadsden, who planned to establish a Southern Pacific Railroad through the area to the Gulf of California.

Expansion and the Slavery Issue

The chiefly industrial North and the largely agricultural South, with their different economic requirements and political policies, had long found themselves at odds. The patriotism engendered by success in the war with Mexico and the subsequent territorial gains was tempered by increasing sectional conflict, as the question of slavery in the newly established states of the expanded west was raised once more.

The Republican North supported the Wilmot Proviso, which suggested that slavery should be outlawed in all the territory ceded to the US by Mexico, with the exclusion of Texas. Democrats in the South rejected the proposal on the grounds that this area was south of the line established by the Missouri Compromise; instead they endorsed the idea of popular sovereignty, whereby settlers in the new territories would decide the issue of slavery for themselves. This was further complicated by California's desire to enter as a free state; when gold was discovered there in 1848 the issue became more pressing as the gold rush began and thousands of people migrated west in a matter of months. Some in the southern states also saw the possibility of employing slaves as miners, and diversifying into industry. In the north, meanwhile, abolitionist feeling continued to grow, not only out of political concerns over power, but increasingly on moral grounds. As a result, continued political stalling and attempts to skirt the issue could no longer be sustained, and a decision on the future of slavery had to be made.

The Compromise of 1850, which included measures designed to satisfy both slaveholders and abolitionists, appeared to many to finally solve the problem, but the provision of popular sovereignty soon sparked violence in Kansas that would last for

several years. It became increasingly clear during the election campaign of 1860 that many in the south saw no alternative to secession from the Union should the Republican candidate, Abraham Lincoln, win the election—which he duly did, without the support of any of the southern states.

The Civil War

Following Lincoln's successful election, South Carolina was the first state to secede, soon to be followed by seven others in the south, which hastily formed the Confederate government. Conflict began in April 1861 as Confederate troops opened fire at Fort Sumter in South Carolina, which they captured. In preparation for war Lincoln began to assemble an army of volunteers and, in response to that, a further five southern states joined the Confederation. The Union planned a naval blockade of the southern coastline, whilst attempting to capture the southern capital of Richmond in Virginia and seizing control of major rivers such as the Mississippi in the west. In the first confrontations, the Union suffered early defeats, despite seeming to hold many advantages. The population of the northern states was much larger, providing greater numbers of available troops and other labor required by the war effort. In addition industry was far more extensive, agriculture more varied and the transportation system of roads, canals, and railroads was better developed and more expansive, providing better communications and supply

Above: Abraham Lincoln, the sixteenth president of the United States.

lines. However, the Confederacy, led by Jefferson Davis, also had certain elements in its favor. To begin with, it had a stronger military tradition, with better disciplined troops and the leadership of experienced officers like Robert E Lee, Joseph Johnston and Thomas "Stonewall" Jackson. Much of the fighting was to take place on the Confederacy's home turf and, ultimately, it only really had to survive in order to win the war, whereas the North was faced with the prospect of having to actively defeat and pacify its enemy if it intended to achieve its objective of restoring the Union.

The South did make forays into Northern territory, notably to Antietam in 1862, and then again to Gettysburg in 1863, but their progress was checked on both occasions. Meanwhile, Lincoln's Emancipation Proclamation was passed in 1863, ending slavery in Confederate states, and accepting black soldiers into the Union army. Although the war had in part resulted from problems surrounding slavery, its abolition had never been an aim of the Union; nevertheless, in an effort to strengthen the Union cause both politically and militarily, it proved to be an important consequence of the conflict, with lasting effects for both the Union and black Americans.

That same year, General Ulysses S Grant captured Vicksburg, securing the Mississippi, and in 1864 was put in overall command of Union forces. A double-pronged attack was then launched, with Grant advancing on Richmond whilst General Sherman advanced to Atlanta and on toward the coast to cut off Confederate troops and supplies. After a long siege at Petersburg, Lee's army retreated to Appomattox, where he surrendered to Grant at the courthouse in April 1865, officially ending the war; Johnston's army, driven north by Sherman, surrendered later that month. Five days after the peace treaty was signed, Lincoln was assassinated in Ford's Theater, Washington by John Wilkes Booth, an actor who had previously conferred with Confederates in planning to capture Lincoln in 1864. The presidency fell to the vice-president, Andrew Johnson, and the process of reconstruction began.

Reconstruction

The Reconstruction Acts of 1867 attempted to set out the means by which the North and South might be reunited, particularly the reorganization of the South and the readmittance of southern states to the Union. However, the nation was to remain deeply divided. The South, not sharing the kind of economic, industrial and infrastructural developments that were taking place in the North, was thrown into even greater turmoil by its defeat in the war, and was faced with potential economic ruin by the abolition of slavery. Meanwhile, although industrialization and urbanization were rapidly growing in the North, this was largely as a result of private, rather than public enterprise. The government was lacking in the means, and to an extent the will, to invest in the South and provide the vast expenditure required for reconstruction to prove effective—and so political struggle persisted.

In 1865, Congress had already established the Freedmen's Bureau, in an attempt to provide food, clothing, medicine, land and education for former slaves, but that same year, many of the southern states, where the idea that blacks were subordinate was more deeply ingrained, passed laws (or "Black Codes") which promoted segregation and the continued subjugation of blacks. These codes were outlawed by the 1866 Civil Rights Act, and the Fourteenth and

Fifteenth Amendments, which provided full citizenship, equal rights, and the vote, but during the 1870s the Southern Democrats were to see a resurgence of support. Fueled by economic inequality between the North and South, and claims of both real and imagined Republican corruption following an electoral controversy in 1876, the Compromise of 1877 was agreed. This saw the end of Union occupation of the South and heralded the return of Democratic state control. Reconstruction came to an end, and white Southern Democrats were once more able to deny the rights of blacks politically, whilst white supremacist paramilitary groups such as the Ku Klux Klan terrorized black citizens.

The Gilded Age

Although Reconstruction was in some ways a doomed project, characterized by a turmoil which has seen it referred to as the "Second Civil War," it was also a period of reform and progress. It was representative of the wider social changes which were taking place, which continued from the end of the Civil War to the turn of the century, as America was transformed into a modern nation. This era is known as the "Gilded Age," a term coined by Mark Twain in the title of a novel in which he attempted to articulate the wealth, expansion, excess, and corruption of the period. Indeed, the massive industrialization, urbanization, and dominance of corporate power which accompanied and spurred America's development from a largely agrarian society had several effects, both positive and negative. The industrial revolution in America, supported by further settlement and exploitation of the resource-rich West, bore witness to dramatic improvements in transportation (the first trans-continental railroad was completed in 1869), communication and other technologies, which in turn fostered economic growth. Whilst there were those motivated by individual gain, and those who pursued corruption as a means of attaining it, there were also those involved in the redistribution of wealth, and ultimately, through the formation of unions and better regulation, energies were increasingly directed toward positive reform.

Similarly, the Gilded Age was a period of social reform as cities developed. The problems engendered by urbanization, a growing population, and mass immigration, prompted the need to address the inequalities faced by minorities and the disenfranchised. There were shifts toward the empowerment of immigrants, blacks and women, and the development of a distinct urban culture. Thus, by the end of the nineteenth century, America had evolved into a culturally diverse, leading industrial power.

The Spanish-American War

The growth of America's domestic industry and economy during the latter part of the nineteenth century precipitated its expansion beyond its borders, and ultimately laid the foundations for American imperialism.

Throughout the 1890s, a great deal of investment was being made in the Cuban sugar trade. However, whilst US businesses were benefiting from high import tariffs, the Cuban economy was suffering. Cuba was a Spanish colony; Cuban nationalists had fought against Spanish rule between 1868 and 1878, and in 1895 instability and disaffection once more spilled into violence as nationalist "insurrectos" rose up against the Spanish, effectively ending trade with America. Atrocities were committed by both sides but, stirred by sensationalist journalism and the threat to American investment, public opinion became increasingly hostile toward Spain.

In 1897, when President McKinley came into power, he was opposed to intervention, but the following year, when the USS Maine mysteriously exploded in Havana, the Spanish were blamed and soon afterward war was declared. In a matter of months, the US had quickly overpowered Spanish forces, and had extended the campaign not only throughout the Caribbean but into the Pacific, invading the Philippines, Guam and Hawaii. All of these were subsequently annexed, along with thousands of Pacific islands, after the rapid defeat of Spain and the signing of the Treaty of Paris which ended the war.

The United States was effectively now an empire, with possessions in both the Atlantic and Pacific. Interest in the construction of a canal across the Panamanian Isthmus was revived (the commercial usefulness of an Atlantic–Pacific waterway having long been recognized). Following an American-aided rebellion in the Columbian province in 1903, Panama gained its independence and was recognized by President Theodore Roosevelt. In return, America was granted a lease to a strip of land from coast to coast. By 1914, when the construction of the Panama Canal was complete, not only had a remarkable feat of engineering been achieved, but America had taken a huge step away from its isolationist roots toward becoming a major world power.

The Partition of Africa

A combination of circumstances drove European expansion and colonialism in Africa, resulting in a swift division of the continent.

Africa at the Beginning of the Nineteenth Century

By the early nineteenth century much of the interior of Africa was relatively little known to outsiders, though internal trading routes ran across the continent and had done for centuries. Africa was, however, moving into a period of dynamic change, with both the arrival of colonizers and the growth of Islam, to cite but two reasons. Ports such as Mombasa were increasing in importance as contact with the rest of the world—whether for trade in materials or in people—also increased.

At the beginning of the nineteenth century, the European presence was largely confined to the coasts. European expeditions into the interior began, motivated by curiosity, the search for raw materials, and sometimes by evangelical zeal. These attracted considerable interest in Europe, and the mapping of Africa by these explorers was instrumental in the outburst of competitive colonialism that followed.

The Scramble for Africa

From the nineteenth century onwards the European attitude to colonialism changed significantly. Originally the European nations had been satisfied with establishing trading posts and minor colonies in Africa. However, the emergence of newly competitive nations and changing economic circumstances precipitated a rush to claim substantial territory. Claims by one European nation would provoke claims in response by others.

The unification of Germany under Bismarck created an emerging nation keen for power of its own; German ambitions in Africa forced the established European powers into an increased programme of colonization. For example, in West Africa, where the British had established several coastal forts by the end of the eighteenth century, annexation was stepped up; by the end of the nineteenth century the British had colonies in Nigeria, Ghana, Sierra Leone, and Gambia. The rush to annex became not just an economic priority, but a patriotic duty.

Belgium and Germany sparked the real "scramble for Africa" at the end of the nineteenth

century. Germany staked a claim to German South West Africa and German East Africa, creating a fear among other nations that if colonies were not claimed quickly there would be nothing left for them. Bismarck set up the Congress of Berlin to decide how Africa should be partitioned, and the outcome was to legitimize King Leopold's claim to the Belgian Congo. In turn this created fears in France, which resulted in the annexation of French Congo; a snowball effect ensued with every nation rushing to consolidate its interests.

This flurry of activity failed to resolve matters; European nations still conspired to outdo each other and settle European rivalries on the continent of Africa. The "scramble" culminated at the headwaters of the River Nile, which the French had claimed to prevent further British expansion. The French came head to head with a superior British force, and a major international incident was only just avoided when the French agreed to withdraw.

The Boer War

Conflict between the European nations in Africa did eventually spill over, in the Boer War of 1899–1902. Vast mineral resources—gold and diamonds—were discovered in southern Africa, in territory occupied by the descendants of Dutch colonialists, the Afrikaners (known in Britain as "Boers"). When the British took the colony from the Dutch during the Napoleonic Wars, the Afrikaners had set up their own nation of Transvaal. There was something of a gold rush, with prospectors from all over flooding into the area and the growth of rampant speculation. Britain became concerned that the Germans and Afrikaners might form an alliance, and gain control of shipping routes to the east, and tension between the communities increased. In October 1899 the Afrikaners besieged British troops which were gathering on their borders, but British reinforcements won several major battles. Despite their adoption of effective guerrilla tactics, the Boers were eventually overcome by the British Army.

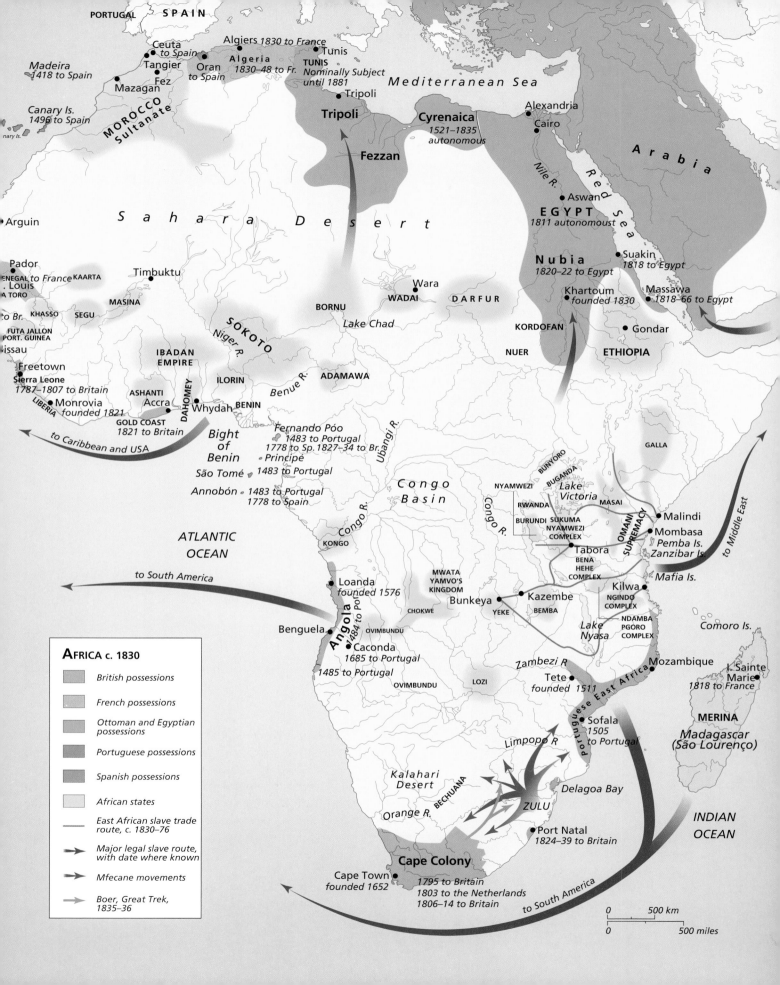

PORTUGAL   SPAIN

Ceuta *to Spain*
Tangier
Mazagan
Fez

Madeira
1418 to Spain

Canary Is.
1496 to Spain
nary Is.

MOROCCO
Sultanate

Oran *to Spain*

Algiers *1830 to France*
Algeria
1830–48 to Fr.

Tunis
TUNIS
Nominally Subject
until 1881

Tripoli

Tripoli

Fezzan

Mediterranean Sea

Cyrenaica
*1521–1835
autonomous*

Alexandria
Cairo

Arabia

Arguin

S a h a r a   D e s e r t

Nile R.

Aswan

EGYPT
1811 autonomoust

Red Sea

Suakin
1818 to Egypt

Timbuktu

Wara

WADAI

D A R F U R

Nubia
1820–22 to Egypt

Khartoum
founded 1830

Massawa
1818–66 to Egypt

ENEGAL *to France*
. Louis
A TORO

KAARTA

MASINA

BORNU

Lake Chad

KORDOFAN

Gondar

to Br.
KHASSO
SEGU
FUTA JALLON
PORT. GUINEA
issau

KHASSO

SOKOTO

NUER

ETHIOPIA

Freetown
Sierra Leone
1787–1807 to Britain

LIBERIA

Monrovia
founded 1821

IBADAN
EMPIRE

Niger R.

ILORIN

ADAMAWA

ASHANTI
Accra
DAHOMEY
Whydah
BENIN

GOLD COAST
1821 to Britain

Benue R.

to Caribbean and USA

*Bight
of
Benin*

Fernando Póo
*1483 to Portugal
1778 to Sp. 1827–34 to Br.*
Príncipe
1483 to Portugal

São Tomé
1483 to Portugal

Annobón • *1483 to Portugal
1778 to Spain*

Ubangi R.

*Congo
Basin*

GALLA

NYAMWEZI

BUNYORO

Lake
Victoria

BUGANDA

MASAI

Malindi

OMANI SUPREMACY

Mombasa
Pemba Is.
Zanzibar Is.

to Middle East

RWANDA
BURUNDI
SUKUMA
NYAMWEZI
COMPLEX

Congo R.

ATLANTIC
OCEAN

Congo R.

KONGO

to South America

Loanda
founded 1576

1484 to Por.

Benguela

Angola

Caconda
1685 to Portugal

1485 to Portugal

OVIMBUNDU

OVIMBUNDU

MWATA
YAMVO'S
KINGDOM

CHOKWE

Bunkeya

YEKE

Kazembe

BEMBA

Tabora

BENA
HEHE
COMPLEX

Kilwa

NGINDO
COMPLEX

NDAMBA
PGORO
COMPLEX

*Lake
Nyasa*

Mafia Is.

Comoro Is.

Zambezi R

Tete
founded 1511

Mozambique

I. Sainte
Marie
1818 to France

LOZI

Portuguese East Africa

Sofala
*1505
to Portugal*

MERINA

*Madagascar
(São Lourenço)*

Africa c. 1830

	British possessions
	French possessions
	Ottoman and Egyptian possessions
	Portuguese possessions
	Spanish possessions
	African states
——	*East African slave trade route, c. 1830–76*
→	*Major legal slave route, with date where known*
→	*Mfecane movements*
→	*Boer, Great Trek, 1835–36*

*Kalahari
Desert*

BECHUANA

Limpopo R

Delagoa Bay

ZULU

Orange R.

Port Natal
1824–39 to Britain

INDIAN
OCEAN

Cape Colony

Cape Town
founded 1652

*1795 to Britain
1803 to the Netherlands
1806–14 to Britain*

to South America

0		500 km
0		500 miles

Japan: 1868–1910

Many years of isolation, upheaval and radical change resulted in the modernization that enabled Japan to gain a role as a major world power.

The "Opening Up" of Japan

For centuries Japan had been reclusive and resistant to foreign infiltration. Nagasaki had been the only city in Japan which could trade with foreigners since the Dutch had negotiated access to the port in 1641. That changed in July 1853 when Commodore Matthew Perry led a small fleet of American ships to Edo, now Tokyo, and refused to proceed to Nagasaki. Threatening the use of superior force, Perry was able to present a letter from President Fillmore which demanded the negotiation of a trade agreement on terms favorable to America. When he returned in February 1854, the Japanese had agreed to all the proposals in Fillmore's letter and the Treaty of Kanagawa was signed in March 1854.

The Meiji Restoration

By 1868 imperial rule in Japan was restored. An emperor had always existed in name but since 1603 the Tokugawa clan based around Edo had run a military dictatorship called the Shogunate. Little power remained with successive emperors, who were based in Kyoto.

Tokugawa rule brought resentment and jealousy from the other clans, but all were too weak to challenge the Shogun alone. But eventually, in 1866, two of the largest rival clans, Satsuma and Choshu, put aside their differences and united in the Satcho alliance to challenge the Shogun's authority. In light of the alliance's military superiority, the Shogun, Tokugawa Yoshinobu, had little choice but to announce the transfer of his powers to the then emperor. The issue was not resolved as the Tokugawa clan made a final stand in January 1868, when Yoshinobu proclaimed the resumption of his power and invaded the emperor's base at Kyoto. This sparked the Boshin War; Satcho alliance forces were able to defeat the Tokugawa invasion and Yoshinobu escaped to Edo. After consolidating control of the rest of Japan, Choshu and Satsuma armies encroached on Edo, forcing Yoshinobu to unconditionally surrender his powers, and the Meiji Era began—the name given by the 122nd Emperor of Japan to his rule.

The Meiji Era

After the restoration, power did not reside supremely with the emperor; he was tied by the demands of the Choshu and Satsuma clans who had achieved restoration on his behalf. The chief aim of the Meiji Era was to rapidly modernize Japan so that it could deal

with the West as an equal and renounce the unequal treaties the West had imposed since Commodore Perry had opened Japan up. They did this through inviting foreign economic advisors to Japan and sending their own students abroad. Furthermore, the new government abolished feudalism and modernized the army by disbanding the Samurai class. It also subsidised the growth of the economy by encouraging the formation of Zaibatsu, large family-owned businesses, including Mitsubishi, Mitsui and Sumitomo.

The Sino–Japanese War

Japan's rapid modernization resulted in its defeat of China in the Sino–Japanese War, marking its emergence as a growing power. China was desperate to maintain its grip on Korea, while Japan was keen to increase its involvement on the peninsula. When a rebellion by reformists in Korea against the ruling elite surfaced in 1894, the Chinese sent in troops to bolster the ailing regime, while the Japanese intervened to strengthen the reformists. War was declared when China refused to acknowledge the new leadership which Japan had appointed. Japan made land advances into Manchuria and crippled the Chinese navy. Japan's military modernization had passed its first test, though this owed as much to Chinese inefficiency as to its own accomplishments. China was forced to sign the Treaty of Shimonoseki in April 1895; in this China accepted Korean independence and ceded Taiwan and the Liaodong peninsula to Japan. A week after the treaty was signed, Germany, France, and Russia forced Japan to return the Liaodong peninsula to China, in a move which demonstrated to Japan that despite success, the great powers would not yet accept an Asiatic power into the "club." This fostered bitter resentment and put Japan on course for a war with Russia.

The Russo–Japanese War

After the "Triple Intervention" by Russia, Germany, and France, Russia had begun moving troops into Manchuria to contest Japan's dominance of Korea. Japan hoped that it could bring Russia to the negotiating table as an equal and work out their respective spheres of influence in the region. However, Russia stalled negotiations and in February 1904 Japan eventually opted for a military solution. The Japanese were very successful, capturing Port Arthur from the Russians, defeating Russia's Pacific fleet and capturing

Above: Emperor Yoshihito, who succeeded his father to the imperial throne in 1912, reigning until his death in 1926.
Opposite: Commodore Matthew Perry bidding farewell to the Japanese Imperial Commission after signing a treaty opening the ports of Shimoda and Hakodate to US trade.

the city of Shenyang. In 1905, Russia's Baltic fleet was sent to bolster the war effort. After sailing around the world, the fleet was defeated before it could accomplish anything in the Battle of Tsushima. The war exacerbated Russia's internal social problems and the country teetered on the brink of revolution; in order to regain control, the Tsar called for a ceasefire. This was the first major victory by an Asian power against a Western one, and Japan was finally accepted as a world power. In the treaty of Portsmouth which followed in September 1905, Russia was forced to cede the southern Sakhalin islands and Port Arthur to the Japanese, to withdraw from Manchuria, and to accept Japanese dominance of Korea, which Japan eventually annexed in 1910.

The Russian Revolution

Growing hardships and resentment, coupled with a series of blunders, led to one of the most formative events of the twentieth century, the Russian Revolution.

The Last Days of the Tsars

The tsars had run Russia as an autocracy since Ivan the Terrible assumed the title in 1547. While other states in Europe were reforming by introducing constitutions to hold their monarchies accountable, the tsars held firm. Any reforms that they granted— for example, the emancipation of the serfs in 1861— were extremely limited in nature and largely designed to maintain, rather than alter, their supreme rule.

However, there were growing—but sporadic— protests and Tsar Alexander II was even assassinated by revolutionaries in 1881. By the time that the last tsar, Alexander's grandson Nicholas II, came to the throne in 1894, a large underground of various subversive groups had emerged, including the first Russian Marxist Revolutionary Group established by Plekhanov in 1883. At the start of the twentieth century the tsar's grip on power was slipping and a series of blunders put the country on the path to revolution.

The Russo–Japanese War

By the turn of the century Japan and Russia were in competition for dominance over the Chinese region of Manchuria. After Russia stalled negotiations on its withdrawal from the region, Japan decided to pursue a military solution in 1904. The resulting war saw Russia's defeat at the hands of Japan which gave rise to feelings of humiliation and resentment within Russia; they had been defeated by what was considered in Europe to be a backward, inferior race. At the height of popular enthusiasm for colonialism, Russia was forced to withdraw from Manchuria and recognize Japanese dominance in the region. During the war with Japan, in January 1905, a priest led a peaceful demonstration through the streets of St Petersburg demanding food and constitutional reform. It was brutally suppressed by the authorities and became known as "Bloody Sunday." These two events—the withdrawal and the savage repression— resulted in strikes and demonstrations spreading across Russia and the country was taken to the brink of revolution. The situation was resolved when the Tsar wisely backed down by introducing the "October Manifesto," in which he promised a constitution and a state parliament as well as relaxation of censorship. This was merely a token reform; all power to appoint the parliament and pass laws had to be approved by the tsar, so the revolution was merely postponed until the next serious mistake.

The Great War

That mistake came in the form of the Great War, a conflict triggered by Russia's guarantee of support to Serbia. This guarantee led it into a war against Germany and Austria–Hungary when the latter responded to the assassination of Archduke Franz Ferdinand in Sarajevo by attempting to crush Serbian nationalism.

The war exacerbated Russia's existing social problems and created even more, proving a massive strain on the Russian economy and society as a whole. Food shortages and conscription became irksome and the Tsar foolishly decided to go to the front to lead the ailing war effort, thus directly implicating himself in any military failures. He left behind his wife, the Tsarina, to rule in his absence: she was German, and thus unpopular during the war. Moreover, her decisions were shaped by the equally unpopular Rasputin, a monk who had seemingly proved to the Tsar that he was the only person capable of curing his only son's hemophilia. Tsar Nicholas's imprudent decisions led to a severe undermining of his authority.

The February Revolution

By February 1917 there was little improvement in the war effort. Food shortages were becoming more acute and soldiers were not adequately fed, leading to massive desertions from the front line. Large-scale rioting occurred in the cities as hunger set in. In order to grasp hold of his authority, Tsar Nicholas attempted to disband the parliament.

The assembly refused and named itself the Provisional Government, then called for the Tsar's abdication. After Rasputin was murdered, the Tsar, who was still at the front, had little choice but to abdicate in favor of his brother Michael, who in turn

Above: Tsar Nicholas II of Russia with members of his family in the private grounds of Tsarskoe Selo, the summer palace.
From left to right: an officer attending, the Emperor, Nicholas II, Grand Duchess Tatiana, Grand Duchess Olga, Grand Duchess Marie,
Grand Duchess Anastasia and (in front) Tsarevich Alexis and one of the sons of the Emperor's eldest sister Grand Duchess Xenia Alexandrovna.

refused the throne. This new provisional government, led by Alexander Kerensky, decided that it would carry on with the war. As the war was exacerbating all Russia's social problems, another upheaval was likely.

The October Revolution

The Provisional Government was inherently flawed, owing to its nature as a weak coalition of diverse interest groups and the absence of any mandate to rule. Its decision to continue the war effort meant that it was unable to address popular concerns, such as food shortages and land reform. The Bolsheviks, a Marxist revolutionary group, were the only one of the many competing interest groups to call for an end to

the conflict, which gained them increased support amongst the war-weary population.

In April 1917 the Bolshevik leader, Vladimir Ilich Lenin, returned from exile after the Provisional Government announced an amnesty for political prisoners. In his so-called "April Thesis," Lenin called not only for "peace" but also for "land" and "bread" for the population. He fled into exile again in the summer of 1917 after a failed uprising, but once again returned in October telling his party to prepare for immediate revolution. On October 25 (on the Julian Calendar, which Russia still used) at a Congress of Soviets, or workers' councils, the majority of delegates called for an end to the Kerensky government and promised support for the Bolsheviks. That same day, the Bolsheviks stormed the Winter Palace, reportedly patrolled only by a women's garrison, and took it in an almost bloodless coup. With St Petersburg under their control, the Bolsheviks took their revolution to the entire country.

Bolshevik Consolidation of Power

In March 1918, Lenin ended the war with Germany by signing the Treaty of Brest Litovsk. The Bolshevik government was forced to accept the loss of swaths of territory, including Ukraine, the Baltic States, Armenia, and Poland. In 1919 the Bolsheviks broke away from the European socialist movement, changing their name to the Russian Communist Party and establishing the Communist International, aiming to spread revolution.

The Civil War

A civil war broke out as soon as the Revolution had occurred between those who supported the Bolsheviks—the "Reds"—and their enemies, the "Whites." The Whites comprised a cross-section of society including army generals, monarchists, and supporters of the Orthodox Church. Once the war in Europe had ended, foreign forces also joined the Whites; these included British, French, and American troops as their governments wished to curb the spread of revolution to the rest of Europe. Even moderate left-wingers fought the Bolsheviks, including Mensheviks and Social Revolutionaries. One of the reasons that the Bolsheviks were successful in the civil war was because the army was placed under the control of Leon Trotsky. Trotsky resisted making radical changes and "communizing" the military so as not to throw his forces into turmoil in a time of war. He reintroduced conscription, homogenized the Army and rehabilitated talented pre-revolutionary generals. The Party also ensured the army was well fed by requisitioning food from the peasantry in a ruthless campaign of War Communism.

Meanwhile, the White counter-revolution was divided; different groups could not be reconciled to the idea of working with one another, and these divisions fed into the field. The White war efforts were disjointed and eventually their counter-revolution fizzled out as Russia once again succumbed to war fatigue. Millions of Russians had been killed or emigrated and famine had become widespread as industrial and agricultural productivity dropped dramatically. The Communists had won, but had to restructure and redevelop the entire nation.

Lenin's Final Years

In order to spark a recovery from the days of War Communism, Lenin launched the New Economic Policy. A market system was implemented in the countryside and state-owned industries were given a degree of autonomy. This helped raise productivity and end famine. This policy was criticized by Marxists for its lack of emphasis on socialist principles; however, Lenin believed it was a necessary temporary stage in order to further develop Russia from an agrarian society into an industrialized one. In August 1918 an assassination attempt on his life was made by Fanya Kaplan, a female Social Revolutionary. This led to a stroke in 1922, after which Lenin had to take a back seat in Soviet politics. A second stroke in December caused him to resign from politics and a third, in March 1923, left him unable to speak. He died on January 21, 1924. He was embalmed and his body placed in a mausoleum in Moscow, where it remains today.

Left: Leon Trotsky, leader of the November Revolution, who was deported from Russia in 1929.

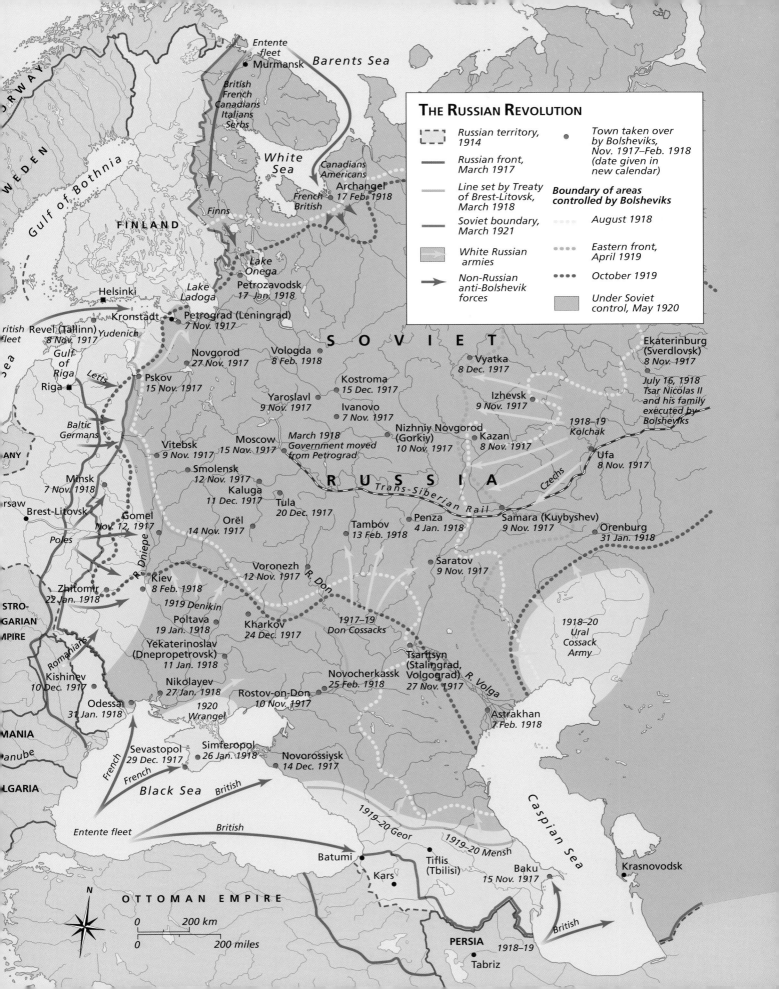

THE RUSSIAN REVOLUTION

Legend:

- *Russian territory, 1914*
- *Russian front, March 1917*
- *Line set by Treaty of Brest-Litovsk, March 1918*
- *Soviet boundary, March 1921*
- *White Russian armies*
- → *Non-Russian anti-Bolshevik forces*
- *Town taken over by Bolsheviks, Nov. 1917–Feb. 1918 (date given in new calendar)*

Boundary of areas controlled by Bolsheviks
- *August 1918*
- *Eastern front, April 1919*
- *October 1919*
- *Under Soviet control, May 1920*

NORWAY
SWEDEN
FINLAND
GERMANY
AUSTRO-HUNGARIAN EMPIRE
ROMANIA
BULGARIA
OTTOMAN EMPIRE
PERSIA

Barents Sea
White Sea
Gulf of Bothnia
Gulf of Riga
Black Sea
Caspian Sea

Entente fleet
● Murmansk

British French Canadians Italians Serbs

Canadians Americans
French British
Archangel
17 Feb. 1918

Finns

Lake Onega
Lake Ladoga

Petrozavodsk
17 Jan. 1918

Helsinki
Kronstadt
Revel (Tallinn)
8 Nov. 1917
Yudenich
British fleet
Letts
Riga
Baltic Germans

Petrograd (Leningrad)
7 Nov. 1917

Novgorod
27 Nov. 1917

Vologda
8 Feb. 1918

S O V I E T

Vyatka
8 Dec. 1917

Ekaterinburg (Sverdlovsk)
8 Nov. 1917

July 16, 1918 Tsar Nicolas II and his family executed by Bolsheviks

Pskov
15 Nov. 1917

Kostroma
15 Dec. 1917

Yaroslavl
9 Nov. 1917

Ivanovo
7 Nov. 1917

Izhevsk
9 Nov. 1917

1918–19 Kolchak

Minsk
7 Nov. 1918

Vitebsk
9 Nov. 1917

Smolensk
12 Nov. 1917

Moscow
15 Nov. 1917

March 1918 Government moved from Petrograd

Nizhniy Novgorod (Gorkiy)
10 Nov. 1917

Kazan
8 Nov. 1917

R U S S I A

Ufa
8 Nov. 1917

Czechs

Warsaw
Brest-Litovsk
Poles

Gomel
Nov. 12, 1917

Kaluga
11 Dec. 1917

Orël
14 Nov. 1917

Tula
20 Dec. 1917

Trans-Siberian Rail

Samara (Kuybyshev)
9 Nov. 1917

Penza
4 Jan. 1918

Tambóv
13 Feb. 1918

Orenburg
31 Jan. 1918

Zhitomir
22 Jan. 1918

Kiev
8 Feb. 1918

1919 Denikin

R. Dniepe

Voronezh
12 Nov. 1917

R. Don

Saratov
9 Nov. 1917

1918–20 Ural Cossack Army

Kishinev
10 Dec. 1917

Romanians

Poltava
19 Jan. 1918

Kharkov
24 Dec. 1917

1917–19 Don Cossacks

Yekaterinoslav (Dnepropetrovsk)
11 Jan. 1918

Tsaritsyn (Stalingrad, Volgograd)
27 Nov. 1917

R. Volga

Odessa
31 Jan. 1918

Nikolayev
27 Jan. 1918

Rostov-on-Don
10 Nov. 1917

Novocherkassk
25 Feb. 1918

1920 Wrangel

Astrakhan
7 Feb. 1918

Sevastopol
29 Dec. 1917

Simferopol
26 Jan. 1918

Novorossiysk
14 Dec. 1917

French
British

Entente fleet
British

1919–20 Geor
1919–20 Mensh

Batumi
Kars

Tiflis (Tbilisi)

Baku
15 Nov. 1917

Krasnovodsk

British

Tabriz

1918–19

N

0   200 km
0   200 miles

World War I

The "war to end all wars" failed to do just that. It brought the deaths of millions and had consequences that affected the whole world in the rest of the century.

The Causes of the Conflict

The causes of the outbreak of World War I reached back over four decades to the Franco–Prussian war of 1870–71. The French defeat included the loss of Alsace and Lorraine, and heavy war reparations of £200 million. From then on, Germany, led at this point by Otto von Bismarck, began to develop its military and industrial strength, increasing its status within the continent. As other countries watched with growing suspicion, in a diplomatic maneuver he formed the Triple Alliance with Austria-Hungary and Italy in 1882. The following year France and Russia signed the Dual Alliance, which then left Britain needing to decide its position within Europe. In 1904, the Entente Cordiale was signed between Britain and France, which then became the Triple Entente when Russia joined in August 1907. Thus, international alliances were sealed, tensions were rife and all that was required for war was a flash point.

Below: Europe's nations now had their first opportunity in forty years to cover themselves in military glory. There was a widely-held conviction that the war would all be over by Christmas. Buoyed by public confidence, young men across Europe rushed to join the fighting forces.

This finally came on June 28, 1914. Archduke Franz Ferdinand of Austria-Hungary, heir to the Hapsburg Empire, had planned a visit to the Bosnian capital, Sarajevo. He was well aware of the dangers of such a move, but was determined to win support from the Bosnians. Austria-Hungary had annexed Bosnia and Herzegovina in 1908 and Serb nationalists wanted to liberate Bosnia, which contained a large number of Serbs. Many Serbs saw this visit as deliberately provocative and a secret Serb society named the Black Hand planned an assassination attempt. This was successful when a member, Gavrilo Princip, shot both Ferdinand and his wife, Sophie. Austria-Hungary, encouraged by Germany, immediately saw this as a Serb challenge to the Hapsburg Empire and issued a 48-hour ultimatum containing many unreasonable demands. The Serbs ignored this and on July 28, the Austrians declared war on Serbia. Two days later, Russia began to mobilize to support Serbia and on August 1, Germany declared war on Russia.

Germany had always been aware that it could be forced to fight a war on both its eastern and western fronts and so the Schlieffen Plan had been devised. This

ALLIANCES ON THE EVE OF WAR, JULY 1914

Austro-German Alliance, 1879–1918

Triple Alliance, 1882–1915

Franco-Russian Alliance, 1894–1917

Triple Entente, 1907–17

Varying independence and nationalist movements sponsored by Russia, 1879–1914

Sympathetic to 'Central Powers'

Sympathetic to 'Entente Powers'

Neutrality guaranteed by United Kingdom

Neutral

Above: Women workers helping to solve the munitions crisis of 1915.
Opposite above: British marines on the march in Ostend.
Opposite below: Even when not under attack soldiers had much to endure in the trenches, which often flooded. Trench foot, a form of frostbite, was common.

was a lightning strike, designed to neutralize the French so that Germany could then concentrate on the Russians. Germany had planned to attack France through neutral Belgium, but the Belgian government disregarded an ultimatum from Germany and refused to allow German troops through the country unhindered. As Germany and Britain had originally been guarantors of Belgian neutrality, both Germany and Belgium looked to Britain for support as the British government considered its position. Finally, the Asquith government decided to honor its commitment to Belgium and in turn gave an ultimatum to Germany to withdraw from Belgium. This was ignored, and on August 4 Britain declared war on Germany.

Trench Warfare

The Germans were the first to initiate the trench lines after the Battle of the Marne in September 1914, digging in to protect themselves from Allied gunfire, while holding onto territory they had gained. The

Allies had little alternative but to follow suit and subsequent battles were played out from these sites, making them a dominant feature of the war. An area of "no man's land" covered in barbed wire would separate the two sides, with subsequent shelling turning the area into a sea of mud and craters. Very few offensive actions were successful as machine guns could fire on attacking troops; the end result was usually little gain and massive casualties. The trenches were usually about seven feet deep and six feet wide and were often waterlogged. On average it took 450 men six hours to dig 250 yards of trench, the British favoring a dogtooth pattern to minimise the destruction from shellfire. German trenches were more elaborate, much deeper and many had electricity and running water. Sandbags were used on both sides of the top to absorb any enemy bullets and steps were cut into the sides to allow soldiers to peer over when on duty. Communication trenches linked the front-line trenches to support trenches in the rear, allowing the movement of men and supplies.

The conditions were brutal with trenches infested by rats, lice, and fleas. The soldiers were frequently wet and cold and trench foot (a painful condition caused by standing in cold water or mud, resulting in dead tissue) was common. Bacterial infections led to trench mouth and soldiers had to become inured to living and fighting surrounded by corpses. Soldiers were constantly vulnerable to attack by enemy snipers and protective headgear was essential. The scaling ladders they used to climb over the top were very steep, making the men sitting targets as they tried to climb over and launch an attack on the enemy. Much of the soldiers' time was spent maintaining and repairing the trenches and on vital sentry duty. Frequently, fighting took place at night, so it was common to catch up with sleep during the day. These trenches were to provide temporary homes for millions of soldiers throughout the course of the war.

Arms

By the early twentieth century, industry was capable of mass-producing weapons and ammunition with huge improvements in their accuracy, rate of fire, and range. Breech-loading weapons along with belt-fed machine guns, quick-firing artillery, and magazine-loading rifles had been developed. Weapon technology continued to be enhanced during the war; machine guns became lighter, sub-machine guns were introduced in 1918, and long-range weapons such as the Paris Gun (with an approximate range of 80 miles) were designed.

The new Mark I tanks were used in battle for the first time in 1916. They were developed in an attempt to break the deadlock of trench warfare. Used to support the infantry, they were reasonably successful, but proved to be difficult to maneuver and prone to

mechanical problems. They housed a crew of eight but due to hot, cramped conditions often led to attacks of delirium and vomiting.

Flame throwers were first used by the Germans at Verdun in 1915. A backpack that contained compressed nitrogen and a mix of coal tar and benzine had a hose attached that was capable of emitting a stream of flames up to about 160 ft.

Germany was the first country to use chlorine gas at the second Battle of Ypres. After the release of 500 cylinders, 5,000 troops died from its deadly effects while a further 10,000 survivors were badly affected. Its psychological effect was devastating and later that year, mustard and phosgene gases were used. The Allies also began to use gas and it was estimated that it caused a total of one million deaths during the war.

Aircraft gradually became more important as the war progressed, and ultimately were used for tactical, strategic and operational purposes. During the course of the hostilities the fighter aircraft was developed with the manufacture of craft such as the Allies' Fokker E1 and the Nieuport 17, and the Germans' Fokker DVII. The British Royal Air Force was formed on April 1, 1918 to fully integrate air power into the offensives. By the end of the war aircraft had become an integrated part of military tactics. About 10,000 aircraft were used and about 50,000 airmen lost their lives, often through inexperience.

Opening Conflicts

In August 1914, the British Expeditionary Force, led by Sir John French, crossed the Channel. They met the German forces at the Battle of Mons on August 23, and although heavily outnumbered, British troops matched the challenge from the German Army. Although they failed to force them back, German forces were held in check and from this moment on the Schlieffen Plan began to unravel as Belgian and French forces moved in against German troops. Germans in the First Army under General von Kluck were forced to turn to the east of Paris to keep in contact with Germany's Second Army. By early September, the Allies had established a new front line just south of the Marne. In the Battle of the Marne, which lasted from September 5 to 10, Allied troops struck and forced the Germans to retreat to a strong position on high ground north of the River Aisne with the Allies in pursuit. However, lacking the resources to continue the pressure, the Allies dug in opposite the Germans resulting in stalemate on both fronts. The two sides then spread out laterally until the start of the month-long Battle of Ypres, which attempted to break the deadlock. October 31, the Germans broke through at Gheluvelt and, despite defending their position, the British Expeditionary Force suffered very heavy casualties. The two sides then dug in for the winter in a line that stretched from the North Sea to Switzerland, as a war that was initially expected to end swiftly turned into a war of attrition.

The Eastern Front

Meanwhile, on the eastern front, Russia had gained a foothold in East Prussia by mid-August. The Austro-Hungarian forces had proved to be very ineffective and Germany was forced to retreat. This prompted Germany to recall from retirement General von Hindenburg who, together with Eric von Ludendorff, transferred from the western front, was able to halt the Russian advance. At this point, the Russian army was split in two by the Masurian Lake from where they planned a pincer movement on the Germans. After intercepting radio messages the German Eighth Army turned upon General Samsonov's troops in the south and scored a decisive victory at the Battle of Tannenburg on August 27, 1914. 30,000 troops were killed and a further 100,000 taken prisoner. Samsonov subsequently took his own life. Hindenburg then gained another victory over General Rennenkampf's forces on September 9–10, restoring East Prussia to German hands.

The second Battle of Ypres began on April 22, 1915, with the Germans using gas for the first time. Despite chlorine's deadly effects, the Allies rallied and when the battle ended on 13 May, stalemate remained.

The Dardanelles

Turkey entered the war on the side of the Central Powers on October 29, 1914. The Allies, under Winston Churchill, First Lord of the Admiralty, planned to

Above: Troops fixing bayonets for a fresh offensive.
Opposite above: In May 1915 a truce was declared at Gallipoli for both sides to bury their dead. The summer brought many more casualties and in the autumn the wisdom of the campaign was finally questioned.
Opposite below: Philippe Pétain, who was replaced as France's military commander by Foch in March 1918.

attack the country through the Dardanelles, the narrow waterway leading from the open sea to Constantinople with the aim of forcing through a passage to their Russian allies. In February, a fleet bombarded the forts at the entrance to the Straits, but progress through the Straits was slow and three battleships were lost to mines on March 18. It was then decided to deploy land forces and on August 25, soldiers landed on the Gallipoli Peninsula from Britain, France, Australia, and New Zealand. In foul weather and on difficult terrain it proved to be a fruitless task. By November, it was clear that retreat was the only option. Fortunately troops were withdrawn successfully by January 1916, but the campaign had cost the Allies 250,000 men and Churchill resigned.

Verdun
The Battle of Verdun began on February 21, 1916. Twelve hundred guns, including the famous 42-centimeter Big Bertha, launched one of the fiercest bombardments of the entire war. Verdun was a symbol

of great national pride and the French under General Pétain were determined to defend it. Their artillery fire inflicted heavy casualties on the German ranks, and French troops were able to keep open a key road to the south of the city, which allowed through the passage of fresh soldiers and supplies. The battle raged on until June, but the Germans were then forced to scale down attacks as the British attack on the Somme, and a major Russian offensive in the east, forced the German commander to redeploy troops elsewhere. During the remainder of the year the French regained all the territory they had lost. The aggregate death toll was 700,000: French losses were marginally greater than German.

The Somme
On July 1, 1916, the Allies launched an offensive on the Somme. However, the artillery attack did not prove to be as effective as hoped against the heavily entrenched enemy, with the firing giving the enemy plenty of warning of the advance. The infantry then came under fierce attack from the Germans' Maxim machine guns and by the end of the first day there were 57,000 casualties: 20,000 of these being deaths. The battle continued well into the autumn with the Allies using tanks for the first time. These were there to support the infantry, but the Germans, after the

initial panic at seeing these vehicles, put up firm resistance, so they did not have the impact originally planned. The battle finally ended on November 19, with over 600,000 Allied and 400,000 German casualties. All that flourished on the battlefields were the poppies that were to become the symbol of the appalling losses on the Somme and in future conflicts.

Conflict at Sea

For the first two years of the war, British and German fleets had avoided a full-scale confrontation but in January 1916, Admiral Reinhard Scheer, new commander of Germany's High Sea Fleet, devised a plan to neutralize Britain's existing naval superiority. He needed to attack to avoid Germany being starved of resources and the plan aimed to split up the enemy fleet to increase his chances of victory. Britain's eastern coast was raided, which forced the British Admiral Jellicoe to deploy a battle-cruiser squadron to Rosyth. This being successful, Scheer then put the second part of his plan into action. He aimed to lure the battle cruisers into open sea by parading some of his own ships off the Norwegian coast. The squadron under Sir David Beatty duly obliged, but the entire High Seas Fleet was waiting near the German outriders. However, and unbeknown to Scheer, British Intelligence had successfully cracked German naval codes and Jellicoe was already steaming in on the attack. The Battle of Jutland began on May 31, 1916 but the *Indefatigable* and the *Queen Mary* exploded within twenty minutes of each other with the loss of 2,303 lives. The Germans were

soon closing in, having the upper hand. However, as soon as Beatty saw the German Fleet, he turned north towards Jellicoe to lure the Germans into a trap. Jellicoe had the tactical advantage and as the two fleets engaged, his ships were arranged broadside across the German line, a manoeuvre known as "crossing the T." The German fleet was heavily bombarded and Jellicoe seemed to be assured of success. However, Scheer effected a complete 180-degree turn and his ships disappeared into the smoke and confusion. He then turned them around and headed back directly towards the British line. Jellicoe decided not to risk the threat of German torpedoes and retreated. By morning the German fleet had slipped away and the Battle of Jutland was over. A total of twenty-five ships and 9,000 lives had been lost. Germany hailed it as their great victory, as their losses were smaller, but they never threatened Britain's mastery of the seas again.

Passchendaele

Field Marshal Sir Douglas Haig then planned a fresh attack on the Western Front. The Battle of Passchendaele began on June 7, 1917 with the British targeting the Messines Ridge, a key vantage point just south of Ypres that the Germans had held for two years. This was successful, and the main offensive was then launched. Although it took much longer than planned, Passchendaele finally fell on 2 November, but at the cost of 250,000 casualties. To keep up this momentum, the Allies then launched one final offensive in 1917. The Battle of Cambrai began on

20 November with over 400 tanks spearheading the attack. The German Army countered and yet again stalemate ensued.

The Russian Revolution

On the eastern front, the Russian Revolution, during the winter of 1916–17, resulted in the abdication of the Tsar in March. The new provisional government had launched a disastrous military offensive on Galicia and the Russian Army began to disintegrate. There was an Armistice between Germany and the Soviet Union in December. German troops were deployed to the west, as they needed to launch an offensive against Britain and France before American troops arrived. Operation Michael was launched on March 21 with the main point of attack between Arras and St Quentin. The German army swept across the Somme battlefield and quickly took Peronne, Bapaume, and Albert, with the British Third and Fifth Armies bearing the brunt of the assault. On 26 March, Marshal Ferdinand Foch became the de facto Supreme Allied Commander on the Western Front. He quickly realized the need to defend Amiens, a key German target. During the following days the Allies strength grew and the German line became overstretched and weak. The advance ended on April 8. Ludendorff tried further initiatives but, by now, American soldiers were flooding the area and German casualties were steadily increasing. On August 8, a combined Allied force launched the Battle of Amiens, backed up by 400 tanks, 2,000 guns and assistance from the recently formed Royal Air Force. The Hindenburg Line was finally breached on September 29 but by then Ludendorff and the Kaiser knew the war needed to be brought to an end. Gradually Germany's allies began to fall and, on November 11, 1918, Germany finally surrendered.

The United States Enters the War

At the beginning of the war the United States had no overseas alliances and on August 19 1914, Woodrow Wilson declared a policy of strict neutrality. In December 1914, General Leonard Wood helped to form the National Security League and argued for a need to increase the size of the US Army. Wilson responded by increasing the army from 98,000 to 140,000. The United States entered the war in April 1917. Conscription was rapidly introduced requiring all males between 21 and 30 to register; four million were ultimately drafted with half of these serving overseas.

Above: The British fleet, viewed from the deck of HMS Audacious. *It was widely believed that Britain still reigned supreme on the seas, although more than a century had passed since Trafalgar.*
Opposite page: The Somme battlefield takes on an eerily bleak quality as winter brings a brief hiatus to hostilities.

Prior to their involvement, the US had assisted the Allies by exporting goods but on February 1, Germany launched a plan of unrestricted submarine warfare. Wilson immediately broke off diplomatic relations with Germany and the country then adopted a policy of "armed neutrality" for two months. By March, three US cargo ships had been sunk and the Zimmerman Telegram had been published: British spies had intercepted a message sent from Germany's Foreign Secretary, Arthur Zimmerman, to Mexico whereby Germany offered to back Mexico in attempt to regain territory in Texas and Arizona in return for Mexican support for Germany. These events intensified many Americans' desire to enter the war and on April 2 Wilson sought approval from Congress to do so; the decision was ratified four days later. The United States army was rapidly mobilized.

The Treaty of Versailles

The Paris Peace Conference began on January 19, 1919 and involved thirty-two nations that represented

Iceland
to Denmark

EUROPE IN 1919

Norwegian Sea

0   200 km
0   200 miles

N

Faeroe Islands
to Denmark

N O R W A Y

Oslo

S W E D E N

Stockholm

F I N L A N D

Helsinki

Leningrad

Tallinn

ESTONIA

Riga

L A T V I A

Baltic Sea

LITHUANIA

Kaunas

Königsberg

U . S . S . R .

North Sea

Glasgow • Edinburgh

UNITED KINGDOM

Liverpool

Birmingham

Amsterdam

Bristol

London

Calais

DENMARK

Copenhagen

Hamburg

Danzig
*free city under
League of Nations*

**East
Prussia**

Warsaw

Brest Litovsk

NETHERLANDS

Berlin

G E R M A N Y

P O L A N D

Brussels

BELGIUM

R. Rhine

Frankfurt

SAAR
*autonomous under
League of Nations*

Prague

CZECHOSLOVAKIA

Cracow

Lvov

Paris

Orléans

F R A N C E

Vienna

A U S T R I A

H U N G A R Y

Budapest

R O M A N I A

Lyon

Bern

SWITZ.

Milan

Genoa

Trieste

Venice

Adriatic Sea

Bucharest

Belgrade

R. Danube

YUGOSLAVIA

BULGARIA

Bordeaux

*ATLANTIC
OCEAN*

Marseille

ANDORRA

Barcelona

I T A L Y

Rome

Sofia

T U R K E Y

ALBANIA

PORTUGAL

Lisbon

Madrid

S P A I N

Balearic Is.

Naples

GREECE

*Aegean
Sea*

Smyrna

Cádiz

Alicante

Athens

Gibraltar
to Great Britain

Almería

Tangier
international
zone

M e d i t e r r a n e a n

*Italian
occupied*

Morocco
to France

A l g e r i a
to France

Tunisia
to France

S e a

Libya

75 percent of the world's population. The defeated countries were not invited and the majority of negotiations were done by the United States, led by Woodrow Wilson, the United Kingdom, represented by David Lloyd George, and France, led by Georges Clemenceau. Woodrow Wilson brought to the negotiations his Fourteen Points, which aimed to create new states with common cultures and languages while reducing arms and creating a new League of Nations to oversee any issues of conflict. However, it proved impossible to create any such states and France and Britain were more intent on reducing Germany's strength. After nine days of talks, five separate treaties emerged, one for each of the defeated nations. All the treaties incorporated the League of Nations covenant, which many countries joined that had not been in the original conflict. The Treaty of Versailles was finally signed between the Allies and Germany on June 28, 1919. Its conditions were harsh, with Alsace-Lorraine returned to France and most of East Prussia integrated into the reconstituted Poland, which also meant Germany lost its access to the sea at Danzig. The Allies were to occupy the Rhineland for fifteen years. The German army was capped at 100,000 and they were no longer allowed to maintain an air force or a U-boat fleet. A clause was also inserted whereby Germany admitted their guilt in causing the war and reparations of £6,600 million were put in place. Although a schedule of payments was agreed, these debts were crippling and were allowed to lapse in the 1920s. At the end of negotiations Germany signed under protest but the United States refused to ratify the treaty.

The Effects of the War

Far from being settled and peaceful, post-conflict Europe was beset by economic hardship and border disputes. The war had left Britain alone close to bankruptcy; the country's final bill was £10 million, of which £7 million was borrowed. The continent's redrawn map left all of the newly formed states with disaffected minorities and Germany continued to remain a problem, having been wounded but not dismembered. The peace terms were punitive enough to provoke an acrimonious response but as events would later show, Germany was not permanently shackled in the way that France had wanted. In 1919, some prescient voices were already warning that the war had not been concluded, merely suspended. Far from being "a war to end all wars," the 1914–18 conflict would eventually be regarded as a prelude to World War II. Sixty-five million men had been mobilized throughout the world and the grim reality of this attritional warfare was that over 10 million had lost their lives.

Below: British and French leaders, pictured during the postwar peace talks. Clemenceau (second left) and Lloyd George (third left) believed that Germany bore full responsibility for starting the war.

The Great Depression

The world's most severe economic crisis, the Great Depression caused massive social, economic, and political changes which would contribute to the start of the Second World War.

The Wall Street Crash

The international economy had never properly recovered since the strain put on it by the First World War and preconditions for the Great Depression were well underway by the time the US stock market on Wall Street collapsed in 1929. Though the United States itself had experienced growth in the 1920s, this was waning by the end of the decade. Improved technology in the countryside had led to increased agricultural productivity, and supply now outweighed demand. This inevitably led to a fall in prices, which impoverished farmers, who could no longer cover the cost of production leading to increased rural debts. This in turn led to unemployment and internal migration, with many people abandoning the land.

Meanwhile, the US stock market had witnessed huge rises in investment in the 1920s, pushing stock prices to record heights. Some forecasters predicted that price rises were unsustainable and a collapse was imminent; this soon became evident and the hysterical selling of stocks occurred, with investors ordering their brokers to sell whatever the price. Events cascaded across America as most investors followed suit. With sharp decreases in funding, companies had to cut costs through massive lay-offs. One result of the massive banking crisis was spiraling unemployment; more than a third of the workforce lost their jobs.

The Effects Spread

As the American economy was the largest in the world, the Depression in America was bound to spread abroad. American government and businesses halted foreign spending and recalled loans, which had been extended to help the world recover from the effects of the Great War. Germany, in particular, was heavily dependent on American loans; they were the only means it had of covering the debt it had incurred as a result of the Versailles treaty agreed after the end of the Great War. In addition, the knock-on effects meant that countries which supplied America and other industrialized nations were badly hit by the drop in production. Soon the whole world was gripped by Depression; only Soviet Russia could remain aloof.

The Effects of the Slump

The initial effect of the slump was for the world to descend into protectionism. The drying up of free trade had greater implications for some countries than others: while Britain and France were able to create protective trading blocs around their empires, countries such as Japan and Germany had no such empires to fall back on. These two countries in particular were highly dependent on imported raw materials, which they could no longer afford, as they lacked sufficient resources of their own—Germany, for example, suffered a drop in output of some 50 percent. They therefore suffered the Depression most acutely and resentment at "Great Power Protectionism" developed into extreme nationalism. This was to have severe repercussions later in the 1930s when the world would once again descend into war.

From Laissez-faire to Intervention

Until the Great Depression the prevailing belief was that governments should pursue a laissez-faire approach to the economy, that is to say a policy of non-intervention. With the mass unemployment and poverty that the Great Depression brought came associated social problems, such as crime and alcoholism. These were problems for the whole of society; not least was the need to feed and clothe the escalating ranks of the many who found themselves quite literally "on the bread line."

Now that these issues had engulfed much of society, governments were called upon to help alleviate the suffering by creating jobs. This required a revolution in the extent to which governments involved themselves in economies. Across the world interventionist policies, traditionally associated with the Soviet model, were now being followed. In the United States, Roosevelt and the Democrats offered the "New Deal," introducing work-creation schemes and helping the state regulate the US economy. In Britain a National Government was formed, comprising all the main political parties, which began attempts to reinvigorate the economy there. Across Europe, from Estonia to Portugal, people saw a need for forceful governments which could intervene and, hopefully, turn things around.

The Consequences

The Great Depression can thus be seen as contributing to the increase in nationalism during the first decades of the twentieth century. The economic failure of the 1920s and 30s provided the more extreme political parties on both the left and the right with popular support that they had not enjoyed before. High unemployment and the loss of confidence in the economic policies of previous leaders led people to accept alternative governments which advocated more nationalistic and economically isolated means of stimulating their economies. Governments began to adopt approaches such as beginning large-scale public works projects as a means of getting the labor force

Above: A breadline at the intersection of 6th Avenue and 42nd Street in New York City during the Great Depression.
Opposite: October 29, 1929: Workers flood the streets in a panic following the Black Tuesday stock market crash on Wall Street, New York City.

back into employment. By 1933 over 36 per cent of the workforce was unemployed in Germany, for instance, and it was to address this that the German Autobahn (highway) system was built. There was also an increased emphasis on rearmament and many of the unemployed found themselves either working in armament factories or conscripted into the armed forces. With this large-scale remilitarization combined with growing militant nationalism, international relations became increasingly precarious, and the situation would continue to worsen until events in 1939 took over.

The Spanish Civil War

Political divisions in Spain finally resulted in the Spanish Civil War which split opinion across the world, and became a rehearsal for World War II.

The Establishment of the Republic

The Spanish Civil War arose out of developments following the collapse of the dictatorship of Primo de Rivera in 1930 when a power vacuum ensued. Elections were held and, as the right had been tainted with the failings of the dictatorship, the socialists were able to win over even the support of some of the middle classes to ensure victory. The socialists had blamed the king for allowing the dictatorship, and the election was widely viewed as a referendum on the monarchy; on April 14, 1931 King Alfonso XIII went into exile, and the Republic was formed. As a result of

Below: General Franco was appointed generalissimo of Nationalist Spain and head of state in October 1936.
Opposite: Civilians man the barricades in Barcelona during the Civil War.

socialist rule, the right wing in Spain recovered and united those who disliked socialism—including the army, big businesses, and the monarchists—into a coalition. The Republic also made an enemy of the Catholic Church by secularizing education and dissolving the Jesuit order.

The Collapse of the Republic

Many expectations had been laid upon the Republic and while any reform dismayed the right, the slow pace of change angered many on the left. The peasants, for example, lost enthusiasm for the government as they felt the pace of land reform was too slow, and the failure to redistribute land was compounded by a drought resulting in a bad harvest. Faced with the realities of power and the need to appease all interest groups, the government—though it had its roots in a series of workers' parties—was coming to be viewed by workers as essentially bourgeois. Attempts to democratize the army to ensure equal access for all meant that any support the military had initially given the socialists also vanished. The right regained power through the ballot box in 1933.

This produced a fierce reaction in Catalonia, which feared that the new government would try to encroach on the autonomy the region had gained during the socialist tenure. There was a general strike and eventually Catalonia declared independence on October 6, 1934; this was brutally suppressed by the government in Madrid. Many left-wing groups responded by uniting into the Popular Front and the left once again won a general election, in 1936. The Popular Front was united by a conviction that both the constitution of 1931 and parliamentary democracy must be upheld but the coalition was weak, fractured as it was between extremists and moderates.

A similar coalition, but right-wing and comprising conservatives, monarchists, and a Catholic confederation, had also developed. These Nationalists were angered by their defeat and enraged that the Popular Front had replaced the right-wing president, Zamora, with their own candidate, ex-Prime Minister Azana. The military and the right conspired to overthrow the elected government and when, on

July 18, 1936, the monarchist leader Calvo Sotelo was assassinated it formed the pretext the conspirators were waiting for. Their rebellion was launched. As a result of this rebellion, the army on mainland Spain was disbanded by the government. Many escaped and joined the rest of the army stationed in Spanish Morocco.

The Civil War

On July 19, 1936, the right-wing General Franco, who had been previously exiled by Azana to the Canaries, arrived in Morocco to assume command and use the territory as a springboard to capture the mainland. His troops were airlifted across the Mediterranean by the German and Italian air forces, as both countries had taken the decision to intervene militarily on behalf of Franco's forces, representing as they did the right-wing Nationalist coalition.

A Fascist takeover in Spain would benefit both Germany and Italy as it would weaken France's position on the continent, and also provide an excellent training ground for their new weaponry and conscripts. The German Luftwaffe's aerial bombardment of the Basque city of Guernica in April 1937, immortalized in Picasso's painting, instilled terror across Europe, as the new, devastating potential of modern mechanized warfare was displayed for the first time.

While Germany and Italy supported the Nationalists, Britain and France failed to come to the aid of the Republic. Anglo-French non-intervention can be seen in terms of a wider general policy which became known as Appeasement. Neither country was in a position to challenge Germany in Spain, or anywhere else, and particularly did not wish to antagonize that newly-powerful country on behalf of a left-wing regime with which London in particular felt little ideological sympathy. However, the German attack on Guernica did encourage both Paris and London to improve their own anti-aircraft defenses in case of a future war.

As the democracies had abandoned the Republic, it was forced to accept aid from the Soviet Union to counterbalance Fascist aid to Franco's Nationalists. This served to divide the Republic between extremists, who welcomed Soviet assistance, and moderates who did not. Such divisions filtered into the military campaign and eventually caused the Republicans to lose Barcelona. Soviet aid did not come cheaply and the entire Spanish gold reserve, estimated at $518 million, was shipped to Moscow as credit for armaments. The Republic was also assisted by the International Brigades, individuals who shared ideological or political sympathies with the Republicans, and traveled to Spain to defend democracy or socialism. Their assistance was courageous but far from enough to save the Republic.

The End of the War

In April 1939, after almost three years of civil war, the Republicans agreed to an unconditional surrender. Madrid had fallen in March and Britain and France had recognized Franco's Nationalist regime in February. The outcome of the Spanish Civil War was essentially dictated by the differing levels of foreign assistance. While the Nationalists were supported by both Germany and Italy, the Republic's dependence on costly Soviet aid undermined, rather than enhanced, its chances of success. In the end the Soviet Union ended its assistance and Franco's victory was assured, though the Civil War left a bitter legacy. Spain was able to remain neutral in the Second World War, allowing Franco to consolidate control, a repressive control which he retained until his death in 1975.

Germany and the Rise of Hitler

Germany in the 1920s was a breeding ground of extremism, enabling Hitler's rise to power and the development of one of the most repressive regimes the world has seen.

The Weimar Republic

The government of Germany between the Second and Third Reichs, between the rule of the Kaiser and that of Hitler, is known as the Weimar Republic, after the town in which it first convened. Its tenure was shaped by the Treaty of Versailles which was widely unpopular in Germany, because of the huge war indemnity Germany was forced to pay and the war guilt which Germans had been forced to admit. People grew increasingly weary of the limitations the treaty placed on their freedom; they had been a great power and now they had to face the loss of their colonies and their military, French occupation of the Rhur, and severe inflation.

By the late 1920s many of these hurdles had been overcome. Under Gustav Streseman hyperinflation was ended, France had to withdraw and Germany joined the League of Nations. By 1924 the Dawes Plan worked out a better repayment plan for the war debt and later, under the Young Plan, the sum total was reduced; by 1932 a moratorium on reparations payments was announced. This period was known as the "Golden Era;" however, by the end of the 1920s Streseman had died and the territory given up at Versailles had not been regained. Extremist parties were able to tap into popular dislike of the treaty, while democratic Weimar politicians were tainted with collaboration.

Germany and the Wall Street Crash

On October 29, 1929 the American stock market collapsed and reverberations were felt across the world; American loans were recalled and trade dried up as the Great Powers returned to protectionist policies. Germany's economic lifeline was vanishing

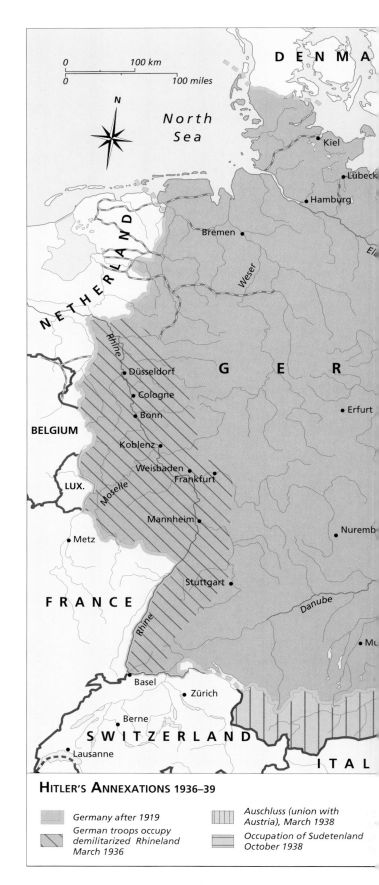

HITLER'S ANNEXATIONS 1936–39

| | Germany after 1919 | | Auschluss (union with Austria), March 1938 |
| | German troops occupy demilitarized Rhineland March 1936 | | Occupation of Sudetenland October 1938 |

SWEDEN

Bornholm

B a l t i c   S e a

Danzig
Free
State

Memel
Territory

LITHUANIA

Königsberg

*Annexed by
Lithuania
October 1939*

Vilna Stri

tock

Stettin

Danzig

*E a s t
P r u s s i a*

U.S.S.R.

Oder

Berlin

Bydgoszcz

Bialystock

zig

A   N   Y

Vistula

Warsaw

Bug

Brest-Litovsk

Dresden

Warta

Poznan

Lodz

P   O   L   A   N   D

Lublin

*Final partition
line established
30 September 1939*

Breslau

Vistula

Lvov

B o h e m i a

Prague

Vitara

Dneister

M o r a v i a

S l o v a k i a

R u t h e n i a

Linz

Danube

Vienna

Bratislava

Salzburg

A   U   S   T   R   I   A

Debrecen

R   O   M   A   N   I   A

Budapest

H   U   N   G   A   R   Y

Graz

Tisza

Czechoslovakian border 1919–38		Moravian territory to Poland October 1938	Protectorate of Slovakia territory to Hungary Nov. 1938	Conquest of western Poland September 1939
Formerly Czechoslovakia occupied March 1939		Memel territory to Germany March 1939	Czechoslovakian territory to Hungary March 1939	Polish territory seized by USSR September 1939

and so too was its relative stability. The Weimar government, now under Heinrich Brüning, pursued a policy of austerity, which did little to ameliorate rising unemployment, and people increasingly turned to extremist parties. On the left was the German Communist Party, the KPD, and on the far right was Adolf Hitler's National Socialist German Workers' Party, the NSDAP, also known as the Nazis. The Nazis were adamant supporters of immediate revision of the Treaty of Versailles and were inspired by the idea of creating a "*volksgemeinschaft,*" a community of German-blooded peoples, or "Aryans." They promised to create jobs by increasing public spending and trimming the workforce of groups they considered to be "undesirable."

Hitler Rises to Power

In the wake of the Depression, support for the Nazi Party increased and they came from nowhere to win 18 percent of the seats in the Reichstag. Farmers, conservatives, and the middle classes accounted for this boost. The Nazis then targeted workers, leading to greater success in the June 1932 elections, when they became the biggest party. Alarmed at this, the previous chancellor, Fritz von Papen, persuaded President Hindenburg to give Hitler the post of chancellor. He hoped Hitler would prove easily controllable, and that the influence of the rest of the party would diminish. Hitler assumed the chancellorship on January 30, 1933.

Hitler's Consolidation of Power

In the March 1933 elections the Nazis gained 44 per cent of the vote and by absorbing another far-right party, the DNVP, secured a majority in the Reichstag. From this platform Hitler was able to pass the Enabling Act, through which the Nazi government became the main legislative body. The act allowed Hitler to ban opposition groups, although the Nazi Party's main rival, the Communists, had already been eliminated under the Reichstag Fire Decree of January 1933. This decree was in response to an arson attack on the Reichstag in which the Nazis were able to implicate Communist agitators. It led to a reduction in Communist support in favor of the Nazis, explaining their increased success in the March elections.

Disquiet over Nazi policies was resolved through intimidation carried out by a comprehensive secret police, ranging from the infamous Gestapo down to civilian informants. The next step was the so-called "Night of the Long Knives" where Hitler turned on the SA, the Nazi militia, because he feared a coup if they became too powerful. On the night of July 1, 1934, he purged the SA and arrested its leader, Ernst Rohm. The last obstruction to Hitler's supreme rule was removed on August 2, 1934 when Hindenburg died. Presidential powers were merged with those of the chancellor to form a new role, the Führer. Hitler's domestic control was supreme; in foreign policy, prominent conservatives in the military and the foreign office still had to be appeased.

Expansion of the Reich

Hitler initially moved cautiously, making a non-aggression pact with Poland and agreeing to negotiate with other European powers over disarmament. He eventually managed to consolidate his control by promoting party members to key positions in the foreign office and the military; most importantly replacing the non-Nazi Foreign Minister Neurath with the faithful Ribbentrop in 1937, and removing the conservative generals Bloomberg and Fritsch.

As the 1930s progressed the external situation also became increasingly favorable for Hitler. America was still recovering from the Depression and was not involved in European concerns. In Italy, Mussolini had warmed to the Reich since Hitler had renounced claims to South Tyrol; ideological similarities gave rise to cooperation. The Soviet Union was concerned with domestic matters; Stalin was pursuing industrialization and collectivisation and the purges had severely undermined the Red Army. France was verging on a political crisis which often led it to follow Britain in foreign policy, and Britain was set on a policy of appeasement. Therefore the Great Powers were not in a position to deter Hitler's expansionist ambitions.

Appeasement

Chamberlain met Hitler at Munich in September 1938, by which time Germany had already annexed Austria in a union forbidden under the Treaty of Versailles. Chamberlain left Munich agreeing to German annexation of the Sudeten areas of Czechoslovakia, which had a sizeable German population. Such a move, Chamberlain announced, was a guarantee of "peace in our time." The choice to adopt appeasement was carefully calculated in view of Britain's military and economic weakness and its overstretched commitment of limited resources to its vast empire. Furthermore, pacifist public opinion played a strong role; this was conditioned by the memories of the First World War and a belief that German demands for a revision of the Treaty of Versailles were reasonable.

Hitler Reneges on Munich

The occupation of the Sudetenland was completed in October 1939, and the remainder of Czechoslovakia was outflanked by the Reich. The following March, Hitler reneged on the Munich Agreement and invaded it. The French were in no position to fulfil, their guarantee of support to the Czechs, and Britain claimed its guarantee could not be activated under the circumstances. However, the British public was incensed that Hitler had lied to them; instead of appeasement, people now demanded action, and Chamberlain was forced to offer guarantees to uphold the sovereignties of Poland, Romania, and Greece— should Hitler invade, Britain would declare war. On September 1 Hitler invaded Poland, and two days later Europe was again at war.

Nazi Domestic Policy

Social policy in the Third Reich was based on the need for cultural purification and the creation of a national community. Young people were indoctrinated through state-controlled education and youth organizations; boys were prepared for war and girls for a life in the home. Nazi society was patriarchal; women were expected to stay at home and raise children.

Anything, from artwork to human beings, that did not meet Nazi social or cultural standards was condemned. Abstract art was branded degenerate, while certain books and films were burned and banned. Any humans of undesirable ethnic or social backgrounds also came under criticism. The Nazis embarked on the T-4 Euthanasia and Compulsory Sterilization campaigns to ensure that the German race remained free from "imperfections" by murdering or sterilizing those with physical or mental disabilities. However, the euthanasia programme was halted owing to the weight of public criticism.

The Nazi Party was resolutely anti-Semitic; it claimed that Germany had a Jewish problem and played on traditional propaganda to encourage persecution. The Nuremberg Laws revoked the citizenship of German Jews and other racial policies restricted their life further. The Jewish community was subjected to increasing persecution, but Kristallnacht ("night of broken glass") on November 9, 1938 can be singled out as the first nationwide attack. It was in response to the assassination of a German diplomat in Paris by a Jew; almost all of Germany's synagogues were damaged and many Jews were rounded up and deported to concentration camps.

Below: German troops in Berlin swear an oath of allegiance to Adolf Hitler in 1934.

The Second World War

The Second World War was the biggest and worst military conflagration ever known, involving countries all over the world and causing millions of deaths.

The Outbreak of War

Guarantees to protect the sovereignties of Poland, Greece, and Romania on the part of Britain and France came under severe pressure when, on August 23, 1939, Stalin and Hitler signed a non-aggression pact. This effectively annulled the risk of the Soviet Union coming to the defence of its Polish neighbor, should Germany attack. Germany then renewed its demands for lands in the "Polish Corridor," gambling on being able to negotiate with Britain and France not to pursue their pledges to defend Poland.

Throughout late August 1939 the prospect of war became increasingly likely. As Germany mobilized on its border with Poland, Britain and France began calling up reservists, moving national treasures to places of safekeeping and, on August 31, the evacuation of millions of British children to places of safety began.

At 5.45 am on the morning of September 1, the first of a contingent of 1,250,000 German troops invaded Poland, following heavy aerial bombardment. Fast-moving mechanized armored divisions, supported by combat aircraft, moved swiftly east from the German–Polish border and south from East Prussia. Polish forces, unprepared for this type of warfare, found it difficult to retaliate and within days the German Luftwaffe had control of the skies and the Polish railway system was out of commission.

For two days Britain and France attempted, via diplomatic channels, to call a halt to this attack on Poland, each sending an ultimatum to the Nazi government to withdraw its troops or else face war with the two most powerful nations in Europe. Britain's prime minister, Neville Chamberlain, had been hesitant to issue an ultimatum, aware of the consequences of Germany's refusal to comply. However, pressure from the House of Commons and members of his own Cabinet saw the delivery of the ultimatum at 9.00 am on Sunday, September 3.

When, two hours later, at 11.00 am, it was clear that Germany would not accede to British demands, Chamberlain made a radio broadcast, announcing that "This country is now at war with Germany." The French sent a similar ultimatum during the day and at 5.00 pm that evening France too declared war on Germany. The following day French troops crossed the German frontier. The Second World War had begun.

The "Phoney War"

The declaration of war on September 3, 1939 saw a flurry of activity in both Britain and France. Their regular armies were mobilized and more reservists

Below: The Parliamentary Home Guard is inspected by Winston Churchill.

called up. Civil defence precautions, devised earlier in the year, were put into place and major evacuation plans, begun days before the outbreak of war, gained momentum. Hundreds of thousands of children and vulnerable adults were moved from the major cities and towns in Britain to safer areas where they could be protected from the physical effects of aerial bombardment.

On September 5 US President Roosevelt declared America's intentions not to become involved in the war, but to try to broker peace talks. He also stated that none of the warring parties would be able to purchase weapons from the US, a position modified just two months later when Congress agreed to sell weapons to the Allies. Later in the war, in March 1941, the Lend and Lease Bill allowed Britain to be supplied with American weapons on the understanding that they would be paid for once the war was over.

In Europe there was little actual fighting throughout the winter of 1939–40. By the second week of September 1939 troops of the British Expeditionary Force had crossed the Channel to meet up with French forces; they moved to defend the Belgian border. The legacy of the First World War, "the war to end all wars," together with the policy of Appeasement, meant that these soldiers were poorly equipped and ill-trained, unready for battle. Nevertheless, they dug in and waited. For several months, neither side mounted any major offensives and this, together with the fact that there was also little activity in the air war, earned this period the soubriquet of the "Phoney War." Only at sea was there any activity; attacks from German submarines— U-boats—and magnetic mines threatened Allied merchant shipping and challenged Britain's Royal Navy, at that time the dominant military fleet in the world.

Blitzkrieg

On land it was not until April 9, 1940 that the German High Command made any moves to break the relative stalemate of the Phoney War. Attacks on Denmark and Norway were swiftly followed by attacks on the Low Countries, and then on France itself. This blitzkrieg or "lightning war" saw major defeats of Allied troops: 2,000 German soldiers trained in winter warfare forced the withdrawal of a 13,000-strong Allied force at

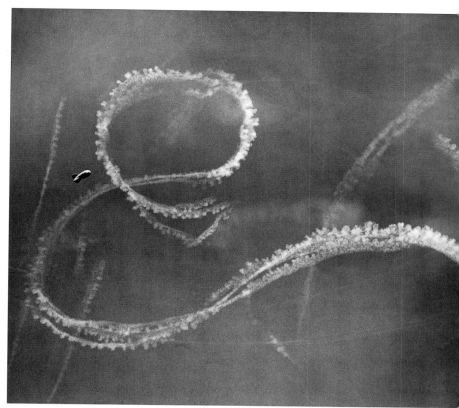

Above: Daytime dogfights marked by vapor trails as British fighters engage the Luftwaffe during the Blitz.

Trondheim in Norway and, most famously, the German advance necessitated the evacuation of 338,226 men under Allied command from the northern French beaches of Dunkirk between May 28 and June 3, 1940.

By the time of the retreat from Dunkirk, Germany had occupied Norway, Denmark, Holland, Belgium and Luxembourg. In rescuing their own troops and others such as the Free Polish Army from France, Britain had a measure of success, surviving to fight another day. However, French troops were left to fight the might of the highly trained and well equipped German military machine as it launched an all-out attack on the country. On June 22, France surrendered to Germany and Britain, protected only by its island status, was left to fight alone.

The momentous events of the spring of 1940 had profound political effects in Britain as well as continental Europe. Chamberlain was forced to resign his premiership as a result of his failure to prevent the occupation of large areas of Western Europe and on May 10 Winston Churchill took over as prime minister, at the head of a coalition government.

The Battle of Britain

Sensing the advantage gained after the retreat from Dunkirk, Hitler made plans for an invasion of Britain. The plan, codenamed "Operation Sea Lion," was to land troops by sea on September 15, 1940, the tides being most favorable on that date. In order for troop ships to land unharried by any air attack, the German Luftwaffe needed to destroy Britain's Royal Air Force. So began the Battle of Britain: two military air forces locked in aerial battles throughout the summer of 1940.

At the start of the battle, the Luftwaffe—with 2,800 aircraft stationed in France, Belgium, Holland, and Norway—outnumbered the Royal Air Force by four to one. Germany, having fought in the Spanish Civil War, had more combat-experienced pilots and first-rate aircraft in the Messerschmitt 109, the Messerschmitt 110, and the Junkers "Stuka" dive-bomber. Although fewer in number, RAF Fighter Command, under the leadership of Air Chief Marshall Sir Hugh Dowding, were well served with the Hawker Hurricane and the Supermarine Spitfire. British fliers also had the advantage of being closer to their airfields and battling over their own country. If they had to bale out or land a damaged plane, the flier and the machine could usually be restored to operational fitness; German pilots and airplanes downed over Britain were lost to Luftwaffe Command.

By the date set for the invasion the RAF had lost 915 planes, the Luftwaffe, 1733. Unable to provide aerial cover for invading troops, Hitler called off his invasion.

War in the Air

With the abandonment of the invasion of Britain, other platforms in the German High Command's tactics came to the fore. As part of Germany's invasion plan, air attacks on London had been an important part of the strategy to defeat and destroy Britain's Royal Air Force. However, attacks on the capital city were also intended to have a symbolic effect. That Germany could attack the seat of government and the administrative heart of the British nation, the Commonwealth and the Empire was an immensely powerful message.

The first of a series of aerial attacks on London began on September 7, 1940; these lasted, with unbroken regularity, for fifty-six days, a period which became known as the Blitz. Initially the raids took place during the day and night, but Luftwaffe losses were large and after a week the bulk of the raids took place under cover of darkness. Although the capital city suffered bombing virtually every night until May 1941, all of Britain's major towns and cities were within range of German bombers, and many of them suffered intense bombing raids. An air raid on the midland town of Coventry in November 1940 marked a change in the tactics of the German High Command; Britain's industrial base was targeted in an attempt to destroy the means by which the country could continue to prosecute the war. Birmingham, Sheffield,

WORLD WAR II AXIS EXPANSION 1938–42

- Germany, 1937
- Added to the Reich to 1939 and conquered by end 1940
- Axis satellites, 1939–44
- Eastern territories and Balkans conquered, 1941
- → Axis invasions 1939–42
- → Soviet attacks, 1940
- → Allied landing in Greece, withdrawal to Crete then Egypt, 1941
- Conquered, 1942
- Controlled by Vichy, 1942
- Allied controlled, late 1942
- Neutral states
- Major Allied convey route

North Cape

Norwegian Sea

Narvik

Arctic Circle

Luleå

FINLAND

NORWAY

SWEDEN

Oslo

Helsinki

Stockholm

Leningrad

Baltic Sea

DENMARK

Lost to Axis 1942

Moscow

Königberg

East Prussia

SOVIET UNION

Hamburg

Berlin

Warsaw

POLAND

Kursk

GERMANY

Frankfurt

Prague

CZECHO SLOVAKIA

Kiev

Stalingrad

TH.

Munich

Vienna

Budapest

HUNGARY

Aug. 1940 to Hungary

ROMANIA

Caspian Sea

Bern

AUSTRIA

SWITZ. Geneva

Milan

Venice

Bucharest

R. Danube

Ar Se

Genoa

YUGOSLAVIA

Belgrade

Sofia

Black Sea

Adriatic Sea

BULGARIA

Corsica

Rome

ITALY

ALBANIA

Istanbul

TURKEY

PER (IR

Sardinia

GREECE

Aegean Sea

Taranto

Athens

Cyprus

SYRIA

IRAQ

terranean

Sicily

Lebanon

Tunis

Crete

KU

Malta to Britain

Sea

Palestine

Trans-Jordan

Tripoli

Benghazi

Alexandria

SAUDI ARABIA

Libya to Italy

EGYPT

Manchester, Glasgow and other centers for the production of aircraft, military vehicles, weapons, and munitions suffered devastating raids. So too did ports like Southampton, Bristol, and Liverpool as the naval dockyards and ships of the Royal Navy and merchant fleets were targeted.

Aerial Warfare—Retaliatory Raids

British bombing of German cities began at the beginning of September 1940. Initially the raids were in retaliation for attacks on British cities. Hamburg, Berlin, and Munich all suffered bombing by the Royal Air Force in this period. As German raids on Britain became more intense, British Bomber Command's attacks became more severe. Public opinion in Britain was hugely supportive of such tactics and when the raid on Coventry destroyed its medieval cathedral and much of the city center, the RAF dropped 2,000 bombs on Hamburg two days later. However, in March 1942 a change in the tactics employed by Bomber Command, led by the newly appointed Air Chief Marshall Sir Arthur "Bomber" Harris, meant that RAF raids were no longer simply retaliatory. Bombing raids were carried out on the Baltic ports and industrialized areas, such as the Ruhr valley, in a bid

to destroy Germany's manufacturing base which provided the weapons and munitions with which to progress the war.

As Germany prepared for an assault on the USSR in June 1941, bombing in Britain petered out. Air raids by the Luftwaffe continued, but they were infrequent. It was not until April 1942 that a new air assault on Britain was launched. In response to the effects of the devastating bombing of German industrial areas and ports by the RAF, the Luftwaffe launched a new offensive. This time, instead of targeting major industrial centers, less heavily protected towns and cities were chosen in an attempt to cause most public distress. These towns appear to have been selected from their entries in Baedeker's travel guide to Britain and the subsequent raids became known as the "Baedeker raids". Consequently, the targets included some of the most beautiful and historic towns in Britain—Exeter, Bath, Norwich, and York.

Aerial Warfare—"Terror Bombing"

Aerial bombardment continued to be a major tool in the weaponry of both sides. With US entry to the war in December 1941, the Allies had huge resources to call on in the air war, and from the beginning of 1943, the Allies' change in tactics, first seen in March 1942, was intensified. A policy aimed at the total destruction of Germany's industrial base was adopted.

Britain's Royal Air Force, equipped with night radar, carried out raids under cover of darkness, which were followed up by high-risk daytime raids flown by the US Air Force. Larger and more destructive bombs, and bigger aircraft, able to carry greater bomb loads, were developed, as well as the "bouncing bomb" which had the ability to skim the surface of a body of water before sinking and exploding. These bombs, designed in Britain by the engineer Barnes Wallis, were utilized in raids on the Ruhr dams in May 1943, when the Mohne and Eder dams were breached.

However, the policy of destruction of Germany's manufacturing base developed, under the guidance of Bomber

Above: German bombers attacking over Britain.

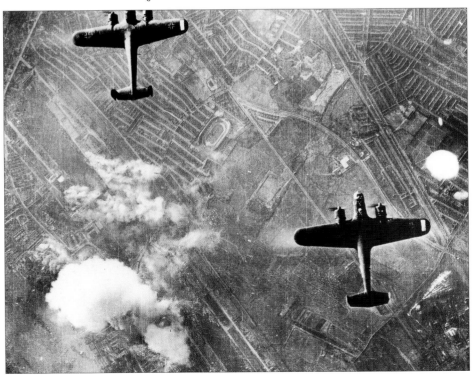

Above: Members of the German Safety Service tackle a blaze caused by incendiary bombs dropped on Berlin.

Command's Sir Arthur Harris, into a policy of "terror bombing" in an attempt to coerce the German public into suing for peace. This policy saw its apotheosis in the attack on the beautiful and historically important German city of Dresden in February 1945. By night, 800 RAF Lancaster bombers attacked the city, followed by more than 400 USAF B-17s during the daylight hours. As the city's population was swollen by people who believed it to be a safe area, it has always been difficult to give exact numbers of those killed but it is generally accepted that at least 35,000 died in the firestorm that swept through and destroyed the city.

Terror bombing was, however, not confined to the Allies. In June 1944 the first of Germany's pilotless bombs landed in southern England. The V1 "flying bombs" were launched from bases in northern France. Without a piloted plane to shoot down, these bombs, nicknamed buzz bombs or doodlebugs, seemed almost invincible and struck fear into the British public. As German bases in France were gradually overrun by the invading Allied troops, the V1 bombs were superseded by the longer range V2 rocket bombs which were more destructive, carrying one-ton warheads, and could be fired from a simple concrete base.

The War at Sea— The Battle for the Atlantic

After the fall of France and the failure of Hitler's British invasion plans, Britain's best hope of defense was the fact that it was an island. But its island status also made

it vulnerable. While everything was done to grow more food and source more raw materials within Britain, the country needed imports. The main source of imported raw materials, food and military equipment was the US. While it was still uninvolved in the fighting, the Lend-Lease Act of March 1941 allowed America to lend military equipment to a country whose defense was perceived necessary for its own safety.

At the start of the war the German Navy had twenty-eight submarines, or U-boats, and even this small number, matched with conventional military vessels and some converted merchant ships, was successful in attacking large numbers of Allied ships, both military and merchant. The success of the U-boat in being able to attack ships virtually undetected encouraged Hitler to build more. Once available in large numbers, several U-boats would group together for safety and in order to be able to attack the convoys of merchant ships, escorted by military vessels, as they crossed the Atlantic. These groupings became known as "wolf packs" – they stalked their prey together.

As the war progressed, the development of sonar, radar, radio intercepts, and air cover gradually enabled the Allies to have some successes in the sea war, such as the sinking of the *Bismarck*, Germany's newest and fastest battleship, in May 1941. However, the threat to convoys of merchant ships protected by Royal Navy vessels remained high, and increased when Russia entered the war in June 1941. Convoys taking supplies to the USSR ports of Murmansk and Archangel via the north Atlantic route were also at risk of attack. In July 1942, Convoy PQ17 lost twenty-two supply ships, followed in September by further German attacks on Convoy PQ18 which lost thirteen vessels. This was despite the fact that in the same year some eighty-seven U-boats were destroyed.

Hitler and Stalin

The Nazi–Soviet non-aggression pact, signed by Hitler and Stalin in August 1939, was a major factor in setting the conditions for the outbreak of the Second World War. With the confidence that Poland could be attacked without the risk of taking on the weight of the Soviet Red Army, Hitler hazarded pursuing his expansionist aims, thus drawing Germany into direct conflict with Britain and France.

For Stalin, the pact had the advantage of allowing the USSR the opportunity to pursue its own hunger for territory. Just two weeks after the declaration of war, the Red Army marched into eastern Poland and by the end of September the country had been partitioned between USSR and Germany. Further Soviet expansionism came in November 1939. Claiming that Soviet control of parts of the Karelian peninsula was vital to bolster the defenses of Leningrad, the Red Army moved into Finland. Despite a heroic struggle by the Finns, fourteen weeks later the Soviets finally overwhelmed the country after a series of bitter battles in sub-zero temperatures which cost the lives of nearly 50,000 Red Army soldiers. A Russian–Finnish peace treaty, signed in March 1940, prevented the actual occupation of Finland, but the war had kindled anti-Soviet feeling amongst the Finns who had intended to remain neutral throughout the bigger conflict.

Always fearful of Hitler's intentions, Stalin believed that sooner or later Nazi ambitions would demand an attack on the USSR. The annexation of Poland, the Winter War with Finland, and the unresisted occupation of the Baltic States—Lithuania, Latvia, and Estonia—in June 1940, were all part of a plan to provide the USSR with a buffer against German attack. Indeed, Hitler's plans for a "thousand-year Reich" were dependent upon the wealth and resources that Russia could supply.

Operation Barbarossa

Germany's attack on the USSR, codenamed "Operation Barbarossa," came on June 22, 1941 when a hundred German army divisions, supported by Finnish and Romanian troops, invaded across a front that stretched from the Baltic to the Black Sea. Although Stalin had advance intelligence of the attack, the information was not communicated to commanders in the field. Taken by surprise, and faced with the sophisticated German

Below: Factories and an airfield in Berlin burn after heavy bombing.

tactics of blitzkrieg, the Red Army was pushed back rapidly so that by the end of June the Russian city of Minsk had fallen, and the German Panzer divisions pressed on toward Moscow.

In comparison with the highly trained and well-equipped German army, the seven-million-strong Soviet army came a poor second. Years of under-investment in equipment meant that soldiers' uniforms were old and outdated, as was their weaponry, including guns and tanks. Additionally, while once the Red Army was home to several brilliant military strategists, Stalin's purges had robbed it of many of its most talented officers and leaders: 30,000 officers had been imprisoned, tortured, or executed as Stalin attempted to consolidate his power.

One immediate consequence of Operation Barbarossa was that Russia and Britain became Allies. By the end of 1941, the first tanks for the Russian Front had rolled off assembly lines in Britain; they were vital to the war on the Eastern Front. German tanks were modern and manned by highly skilled troops; most of the thousands of tanks at the disposal of the Red Army were obsolete, with fewer than 2,000 modern KV-1s and T-34s available.

Hitler had launched Operation Barbarossa a year after he had successfully subdued and occupied most of Western Europe. Although it had not been possible to execute the planned invasion of Britain, the Nazi regime was at the height of its powers and had tried and tested its blitzkrieg tactics to stunning effect. The US had shown no inclination to engage in military action and with Japan, a Nazi ally, holding territory on the USSR's eastern border, Hitler felt confident that he could take Russia. He was also aware that it was important to move swiftly and establish territorial gains quickly, knowing that it would be difficult to maintain long supply lines in the face of the Russian winter.

The Battle of Stalingrad

Initially, Germany's invasion of the USSR made progress. By September, Leningrad was surrounded; Kiev fell in October and by the end of November 1941 German troops had reached the outskirts of Moscow. Under Stalin's orders the retreating Russians had followed a "scorched earth" policy, whereby everything that might have been of use to the Germans was destroyed, including bridges, railways, and fields of crops.

Russia was ready to defend Moscow and Leningrad, and at the end of 1941 a counter-attack was launched against the Germans, who were now faced with the problem of the dreaded Russian winter. The freezing temperatures grounded Luftwaffe aircraft and oil froze in the sumps of the Panzer divisions' tanks. The human tools of war fared little better; German soldiers were often ill-equipped for the below-zero temperatures and lacked winter camouflage.

The Red Army held out over the winter and had some success in pushing the Germans back from Moscow in January 1942, but by May the German Army had regrouped and was ready to launch a new offensive. The plan was now to attack the Crimea in the south, prior to seizing control of the Caucasus which had vital supplies of oil. June and July saw successes, with the capture of Rostov and Sevastopol but, as it turned north the German advance was slowed by fierce Russian resistance and was finally checked in the suburbs of the city of Stalingrad.

This was to be desperately defended and, as the winter of 1942 set in, the Russians under Soviet General Chuikov launched a counter-offensive, inflicting heavy casualties, surrounding the Germans to both the north and south of the city. Trapped, the German forces of the Sixth Army and the Fourth Panzer Division awaited resupply and the arrival of a relieving army, but by December any such attempts were an evident failure. For several weeks Stalingrad saw a bitter stalemate in which whole companies of troops fought through the city house by house in order to gain any territorial advantage they could. Hitler refused the now-surrounded German troops permission to surrender. But, on January 31, 1943, lacking supplies of winter uniforms, food, and medicine, and with temperatures reaching 24 degrees below freezing, the German commander Field Marshall Paulus disobeyed the Führer's orders. This surrender marked the German army's greatest defeat.

The Axis Powers

Germany had a number of allies throughout the war. Some were puppet states, like Vichy France and the Norway of the German collaborator Quisling, but the major European ally—and an ideologically analogous state—was Italy. Like Germany, Italy was a fascist dictatorship, led by Benito Mussolini. In May 1939 the two countries signed the Pact of Steel, forming a political and military alliance, with a resolution to support each other in time of war.

However, it was not until June 10, 1940, when

Germany was well on the way to victory in France, that Italy declared war on Britain and France. At this point in the war Italian troops did not fight alongside the German Wehrmacht. Instead, Italy began offensives against British Somaliland in August 1940 and against Egypt in September. The following month Mussolini ordered an invasion of Greece. Ten divisions of Italian troops moved across the border from Albania, the nation occupied by Italy in April 1939.

September 1940 saw not only the beginning of the Blitz on Britain and the Italian invasion of Greece but, on the political front, saw Japan sign a ten-year pact with Germany and Italy. The military axis between Berlin and Rome was expanded into a tripartite axis to include Tokyo. The Axis Powers, as they became known, joined the three most territorially aggressive nations in the world in an alliance that spanned the globe.

One of the major intentions of the pact was to dissuade the US from entering the war. While US President Roosevelt was not averse to bringing his country into the fray on the Allies' side, there were still strong feelings in the nation that the war was a strictly European affair. Despite this attitude, the US had been a staunch supporter of Britain and France.

However, the Pacific region, on the western doorstep of the United States, was already destabilized by Japan's territorial aggression. In 1931 Japan had annexed a large portion of China, the province of Manchuria, which became known as Manchukuo. From this starting point, the Japanese Army moved to take control of the whole of China. Just days before signing the pact with Hitler and Mussolini, Emperor Hirohito gave the orders for Japanese troops to strike into French Indochina, crossing the border from Manchukuo into Tonkin.

North American Neutrality

With the outbreak of war in Europe in September 1939, the US was determined to remain neutral,

Below: Americans gather to enrol for the US Air Force in New York.

adopting an "isolationist" policy. Seeing the war as a strictly European affair and keen to establish itself as free from Europe's squabbles but a major influence in its own region, there was little appetite for military engagement thousands of miles away. This was especially the case as it was so soon after the First World War. Eager to establish its position legally, several Neutrality Acts were passed by Congress, the first as early as August 1935.

Within days of the declaration of war it was made clear that the US would supply arms to neither side, but in November 1939, following urgings from President Roosevelt, Congress relented and sanctioned the purchase of arms and ammunition by Britain and France. The US was also a major source of food and raw materials for Britain during the year-long period in which it stood alone against Germany and Italy. When the USSR, in the face of invasion by Germany, joined the Allies, Roosevelt pledged to help the Soviets any way possible, short of military engagement.

Thus, it was clear that throughout the first two years of the war, the US was pushing at the bounds of neutrality. There was an pseudo-military involvement with the Allies and against the Axis powers: American naval observers had been attached to the Royal Navy since 1940 and in 1941, as US supplies became more vital to the survival of the European Allies, anti-U-boat patrols began off the coast of North America. After the US destroyer *Greer* was attacked by a German submarine, Roosevelt ordered that any Axis vessels within the American Defense Zone should be fired at on sight.

Despite the harrying of American vessels in the Atlantic, it was not German actions that drew the US into the armed conflict, but a devastating attack by Japanese aircraft on the US naval base at Pearl Harbor on December 7, 1941. The day after the attack the US and Britain declared war on Japan. With the entry of America to a combat role and fighting in Asia, Russia, Europe, and Africa, the conflict had assumed a truly global scale.

Battle for North Africa

As the Battle of Britain raged in the skies of northern Europe in the summer of 1940, Mussolini widened the offensive by launching a campaign in North Africa. In September, following an unsuccessful foray into British

Above: A roll call for some Egyptian fighter pilots.

Somaliland in August, Italian forces attacked the British colony of Egypt from their own colony of Libya. Capturing Sidi Barrani and then halting the advance fifty miles into Egypt, there was no action until December, when General Wavell launched the first British offensive against Italian forces. Sidi Barrani was recaptured, and by the end of the month British and Commonwealth troops had forced the Italians into retreat, driving them well back into Libya.

However, British gains in Libya suffered a reverse when, in March 1941, the German General Erwin Rommel and his Afrika Korps launched an offensive. Not only did they regain Libya, but they drove British and Commonwealth troops back through Egypt, to within striking distance of the Suez Canal.

Throughout the remainder of 1941 and early months of 1942, skirmishes in the deserts of North Africa took place between Rommel's Africa Korps and the British and Commonwealth troops, reorganized as the Eighth Army under General Auchinleck. For much of the time Rommel had the upper hand and in May 1942 he launched an attack on the Eighth Army, which was outflanked and forced into a rapid retreat to Tobruk. After the fall of Tobruk, Auchinleck was replaced by General Montgomery and, with reinforcements, a line was held at El Alamein.

By October 1942, with a complement of 200,000 men and bolstered by new US Sherman tanks

North Cape

ICELAND

Norwegian Sea

Narvik

0   200 km
0   200 miles

N

NORWAY

SWEDEN

FINLAND

OSLO

STOCKHOLM

Baltic Sea

HELSINKI

Leningrad

**SOVIET
UNION**

*North
Sea*

Edinburgh

DENMARK
Copenhagen

**REICHSKOMMISSARIAT
OSTLAND**

Königberg

**East
Prussia**

**UNITED
KINGDOM**

Hamburg

DUBLIN
IRELAND

AMSTERDAM **Neth.**

BERLIN

Warsaw

Poland

**REICHSKOMMISSARIAT
UKRAINE**

LONDON

GERMANY

BRUSSELS
Belgium

Frankfurt

PRAGUE
Bohemia

SLOVAKIA

PARIS

Munich

VIENNA

*ATLANTIC
OCEAN*

FRANCE

BERN
SWITZ.
Geneva

Austria

BUDAPEST

HUNGARY

ROMANIA

Milan

Venice

Banat

BUCHAREST

Genoa

CROATIA

*Adriatic
Sea*

Danube

BELGRADE
SERBIA

Marseille

ITALY

Mont

SOFIA

BULGARIA

PORTUGAL

S P A I N

Corsica

ROME

ALBANIA

GREECE

*Aegean
Sea*

MADRID

Sardinia

Taranto

TURKEY

LISBON

Balearic Is.

ATHENS

M e d i t e r r a n e a n

Algiers

Bone

Tunis

Sicily

*Malta
to Britain*

Crete

French North Africa

S e a

and self-propelled guns, Montgomery was ready to attack Rommel's Afrika Korps. The Eighth Army drove the German troops back from Egypt and into Libya. The victory at El Alamein, celebrated on November 15, 1942, was a significant one for the Allies. With the surrender of the Vichy French troops defending French North Africa following an invasion of British and American forces, led by US General Eisenhower, in the same month, the Allies were set to challenge Axis strength in the Mediterranean.

Italy Surrenders

Allied victories in North Africa opened the way for an attack on Italy. Using North African bases, the assault began in June 1943 with the heavy aerial bombardment of the island of Pantelleria. After two days of bombing the island's commander surrendered and Allied troops then landed. By the end of July Eisenhower's troops were in control of Sicily's capital, Palermo.

On July 25, in the face of the loss of its islands and an Allied air attack on Rome, Mussolini was deposed and imprisoned. King Victor Emmanuel took command of the Italian military and the anti-Fascist Marshall Badoglio was appointed Prime Minister. With political change came Italy's official surrender on September 8, and many German soldiers became prisoners of war when their former allies, the Italians, handed them over to the Allies. However, many German divisions escaped capture and turned into an occupying force in the northern half of the country, retaining control of Rome for many months.

The fact that Germany maintained a strong presence in the region enabled an audacious raid by German glider pilots to free Mussolini from his remote mountain prison. He was flown to Munich and later returned later to Northern Italy, where he remained until the final days of the war in Europe. He was discovered in hiding by Italian partisans and summarily tried and executed, along with his mistress and aides. Their bodies were hung up by the heels and displayed in the Piazza Loretto in Milan.

The Assault on "Fortress Europe"

"Fortress Europe," as the occupied and heavily defended countries of western Europe had been dubbed, and from where the British Expeditionary Force and the remnants of its Allies had been expelled in June 1940, needed to be breached if Germany was to be defeated. An attempt to land troops by sea on the French coast had been made in August 1942. More than 6,000 soldiers drawn from British, American, Canadian, and Free French divisions, supported by air and naval cover, landed at Dieppe. Fighting lasted nine hours before the Allies were overwhelmed. Losses from the raid were high—more than 1,000 men dead and 2,500 taken prisoner, with tremendous losses of heavy equipment, including invasion barges, tanks, troop carriers, and other ships, and almost a hundred Allied aircraft. The operation, headed by Britain's Admiral Lord Louis Mountbatten, was disastrous but was claimed to have only been a reconnaissance mission and not an attempt at a full-scale invasion.

Whatever its actual purpose, the Dieppe raid gave the Allies valuable lessons in what would be required for an all-out attack. US General Eisenhower and the commanders at Allied Supreme Command used the experience when preparing the strategy for the D-Day landings. By April 1944 Britain had become a gigantic armed camp with British, American, and Commonwealth troops, as well as remnants of European armies such as the Free French and the Poles, stationed throughout the country. Throughout the length of southern Britain large-scale military exercises were under way, with troops practicing coastal assault techniques.

Elaborate steps were taken to ensure that no details of the planned offensive reached the German High Command. For ten miles inland, the southeastern coast of Britain was off-limits to all but the military. In March, travel to Ireland had been banned to try and prevent information being passed to diplomats in enemy consulates in Dublin. This ban was followed in April by a restriction on all foreign diplomats in London who were prevented from traveling and from sending dispatches without inspection. Further strategies to disguise the Allied plans included the use of decoy ships and troops to suggest concentrations of troops and equipment in regions other than the intended embarkation areas.

The D-Day Landings

The invasion of Europe began on the morning of June 6, 1944, known as D-Day. In the early morning light troop barges came ashore on the beaches of Normandy. British and Canadian Forces landed at beaches codenamed Gold, Juno, and Sword to the north of the port of Caen; US troops landed further west, closer to the Cherbourg peninsula, at Utah and Omaha beaches. The invading troops came under heavy fire but the Germans had been taken by surprise, believing that the invasion would come in the Pas de Calais, farther east. Considering the Normandy maneuvers to be a bluff to draw the defenses, the German High Command maintained a strong presence in north-eastern France. The less heavily defended Normandy coast was further bolstered as a landing place by the heavy bombing of rail links and bridges in the area prior to D-Day, which meant that the Germans found it difficult to move troops and supplies to the front. Immediately prior to the sea-borne landing, from midnight to 5.30 am, parachutes and gliders had landed behind enemy lines to take key points by surprise. The combination of these factors made Operation Overlord, as the landings were codenamed, a success from day one. By midnight on June 6 the Allies had moved several miles inland across a broad front, having landed 155,000 men for a loss of 9,000.

Building on the success of D-Day in the following days was an immense undertaking. Not only were the Allies engaged in ferocious fighting for virtually every inch of land, especially around Cherbourg, but it was also necessary to establish supply lines from Britain. Artificial, or "Mulberry," harbors were constructed off the Normandy coast to allow ships to dock to unload more troops and supplies. Six days after the initial landings the various Allied divisions had linked their beachheads to establish a broad front which pushed through Normandy, to be refreshed and supplemented by new troops from Britain.

By the end of July the German resistance in Normandy was broken. The failure of the German High Command to be able to re-supply their divisions in Normandy with either men or equipment due to Allied air strikes on the supply routes, together with the overwhelming strength of the Allied troops, meant that despite the ferocious defense by some German soldiers they were unable to defeat the odds. The fall of the Norman town of Caen allowed the Allies a clear route to Paris which was liberated amid emotional scenes of celebration on 25 August 1944.

The Holocaust

As the Allies pushed into German-held territory, the true horror of what the Nazi concentration camps actually meant was revealed to a shocked world. Auschwitz was relieved in January 1945 by the Russians, and in April the Western Allies revealed the camps at Bergen-Belsen,

Buchenwald, and Dachau. The existence of the camps had been known for several years, as were Hitler's views on Germany's supposed "Jewish problem," but few could have guessed the extent of the inhumane treatment of those sent to the camps.

Initially, the camps were seen as a place to house anyone who did not fit in with Nazi ideals, principally the Jewish population of Europe, but others including Poles, Slavs, the Roma people, homosexuals, and Jehovah's Witnesses were also incarcerated. In the camps conditions were appalling, with starvation rations; people were worked until they died. Illness from infections, starvation, and disease took its toll on those consigned to them, but the majority of the six million Jews who died in the Holocaust were killed as part of a policy of genocide.

Heinrich Himmler's "Final Solution" to Hitler's "Jewish Problem" was the elimination of all Jews in German-occupied lands. This required killing on an industrial scale, and to this end large areas were built which could be filled with poison gas, killing hundreds of men, women, and children at one time. The Nazi regime even built huge incinerators which could deal with the thousands of bodies the policy delivered.

Many of those who survived until the liberation of the camps by the Allies died in the aftermath as, despite immense amounts of medical aid and food, they were so weakened that they did not have the strength to live. Those who did survive into the post-war era lived with the scars of the suffering that the inhumanity of their treatment, and the treatment of those around them, had inflicted.

Divisions in Europe

From the beginning of 1945 it was obvious that the defeat of Germany was imminent. Between February 4 and 11, Roosevelt, Churchill, and Stalin—as the leaders of the "Big Three" – met at Yalta in the Crimea to discuss the post-war division of Germany.

On March 24, the Western Allies crossed the Rhine, a major defence point for the Germans. Devastating bombing raids on major German cities like Dresden and Berlin supported the ground troops' efforts as they pushed on towards Berlin. The Red Army crossed the Oder and, by April 25, had surrounded Berlin. As they stormed through the city, Hitler committed suicide on April 30. The war in Europe was all but over and on May 7, General Jodl signed Germany's unconditional surrender.

At a further conference of the Big Three at

Potsdam in July 1945, the alliance between Britain, the United States and the USSR broke down. The death of President Roosevelt just weeks before victory in Europe meant that the US was represented by Truman. Clement Atlee, Prime Minister since Churchill's defeat in the British general election immediately after the war, was Britain's envoy; only Stalin still held office. He refused calls for elections in Eastern Europe, and no agreement could be reached about exactly where Germany's frontiers should be drawn.

The discord at Potsdam prefigured the Cold War, and Churchill complained that an "Iron Curtain" was being brought down across Europe.

Trial and Retribution

While Hitler, the central architect of the Nazi vision, had escaped trial by his suicide, there was widespread agreement that others should stand trial for war crimes. Some had escaped in the confusion of the final days of the conflict, and Goebbels and Himmler had also avoided justice by taking their own lives.

Those Nazis captured by the Allies were brought before an International War Crimes Court at Nuremburg in November 1946. Of the twenty-one defendants, three were acquitted, seven received prison sentences, ranging from ten years to life, and the remainder were sentenced to death. Of those to be executed, the most notable were Goering and von Ribbentrop. Hours before he was due to be hanged, Goering committed suicide by swallowing a cyanide capsule which he had kept hidden throughout the trial. On October 16, 1946, the execution of the others took place. Their bodies, together with that of Goering, were taken to Munich to be cremated and, according to the official announcement, their ashes were "scattered in a river somewhere in Germany".

Below: General Leclerc's armored division passes through the Arc de Triomphe.

The War in the Pacific

The war in the Pacific grew from relatively small beginnings into a large part of the global conflict, and saw the dropping of the atomic bomb before it finally ended.

Japan Expands into Manchuria

Japan had been devastated by the Great Depression. In order to alleviate this, Japan successfully embarked upon a full colonization of nearby Manchuria, where it had had an interest since the Sino–Japanese War. This would, it was thought, gain an external market for Japanese commodities, land for Japanese farmers, and ready access to many raw materials. Although Manchuria did not produce the dividends as quickly as had been hoped, the Japanese population was whipped up into a popular fervor for further expansion. The two main wings of the military, the army and the navy, were keen to cash in on this popularity and pushed for further military expansion. While the army saw glory on the large battlefields of China, the navy saw its worth in the colonization of the countless islands in South-East Asia with their treasure troves of natural resources, especially oil—a vital commodity for sustaining the navy's growing requirements.

The army's wishes were fulfilled first with further penetration into China from 1937, under the auspices of bringing stability to her troubled neighbor. The army was quickly drawn into a stalemate and brutal Japanese tactics, for example the "Rape of Nanking," incurred widespread international condemnation. This led the British, Americans, and the Dutch to impose an oil embargo so as to further hinder the Japanese invasion. The stalemate and the now desperate need for oil allowed the navy to assert the merits of its "Southern Policy" to divert attention from the Chinese theater.

The Problems of a Southern Policy

The areas Japan sought for expansion were already colonized by the European powers, and this quest for colonies therefore placed Japan on a spiral towards inevitable war in the Pacific. France owned Indochina, while the British had colonies in Burma, Malaya, and Singapore and exerted pressure over Siam (now Thailand). The Dutch Empire sprawled across the resource-rich East Indies and even the Americans had claims over the Philippines. This led, unsurprisingly, to a feeling in Japan of encirclement—the Great Powers, the Japanese believed, were encroaching on Japan's

natural sphere of influence. Infuriated that their own backyard had been taken over and nowhere left for them, the concept of pan-Asianism gained ground amongst the Japanese public. The idea was that Asia should be for Asians, and that owing to her natural military and economic weight Japan should be at the head of this "New Order in East Asia." The Japanese public believed that its invasion of South-East Asia was a move to liberate its Asian brethren from European colonial repression.

A New Opportunity for Expansion

In 1940, the situation in Europe became favorable for Japan. Germany, now Japan's ally, had crushed the French and the Dutch by June, and the maintenance of their empires came into question. Pétain's new French puppet government at Vichy had little choice, owing to German pressure, than to allow Japan to step in to "assist" in French Indochina. The Dutch administration in the East Indies managed to stand firm for the time being. Britain could now no longer guarantee the security of her colonies, given her lonesome war effort against Germany in Europe. By 1940, therefore, the only real restriction on Japanese expansion was the United States.

The Road to Pearl Harbor

The United States was far superior in population size, territory size, and industrial output to Japan. The decision to go to war against such a foe could not be taken lightly, even though the Americans were proving irksome to Japanese expansionist aims. Massive American military and economic aid to the Chinese nationalists was drawing the Japanese army into a quagmire in Asia and this brought resentment. American oil interests in South-East Asia also undermined the ability of the Japanese navy to drive southwards. Furthermore, America refused to acknowledge Japanese dominance of Manchuria.

By late 1941 Japan was poised to move into South-East Asia, and diplomacy was the last option open to America. By November 1941, however, diplomacy had failed; Roosevelt was keen not to be seen appeasing Fascism, as Chamberlain had been criticized for doing,

Above: The destroyer USS Shaw after the attack on Pearl Harbor.

and therefore thwarted Japan's overtures for a meeting with the Japanese premier. At this point Tokyo saw no other option but war, and realized the merits of a pre-emptive strike on America's Pacific Fleet while it remained in harbor. The weather would make an assault difficult during the first few months of 1942 and by the summer Japan's oil reserves would have been severely depleted. So an attack was launched immediately: on December 7, 1941 (in Washington), December 8 (in Tokyo), the Japanese launched a surprise attack on Pearl Harbor, Hawaii, dislocating the US Pacific Fleet in its home port.

Japan in the Ascendancy

Initially, Japan had a free hand in South-East Asia, as Roosevelt had declared a "Germany First" policy. Japan tightened her grip on the region, capturing two major British-administered cities, Hong Kong and Singapore, on December 25, 1941 and February 15, 1942 respectively. By early 1942 the Japanese had completed invasions of the Dutch East Indies, Burma, Malaya, Sumatra, and the Philippines—and were at the apex of

their power. However, in May 1942 the Allies scored a victory in the Battle of the Coral Sea, in the first clash fought between aircraft carriers. Although the Allies suffered a greater defeat militarily, they managed to inflict enough damage on the Japanese to thwart an attack on Port Moresby in New Guinea. Port Moresby proved a vital foothold for the Allies in the Pacific and, furthermore, had the Japanese captured it, they would have been well placed to invade northern Australia.

The Battle of Midway

A month after the Battle of the Coral Sea, Japan attacked the mid-Pacific island of Midway, home to an American naval base. This was in retaliation for an air raid on Tokyo in April 1942, called the Doolittle Raid, the first attack on Japanese home soil. It had been organized by Lieutenant Colonel James H Doolittle and was launched from an aircraft carrier in the Pacific. The assault had shaken Japanese domestic opinion, which was unprepared for the reality of aerial warfare.

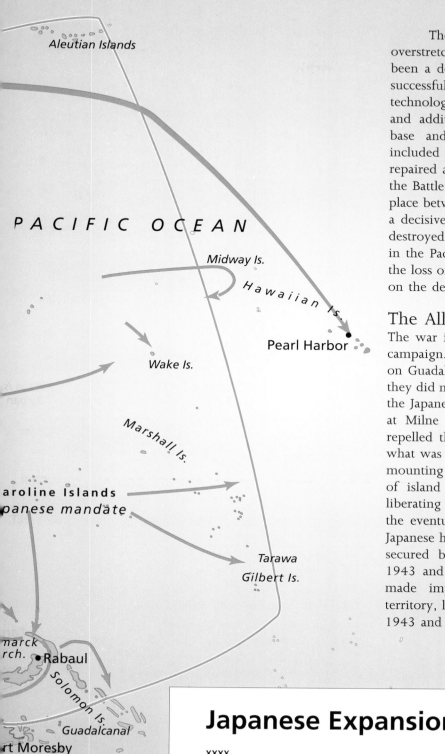

The daring Japanese raid on Midway severely overstretched their line of defence, but would have been a decisive defeat for the Americans had it been successful. However, their superior communications technology had alerted the Americans to Japan's plans, and additional ships were dispatched to relieve the base and launch a surprise counter-attack. These included the carrier, USS *Yorktown*, which had been repaired at lightning speed after sustaining damage in the Battle of the Coral Sea. The Battle of Midway took place between 4 and 7 June 1942, and America scored a decisive victory: four Japanese aircraft carriers were destroyed. This battle is often seen as the turning point in the Pacific War; Japan was unable to recover from the loss of the aircraft carriers and this put the country on the defensive.

The Allies Fight Back

The war in the Pacific was for the most part a naval campaign. In August 1942 American marines landed on Guadalcanal and a fierce land battle ensued which they did not win until February 1943. In August 1942, the Japanese launched an attack on the Australian base at Milne Bay in New Guinea. The Australians had repelled the Japanese invasion by early September in what was the first Allied victory in a land battle. With mounting successes, the Allies embarked upon a policy of island hopping; jumping from island to island, liberating them from the Japanese as they went, with the eventual goal being to come within reach of the Japanese home islands. The whole of New Guinea was secured by the Australians and Americans in early 1943 and over the next two years the United States made impressive headway into Japanese-occupied territory, landing in the Solomon Islands in November 1943 and on Saipan Island by mid-1944.

Japanese Expansion December 1941 – July 1942

XXXX		
14 Japanese Army	Aircraft carrier attack on Pearl Harbor	**Colonial possessions 1941**
Japanese Empire early 1941		British (Commonwealth)
Occupied by Japan December 1941 – July 1942	Japanese offensive operations December 1941 – March 1942	Dutch
China	Approximate limit of Japanese advance July 1942	French
		Portuguese

Above: The vast mushroom cloud which rose some 20,000 feet above Nagasaki, the second Japanese city to be devastated by the use of the atomic bomb.

The Battle of Leyte Gulf

In October 1944 the Battle of Leyte Gulf in the Philippines took place: the largest naval battle in history. An outnumbered Japanese force attempted to obstruct the Allied takeover of the Philippine island of Leyte, and the battle is often credited as being the point at which the Japanese navy was finally destroyed as a credible force in the Pacific. This battle was the first in which Kamikaze pilots were used, and a rise in fatalist attitudes among the Japanese has been deduced as a result of the deployment of this extreme technique. Japanese suicide pilots would fly their

aircraft into the sides of enemy ships to inflict maximum potential damage. This first recorded instance of a Kamikaze attack was on the Australian ship HMAS *Australia* on October 21, 1944.

After the Battle of Leyte Gulf was won there were still two months until the scheduled invasion of Okinawa, and therefore the Allies decided in the interim to capture the island of Iwo Jima and the Japanese airbases located there. The attack began in February 1945 and was fiercely fought as Japanese soldiers were by now being told to fight to the death, taking as many enemy soldiers with them as possible. The island was finally secured by March 1945 in time for the invasion of Okinawa.

The Battle for Okinawa

By March 1945 the Americans began their regular firebombing campaign over Japanese cities, which would eventually claim many thousands of lives. The British were able to force Japan's retreat from Burma and the Americans began their invasion of Okinawa in April. Okinawa was in the Ryukyu Islands and therefore part of Japanese home soil. Unlike Iwo Jima, there was a large civilian population in residence which was directly affected by the battle. Over 100,000 Japanese are estimated to have been killed or to have committed suicide after being given propaganda accounts of American barbarity. Okinawa was occupied by the end of June and was to become the last major battle of the Pacific War, although that was by no means certain at the time.

The Dropping of the Atomic Bombs

The estimated 12,000 Americans who died at Okinawa (and the 100,000 Japanese) contributed to US President Truman's decision to finish the war quickly, by any means possible. The Allies were exhausted by prolonged fighting and, after the jubilation of Victory in Europe, few had the energy to invest the required might for a conventional assault on the Japanese home islands. Fewer still would have been prepared for the massive loss of Allied lives this would have entailed. The War in Europe was over and the Russians were preparing to begin an offensive to liberate Manchuria. Truman, however, was keen to stem his Russian ally's expansion into the region. As a result of these considerations, on August 6, 1945 an atomic bomb named Big Boy was dropped by the *Enola Gay*, completely devastating the city of Hiroshima; this was followed by a second atomic bombing on the port

of Nagasaki on August 9. Six days later, on August 15, Japan surrendered and the War in the Pacific, and indeed the entire Second World War, was finally over.

The Aftermath

From 1945 until 1952 Japan was placed under direct American occupation, under the supreme command of General Douglas MacArthur. The Japanese Emperor Hirohito was not tried as a war criminal, instead being rehabilitated and reinstated as Emperor: however, his powers were revoked. His figurehead status was subsequently used to encourage the Japanese people to support both the American Occupation and a new constitution. The new constitution insisted upon the disarmament and demilitarization of Japanese society. It also enfranchised women and ensured that the Japanese educational system remained free from indoctrination by revoking the Imperial Rescript on Education, which had been partly responsible for the growth of extreme nationalism in Japanese society.

The International Military Tribunal for the Far East took place at Ichigaya and was the Pacific War's equivalent of the Nuremburg trials. Trials took place between 1946 and 1948 and the principal charges

Above: On June 16, 1948 a ceremony took place in Cardiff, Wales, as the remains of over 4,000 American soldiers, were loaded aboard the US Lawrence Victory bound for New York.

were for waging aggressive warfare and the mistreatment of prisoners of war. Many eyewitness accounts of the Rape of Nanking were used in evidence against the accused, who ranged from former premiers and foreign ministers to generals and racial theorists. Aside from those who died during the course of the trial, all were found guilty, though only seven out of twenty-five were sentenced to death. Hirota and Tojo, two former Japanese premiers, were among them. They were hanged in the early hours of December 23, 1948.

The Peace

By 1950 the communist invasion of South Korea required the United States to divert its attention and resources from Japan and power was steadily transferred to Japanese politicians. This process culminated in the final peace treaty, the Treaty of San Francisco, signed on September 8, 1951. It came into effect in April 1952 and the American Occupation was formally ended.

India: The Road to Independence and Partition

Independence on the Indian subcontinent saw the rise of charismatic leaders and eventual success, despite inter-community conflict and division on religious grounds.

Discontent and Nationalism

Despite India's initial loyalty to Britain at the outbreak of World War I, the hardships which were endured by India as a direct result of the conflict bore witness to steadily growing discontentment. Throughout the 1920s and 30s, during the years between the First and Second World Wars, India's struggle for independence gained momentum and saw a revival of nationalist sentiment. Furthermore, although some concessions were made on the part of the British—notably with the India Act of 1919, which admitted Indians to provincial government—Britain refused to completely relinquish its control, leading to increased unrest amongst the Indian population. This took the form of both peaceful protest and violent clashes. Despite the tide of growing nationalism, the marked divisions between the Hindu Congress and the All-India Muslim League, which had been unsuccessfully exploited before the war, with the attempted partitioning of Bengal by the British, and which were temporarily resolved during the war years, were also resurfacing. During this period, three men in particular were to take centerstage and be largely responsible for shaping India's political future. They were Mohandas Gandhi, Jawaharlal Nehru, and Mohammed Ali Jinnah.

Gandhi

Gandhi was a medium-caste Hindu who had trained in Britain as a lawyer before spending some twenty years working for Indians in South Africa, where he had encountered and opposed discrimination. In 1915 he returned to India and, following the First World War, reorganized Congress and began to mobilize nationalist support, leading campaigns of peaceful civil disobedience such as strikes, boycotts and the refusal to pay

Above: Lord Louis Mountbatten of Burma, the last Viceroy of India and overseer of the partition of India into India and Pakistan with his wife and Mohammed Ali Jinnah, leader of the All India Muslim League, after talks at the Viceroy's House, New Delhi, India, April 1947.
Opposite: Mahatma Gandhi (Mohandas Karamchand Gandhi).

taxes. The British responded by imprisoning thousands of Indians, Congress leaders amongst them, and Gandhi himself was imprisoned for two years in 1922. Following his release, Gandhi began to turn his attentions more towards the most disaffected elements of Hindu society, working with the lowest caste "untouchables," encouraging them to abandon machinery and to return to a more simple way of life. The politically aware middle classes supported him for having made the Congress a more accessible institution, and the peasants followed him for his holiness and attempted social reforms: by these methods, Gandhi managed to unite Hindu India with a common goal of independence. He also attempted to promote Hindu–Muslim unity but by 1930 the first calls would come for a separate Muslim state to be established in parts of northern India.

The Path to Independence

In 1928 during all-party talks and Congress meetings, India requested that dominion status be granted, with the threat of a return to mass civil disobedience

should Britain not comply. Following a meeting in December 1929, at which the recently elected president of Congress, Jawaharlal Nehru, demanded total independence, such campaigns were renewed throughout India. January 26, 1930 was declared as the "Purna Swaraj", or Independence Day, and between March and April Gandhi led perhaps the most famous of his protests, the Salt March (or Dandi March), walking around 250 miles to illegally harvest salt from the sea, in protest at the salt taxes enforced by the British. Shortly afterwards Gandhi was once more imprisoned. During this time, the first round table discussions were held in London, with the aim of resolving "the India problem," but with Gandhi and other leaders in prison, Congress refused to attend.

After his release in 1931, Gandhi agreed to cease civil disobedience in return for the release of political prisoners under the Gandhi–Irwin pact, and he attended the second round table discussions, representing Congress. However, he was dissatisfied with the outcome of these talks and resolved to restart the non-cooperation movement in 1932. Until 1935

Congress and the British Government were deadlocked but in 1935, under the viceroy Lord Willington, another India Act was passed which took much greater steps towards independence on the subcontinent.

Following elections, eleven self-governing provinces were established, eight of which were won by Congress, whilst in the remaining three, coalition governments were formed with the Muslim League. However, for Gandhi, Nehru, and many of their supporters, these measures still did not go far enough; only complete independence would satisfy their demands. Meanwhile, many Muslims, under the leadership of Mohammed Ali Jinnah, feared that they would be repressed by the Hindu majority, and their desire for independence not only from Britain, but from Hindu-dominated India, began to strengthen.

World War Two and India

In 1939, at the outbreak of World War II, the Viceroy Lord Linlithgow declared India's participation with no consultation of the provincial governments, prompting Congress ministers to resign in protest and refuse to offer their support. However, as the Japanese advanced towards the Indian frontier, Britain decided to offer India full independence after the war in return for cooperation. Vast numbers of Indians were mobilized in support of the British and fought alongside the allies. However, Subhash Chandra Bose, who had twice been president of Congress, broke away to form a new party—the All India Forward Bloc—before escaping to Germany. Here he enlisted

support from the Germans and Japanese to form the Indian National Army, which fought against British and Indian troops in Burma and north-eastern India, and briefly established a provisional government in exile on the Nicobar Islands.

Jinnah's demands for a separate Muslim state of Pakistan were given further weight during the war, with the British not only advocating post-war independence, but also a clause which would enable provinces to opt out of the federation. Gandhi and Nehru opposed any such plan, launching the "Quit India" campaign in 1942 as an attempt to force new negotiations with the British. Once more, this heralded mass civil disobedience, which saw Gandhi and Nehru imprisoned almost immediately, along with most other Congress leaders. The British suspected that the Japanese would soon invade and give power to Congress.

Independence and Partition

Before the Japanese were able to invade India, their surrender was assured with the dropping of atomic bombs on the cities of Hiroshima and Nagasaki: but by 1945, the British Government under Attlee was determined to give India its independence anyway. Britain wished for India to maintain a federal structure, whilst Congress demanded a unified India with a centralized government; the Muslim League, meanwhile, remained committed to the idea of an autonomous Pakistan. A political stalemate arose following the Indian elections of 1945, leading to widespread rioting and violence between Hindus and Muslims. The British army intervened, but it was clear that India was on the brink of civil war and some form of political agreement had to be forged in an attempt to avoid further bloodshed. Somewhat surprisingly, on June 3, 1947, Britain announced that it would transfer all power to India by August, and that Lord Mountbatten, commander of allied forces in South-East Asia during the war, would be the last viceroy.

Despite Mountbatten's attempts to encourage a divided India to unite, Jinnah was determined that partition should take place. Although Gandhi remained committed to the rule of Congress over all of former British India, in the end Nehru relented. On August 15, India finally gained its independence, with Nehru as prime minister, and the establishment of East and West Pakistan. Three provinces, however, had not pledged to join either India or Pakistan. These were

Junagadha, Hyderabad, and Kashmir. The first two were rapidly absorbed by India but the situation in Kashmir, poised as it was between India and Pakistan, was to prove more problematic. Both Muslim and Hindu forces moved in, dividing the region and beginning a conflict that would rage until 1949. Violence erupted elsewhere too, as millions of Hindus and Muslims fled across the newly established borders to settle in either Hindu-dominated India or Islamic Pakistan, and many who were left behind in both countries were massacred. Gandhi, who had returned to social work in Bengal, now took a stand to end the violence, pledging to starve himself to death if the persecution of Muslims in India did not cease. His protest was successful, but a few days later he was assassinated by a Hindu Brahmin who regarded him as a traitor.

India after Independence

Since independence, India's history has continued to be marked by periods of sporadic upheaval. Jawaharlal Nehru successfully ruled as prime minister until his death in 1964, guiding the nation through a period of relative peace and stability, to be succeeded by his daughter, Indira Gandhi. She too was a powerful leader, but was indicted for corruption in 1975 and briefly imprisoned in 1978. She was re-elected the following year, but was assassinated in 1984 by Sikh terrorists. The Congress Party remained the dominant political party in India except for brief periods in the late 1970s, and from the late 1980s until the mid-1990s. In the early 1990s, the BJP, or Bharatiya Janata Party, the Indian People's Party, emerged as a contender for national leadership and was successfully elected with a large majority in the late 1990s. India boasts a long history of democracy, but that history has also been characterized by underlying tensions between various ethnic or political affiliations, particularly between Hindus and Muslims, which has seen distrust between India and Pakistan persist to this day.

Below: October 28, 1950: Indian Prime Minister Pandit Jawaharlal Nehru by a lily pond in the garden of his New Delhi home. With him are his daughter Indira Gandhi (Indira Priyardarshini Nehru), and her son Rajiv, who both succeeded him as Prime Minister.
Opposite: Nehru and Gandhi engaged in discussion.

The United Nations

The UN grew out of the need for a peacekeeper and international arbiter following World War II. In a changing world, it continues to pursue global development.

The Creation of the UN

On August 14, 1941 US President Roosevelt and British Prime Minister Winston Churchill met on HMS *Prince of Wales* in the Atlantic Ocean and signed the Atlantic Charter, setting out a series of principles which were to form the basis for future international peace and security. The Charter was effectively to replace the League of Nations, the organization that had been founded in 1920 to act as an international arbiter and to preserve peace. The League of Nations had been advocated by US President Wilson at the end of World War I; however, disagreement over the contentious Treaty of Versailles resulted in the disassociation of the United States from the League.

In January 1942, 26 nations allied against Axis aggression met to sign the Atlantic Charter, and the term United Nations was first applied. The big three, Britain, America, and the Soviet Union, reaffirmed the idea of using the Atlantic Charter as a basis for an international institution at the Tehran meeting in December 1943. The proposals for such an organization were outlined at a series of conferences at Dumbarton Oaks in Washington DC. In the final days of the War, a meeting was held in San Francisco to draw up the charter and, on October 24, 1945, the United Nations Charter was ratified and the organization officially came into being.

In January 1946 both the Security Council and the General Assembly met for the first time in London. By the end of the month, the General Assembly had adopted its first resolution; to eliminate atomic weapons and other weapons of mass destruction. The headquarters of the United Nations was moved to New York.

The United Nations System

The UN system was conceived as a network of international organizations, the main six being the Security Council, the General Assembly, the Economic and Social Council, the International Courts of Justice, the Secretariat, and the Trusteeship Council.

The Secretariat is the command center for the whole of the United Nations, headed by the Secretary General who personally oversees the appointments of all staff on the Secretariat. The Secretary General supervises the implementation of Security

ORIGINAL MEMBERS OF
THE UNITED NATIONS 1945

Original Members

Security Council Members

Council resolutions and is directly involved in administering peace-keeping operations. The International Courts of Justice, located at The Hague in the Netherlands, was designed to arbitrate in disputes between states or to advise the General Assembly on legal matters. It consists of nine judges, all appointed by the Secretary General. Five of these, however, must come from each of the five permanent members of the Security Council. The Trusteeship Council was charged with ensuring that UN trusteeships were governed in the best interests of the population living there and to draw up plans for eventual independence. These trusteeships were often territories confiscated from the Axis after the Second World War, or were mandates inherited from the League of Nations. The final trusteeship to gain independence was Palau in 1994 and shortly after this the Trusteeship Council suspended its operations as its mission had been completed.

The Economic and Social Council presides over an array of programmes, funds and agencies, most famously including UNICEF (the United Nations Children's Fund), UNCTAD (UN Conference on Trade and Development) and UNHCR (UN High Commission for Refugees). Many other organizations come under the umbrella of the council, including programes for the environment, women, drug controls, human settlement, food provision, transportation, labor, and reforestation. The Economic

and Social Council also presides over a series of specialized agencies such as the World Health Organisation, UNESCO (UN Educational Scientific and Cultural Organisation), and the World Bank Group, which includes the IMF (International Monetary Fund). The council also runs specific regional development missions; UNRWA (UN Relief and Works Agency) is designed to assist Palestinian refugees and economic commissions have been established for Europe, Africa, Asia–Pacific, and Latin America and the Caribbean.

The Big Five and the Security Council

Roosevelt believed that the failure of the League of Nations was that it did not recognize the fact that there was an unequal distribution of power in the world. He believed that the new organization should reflect this and so the idea of a Security Council was adopted: an executive body of the four great powers, Britain, America, the Soviet Union, and China, who—as the greatest powers—had the responsibility to "police" the world. Fearing Soviet penetration into Western Europe, Britain improved its relationship with France. As part of this process, Britain negotiated France a permanent seat on the council. Each of these members has the power to veto resolutions that they do not support, in which case the United Nations cannot intervene. According to the Nuclear Non-Proliferation Treaty only the five permanent members of the Security Council can possess nuclear weapons.

Debates have now arisen over the legitimacy the Big Five have to maintain their positions on the Security Council. Germany and Japan, as leaders of the global economy, are key contenders for membership, shortly followed by India and Brazil as two of the most populous countries. The Netherlands and Italy advocate a single European Union seat, which would require Britain and France to relinquish their seats, but they are unlikely to do so. As well as the permanent members, there is also space for ten other members—comprised of a selection of all the other member countries of the United Nations, the selection rotating after a period of two years. These ten do not have the right of veto, but for any resolution to pass, it requires the approval of nine out of the fifteen members. Provided there are no vetoes by the permanent members, the non-permanent members are able to influence UN policy through this mechanism.

The General Assembly and Non-member States

The General Assembly is the only UN organization where all the member states are represented. There are currently 191 member states in the United Nations. The Papacy and the Palestinian Authority are not members but have observer status, which means they can be present during proceedings. Taiwan is not a member because mainland China refuses to view it as a separate country and could use its veto to block its entry. Similarly the territory of Western Sahara is not seen to have its own sovereignty and is represented by Morocco. The Assembly can debate a wide range of issues from budgetary matters to cultural concerns. In order to pass a resolution, the assembly requires a two thirds majority. However, even if this is attained, the resolutions are not legally binding; they can form the basis for a recommendation to the Security Council to approve a similar resolution, in which case they would become legally binding. The General Assembly has become a crucial lobbying point for developing nations to petition the developed world—owing to their numbers, the developing world make up the majority of the Assembly, and so the debates often reflect issues pertaining to development and poverty.

The Future of the United Nations

In recent years the future of the United Nations has come under question. Since the end of the Cold War, the United Nations Security Council no longer reflects the balance of power. American power has dramatically increased since the removal of the Soviet Union as a counter-balancing force, and the United Nations has therefore become increasingly reliant upon the support of the United States. The relationship has not always been harmonious as events surrounding the 2003 invasion of Iraq demonstrate. Although American hegemony has resulted in a weakening of the UN's ability to provide international security, the UN's wide array of economic and social programs are not affected by this and will continue to pursue global development.

Below: The Headquarters of the United Nations in New York City.
Opposite: Kofi Annan became Secretary-General of the United Nations in January 1997, succeeding Boutros Boutros-Ghali of Egypt.

Revolutions in Latin America

The twentieth century in Latin America has been one of upheaval, of military coups and dictatorships from all sides of the political spectrum.

The Twentieth Century

The majority of Latin American countries had secured independence from their European colonizers in the earlier half of the nineteenth century, largely as a result of resentment towards the Spanish and Portuguese, and inspired by the freedom won by North America from the British. However, Latin American countries were overshadowed by the mounting economic strength of their powerful neighbor north of the Mexican border; unable to compete, many became dependent upon the United States. World War I brought the first economic blow, with European trade and investment in Latin America abandoned in favor of the US, which was correspondingly able to bring its own manufacturing companies into the region. The second blow was the Great Depression, precipitated by the Wall Street Crash. US financial support was cut off, debts were called in and world market prices of Latin America's primary products plummeted.

The result was rapid industrialization and a collapse in the confidence of the workers and the urban classes, and from 1930 a wave of revolutions across the region ushered in a number of dictators, such as Vargas in Brazil and Perón in Argentina. For the most part, these revolts did nothing to close the increasingly large gap between rich and poor, and whatever social reforms had been initiated in the 1930s had mostly declined by the middle of the 1940s, while the effects of industrialization only served to exacerbate the situation. This was not improved by the onset of World War II. Economic development declined further, and population growth simply increased the numbers of those living in poverty. As a result, the 1950s was again a period of revolution and military coups, with Guatemala, Bolivia, and Cuba undergoing radical political transformation.

Dictatorships

Much of the history of twentieth-century Latin America is that of the rule of various dictatorships and military juntas. The economic and social problems experienced by most of the countries and islands of the region meant that the inhabitants began to look towards other models of government, in particular to the extremes of Fascism and Communism seen in Europe.

Right: Marxist President of Chile, Salvador Allende, who was killed after the army seized power in 1973.

In Brazil the first dictatorship of Getulio Vargas began in 1930. With military support, Vargas assumed power despite having being defeated in the democratic process, in which he stood as a candidate for the Liberal Alliance. The bloodless revolution that brought in Vargas was essentially a liberal bourgeois coup, which resulted in further capitalist development and industrialization. However, Vargas' dictatorship gradually began to model itself upon European Fascism. His capitalism was without liberal reforms and his rule saw the use of repressive tactics similar to those used by Mussolini in Italy and Salazar in Portugal; he also tolerated anti-Semitism. He was forced to step down from the presidency in 1945 due to his own constitutional reforms—which ruled against any leader succeeding him—but returned in 1951, ruling until his suicide four years later.

In Argentina, 1930 saw a military coup in which the elected president was forced out of office. During the following decade a series of governments took control; these advocated more conservative principles and when, in 1943, the army intervened again, they gave Juan Perón the presidency. Perón had enough popular support within Argentina for him to be able to rule despite the opposition of some elements of the army and in 1946 he won a democratic election which kept him in power. Despite his essentially Fascist principles, Perón pursued social changes that would benefit the working classes and was at the helm of an economic boom which eventually collapsed in 1955. Perón's popularity had begun to wane in 1952, with the death of his wife Evita, who had had as much to do with his appeal to the workers as had his policies. He was deposed in 1955 by the armed forces, following disputes with the Catholic Church and charges of corruption. Perón returned to the presidency in 1973, winning another election, despite not having been permitted to stand in the original elections held earlier that year. He died the following year.

A more violent revolution had taken place in Bolivia during 1952, when Communist forces led the civilian population into overthrowing the military junta. Bolivia, now one of the most underdeveloped of Latin American countries, then began to suffer as a result of economic policies which followed a course of nationalization and enfranchisement.

Communism was most famously embraced in Cuba during the 1950s. The Cubans had overthrown their US-backed military leader, Gerardo Machado, in 1933 and a period of short-lived governments had followed until the assumption of power by Fulgencio Batista in 1940. Batista's rule was harsh and oppressive and he was to remain in power, despite an interregnum period, until 1959, when a further revolution ousted him. This revolution was instigated by a lawyer, Fidel Castro, who initiated a guerrilla campaign against the Batista regime in 1956. Batista's unpopularity provided Castro's movement with the opportunity to wrest control during a period of bloody fighting and Batista fled to the US in January 1959. Castro's Communist regime sought to remove all opposition to its position, and thousands of Cubans fled. However, the adoption of a Communist ideology did lead to social and economic reforms which improved the prospects and standard of living for some of the working population. Castro's Communism also resulted in increased hostility from the US, and the country became a pawn between the USSR and the US during the Cold War.

Marxism had also seen historic popular support in Chile, and during the 1970s this helped to usher in the presidency of Salvador Allende. Allende's economic reforms did little for the Chilean economy, however, and he in turn was overthrown in a bloody military coup, bringing in the dictatorship of General Augusto Pinochet, which lasted until 1988.

Growth and Recovery

The majority of Latin American dictatorships are no longer in existence. Argentina, struggling with a crushed economy, though with the added benefits of rich natural resources and a high literacy rate, is now a democratic republic. In Guatemala, thirty-six years of civil war were ended with the signing of a peace treaty in 1996, and foreign investment is gradually beginning to bolster the once ailing economy. Chile has begun to benefit from growing tourism, a highly successful wine trade and a modern telecommunications industry. In addition, the recent signing of free-trade agreements with the US, the European Union, and Canada have served to improve the possibilities of foreign investment. Trade agreements have also been particularly important to countries such as Mexico, where foreign trade, particularly that with the US and Canada, has tripled during the past decade. Tourism has also proved to be vital to the development of countries such as Costa Rica and the islands of the Caribbean.

Communist China

The twentieth century has been one of turmoil in China, but has also seen astonishing growth and modernization, though this has been an often painful process.

The Beginnings

The first Chinese republic, established in 1911, failed to address the country's social and economic problems, and the early decades of the twentieth century saw China descend into a state of near-anarchy. Local warlords seized power and behaved with sometimes astonishing brutality; and though a fragile balance of power existed between the warlords and other groups, nothing could be achieved. The war with Japan at the end of the nineteenth century had also left considerable complications in its wake.

The first war between the north and the south of the country started in 1917; this resulted in a full civil war. The republican leader, Sun Yat-sen, formed his own southern governments in 1917, 1921 and 1923 and created a political party, the Kuomintang or Nationalist Party, with the aim of achieving some sort of unity. He also wanted to build links with the Chinese Communist Party which, although still small, was growing. In these aims he was unsuccessful, dying before any of them could be achieved.

Civil War

Successive Japanese governments turned their attentions to China, and to their "interest" in Manchuria, which they fully invaded in 1931. During the war which eventually broke out with Japan, from 1937 to 1945, the Chinese Communists and Nationalists, the latter now led by Chiang Kai-shek, formed a united front. The aim was to concentrate on the defeat of Japan rather than weaken themselves through civil war; their alliance was, however, fragile.

After the war their conflict resumed. The brunt of the war against Japan had been shouldered by the Nationalists, and they were severely weakened and unable to thwart Communist progress through the countryside. The Communists were led by the son of a peasant from Hunan province, Mao Zedong, who

Right: Dr Sun Yat-sen formed the Kuomintang or Nationalist Party.

had seen off competitors to his authority during the war years. The Communists prided themselves on discipline and had won much support amongst the peasants, while the Nationalists were associated by the majority of people with corruption and hyperinflation. After Beijing was captured in January 1949, the rest of China's cities fell to the Communists throughout the year. On October 1, 1949 Mao proclaimed the establishment of the People's Republic of China, but it was not until December that the Communists took Chengdu, the last Nationalist-held city. The Nationalists fled and exiled themselves on Taiwan, a large island in the South China Sea relatively close to the mainland.

Communist Consolidation of Power

After the flight of the Nationalists China had its first strong, united government for decades. Immediately after unification, China intervened in Korea, where an American-led United Nations invasion force was able to push the advance of the Communist North Koreans back toward the Chinese border. Once the war was settled—after a protracted stalemate—Mao set about consolidating his regime, launching a "five-year plan" in 1953.

Following Stalin's example, emphasis was placed on the development of heavy industry and collectivization. Private enterprise was abolished; factories, banks, and trade were nationalized; and price controls were established to end the inflation brought on by the Nationalists. In rural areas, land redistribution got under way and landlords' estates were shared amongst peasant collectives. In addition the Chinese alphabet was simplified to increase literacy. The 1950s saw an increase in overall standards of living and economic growth. In 1956, in order to encourage further growth, the Communist Party decided to invite intellectuals to give constructive criticism of the regime in the "Hundred Flowers" campaign under the slogan "Let a hundred flowers bloom, let the hundred schools of thought contend." After a long period of reluctance, intellectuals sent in millions of criticisms of the Party's policies. By June 1957 Mao was humiliated; he claimed the comments were subversive and not constructive, and abruptly halted the campaign in July. He then furiously launched the anti-rightist campaign, alleging that many of the intellectuals who had responded were rightists. He used this new campaign to have them purged, and in doing so created a long-lived distrust between the Party and Chinese intellectuals.

The Great Leap Forward

In an early sign of a pending Sino-Soviet rift, Mao decided that the Soviet path to socialism was not entirely applicable to China and desired to put China on its own course. He believed that China should no longer follow Stalin's model of costly mechanization and an emphasis on collective farms and heavy industry. Instead, he believed that his country should take advantage of its huge population and carry through rapid development by utilizing its massive workforce.

The population was mobilized into communes, which were much greater in scale than the Soviet collective farms. Family units would pool resources on a massive scale in a bid to reduce waste, and each commune was to focus upon agricultural production and light industry. Steel was the main focus of the light industry drive, with the aim of outpacing British production within fifteen years. Back-yard furnaces were developed in the communes for people to melt down scrap and make steel. Initially the scheme was successful; this encouraged Mao to step up the quotas the government demanded from each commune. However, as the demands grew they became unsustainable; regional Party leaders began lying about attaining their quotas; in order to meet the government's ever-increasing demands, the peasants had to use grain set aside for subsistence. Severe, widespread famine ensued, resulting in millions of deaths. Furthermore, in order to meet their steel quotas the population had melted down all available utensils—for example, woks which were vital for cooking—which only resulted in the creation of useless scrap metal that was much lower in value than the items had been before they were melted. The Great Leap Forward was an unmitigated disaster that resulted in economic stagnation and an estimated twenty million deaths.

The Cultural Revolution

After the failure of the Great Leap Forward Mao was forced to take a back seat in Chinese politics, yet remained Chairman in name. In the meantime Liu Shao-chi and Deng Xiaoping assumed control, putting forward a policy of "practical socialism," which advocated putting economic efficiency above ideological purity. By the mid-1960s, Mao wanted to stage his comeback and used the alleged weakening of ideology as a result of practical socialism as his pretext. He launched the Great Proletarian Cultural Revolution in 1966 to kill two birds with one stone: to reinvigorate Communist ideology among the Chinese population, and to regain personal control of China. The call for revolution was taken up by students, who had spent all their life in a Communist society; anarchy grew in schools across the country as they formed "Red Guard" units and occupied the classrooms, denouncing their teachers and terrorizing their neighborhoods. Mao, meanwhile, used the Cultural Revolution to purge moderates from the Party at all levels, intimidating those remaining into following him.

The Cultural Revolution spun out of control when it was taken up by workers as well. The workers, like the students and Mao, used the Cultural Revolution as a pretext to denounce people in positions of authority, and all work in the factories ground to a halt. Mao had unleashed a generation's frustration. It proved difficult to control and by the end of the 1960s Mao realized that he had proved his point. With his power restored and his personality cult at extreme heights, Mao ordered the Red Army to disband the Red Guards and send them to the countryside to learn from the peasants, where many remained until after Mao's death.

Mao's Death

Mao was in his seventies during the Cultural Revolution and the question of his succession soon began to surface. By 1970 Lin Biao, the head of the army, had emerged as Mao's clear successor; however Lin was killed in a plane crash as he was trying to flee the country. The suspicious circumstances of his death led to a rash of conspiracy theories asserting that Lin had attempted a failed assassination of Mao; whatever the truth of the matter, Lin's death had reopened the question of Mao's successor. On September 9, 1976 Mao died, and a power struggle immediately broke out between the "Gang of Four" on the far left—who were led by Mao's widow and advocated continuing the Cultural Revolution—and the reformers on the right of the party, led by Deng Xiaoping, who had again re-emerged after being purged during the Cultural Revolution.

To everyone's surprise, Mao had named Hua Guofeng, who belonged to neither group, as Chairman of the Party. Hua turned against the Gang of Four and had them arrested; all were given death sentences, commuted to life imprisonment. Meanwhile, Hua was faced with the difficulty of challenging Mao's authority. As his successor, Hua drew legitimacy from

Mao and therefore decided to follow the "Two Whatevers" – whatever Mao said and whatever Mao instructed would be followed. But throughout the late 1970s Deng increased his control over the Party by drawing loyalty from the army, and denounced the Cultural Revolution. He thereby discredited Hua for following the "Two Whatevers" and weakened the remaining Maoists in the Party. By 1981 Deng and his reformist associates had managed to oust Hua from key leadership positions and were pursuing reform. Hua was, however, allowed to remain a member of the Central Committee until 2002.

Deng's Reforms

Deng was intent on modernizing the economy and wanted to achieve this pragmatically, by "seeking truth from facts." His aim was to modernize China by gearing it towards a socialist market economy, where the means of production were transferred from state hands to private enterprises. Deng pursued a policy of attracting foreign investment to China, initially by developing special economic zones, such as in Shenzhen in 1980. These were small enclaves where liberalized economic laws applied; quite out of keeping with Marxist ideology, they offered tax incentives to attract foreign firms to forge joint ventures with Chinese companies. With the revenue provided by this new-found foreign trade, Deng aimed for the "Four Modernizations" in the sectors of agriculture, industry, science, and technology; and the military and Chinese students were sent to study abroad. Here they gained insights into capitalist economic methods, encouraging further modernization. Deng also sought to improve diplomatic relations with the outside world and even visited President Carter at the White House in 1979. In 1984 he negotiated the return of Hong Kong from Britain, scheduled for 1997. Increased modernization and foreign relations paid off, as by the end of the century China was experiencing massive economic growth.

Tiananmen Square

By 1989, however, many people had grown dissatisfied with the regime. Students and intellectuals demanded democratization to accompany the economic liberalization of the 1980s, and were spurred on by the political liberalization occurring in Eastern Europe. Workers were also dissatisfied with the economic reforms, as increased marketization had ended job security and precipitated price inflation. The death of Hu Yaobang provided the trigger for the protests, as Hu had been considered to be in touch with the people, yet had been dismissed in 1987, in circumstances that were widely thought to be unfair. On May 4, 1989, on the eightieth anniversary of a nationalist uprising, thousands of people descended on Tiananmen Square in Beijing to protest. The protest attracted more and more people until an estimated 100,000 people had flooded the square. The event was well covered by the foreign press who were in Beijing to report on the visit of Mikhail Gorbachev. On May 20 the authorities declared martial law and on the night of June 4 they took the decision to clear the square using force; they feared the collapse of their authority or a repeat of the anarchy of the Cultural Revolution. An unknown number of people died; some estimates place the figure as high as 5,000. The crackdown gained widespread criticism from the outside world and the United States and the EU announced an embargo of weapons sales to China. However, economic growth has continued and political discontent has quietened down; but without adequate reforms it is likely that it will resurface at some time.

Below: Pro-democracy students march on Tiananmen square to join thousands of others demonstrating at the funeral of reformist policitician Hu Yaobang.
Opposite: A young member of the Red Guard gives an honorary armband to Mao Zedong in 1966.

Communist Russia

Communist rule in Russia lasted just over seventy years and saw astonishing upheavals, from Stalin's oppression to Gorbachev's liberalization, changing the country forever.

Stalin's Rise to Power

In 1922 Stalin became General Secretary of the Communist Party of the Soviet Union and strengthened the executive powers of this position until it became the most powerful role in the Party. Before his death in 1924, Lenin warned against allowing Stalin too much power; Stalin had this information suppressed as he began his quest for control. His main rival was Trotsky; but other prominent Politburo members such as Zinoviev, Kamenev, and Bulganin were also contenders. Stalin eventually aligned himself with Bukharin and Rykov on the right; after a brief alliance with Zinoviev and Kamenev, he propounded the idea of "socialism in one country" rather than "permanent revolution" – the traditional Marxist idea favored by

Trotsky. Stalin's policy meant that socialism should first be consolidated in Russia rather than spread to other countries immediately. His victory against Trotsky can be dated to 1928, when he announced his first five-year plan and Trotsky fled into exile. Stalin turned on Bukharin and Rykov, who had facilitated his rise to power, in a bid to reign supreme; however, his control did not become total until he initiated the Great Purges in 1936.

Stalinism

Stalin's first two five-year plans saw a rapid rate of industrialization, albeit from a very low base. He replaced Lenin's New Economic Policy with a centrally planned economic system. Industrialization was funded through the confiscation of property from the peasantry and was sustained by putting constraints upon wages and individual consumption. To assist industrialization in the cities, Stalin embarked upon collectivization in the country-side. The idea was to replace many hundreds of small, inefficient farms with new massive collectives which would produce surplus food and less waste. Collectivization was not as successful as Stalin had hoped and production levels dropped leading to widespread famines in which millions died.

In 1936 Stalin launched his Great Purges, the removal of supposed enemies of the State, which either resulted in execution after a show trial or deportation to a Gulag, an extremely harsh prison camp, often in Siberia. Initially much of the Communist Party was

purged; more than half of the delegates at the Seventeenth Party Congress of January 1934 are thought to have been victims. This process was completed with the assassination of Trotsky in Mexico in 1940. Then the Purges were applied to the whole of Soviet society; anybody displaying alleged anti-Soviet tendencies was liable to be deported or executed. Senior officials in the Red Army were purged between 1937 and 1939 so as to forestall any coup attempts. Finally, came the "Purge of the Purgers," as the NKVD (the state secret police) leadership was examined; the incumbent head of the NKVD, Yezhov and his predecessor, Yagoda were executed.

The Great Patriotic War

On August 23, 1939, Molotov, Stalin's Foreign Minister, signed an agreement with Ribbentrop, the Nazi Foreign Minister, agreeing to a non-aggression pact and the division of Poland between the two. In mid-September Red Army troops occupied the eastern parts of Poland and later annexed the Baltic States as well. But in June 1941, following a successful campaign against France in the West, Hitler invaded the Soviet Union.

The war was initially a disaster for Russia, with millions of Russians killed and a German advance

Above: Soviet leader Joseph Stalin with British prime minister Winston Churchill at the Crimea conference, Yalta in 1945.
Opposite: Russian revolutionary leader Vladimir Ilyich Ulianov, better known as Lenin, (L) poses in Gorki in 1922 with Yossif Vissarionovitch Dzhugashvili, better known as Joseph Stalin, who became secretary general of the Soviet communist party in 1922.

which neared Moscow at its peak. Germany's preoccupation with acquiring oil from the Caucasus saw a bitter campaign culminating in the Battle of Stalingrad, which turned the tide of the war; the Soviet army was beginning to recover from the Purges and the Germans were severely overstretched. After Stalingrad, Soviet troops were successful in pushing German troops all the way back to German territory, eventually capturing Berlin in May 1945.

The Last Years of Stalin

After the war, Red Army troops were in direct occupation of the whole of Eastern Europe. Stalin hoped that when the United States withdrew from Europe, the Soviet Union could become the leading power on the continent. However, the Americans had decided upon a policy of containment of Soviet influence and set about undermining Communist Parties across Western Europe.

U.K.

North
Sea

NORWAY

SWEDEN

DEN.

GER.

Oslo

Stockholm

Baltic Sea

Gdansk

LAT.

Riga

LITH.

POLAND

Warsaw

BELARUS

Minsk

Kiev

UKRAINE

MOLDAVIA

Odessa

Black Sea

TURKEY

SYRIA

Mossul

Bagdad

IRAQ

K.

SAUDI

ARABIA

Q.

Persian Gulf

FINLAND

Helsinki

Murmansk

Arkhangel'sk

St Petersburg

Novgorod

Moscow

Nizhniy
Novgorod

Kirov

Perm

Yekater

Chelyabinsk

Samara

Volgograd

Volga

Astrakhan

Groznyy

GE.

Tiflis

AR.

AZ.

Baku

Caspain Sea

Tabriz

Tehran

IRAN

Herat

Kabul

AFGHANISTAN

Barents
Sea

R U S

K A Z A K H S T

Aral
Sea

UZBEKISTAN

Urgench

TURKMENISTAN

Ashgabat

Samarkand

Tashkent

TAJIKISTAN

Amu Darya

PAKISTAN

AR. = ARMENIA
AZ. = AZERBAIJAN
DEN. = DENMARK
EST. = ESTONIA
GE. = GEORGIA
GER. = GERMANY
LAT. = LATVIA
LITH. = LITHUANIA
Q. = QATAR
U.K. = UNITED KINGDOM

USSR TO **RUSSIAN FEDERATION**

Former boundary of USSR
to 1991

Member of Commonwealth
of Independent States from 1991

Khrushchev and "De-Stalinization"

After Stalin's death Nikita Khrushchev maneuvered himself to the center of the Party apparatus and, with the assassination of his main rival Beria in December 1953, became the leader of the Communist Party. It was not until 1958 that he ruled the Soviet Union supreme when he assumed the position of prime minister as well. In 1956, at the Twentieth Party Congress, Khrushchev surprised all the delegates with a speech denouncing Stalin for his cult of personality and excessive brutality during the purges.

At the same conference he espoused the need for peaceful coexistence with the West. By 1964, even Khrushchev's closest allies were concerned about his erratic style of rule and much of the Party was frustrated that he had yielded to the Americans in the Cuban Missile Crisis. While he was away from Moscow on holiday, Mikoyan, Kosygin, and Brezhnev engineered his downfall. He was placed under house arrest until his death in 1971.

Brezhnev: Stagnation and Intervention

Brezhnev initially had to rule alongside Mikoyan and Kosygin, but was soon able to outmaneuver them and become supreme ruler. He reversed the de-Stalinization process initiated by Khrushchev by praising Stalin as the leader of the wartime USSR on the twentieth anniversary of victory.

Early in his leadership, Brezhnev was forced to deal with the "Prague Spring." In January 1968, the Czechoslovakian leadership under Alexander Dubcek began a liberalization of party rule. This contravened Brezhnev's personal ideology, so he commanded an invasion of Czechoslovakia to restore Soviet influence and end the liberalization of the Party there. Brezhnev asserted the right to use Soviet intervention in order to maintain Communism in its Eastern Satellites in what was to become known as the "Brezhnev Doctrine."

Under Brezhnev the economy began to stagnate because of its over-reliance on an agricultural industry which had not sufficiently recovered from the days of collectivization. High levels of military spending placed

Above: A Russian tank in the heart of war-torn Budapest in 1956. Following uprisings in East Germany and Poland, the USSR sent troops into Hungary after Hungarian rebels announced that it would withdraw from the Warsaw Pact.
Opposite: President Gorbachev who initiated the policies of Perestroika and Glasnost.

Stalin therefore tightened his grip over Eastern Europe, developing a series of Communist satellite states which remained in power until the 1980s. Stalin's power within the USSR became even greater; he had, after all, presided over the victory, and the purges began again. He embarked on a further purge called the Doctors' Plot, which was effectively a purge of the Jewish population in the USSR. Stalin's justification was that he believed all Jews were American agents. The Doctors' Plot was brought to a halt with the death of Stalin on March 5, 1953. The official report stated that he had died of a cerebral hemorrhage, but many conspiracy theories have developed suggesting he was murdered.

a heavy burden on this already weak economy. Furthermore, the rigid, centrally planned system gave little scope for innovation in science and technology. Combined with the absence of competition for jobs, this led to reduced efficiency, lower overall quality, and low output. Living standards fell with the decline in output, giving rise to a black market in consumer goods. This led to widespread corruption, and particularly susceptible to such corruption were Brezhnev and the leading Party members. The Brezhnev tenure became known as the "era of stagnation."

Gorbachev and Reform

The USSR was for a short time ruled by Andropov until his death in 1984; he was followed by Chernenko, whose rule was even briefer. Andropov offered a brief respite from the Brezhnev era by investigating official corruption; however, under Chernenko moves were made to return to the Brezhnev era and the investigations into corruption was halted. Chernenko was often ill and his rule was interrupted by long absences when he was in hospital; he eventually died on March 10, 1985.

The following day, Mikhail Gorbachev was appointed General Secretary of the Party. By 1987 he felt he had consolidated his control of the Party sufficiently to introduce his reform policies, *Glasnost* and *Perestroika*. *Perestroika* was the reconstruction of the Soviet economy in order to remedy the years of stagnation under Brezhnev. One typical law passed as part of *Perestroika* was the law on state enterprise, which allowed companies to determine their own output based upon the demand for the goods they produced. Furthermore the government was no longer expected to bail companies out if they went bankrupt. Another law, on "Cooperatives," allowed private enterprise for the first time since Lenin's New Economic Policy. Simultaneously with his launch of *Perestroika*, Gorbachev initiated *Glasnost*, a policy of openness and freedom of speech. *Glasnost* was designed to open the debate on economic reform, and also make it more difficult for conservative Party members to criticize reform. *Glasnost* ultimately undermined the regime as it revealed the superior living standards of most people in western societies in comparison to those within the USSR. People became disenchanted with the slow pace of *Perestroika* and reform was not achieved in time to prevent the collapse of the Union.

The Collapse of the USSR

When the extent of the economic crisis was revealed by *Glasnost*, each of the fifteen constituent republics began withholding raw materials, manufactured goods and hard currency from the Union. *Glasnost* also gave rise to an increase in anti-Russian sentiments in the outlying republics. These republics began calling for independence; in Azerbaijan and Lithuania, nationalist uprisings were crushed by the Red Army. However, a relaxation of the censorship laws allowed reports of this recent Soviet repression to spread and further encouraged nationalist groups.

In August 1991, conservative Party members made a final attempt to undermine Gorbachev and halt his reforms. While Gorbachev was holidaying in the Crimea he was placed under house arrest. The coup instigators were forced to back down when Yeltsin, the leader of the Russian Soviet Republic, refused to back them. Gorbachev returned to Moscow, but his power was severely compromised. While he had to arrest much of his Politburo for involvement in the coup, Yeltsin's position as Speaker of the Supreme Soviet of the Russian Federation had strengthened. Russia decreed that it no longer followed the Soviet Union's laws and therefore Union control of the largest republic was essentially lost. The other fourteen republics made similar announcements successively in order to avoid Russian dominance in place of the USSR. On Christmas Day 1991, Gorbachev resigned and passed his executive powers on to Yeltsin. The USSR was dissolved and fifteen republics took its place.

The Cold War

The Cold War overshadowed the post-war world, as the superpowers jostled for the upper hand. Most countries were affected by the consequences of this struggle for dominance.

Origins

In spite of their ideological differences, Britain, America, and the Soviet Union were allies during the Second World War. In February 1945 the "Big Three" met at Yalta and agreed to divide Europe into different zones of occupation; the Soviets in the East, the Americans and the British in the West and in the Balkans.

However, the Allies' differing opinions on the nature of the post-war world could not be reconciled owing to their divergent ideologies. In their respective zones each sought to implement political and economic structures to mirror their own. For Britain and America this meant encouragement of pluralism and free trade. The Soviet Union sought the establishment of centrally planned economies and Communist Party monopoly of power. America undermined Communist Parties in Western Europe and the Soviets were displaying expansionist tendencies towards Iran, Turkey and Greece. As a result, George Keenan wrote his "long telegram," which was to form the basis of President Truman's foreign policy. Keenan claimed that peaceful coexistence would be impossible as Soviet leaders were highly paranoid about Western intentions. The British Empire was no longer strong enough to keep Soviet expansion at bay, and in 1947

Below: British Prime Minister Winston Churchill (L), US President Franklin D. Roosevelt (C) and Soviet Premier Josef Stalin (R) at the Conference of the Big Three at Yalta in February 1945.

ORIGINS OF THE COLD WAR,
EUROPE AFTER WORLD WAR II
1945–1949

Soviet Union from May 1945

Western limit of Soviet occupation or
influence mid-1945

Occupied by western forces or
pro-western in sympathy

Soviet occupied or control

Soviet zones of Germany and Austria

Franco's Pro-western Falangist
regime isolated

Yugoslav–Soviet rift 28 June 1948
becoming non-aligned

Civil war 1946–49 Pro-western Forces
gain control

Original members of NATO
4 April 1949

Colonial territories

Neutral

(1) From Germany to Poland 1945

(2) from Germany to USSR 1945

(3) Returned to
Czechoslovakia from

(4) Returned to Romania
from Hungary 1945

(5) From Hungary
to USSR 1945

(6) From Romania
to USSR 1945

(7) To USSR 1940,
lost 1941, retaken 1944

(8) To USSR 1940, lost 1941–44,
returned 1947

(9) To USSR 1947

(10) Federal Republic of Germany
formed Sept. 1949

0   200 km
0   200 miles

Norwegian Sea

North Sea

Edinburgh

IRELAND
Dublin

GREAT BRITAIN

London

Atlantic Ocean

Amsterdam
NETH.
Brussels
BELGIUM
LUX.

Hamburg
British zone
Berlin
G E R M A N Y
U.S. zone

FRANCE
Paris

Luxembourg
Independent 1945
(incorporated into
Germany 1940–45)

Alsace Lorraine
Returned to
France 1945

Small border
areas returned
to France 1945

Returned to
France 1945

Genoa

SWITZERLAND

French zone

Fr. zone
U.S. zone
Br. zone
AUSTRIA
Vienna

Prague
CZECHOSLOVAKIA
Communist coup February 1948

Stuttgart

HUNGARY
Budapest

Copenhagen
DENMARK

Baltic Sea

S W E D E N

N O R W A Y

FINLAND

Estonia
Latvia
Lithuania

Warsaw

P O L A N D

Cracow

U S S R

R O M A N I A
Bucharest

BULGARIA

YUGOSLAVIA
Yugoslav–Soviet rift 28 June 1948
becoming non-aligned

Adriatic Sea

ALBANIA

GREECE
Civil war
1946–49
Pro-western Forces
gain control

Athens

Aegean Sea

S P A I N
Franco's Pro-western
Falangist regime isolated

Oporto
PORTUGAL
Madrid
Lisbon

ANDORRA

From Italy
1947–54

Rome
Naples

I T A L Y

Corsica

Sardinia

Sicily

Balearic Is.

Tangier
International
zone
Morocco
(Spain)

Gibraltar (Britain)

Morocco
(France)

Algiers
ALGERIA
(France)

Tunis
TUNISIA
(France)

Malta
(Britain)

M e d i t e r r a n e a n   S e a

Crete

Above: American tanks and troops at the American sector checkpoint in the Berlin Wall in Germany.

Truman decided to pursue a policy of containment, though ships were sent to patrol the Mediterranean and the US provided economic assistance to defeat the Communists in the Greek Civil War.

Washington feared that communism could spread westward since Western Europe had been economically devastated after the Second World War, and so massive amounts of American aid were to be given to Europe under the Marshall Plan. Marshall Aid was even offered to Eastern Europe so as not to directly antagonize the Soviets, but Moscow saw this as an attempt to undermine Soviet control in its sphere of influence. The Marshall Plan placed Western Europe firmly into the American bloc and consequently forced the USSR to further tighten its control in the East. The Cold War—a remorseless struggle for dominance by any means short of actual hand-to-hand fighting—had begun.

The Warsaw Pact and the North Atlantic Treaty Organization (NATO)

The North Atlantic Treaty was signed by twelve nations in 1949. It stemmed from the Brussels treaty, which had been signed by Britain, France, Belgium, the Netherlands, and Luxembourg as a defensive arrangement for Western Europe against the Soviet Union. However, the Brussels group was not strong enough to keep communist infiltration into Western Europe at bay, so the Treaty was expanded to incorporate the United States, Canada, Denmark, Iceland, Italy, Norway, and Portugal. Together, these nations signed the North Atlantic Treaty in order to provide mutual assistance if any one of them was attacked by a non-member state. In 1955 West Germany was included in the treaty, which the Soviet Union viewed as a deliberately antagonistic move.

As a result it created the Warsaw Pact, a "Treaty on Friendship, Cooperation and Mutual Assistance" in order to counterbalance NATO. It was signed by states under Communist Party control, including Czechoslovakia, Poland, Hungary, Bulgaria, East Germany, Romania, and Albania. The initial aim of the Warsaw Pact was as a mechanism of control for the USSR over its new satellites. However, as it progressed, it provided a forum for inter-party debates where regional stability could be discussed. Although the Warsaw Pact was dissolved in 1991, NATO has continued, with many of the former Warsaw Pact states signing up.

Berlin

At the end of the Second World War, the capital of the Third Reich was divided into four occupying zones. Eventually, the British, French, and Americans amalgamated their sectors, forming West Berlin, while the USSR held on to the East. Germany was similarly divided and in 1949 the Federal Republic of Germany (West Germany) and the German Democratic Republic (East Germany) were formed. West Berlin was deep inside East Germany and this was to prove contentious throughout the course of the Cold War. In June 1948, the Communist authorities in the East imposed a blockade of western goods getting to West Berlin through East German territory; this was intended to try and starve West Berlin and pressure this sector of the

Below: The historic first meeting between Soviet leader Nikita Khrushchev and newly-elected American President John F Kennedy in Vienna in June 1961.

city to come under Soviet control. The Truman administration in the US responded quickly by embarking upon the Berlin Airlift, a daily delivery of vital supplies by air for well over a year, which caused the Soviet government to end the blockade.

During the 1950s Berlin remained a divided city, yet with a pass people could still move between the zones. However, this movement was actually only in one direction, from East to West, and the East German authorities required a rapid solution to stop the mass exodus of its citizens. On the morning of August 13, 1961 Berliners awoke to find their city literally divided by huge barbed-wire fences, which were later to be replaced with a concrete wall: the Berlin Wall. All transport links between the two sectors were cut, and guard posts set up along the border. In 1963, with West Berliners' morale particularly low, President Kennedy visited the city and delivered his famous "Ich bin ein Berliner" speech. The sentiment

Below: Fidel Castro became prime minister of Cuba in 1959 when he led the Communist overthrow of Batista.

was that West Berlin was a symbol of liberty and that all freedom-loving people were in effect citizens of Berlin. This boosted the morale of West Berliners.

The Korean War

At the end of the Second World War the US and the USSR negotiated a joint occupation of the Korean peninsula after it was liberated from Japan. The border dividing the zones ran along the thirty-eighth parallel. To the north of this, in Soviet-controlled territory, Korean communists were given key positions in government, and in the south, the Americans ensured nationalists and conservatives were prominent. When it came to finding a solution to reunite the two zones and provide independence, the two governments were irreconcilable.

Both regimes saw themselves as the legitimate government of the whole of Korea, and made it their aim to destroy the other and rule supreme over the entire peninsula. After several years of minor skirmishes, Kim Il Sung, the leader of the North Korean communists, finally gained Stalin's agreement to an invasion of the South, which began on June 25, 1950. In response, Truman convinced the American government to militarily assist the South by likening the North's attack to Nazi aggression and non-intervention to the much discredited policy of appeasement. The United States also managed to engineer UN support for a war against North Korea because the USSR was boycotting the UN Security Council in protest over its failure to recognize Communist China. The UN counter-offensive was successful, and drove the communists beyond the previous border. The UN forces crossed the thirty-eighth parallel and, at the greatest extent of their advance, neared the Chinese border.

But crossing the demarcation line had grave consequences: the People's Republic of China decided to come to the aid of its communist allies in North Korea and pushed the UN forces back into Southern territory. A war of attrition continued for two more years, leading the Chinese, the Americans, and the UN to agree to an armistice which was signed in July 1953, with the border having changed very little from its pre-war position.

The "Spy Plane" Incident

On May 1, 1960 the Soviet Union shot down an American U2 spy plane and captured the pilot, Gary Powers, together with photographs of Soviet military

Above: American troops assault North Korean positions beyond the thirty-eigth parallel with heavy shelling from 155mm self-propelled guns.

installations. President Eisenhower was forced to admit that he had authorized the flight, so as not to undermine the pending "Big Four" summit in Paris. This meeting between Britain, France, the US, and the Soviet Union was designed to reduce Cold War tensions, but the spy plane incident overshadowed the entire event. Khrushchev refused to proceed unless Eisenhower issued an apology. Eisenhower refused and the talks failed; soon after, the Cold War escalated with confrontation over the construction of the Berlin Wall and the over the Soviet stationing of missiles in Cuba.

The Cuban Missile Crisis

In 1962, President Kennedy announced that US intelligence had discovered that the Soviet Union was developing missile bases less than a hundred miles away from American territory, in Cuba.

The United States had been trying to topple Castro's communist regime since its inception. In 1961, the CIA had trained Cuban exiles to instigate a counter-revolutionary assault on the Bay of Pigs in Cuba. Meanwhile the Soviet leadership under Khrushchev was anxious that the Cold War was not progressing in their favor; talks were stalling over Berlin, and the United States not only had a greater nuclear arsenal, but also had missiles stationed in Turkey, within striking distance of Soviet territory. Moscow was keen to redress the nuclear balance of

power and, as Castro needed assistance to consolidate his rule, stationing Soviet missiles on Cuban soil was mutually beneficial.

Kennedy, meanwhile, as a young, Democrat president, needed to demonstrate firm resolve to a sceptical public in containing the "red terror." Therefore he was not in a position to back down when he announced that the USSR must withdraw the missiles and ordered a naval blockade of Cuba to stop Soviet ships reaching Cuba. In response to the blockade, Khrushchev authorized Soviet commanders to launch their nuclear weapons if the Americans launched a ground assault. Trapped in a deadlock which took the world to the brink of nuclear war, neither man could easily budge from his position. Finally, the older of the two statesmen, Khrushchev, decided to back down in order to avoid a third world war. On October 28, seven days after the crisis began, he ordered Soviet ships to return and agreed to dismantle Soviet nuclear weapons in Cuba.

The Cold War and the Third World

The Second World War had damaged Britain, and France's abilities to maintain their empires, and the process of decolonization began immediately. Over the coming decades most of the European colonies were

Inset map labels:

CHINA
Lao Cai
Cao Bang
Nanning
CHINA
BURMA
Dien Bien Phu
Lang Son
Tonkin
Red
Hanoi
Haiphong
Gulf of Tonkin
20°
Sam Neua
Luang Prabang
Mekong
Phat Diem
Hainan
L A O S
Vinh
Vientiane
Yankee Station
US 7th fleet
THAILAND
Mekong
Donghoi
DMZ
16°
Pakse
Hue
Tourane
I CORPS
Quang Ngai
Bangkok
Kontum
Pleiku
Qui Nhon
Siem Reap
II CORPS
CAMBODIA
Ban Me Thuot
Nha Trang
Kratie
12°
N
Gulf of Thailand
Phnom Penh
Loc Ninh
Phan Rang
Dixie Station
III CORPS
Bien Hoa
Saigon
Sihanoukville
1973 US military evacuation
IV CORPS
Cau Mau
0   100 km
0   100 miles

Legend 1:

VIETNAM WAR 1959–75

Communist-held area January 1973 "ceasefire"

U.S. corps command area

North Vietnam subject to air attack

Communist-controlled area in Laos and Cambodia 1950–75

Controlled by Khmer Rouge c. 1975

Controlled by Pathet Lao c. 1975

Area of Communist guerrilla activity c. 1975

Legend 2:

COMMUNIST SUPPLY ROUTES

Ho Chi Minh Trail

Sihanouk Trail

Sea supply routes

Communist-held area 1959–60

Main map labels:

Ha Giang
Nanning
NORTH VIETNAM
CHINA
Hanoi
Haiphong
Nam Dinh
Ninh Binh
Gulf of Tonkin
Thanh Hoa
Hainan
Vinh
Yulin
Nape Pass
HaTinh
Mu Gia Pass
Ben Kari Pass
Dong Hoi
Thakhek
DMZ
Quang Tri
Tchepone
Khe Sanh
Savannakhet
Hue
LAOS
Da Nang
Ubon Ratchathani
Quang Ngai
Kontum
CAMBODIA (KAMPUCHEA)
Qui Nhon
Battambang
Pursat
Kratie
Nha Trang
Kompong Chhnang
Mekong
Kompong Cham
Cam Ranh Bay
Phnom Penh
SOUTH VIETNAM
Gulf of Thailand
Ho Chi Minh City (Saigon)
Kompong Som (Sihanoukville)
My Tho
Can Tho
Vonh Loi
South China Sea
2000
1000
500
200
0 m
0   100 km
0   100 miles

granted independence and the new superpowers, the USA and the USSR, stepped in to fill the vacuum that the Europeans had left behind. The Soviet Union was keen to nurture the growth of Communism, while the USA meanwhile wished to stimulate markets in these newly-independent countries.

However, the new regimes were keen not to replace their previous colonial masters with others in either Washington or Moscow, and many of the new states joined the Non-Aligned Movement, in order to manipulate both sides and gain more funding. Frequently the decolonization process was not smooth, as different interest groups vied for power. In order to propel themselves into government rather than rival groups, many enlisted Soviet or American support. Angola is a case in point. When it was granted independence from Portugal in 1975 the three main parties refused to work with one another. The Marxists obtained assistance from Cuba and the USSR, while the US and South Africa gave support to the nationalist UNITA. This led to a prolonged civil war, which long outlasted the Cold War. America was particularly keen to maintain US dominance of the Third World countries of the Americas and was involved in challenging communists in Chile, Cuba, El Salvador, Grenada, and Nicaragua.

Vietnam War

After the Vietnamese defeated the French in the war for independence a peace agreement was signed in Geneva in 1954. The result was to split the country in two, between a communist North and a capitalist South, pending elections and unification. Unification became impossible as both the North and the South began implementing contrary socio-economic systems. Moreover, by the late 1950s the communist Vietcong, with Soviet support, was trying to subvert the US-sponsored regime in the South, a government which was rendered more unstable following a coup d'état in 1963. In 1965, the American President, Lyndon B Johnson, decided upon direct military assistance to the South to destroy the Vietcong guerrilla campaign and the North Vietnamese Army. American forces were unable to defeat the Vietcong by conventional methods owing to the jungle terrain and widespread sympathy for their cause. Additionally, the North Vietnamese Army was sustained by financial and technical support from both the USSR and China. The Americans were unable to win the "hearts and minds" of the South Vietnamese because they employed severe tactics to

root out Vietcong from amongst the villagers and used napalm and herbicides to destroy farmland, killing many people in the process. Ironically, the United States' intervention increased support for the communists. By the late 1960s it became clear to America that the war was unwinnable; it was costing too many American lives, and resulting in considerable public protest at home and abroad.

After Nixon became president, he promised a "Vietnamization" of the war—the removal of US troops leaving the South Vietnamese regime to oppose the North by itself. After the US withdrawal in 1973, the North's victory was in sight, but did not arrive until April 1975, when the government in the South finally surrendered.

Détente

The Cold War was punctuated by periods of détente (a relaxation of tension.) The main period of détente can be discerned from the beginning of the Strategic Arms Limitation Talks (SALT 1), which were held between 1969 and 1972, when the Vietnam War was drawing to a close. Both sides had achieved second-strike capability since their deployment of nuclear submarines. This had reinforced the realization of the potential for mutually-assured destruction, or MAD—the understanding that any nuclear war would devastate both sides—and made both sides more amenable to negotiation. Furthermore, in the early 1970s the impasse over Berlin was broken, as Willy Brandt attempted to re-establish links with East Germany. By 1972 SALT 1 had resulted in agreements to reduce nuclear arsenals on both sides, especially anti-ballistic missiles. The period of détente was sustained by the Helsinki Accords of 1975, which were the final act in the establishment of the Organization for the Security and Cooperation, in Europe. The Accords became the touchstone of détente; agreement was reached on security, economic cooperation and environmental degradation, and every European nation was in attendance except Albania. A section on human rights was also included, which the Americans planned to use as a platform to petition the USSR to end human rights abuses.

Afghanistan and the New Cold War

On Christmas Day 1979 détente effectively collapsed with the Soviet invasion of Afghanistan. However, the seeds of the collapse had been sown beforehand, when

the Carter administration in the United States used the Helsinki agreement to reproach the Soviet Union's human rights record. The USSR intervened in Afghanistan to stop a rebellion by the Islamic fundamentalist groups, the mujahedeen, who were opposing the pro-Moscow government. In reaction, the United States funded the mujahedeen and after the brief spell of détente the two superpowers were once more engaged in indirect conflict.

Unable to defeat the Islamic resistance, the Soviet intervention lasted until 1989, making it a costly conflict in terms of lives, money, and resources. Partly resulting from Soviet escalation of the Cold War and the Iranian hostage crisis in January 1981, the Americans returned the Republican Ronald Reagan as their new president. In 1984 Reagan implemented the NATO Dual Track decision to update the Intermediate-range Nuclear Forces (INFs) in Western Europe to Pershing II warheads in response to Soviet deployment of updated SS20s in 1976.

Reagan talked tough on communism, delivering his famous "Evil Empire" speech, directed at the USSR

Above: Russian soldiers invade Afghanistan in December 1979, only withdrawing their troops in 1989.

and proclaiming the need for a Star Wars-style missile defense shield. He also acted tough, attempting to topple the Sandinista regime in Nicaragua and engaging in direct military intervention in Grenada.

COLD WAR ALIGNMENTS TO 1991

NATO member, 1990

US influence or intervention, 1981–89

Star Wars defense system

USSR, 1990

Warsaw Pact member, 1955 to 1991 (formally dissolved July 1991)

Soviet troop withdrawal, 1989

Soviet troop withdrawal, 1990–91

Simultaneously, however, Reagan told the USSR that if they proved willing to negotiate, he would be prepared to listen.

Above: Soviet leader Mikhail Gorbachev stands alongside US president Ronald Reagan in 1986.
Opposite: Former shipyard worker, Lech Walesa, became leader of the Solidarity movement in Poland.

Gorbachev and Reagan

In March 1985 Mikhail Gorbachev assumed power in the Soviet Union. As a moderate reformer, he applied a "new thinking" to his foreign policy. He initiated a rapprochement with the West in order to end the Soviet Union's unsustainably large defense budget. In line with "new thinking" a series of summits were arranged; they were designed to reduce nuclear arsenals and improve the relationship between the two blocs.

The first summit at Geneva broke the deadlock between the two sides who had not met in six years but the next meeting at Reykjavik in 1986 failed as Reagan refused to give way on his plans for a Strategic Defence Initiative, SDI. A series of meetings between Gorbachev and Western leaders culminated in the Washington Summit in 1987, where the arms race came to an end as both sides agreed to decrease their arsenals of intermediate range nuclear missiles—and so the Cold War was ended. Further talks in 1991—called START I—reduced the number of long-range nuclear weapons. These were followed by START II in 1993, and the Treaty of Moscow in 2002 saw further reductions of both Russian and American nuclear armaments.

The Collapse of Communist Regimes in Eastern Europe

The Eastern European communist regimes had formed a vital part of the Soviet Union's security system during the Cold War. However, with the improvement of longer-range missile technology, they had become less strategically useful to Moscow and instead developed into an economic burden. In 1988 Gorbachev announced that the Brezhnev Doctrine was officially over; the USSR would no longer prop up its allies in Eastern Europe as it had done in Czechoslovakia in 1968.

Without Soviet assistance the regimes were forced to go it alone. With the removal of the threat of Soviet military intervention, opposition movements became increasingly proactive in launching demonstrations and strikes. In Poland and Hungary, the communist parties were forced into round-table talks with opposition groups as it became clear the population would no longer stand for Party rule. In these so-called "negotiated revolutions," the talks

resulted in freer elections for both countries. In Poland, Solidarity emerged as the main opposition movement under Lech Walesa after the organization had been suppressed by the authorities following a failed uprising in 1980. Walesa was eventually appointed as Poland's first non-communist president in 1990.

The changes in Poland and Hungary set a chain reaction in motion across the entire bloc. The Communist monopoly of power in both Bulgaria and Czechoslovakia soon ended as their populations learned from the example being set in the neighboring countries and demanded reform. Increased freedom of movement resulting from these revolutions meant that East German citizens had now gained an easier means of reaching West Germany; the Austria–Hungary border was opened and East Germans poured into West German embassies across the Soviet bloc demanding asylum. Faced with a rapidly declining population and weekly protests Egon Krenz, the new East German leader, had little choice but to allow freedom of travel.

On the evening of November 9, 1989, East Berliners gathered along the Berlin Wall, and owing to a misinterpretation of Krenz's new travel laws, began tearing it down and walking freely into the West. The collapse of the Wall did not remedy the economic stagnation nor halt the decline in population and eventually the East German authorities were forced to agree to reunification, which occurred on October 3, 1990.

The revolution was only violent in Romania, where the leader, Nicolae Ceausescu, had developed a stronger grip on power than his neighbors through extensive repression and a strong personality cult. However, information about revolutions in Eastern Europe and of Ceausescu's repression and ethnic cleansing were quickly disseminated through radio broadcasts from neighboring countries. This resulted in protests and street fighting; the civilian population together with the Army rose up against Ceausescu loyalists. In a bid to end the fighting, Ceausescu was promptly tried and executed on Christmas Day 1989.

The Middle East Since 1948

The establishment and existence of Israel led to a series of conflicts with its neighbors in the Middle East, resulting in continuing problems across the region.

The Israeli War of Independence

Soon after the British withdrew from Palestine in 1948, the Israeli War of Independence began. On May 15, 1947 the declaration of the State of Israel was made, but many Arabs formally rejected the Partition Plan put forward by the United Nations in November 1947. It had proposed the establishment of both a Jewish and an Arab state in Palestine. Instead, Jewish and Arab militias began a campaign to control territory beyond the UN-designated borders with the Palestinian militia assisted by Iraqi, Syrian, Egyptian, Jordanian, and Lebanese troops. Up to a million Palestinian refugees left Israeli territory and 600,000 Israeli refugees left Arab territories across the Middle East. While Israeli refugees were incorporated into the new state, Palestinian refugees received very little assistance from the rest of the Arab world, and were forced to set up homes in refugee camps across the region, where many remain to this day. There were some exceptions; the Moroccan king refused to expel the Jews there and the leaders of the Israeli town of Haifa encouraged Arabs to remain. A ceasefire came with the signing of an armistice at Rhodes in 1949, but a peace treaty was not signed.

The Suez Crisis

Israel joined Britain and France in an invasion of the Sinai peninsula in Egypt in 1956 to forcibly reverse Egyptian President Nasser's nationalization of the Suez Canal and his blockade of the Straits of Tiran. Israel was keen to open the canal to its shipping, while Britain and France wanted to retain their pre-existing shipping interests, which had been adversely affected by Nasser's nationalist campaign. The invasion was initially successful; however, the United States was forced to intervene against its three closest allies, who then had no choice but to withdraw under the threat of American economic pressure. In return for Israel's withdrawal from the Sinai peninsula, it was granted shipping rights in the canal. The United Nations adopted a resolution and proceeded to send troops into the area in order to maintain peace and order whilst a political settlement was worked out.

The Six-Day War, 1967

The political situation following Suez had not been suitably resolved, as Egypt once again blockaded the Straits of Tiran and expelled United Nations troops from Sinai, replacing them with Egyptian forces.

Right: British prime minister James Callaghan meets President Anwar Sadat of Egypt in 1978.
Opposite page: Israeli chief of staff David Elazar (second right) and later Israeli premier Yitzhak Rabin (left), land near frontline positions on the Golan Heights during the Yom Kippur war in 1973.

Furthermore, Nasser called upon all Arabs to assist in the destruction of Israel. As a result, Israel decided to launch a pre-emptive strike into Egypt and an initial air strike destroyed much of the Egyptian air force while it was still on the ground. This attack was compounded by a ground assault in which Israel managed to capture the Gaza Strip and Sinai once again. Taking advantage of this Israeli offensive in the south west, Syria and Jordan attacked it from the north and east. Their attack was easily repelled by Israel which used it as a reason for occupying the West Bank (previously Jordanian territory) and the Golan Heights (previously Syrian). The war had a crucial outcome on the balance of power as Israel was now seen as a regional force to be reckoned with.

The Yom Kippur War, 1973

On October 6, 1973, the Jewish holy day of Yom Kippur, Egypt and Syria launched a simultaneous attack on Israel to regain Sinai and the Golan Heights respectively.

Initially they were successful, but after several weeks of fighting America came to Israel's aid with an airlift of essential munitions and supplies. American involvement helped broker a ceasefire, but Israeli public opinion had been severely shaken by heavy losses of both men and aircraft. The deal negotiated by American secretary of state Henry Kissinger saw another Israeli withdrawal from the Sinai peninsula and a multinational force was provided to monitor the border. This led to both Israel and Egypt signing the Camp David Accords in 1979, which was the first peace treaty between Israel and an Arab state. It resulted in Egypt's expulsion from the Arab League and the assassination of the then Egyptian Premier, Anwar Sadat, by Islamic extremists in 1981.

The Syrians were less successful than the Egyptians. The Israeli advance had placed them within shelling distance of the Syrian capital, Damascus, and they were forced into a ceasefire in which they agreed to return to their pre-war borders, with continued Israeli control of the Golan Heights.

The Israeli–Lebanese War

As a civil war raged in Lebanon, Yasser Arafat's Palestine Liberation Organization was able to carve out a semi-autonomous enclave in the south of the country, within striking distance of Israel. After a series of raids on its citizens, Israel decided to respond by invading Lebanon. This successfully removed the PLO threat, as it was forced to relocate to Tunisia, but it did bring widespread international criticism. In addition, the Maronite Christian massacres of more than 1,000 Palestinian refugees in camps in West Beirut tarnished Israel's international reputation, as it was seen as having failed to prevent them happening. Although the PLO were banished, the Israeli occupation begat more opposition from other Arab militia groups, especially Hezbollah. By 1985, Israel had retreated from all but the far south of Lebanon near the border with Israel. It was not until 2000 that Israel completely withdrew from Lebanon; however, Hezbollah claim that it is still occupying the small area of Cheeba Farms.

The First Intifada

After years of Israeli military control the Palestinian population in the West Bank and Gaza Strip grew angry at the conditions there and, furthermore, both Egypt and Jordan were loosening their claims to the Gaza Strip and the West Bank respectively. All that was needed to spark widespread insurrection was a trigger, which came in 1987 when an Israeli settler shot a Palestinian schoolgirl in the back. The PLO, in exile in Tunisia, were keen to coordinate this spontaneous protest, but they were now rivaled by two other groups, Palestinian Islamic Jihad and Hamas, both vying for grassroots control of the opposition movement. These three main interest groups, with differing agendas, prolonged the uprising. Israel, with superior military capability, was successful in containing the Intifada, though not without creating internal problems. Allegations of human rights abuses divided Israeli domestic opinion, giving rise to the election of a moderate leader, Yitzhak Rabin, in 1992. His willingness to negotiate led to the peace process, which eventually culminated in the Oslo Accords, a series of agreements.

The Oslo Accords

The Oslo Accords ultimately agreed an Israeli withdrawal from the Gaza Strip and the West Bank which would form the first step to the creation of a Palestinian state. The Israeli President, Yitzhak Rabin, and the PLO leader, Yasser Arafat, famously shook hands on the White House lawn and signed the Declaration of Principles on September 13, 1993. For

Below: PLO Chairman Yasser Arafat pictured in 1988.
Opposite: US President Bill Clinton, left, meets Israeli prime minister Ehud Barak in 2000 during the Arab-Israeli summit at Camp David.

the first time in history the PLO and the state of Israel formally recognized one another. However, despite international jubilation, contentious issues such as the Israeli settlements in the West Bank and Gaza, rights to Jerusalem and border security were not dealt with.

The Accords allowed Jordan to sign a peace treaty with Israel in October 1994. The two countries had not been at war since 1967 and so agreement was more easily reached than with either Lebanon or Syria. These negotiations had not sufficiently developed by November 1995 when Yitzhak Rabin was assassinated by a man who was opposed to negotiating with the Arab world. His assassination came at a time of widespread discontent with the Oslo Accords, as it was felt that these had not adequately dealt with the divisive issue of the Israeli settlements. Subsequent Israeli governments under Benjamin Netanyahu and Ehud Barak refused to meet Palestinian demands and the peace process collapsed when Arafat walked out of talks. Israel's relations with the rest of the Arab world also suffered; relations with Jordan were not normalized and as Israel failed to withdraw from the Golan Heights, an agreement with Syria became impossible.

The Second Intifada

In September 2000 the main Israeli opposition leader, Ariel Sharon, visited the controversial site of the Temple of the Mount and proclaimed it forever part of Israel. While this is the holiest site in Israel, the Temple also occupies the same site as the Al-Aqsa Mosque, the third holiest site in Islam. Moreover, the sovereignty of the site is fiercely debated. It was occupied by Israel during the 1967 war, and ownership was not settled by the Oslo agreements. Sharon's proclamation met with an emotional reaction in the Muslim world and rioting spread across Jerusalem and the West Bank. When the shooting of a twelve-year-old Palestinian boy by Israeli security forces was captured by the world's news crews, the rioting became so widespread that it fused into a Second Intifada. In February 2001, Sharon was elected as Israel's prime minister and soon after began to formally reoccupy the West Bank, meeting widespread international condemnation. Suicide bombing became a prevalent tactic in the uprising, and Israel has defended its strong reaction as part of the wider global "War on Terror," building a controversial wall around the West Bank to stop terrorists entering Israel.

Division and Conflict in the Arab World

Religious and ethnic divides in the Middle East have precipitated many conflicts, while its oil reserves have made it a focus of international attention.

Oil and Development

The discovery and exploitation of oil reserves has conditioned much of the history of the Middle East in the twentieth century. The area had long been occupied by the Ottoman Turks, which gave rise to Arab nationalism. When the Ottoman Empire collapsed at the end of the First World War, the British and French held the area between them as mandates and independence was finally granted after the Second World War. Owing to centuries of non-Arab rule, a pan-Arab movement accompanied the decolonialization movement. Attempts such as the United Arab Republic, a union of Syria and Egypt between 1958 and 1961, can be seen as part of this trend. However, pan-Arab nationalism failed because new rulers were unwilling to relinquish their control. Also, different countries had different levels of wealth owing to the unequal distribution of oil across the region. Religion also proved divisive as the Arab population is split between Shiite Islam, Sunni Islam, and Christianity. After the Israeli War of Independence, Palestinian refugees set up homes in refugee camps across the region, and the fact that other Arab governments have refused to grant Palestinians citizenship—despite many having been born in these camps—continues to highlight the unfeasibility of pan-Arabism. Additionally, there are countries in the Middle East dominated by non-Arabic populations including Turkey, Egypt, and Iran.

The Iranian Revolution

In 1951 the popular Iranian Prime Minister Mohammed Mussadiq engineered the nationalization of the Anglo-Iranian Oil Company. America encouraged the Shah of Iran to dismiss Mussadiq, which resulted in the people supporting him rather than the Shah, who was seen as an American puppet and fled into exile in order to pre-empt a possible revolution. Eventually, the United States managed to restore the Shah, but in the eyes of his people he had become all the more tainted by association with the

US. In response to the dissatisfaction this caused, the Shah employed repression to avoid further insurrection. For the next two decades he embarked on a successful period of industrialization and military build-up, by the late 1970s, overspending on defense had led to a budget deficit and an economic crisis. Meanwhile Iranian society had been transformed; a narrow westernized élite had developed. Rapid industrialization resulted in a sharp increase in urban immigration and had given rise to poverty and unemployment. The Shah's censorship laws meant that social dissatisfaction could not be expressed through the media or public rallies, and only the mosques remained as a possibility for expressing freedom of thought. Here those who wished to overthrow the Shah became susceptible to the ideas of the Shiite clerics and, in particular, those of Ayatollah Khomeini, who wanted the revolution to create an Islamic republic and end the secularization and westernization occurring in the country. At the end of 1978 an article appeared in the official press criticizing Khomeini, which met with widespread public protests. Conscripts refused to fire on the protesters and switched sides. Khomeini, still in exile, called for an Islamic republic and, without the support of his army, the Shah fled. On February 11, 1979 an Islamic Republic was proclaimed in Iran. Immediately the new regime set out to disassociate itself from the West; Khomeini loyalists stormed the American Embassy in Tehran in November 1979 precipitating a hostage crisis which cost US President Carter the presidential election in 1980 and which did not end until January 1981. By this time the Shah had died in exile and the new president, Reagan, had promised to unfreeze Iranian assets. The revolution was still being consolidated when neighboring Iraq instigated a war against Iran in 1980.

The Iran–Iraq War

Saddam Hussein was keen to promote Iraq as a regional power and Iran was a prime target. Iran and

IRAQ ETHNIC AND RELIGIOUS GROUPS

- Sunni Kurd
- Sunni Arab/Sunni Kurd
- Sunni Arab
- Shia Arab/Sunni Arab
- Shia Arab

Terrorist attacks to January 2005

- Against civilians
- Against the military

RUSSIAN FEDERATION

GEORGIA

ARMENIA   AZERBAIJAN

Ozero
Sevan

TURKEY

to
AZER.

Van Gölu

Lake
Urmia

IRAN

SYRIA

Zäkho

Rawandiz

Tel Afar   Mosul   Arbil

Kirkuk

Baiji   Tuz

Tigris

Tikrit

Euphrates

Hadithah

Balad   Miqdadiyah
Bani Sad   Ba'qubah
Ramadi
BAGHDAD
Fallujah
Suwayrah
Musayyih   Mahawil
Hillah   Numaniyah
Karbala
Najaf   Amarah

Rutbah

Anbar

I   R   A   Q

JORDAN

SAUDI
ARABIA

Samawah

NasiriyahKurnah

Basra
Safwan

N

0   100 km

0   100 miles

KUWAIT

Persian
Gulf

Iraq had long-standing border disputes over the strategic Shatt al Arab waterway and the oil-rich province of Khuzestan. Iran appeared to be weakened by its recent revolution, though Khomeini was still extremely critical of Hussein's secular rule. Hussein was himself a Sunni Muslim and was renowned for his ill-treatment of Shiites in Iraq. As Iran also seemed weakened by an army purge Hussein decided to strike, basing the invasion upon evidence of Iranian support for an assassination attempt on the Iraqi foreign minister, Tariq Aziz. Iraq's war effort was financially backed by oil-rich Kuwait and Saudi Arabia, which both feared that their own Shiite minorities might be spurred on to revolution by the example set in Iran. Iraq was able to buy weapons from the USSR and its satellites as well as from much of the Arab world, while in Iran the removal of the Shah had also signaled the removal of American weapons. Iran's war effort, therefore, often employed antiquated tactics, including the widespread use of children to clear Iraqi minefields on the front line, so as not to burden Iran's small tank corps. By 1982, Iran was beginning to gain some success on the battlefields, and the United States and her allies began to intervene on behalf of Iraq, providing it with chemical and biological weapons and protecting Iraqi oil tankers. Meanwhile it became apparent that the Reagan administration was also supplying weapons to the Iranians in what became known as the "Iran–Contra" affair. In 1982, Iraq offered to negotiate with Iran. Iran refused as the ruling clerics were intent on toppling Hussein.

A stalemate dragged on for another six years until 1988, when Iraq began bombing Iranian cities including the capital, Tehran. Iran then suggested a peace agreement and Iraq agreed; protracted warfare was taking its toll on the economy and civilian morale. An estimated 1.5 million people were killed in a war which did very little to alter the borders in either side's favor. Iraq was left with a huge war debt, especially to Kuwait to whom it owed $14 billion, which contributed to the reasons for Saddam Hussein's invasion of Kuwait in 1990.

The Gulf War

Iraq believed that it had done a great service to all the nations in the Arab world by weakening Iran and preventing the spread of revolution, and that therefore its war debt should be canceled. During the Iran–Iraq war, Kuwait had begun drilling for oil inside Iraqi territory and, in order to get a favorable resolution

from the UN for this border dispute, Kuwait raised its production, which caused a drop in the oil price. This was against the interests of Iraq which needed to keep oil prices high in order to repay its war debt; furthermore, Iraq was keen to extend its access to the Persian Gulf by annexing some of Kuwait's coastline. This combination of factors ensured that an Iraqi invasion was almost inevitable. It began in August 1990 and the Iraqis quickly overran the country.

The United Nations immediately passed a resolution demanding the withdrawal of Iraqi troops followed by the implementation of economic sanctions. International intervention was decided upon when it was feared that Hussein would use Kuwait as a springboard to Saudi Arabia's Hama oil fields. These were among Saudi Arabia's most lucrative; if they came under Iraqi possession, Iraq would have a monopoly over the oil industry. Oil importing countries, like Japan and the US, would then have little choice but to negotiate with the regime. American troops moved into Saudi Arabia throughout August to protect the kingdom's oil fields. In November 1990 the United Nations Security Council passed Resolution 678, which stated that Iraq should withdraw from Kuwait by January 15, 1991. The deadline expired without any Iraqi withdrawal and subsequently the American-led, thirty-four-member coalition launched Operation Desert Storm, the continued air assault on Iraq. Operation Desert Saber, the ground operation, was launched on February 24. Iraqi troops retreated to the pre-war borders, burning Kuwaiti oil fields in their wake. By February 27, American President George Bush announced that Kuwait had been liberated.

The Lebanese Civil War

Since independence, Lebanon's different national and religious groups had lived in relative harmony. However, resentment grew amongst the majority Muslim population at their impoverishment while the Maronite Christian population appeared to be prospering. In 1975 this resentment culminated in an attempt to assassinate the leader of a prominent Christian political party, the Phalange. Phalangists responded by massacring twenty-seven Palestinians on a bus in Beirut. This was followed by reprisals and counter-reprisals on both sides, resulting in hundreds of deaths. The Lebanese Muslim population allied with those Palestinians living in refugee camps in southern Beirut. Together they occupied West Beirut, while the Christians occupied the east of the city. After fighting had engulfed the entire country, the president invited Syrian troops to intervene. The Syrian occupation gained a few years of calm until the Israeli invasion and Maronite massacres at the Sabra and Shatilla Palestinian refugee camps. The United States intervened to stop the bloodshed. The resulting agreement relied upon all foreign forces to withdraw but, as Israel had retreated to the south and American marines were being pulled out, Syria refused to leave. In the early 1980s violence was sporadic, but included attacks on the US Embassy and the American Univerity of Beirut.

In 1987 the fighting worsened when the Christian president engineered the succession of a Christian, General Aoun, as prime minister. This contravened Lebanon's unwritten understanding that

the prime minister would be a Sunni Muslim. Muslims refused to accept Aoun, and instead followed Salim al-Hoss; from September 1987, East and West Beirut had different governments. Bitter fighting followed until a successful joint Syrian and Muslim attack on Aoun forced him to flee into exile. A peace treaty, the Taif Agreement, was subsequently signed by both sides. This provided an amnesty for all participants in the war and increased political representation for the Muslim population.

The Second Gulf War

After the September 11, 2001 terrorist attacks on America, President George W Bush launched a "War on Terrorism". The initial phase saw an invasion of Afghanistan against the Taliban, a regime which the United States had originally funded in opposition to the Soviet occupation of the country during the 1980s. The aim was to destroy Osama Bin Laden's al-Qaida terrorist network, then based there. The Bush administration believed the invasion had not satisfied that aim, and that Saddam Hussein's Iraq was linked with terrorist organizations. On March 20, 2003, the United States and Britain led a markedly smaller coalition than during the first Gulf War against Iraq, and America failed to get a UN resolution in favor of an invasion. Bush asserted that Saddam Hussein had not destroyed his stockpiles of weapons of mass destruction; however, no trace of them was found by UN inspectors. The actual invasion was completed by May 1, 2003, but a large insurgency has continued with many suicide bombings and televised assassinations of foreign nationals. This was not stopped by the arrest of Saddam Hussein in December 2003.

Left: Former Iraqi president Saddam Hussein pictured in 2001.

The Balkans

An artificially created Balkan state, Yugoslavia held together for over seventy years but split apart under ethnic tensions, generating controversial international involvement.

The History of Yugoslavia

Yugoslavia was first formed after the First World War, when the peacemakers decided that the southern or "Yugo" Slavs of the Balkans should be united under one kingdom. Prior to the war, the region had come under the jurisdiction of both the Ottoman and the Austro-Hungarian Empires. The Balkans had been traditionally influenced by the Eastern Orthodox church since the time of the Byzantine Empire, many centuries earlier. However, under the influence of Ottoman and Austro-Hungarian rule many people had converted to Islam or Roman Catholicism. Religious differences were surpassed, however, by a common Slavic ethnicity, which provided a rallying point for the people of the region to oppose foreign occupation and repression. Therefore, on the collapse of the Austro-Hungarian Empire after World War I, the powers drawing up the Treaty of San-Germain saw benefit in uniting the Southern Slavs, and the Kingdom of Slovenes, Croats, and Serbians was formed in 1918.

By 1929, however, the kingdom of Yugoslavia replaced it. This was ruled by a Serb-dominated autocratic monarchy, whose presence caused resentment in non-Serb national groups. This state was broken up when it was invaded by the Axis Powers in 1941 and the Croats used this as a way of gaining control over the region, at Serbia's expense, by siding with the Axis. In exchange for collaboration, Croatia was granted autonomy and the Ustashe, a Croatian fascist group, was placed in control. Serbia, meanwhile, was under direct German occupation. In a stark precursor for what was to come in the 1990s, the Croatians began a process of genocide against the Serbian population within the borders of Croatia and many thousands were killed.

Within the occupied territories, two main resistance groups emerged. The Chetniks were a nationalist resistance movement connected to the royal government in exile, and the Yugoslavian National Liberation Army, the NLA, was a communist movement led by Josip Tito. When it emerged that the Chetniks had been engaged in secret ceasefire negotiations with the Nazis in order to crush the communists, popular support was thrown behind the

NLA. In 1944 the Nazis withdrew from the region to bolster Germany's defense against the Russian advance. With the Chetniks marginalized, the NLA was credited with expelling the Axis.

Tito's Yugoslavia

Initially the West had tried to rein in Tito by incorporating his communists into an administration with the king's government—although the king himself was exiled—and a Republic was formed under a president. Tito agreed to this arrangement in 1944, but his popularity for expelling the Germans resulted in his election as prime minister and later, in 1953, in

*Above: Former Yugoslav President Slobodan Milosevic appears in front of
the War Crimes Tribunal in 2002 in The Hague.*
*Opposite: Under the leadership of Josip Tito, the Balkan nations were
unified as Yugoslavia, a significant power in post-war Europe.*

suppressed. Although repression was used, Tito realized that this sentiment was widespread, and as a result introduced a new constitution in 1974 which made representation of each republic equal. Tito died in May 1980 but the state remained intact because the 1974 constitution kept all the nationalities content.

The Break-up of Yugoslavia

After the death of Tito, Slobodan Milosevic, the leader of the Serbian Communist Party, emerged as the pre-eminent personality in Yugoslavian politics. Milosevic, as a Serb nationalist, strengthened Serbian dominance—a provocative move in light of Croatia's historical grievances. Milosevic disguised his demands for greater Serbian dominance in a call for greater democratization, in place of the 1974 constitution, at a speech to the fourteenth Party Congress in January 1990. The demand was transparent; the other nationalities realized that democratization would see Serbians forming the majority of the electorate, so the Croatian and Slovenian delegates walked out of the Congress in protest.

In 1990 elections, pro-unionists were elected in Serbia, while independence-minded leaders were elected in Slovenia and Croatia. This caused alarm in Belgrade, leading the Yugoslavian People's Army to call for martial law, a decision which had to be approved by a majority of the republics. The talks resulted in a tie with four votes in favor and four against. The four votes in favor were cast by Serbia and its dependants (Kosovo, Montenegro, and Vojvodina) and the four against by Macedonia, Croatia, Slovenia, and Bosnia, who frequently had to ally in order to override Serbian dominance. Under such a system, progress could not be made and Croatia and Slovenia saw no other option but to declare their independence.

Croatian and Slovenian Wars

The Slovenians voted for independence in December 1990, in a landslide majority. When this was declared on June 25, 1991, Yugoslavia declared war. The war lasted ten days and was designed to break Slovenia's resolve. When it was clear that Slovenia would not forcibly return to the union, the Serbians withdrew.

his election as president as well. In assuming both roles he was able to cement his control. Tito succeeded in uniting Yugoslavia's different republics and minorities behind the idea of a socialist federation. His was the first Communist Party to break away from the Soviet Union's dominance and instead he pioneered the non-alignment movement. This made Yugoslavia a credible actor on the international stage and in turn helped to gel the country together. Tito was not averse to using coercion by the secret police to further unite Yugoslavia; in 1971 the Croatians, once again, rose up in protest against Serbian domination of the union in the so-called Croatian Spring. They were angered that Croatian income was being used to subsidize poorer republics, and that their national culture was being

ETHNIC DIVERSITY OF FORMER YUGOSLAVIA c.1990

Slovenes

Croatians

Serbians

Bosnian Muslims (Slavs
converted to Islam after
the Ottoman conquest)

Macedonians

Germans

Italians

Hungarians

Romanians

Albanians

Turks

Greeks

The bloodless war against Slovenia was not mirrored in Croatia; Croatia, unlike Slovenia, had areas with sizable Serbian populations, especially Krasjina and Slavonia. As a Serb nationalist, Milosevic refused to let these Serbs live outside Serbia. In a bid to bring Croatia back into the union and repatriate the Serb minority there, Serbia began shelling Croatian cities. Croatia's resolve did not break; instead the Serbian invasion increased their will to resist. A long siege of the city of Vukovar in Krasjina ensued until the Serbians were finally successful. Across

Croatia, both sides engaged in "ethnic cleansing:" Croatians were forced into the interior and Serbians were forced out of Croatia altogether. Given the scope of the crisis, the UN agreed to intervene. A protection force was sent in to broker a ceasefire, oversee the Serbian retreat and uphold the peace. Krasjina and Slavonia announced their independence from Croatia and formed an autonomous Serbian republic; this obstructed the signing of a peace treaty until 1995, by which time the Croatians had launched a swift invasion to recapture both provinces and forced the Serbian population out.

Bosnia

Bosnia declared its independence in April 1992. It was the most heterogeneous republic; its three main ethnic groups were the Serbians, the Croats, and the Bosniaks, a Slavic Muslim group. When independence was declared, the Serbian population rose up in protest and occupied the majority of the country, despite the fact that they only accounted for a third of the population. The Croats followed suit, annexing much of the remainder and leaving only a small area for the majority, the Bosniaks. The Bosnian Serbs, with the help of Serbia, waged ethnic cleansing on the Muslim population. Furthermore, in a bid to contain the Bosniak army within Sarajevo and the Croatian army within Mostar, both cities were subjected to long sieges, during which the Serbs would bombard the cities, killing civilians as well as soldiers. While the siege of Mostar lasted nine months, the siege of Sarajevo lasted almost four years.

The Croatians and the Bosniaks were initially in agreement against the Serbs, but as the war raged, a dispute over the little territory the Serbs had left them escalated into a war in 1993. Eventually, a deal was negotiated and this war ceased within a year, but not before the country had been splintered further asunder. In 1993 the UN protection force maintaining the peace in Croatia had its remit extended to cover Bosnia as well. Safe zones were established, including Srebrenica, where in 1995, Serbian forces led by Ratko Mladic entered the zone and massacred more than 7,000 Bosniaks. International opinion was by now firmly against the Serbs as a result of the atrocities in Srebrenica and this was compounded by the Serbs raiding NATO weapons stores and flouting the no-fly zone over Bosnia. NATO was therefore forced to use its military might for the first time since its inception against Serbia. It shot down Serbian fighters and launched air raids on Serbian munitions stores. The Serbian war effort was now futile. They finally agreed to a ceasefire and, later, to sign the Dayton Peace Agreement, where Bosnia was divided, creating a Serbian and a Bosniak-Croat section.

After the war the International Criminal Tribunal for the Former Yugoslavia was established to try war criminals from both sides. Some convictions have been made, but some of the greatest war criminals remain at large; at the time of writing these include Mladic, who was responsible for Srebrenica, and Radovan Karadzic who is thought responsible for ordering ethnic cleansing.

Kosovo

In response to Serbian repression, ethnic Albanians in Kosovo formed a resistance movement in 1996, the Kosovan Liberation Army or the KLA. The KLA began a guerrilla campaign against the Serbian authorities in Kosovo, which resulted in severe reprisals. These reprisals saw thousands of Albanian refugees leave Kosovo for Macedonia, which had the potential to upset the fragile balance of Albanian–Slav relations there. If Macedonia fell to instability, then so could the entire Balkans.

NATO therefore decided to send in peacekeeping forces with Serbia's complicity. This failed to stop the fighting, and after the January 1999 massacre of 45 Albanians by Serbian police and the failure of negotiations, NATO decided upon direct military action. The bombing campaign began on March 24, 1999 and lasted until June 10. In that period Serbian military, economic and communications targets were bombed. A convoy of Albanian refugees and the Chinese Embassy were also bombarded, bringing much international criticism. As NATO began plans for a ground offensive, Russia convinced Milosevic to back down. He finally acquiesced and allowed a NATO occupation of Kosovo. NATO's mandate to intervene came under severe criticism as it lacked a UN resolution; it was also not in keeping with its charter, which only sanctions action if a member state is attacked and Kosovo was not a member state. In the aftermath of the war, hundreds of thousands of Albanians returned; however, thousands of Serbs were driven out. The loss of Kosovo from Yugoslavia was crucial to the popular revolt which overthrew Milosevic in 2000. He was subsequently arrested and put on trial at The Hague for war crimes.

Post-Colonial Africa

The struggle for freedom and independence in Africa took many forms, and the continent's colonial past has left many problems in its wake.

British Decolonization

After the loss of its colonies in the Far East to Japan during the Second World War, Britain increased its economic exploitation of its African colonies. To do this, an increasingly industrialized base was required, giving rise to a black African working class. Meanwhile, in the war with Germany, over 300,000 black Africans were conscripted. After the war both demobbed soldiers and the new working class began to call for greater black African representation in colonial governments.

Britain and France granted this increased representation in the hope that it would permit further post-war economic development, which would in turn benefit the imperial powers. However, development brought with it social discontent, as problems such as unemployment, high inflation, and corruption began to surface. Black Africans were frustrated at the monopolies that the European colonizers had built up over raw materials and trade, and this increasingly led to rioting. The first instance of this was in Accra in the British Gold Coast (now Ghana) in February 1948. In the light of widespread unrest, Britain decided that independence was the most cost-effective avenue to pursue, as policing operations could become protracted, expensive and give rise to international criticism. Furthermore, Britain realized that a change in the political relationship with the colonies would not necessarily denote a change in the economic relationship.

French Decolonization

In 1954 a bitter struggle broke out as Algeria attempted to gain independence from France. Algeria and France were closely linked; not only was Algeria strategically important, it was also home to many

Below: French armed soldiers are on watch in the Algerian capital on March 22, 1962, four days after the Evian agreement.

SPANISH
MOROCCO *1956*
1956 ■ Rabat
MOROCCO
Sidi Ifni □
□ Aajun
1975
SPANISH
SAHARA
WESTERN SAHARA
1975–79
disputed between
Mauritania,
Morrocco, and
local 'Polisario'
guerillas
1965
■ Nouakchott
MAURITANIA
1960
Dakar ■
1960
Bathurst ■
SENEGAL
GAMBIA
Bissau □
1975
GUINEA
Conakry ■
Freetown ■
1958
SIERRA
LEONE
1961
Monrovia ■
LIBERIA
Abidjan ■
IVORY
COAST
1960
GHANA
1957
Accra ■

Algiers ■

ALGERIA
1962

MALI
1960

Niger R.

Niamey ■
Ouagadougou ■
VOLTA
1960
1960
DAHOMEY
TOGO
Lomé ■
Porto
Novo ■

NIGER
1960

NIGERIA
1960

Benue R.

Lagos ■

Tunis ■
TUNISIA
1956

Tripoli ■

LIBYA
1951

Benghazi ■

Lake Chad
■ Fort Lamy

CHAD
1960

SUDAN
1956

Khartoum ■

Cairo ■

EGYPT
1922–54 treaty
with Britain
1956 British military
garrison leaves

Mediterranean Sea

Nile R.

Red Sea

1952 from Italy
to Ethiopia
ERITREA

DJIBOUTI
□ Djibouti

Addis
Ababa ■

ETHIOPIA

1960

SOMALIA
1960

Mogadishu ■

CENTRAL
AFRICA *1960*

Bangui ■

Yaoundé ■
CAMEROON
1960

1975 to Equatorial Guinea
Santa Isabel
Fernando Póo □
Principé
1968
SPANISH
GUINEA
São Tomé
1975
Librevilleé ■
GABON
1960

Congo R.

Ubangi R.

CONGO
1960

UGANDA
Kampala ■
1962
Lake
Victoria

R.
R.
Kigali ■
Bujumbura ■ B.
1962
1962

KENYA
1963
Nairobi ■

TANZANIA
1961

Pemba Is.
Zanzibar Is.

Mafia Is.

Dar es Salaam ■

Lake
Tanganyika

ATLANTIC
OCEAN

CONGO
1960

Brazzaville ■
Kinshasa ■

Luanda □

ANGOLA
1975

ZAMBIA
1964
Lusaka ■

Lake
Nyasa

1964
MALAWI
Lilongwe ■

Zambezi R.

1975

Comoros Is.

MADAGASCAR
Tananarive ■

1960

Harare
(Salisbury) ■

RHODESIA

MOZAMBIQUE

1965 unilateral
declaration
of independence
1980 popular elections
becomes ZIMBABWE

AFRICAN INDEPENDENCE

1966 Date of independence

□ Capital of an
   independent state

■ Capital of a colony
   or dependency

British

French

Portuguese

Spanish

Italian

Never colonized

SOUTHWEST
AFRICA

Windhoek □
1971 South African
mandate declared
illegal by U.N.
1990 fully
independent
as Namibia

BOTSWANA
1966

Gaborone ■

Limpopo R.

Pretoria ■
Mbabane ■
Maputo □
SWAZILAND
1968

Orange R.

Maseru ■
LESOTHO
1966

SOUTH
AFRICA
1910 Self-governing British Dominion
1961 Leaves British Commonwealth

Cape Town ■

INDIAN
OCEAN

N

0   500 km

0   500 miles

French settlers. The French were not prepared to grant independence, so a war of liberation broke out between the FLN, the Front de Libération National, and the French authorities. Although France was able to win the struggle militarily, it could not do so politically. Heavy-handed tactics merely strengthened the FLN's resolve and brought with it international criticism as France was seen as obstructing national self determination. In addition, America feared that FLN could align with the Soviet bloc and therefore put pressure on Paris to seek a more moderate solution.

By 1962 French domestic opinion had become bitterly divided so, for the sake of national unity, President de Gaulle agreed to grant Algerian independence. In a bid to avoid repetition of the bloody Algerian decolonization process, France was reluctant to stem the tide of African nationalism elsewhere, and proceeded to grant independence to all of its African holdings.

Other Decolonization Processes

Most of the European colonial powers learned from France's mistakes in Algeria and were less inclined to stifle demands for independence. In the Belgian Congo, a riot in Leopoldville (Kinshasa) in 1960 led the Belgians to draw up a speedy timetable towards creating an independent state.

Only the Portuguese were able to hold on to their colonies in Mozambique and Angola. Portugal was under the dictatorship of Salazar and was less affected by domestic political criticism over its colonial policies; it was therefore able to suppress nationalist movements in Africa unimpeded. It was assisted by America's failure to criticize Salazar's colonial policies; they were reliant upon his regime granting them military bases in the Portuguese-owned Azores.

The Roots of Apartheid in South Africa

In both Rhodesia and South Africa white settlers were able to gain independence from Britain and continue to suppress black political representation for a time. White supremacists across Africa wished to ensure that the continent's wealth was kept in white hands. This was particularly significant in South Africa, where the discovery of valuable minerals—including diamonds and gold—had led many Europeans to settle there. After the Boer War, South Africa was granted independence by the British. The new government immediately imposed restrictions on the freedom of the black population and segregationist laws were increasingly introduced, starting with the Native Land Act of 1913, which placed restrictions on black ownership of land.

During the Second World War, South Africa underwent similar industrial development to other African states in order to meet the Allies' economic needs. A new black working class increased the demand for a repeal of pre-war segregationist policies. Fearing a threat to their livelihoods and economic dominance, white South Africans voted Daniel Malan's National Party into office. Its election pledge had been the introduction of apartheid, the idea that races should develop separately. Throughout the 1950s efforts were made to separate whites and blacks, with different amenities, residential districts, farmland—and the finest of everything being set aside for whites.

Although many whites were initially alarmed by apartheid, it gained more support as a result of the militant black response. The African National Congress (ANC) was formed by blacks to provide them with representation under the repressive system. The ANC embarked on a policy of armed struggle as a result of the Sharpeville Massacre in 1960, where black demonstrators were shot by the local police, resulting in sixty-seven deaths. The outcome of ANC militancy was the arrest and imprisonment of its leadership, including Nelson Mandela, in 1964. For the following decade there was little challenge to the apartheid system.

The End of Apartheid in South Africa

By the time that rioting began in the Johannesburg township of Soweto in 1976, the situation had changed. Neighboring states such as Botswana, Angola and Mozambique had become independent with black-dominated governments, making the white South African government regionally isolated. These nearby states now provided a convenient haven for black opposition groups. International opinion was also turning against apartheid. In 1977 the UN imposed an embargo on arms sales to South Africa, which followed the murder of Steve Biko, the leader of black consciousness, while in police custody. By the mid-

Above: African National Congress President Nelson Mandela shown shortly after his release from Robin Island prison in 1990.

Opposite: Anti-apartheid militants attend the burial ceremony of Steve Biko in 1977. Steve Biko, born in King William's Town, was the founder and leader of the Black Consciousness Movement and the first president of the all-black South African Students Organization. He was detained four times in the last few years of his life, and died in police custody as a result of the beating he received.

1980s, with the Cold War drawing to a close, America was less susceptible to the South African government's explanation that apartheid was linked to anti-communism. Despite Reagan's veto, the US congress passed the Comprehensive Anti-Apartheid Act, which sanctioned the import of many South African goods and imposed an oil embargo. With other governments already having embargoes in force, or introducing them following America's example, the economic noose tightened around South Africa.

The National Government and its policy of apartheid began to lose the support of big businesses, some of which began negotiations with the ANC in exile. In the 1989 election, the National Party lost the majority of the votes, which forced Prime Minister F.W. de Klerk to announce the end of apartheid on February 2, 1990, and the end of the ban on the ANC. Soon afterwards, Nelson Mandela was released from prison and the ANC was able to win a sweeping victory in the elections of 1994, which gave black South Africans the vote for the first time.

Post-Colonial Problems

Civil War

The transition towards independence has not proved easy in Africa. A Pan-African Union was ruled out from an early stage as the new leaderships which arose from the national liberation movements could not be reconciled to the idea of renouncing their claims to power. Furthermore, tribal divisions were precipitating conflict within the newly defined states—and a Pan-African Union was out of the question.

Civil war has defined post-colonial Africa as different tribes have vied for power or demanded secession. In Nigeria, the predominantly Christian Igbo peoples tried to form the breakaway republic of Biafra in 1966; they resented being united with the Islamic Hausa tribe in the north and the Yoruba in the south, and having to share their oil deposits with them. In Rwanda in 1994, extremist members of the Hutu majority tribe began a campaign of genocide against the minority, yet politically dominant, Tutsis. In Ethiopia a thirty-year civil war ensued over Eritrean independence. Eritrea had been colonized by Italy and was then under a British mandate until the United Nations decided it should join Ethiopia in a federation. Across Africa similar patterns of conflict emerged as new nation states developed with borders that had little relevance to pre-colonial tribal or religious boundaries.

Poverty and Famine

The combination of precarious environmental conditions and susceptibility to the instability of the world economy have led to decades of famine and poverty in Africa. In years of severe drought, governments have been unable or unwilling to assist in famine relief and widespread starvation has ensued.

Ethiopia witnessed a particularly severe famine in the early 1980s when nearly one million people died. The population became reliant upon food assistance as the country, with a largely agrarian population, is prone to drought and desertification. This, combined with overpopulation, which has resulted in deforestation and overgrazing and the reliance on too few cash crops and a limited access to markets has precipitated starvation. By 1984 Ethiopia had become reliant upon oil imports to run its military in its ongoing war with Eritrea and was therefore vulnerable to oil price rises during the 1970s, diverting yet more of the government's spending away from food support programs. These factors all combined to result in severe famine. After a brief respite from the fighting, with the ceasefire in 1991, the war with Eritrea resumed in the late nineties, and so too did the famine.

Debt

After the hikes in oil prices during the 1970s, excess wealth from oil-producing nations was put into western banks. These used the money to provide African countries with often high-interest loans in order to stimulate development. Poor performance by the global economy in the 1980s led to the debt crisis: many African nations were unable to meet their

Above: Refugees return to Rwanda in 1996. Over 800,000 refugees returned to Rwanda after Tutsi rebels successfully routed Hutu militias in several huge refugee camps near the border of Zaire and Rwanda.
Opposite: Bob Geldof, organizer of the Live Aid concerts in London and Philadelphia in 1985 which raised money to alleviate famine in Ethiopia.

repayment dates, leading to ever greater interest tariffs. A large proportion of the budget of many African countries is now spent on debt repayment rather than development of industry, education, and healthcare, and they have found themselves in a vicious cycle of poverty from which they cannot escape. Several suggestions have been made to ameliorate the situation. Less radical solutions include rescheduling the debt burden so that African nations could spend more on internal development, especially on education and healthcare, in order to create an industrial base from which they might repay the debt in the future. But there have been suggestions that the debt should be completely written off.

HIV and AIDS

The lack of sexual education, funding for contraceptives and the use of dirty needles in health care have all contributed to the rise in the number of HIV cases in sub-Saharan Africa. In some African countries it is estimated that more than 25 percent of the adult population is HIV positive. The inability to access anti-retroviral drugs—which are widely available in the developed world—has increased the number of people who go on to develop full-blown AIDS from HIV. In many countries the issue of AIDS remains taboo and governments have been slow to admit the extent of the problem. HIV and AIDS are set to become the biggest challenge for sub-Saharan Africa in the twenty-first century. The disease is forcing an increasing number of people of working age to become economically inactive and dependent upon the state; in addition, very many children are left without parents or older relatives. With a rapidly increasing dependency ratio the states thus affected will run into severe economic troubles in the future.

European Integration

The development of integration and cooperation across Europe has culminated in the existence of the EU and the Eurozone, still expanding and changing today.

The Origins of Western European Integration

Throughout history large swaths of Europe have been integrated: under the Roman Empire, Charlemagne's Frankish Empire, the Holy Roman Empire, Napoleonic Europe and even Nazi-occupied Europe. Most, however, have involved the subjugation of one nation by another.

After the Second World War, the idea of further integration gained increased support; people hoped it could put an end to the national rivalries that had precipitated the conflict. Washington also advocated integration, hoping that it would bring about rejuvenation of Western Europe's economy—excluding Soviet influence as well as re-opening markets for American goods; Western European governments had a similar view. Not only were they keen to stave off the Soviet threat, they also wanted to tie down the West German economy so that it could not resurge and wage aggressive war yet again.

The First Step toward Integration

This was achieved with the creation of the Council of Europe in 1949, which encouraged closer cooperation. It was followed by the Schuman Declaration, made by French Foreign Minister Robert Schuman, which suggested France and Germany's steel and coal industries should be joined. This paved the way for the European Coal and Steel Community (ECSC), an agreement signed in 1951 together with Italy, the Netherlands, Belgium and Luxembourg. Britain refused to join ECSC because London believed that it would interfere with national sovereignty. The ECSC was controlled by the "High Authority," which was the first independent, supranational body on the path to integration.

After the establishment of the ECSC, moves were made towards a political and military federation, under plans for a European Defense Community (EDC) and a European Political Community (EPC). Under the EDC the plan was to fulfil the American request for West German rearmament without upsetting those countries that had recently suffered in the war. However, the French National Assembly refused to ratify the EDC out of fear of Germany; given this failure, attempts to form the EPC were shelved.

The European Economic Community

In 1957 the movement towards a European federation was furthered significantly when the Treaty of Rome was signed on March 25. This was a collective name for the treaties establishing the European Economic Community (EEC) and the European Atomic Agency, Euratom. The EEC's mission was to establish a common market between member states and bring about the "four freedoms" – the free movement of goods, people, capital, and services. Euratom was designed to pool together non-military nuclear capabilities. These two new organizations were combined with the ECSC by a merger treaty, which came into force in 1967. The three organizations streamlined their institutions, creating a single European Commission, a Council of Ministers and a European Parliament. After serving as an executive body for the three institutions they were later taken over by the European Union. In 1979, elections were held for the European Parliament and the citizens of member states elected the parliament directly for the first time.

Enlargement

The founding members of the EEC were France, West Germany, the Netherlands, Belgium, Luxembourg, and Italy. Britain did not join, fearing that joining a customs union in Europe would disrupt trade with the newly formed Commonwealth; during the 1960s Britain came to realize that participation in Europe was more useful, as Commonwealth trade was not providing the hoped-for dividends. The British application for membership was twice rejected by French President, General de Gaulle; it was not until 1973, after his death, that Britain was finally welcomed into the EEC. Ireland and Denmark followed suit; their trade interests were closely linked to Britain's. Norway also showed interest in joining, but a referendum proved unsuccessful. Not long after shedding authoritarian governments in the mid-1970s, Greece, Portugal, and Spain also joined; Greece in 1981 and the Iberian countries in 1986. Further enlargement occurred in 1995 when Austria, Finland, and Sweden joined. Although their nearest neighbors had negotiated membership, the Norwegians again voted against joining.

After the collapse of the USSR and the end of Communist Party rule in Eastern Europe, many East European states wished to join the EU. At a meeting in December 2002 in Copenhagen, it was agreed that ten countries would be admitted: Lithuania, Latvia, Estonia, Slovenia, Malta, Hungary, the Czech Republic, Slovakia, Poland, and Cyprus. These were admitted in May 2004, taking the total to twenty-five. Cyprus was admitted after Greece threatened to veto the other states' entrance unless it was included, and this created difficulties with Turkey, which also desires EU membership. Romania and Bulgaria have negotiated entrance for 2007.

The European Union

The EU came into being with the signing of the Maastricht Treaty on February 7, 1992. It was established as a supranational body and had the task of creating a single market among its member states. As part of this, the EU took over the administration of the customs union, the Common Agricultural Policy and the Common Fisheries Policy. In addition, the EU encouraged member states to adopt a further array of common policies in areas ranging from the environment and transport to culture and road safety.

The European Union has set a series of guidelines for foreign and security policy, which the member states are expected to follow, yet within these parameters states are free to pursue their own foreign policies. The guidelines insist that members must adhere to the UN Charter and the rule of law, and uphold democracy and human rights in their foreign policy. Through this the EU has become an international organization; its member states have used its institutions to negotiate trade and aid agreements or to impose sanctions and arms embargoes. In addition, there are increased links between different police forces, especially over such issues as drug-trafficking, asylum seekers and border control; many of the Union's internal borders were scrapped by the 1990s.

Amsterdam, Nice and a European Constitution

Ultimately the member states are the masters of the EU. The Maastricht Treaty was updated by the treaty of Amsterdam in 1997, which was designed to democratize the EU, giving a greater say to the population. This was criticized for not going far enough to reform the EU's

over-complicated bureaucracy, and was followed by the Treaty of Nice, which came into force in 2003. New rules placed restrictions on the size of European institutions, a vital prerequisite given the EU's pending enlargement. Eventually, this treaty will be replaced by a European constitution, which is designed to replace the overlapping texts of the numerous existing treaties.

The text for the constitution was drafted in 2003 but not agreed until 2004; each country has to agree to adopt the constitution. Some have chosen referenda as a means of deciding, while others have opted for national governments to make the decision. The adoption of a constitution could prove difficult; countries with referenda may vote against it, preventing it coming into effect.

Economic and Monetary Union (EMU)

The EU decided to pursue Economic and Monetary Union in 1992 as Germany was keen to allay the fears of EEC countries, particularly France, over its reunification. The euro became official tender on New Year's Day 2002 in twelve of the then fifteen member states. These twelve also united their economies under the coordinated control of the European Central Bank. Each country wishing to join EMU has to meet a set of criteria ensuring that their economy is stable enough. Britain, Sweden, and Denmark have chosen not to join the euro. Britain and Denmark were able to negotiate opt-out clauses by threatening not to sign the Maastricht Treaty. They are not expected to join, unless their national governments decide otherwise. Sweden, however, does not have such a clause and is obliged to adopt the euro at some point, but it may be difficult for the EU to force acceptance.

The primary aim of the single currency is to promote the single market, by removing the cost of exchanging currency and also by encouraging freer movement of people within the Eurozone.

The Changing World

The Ozone Layer and Global Warming

Climate change is one of the most well known of the environmental concerns facing today's society. The climate is always changing; however, many scientists believe that many of the changes we are now experiencing are as much a result of human activity as of natural causes. The greenhouse effect is believed to pose the greatest threat to the world's climate. Gases in the earth's atmosphere are vital for keeping the planet warm and sustaining life in all its forms, but the human release of extra greenhouse gases—in the form of pollutants—are having a detrimental effect upon the atmosphere and are responsible for the erosion of the ozone layer. Climate change, in particular global warming, is generally held to be responsible for the increases in more extreme weather conditions across the globe, such as a rise in the number of droughts and the dramatic raising of sea levels as the polar ice caps begin to melt more rapidly. In 1992 the United Nations agreed to address the issue of climate change, acknowledging the role that human activity was having on the atmosphere. Then, in 1997, the UN convention for climate change met at Kyoto in Japan in order to draw up a protocol which requires participant countries to reduce their emissions in a bid to resolve the problem. The Kyoto agreement was finally made international law in February 2005; however, its impact on climate change is negligible. Only those countries who have agreed to the protocol are required to reduce their emissions and among those who refuse to recognize the Kyoto agreement are the US and Australia, two of the largest energy consumers on the planet.

Energy Consumption

High levels of energy use are determined by several basic factors, the most crucial being that of industrial development. Those countries that have highly industrialized infrastructures will inevitably use more energy, be it from oil, coal, electricity, or nuclear sources, than those without. In addition, high energy consumption is affected by the size of the population: the greater this is, the greater the need for energy. As a general rule, therefore, the countries that are most responsible for energy consumption are those that tend

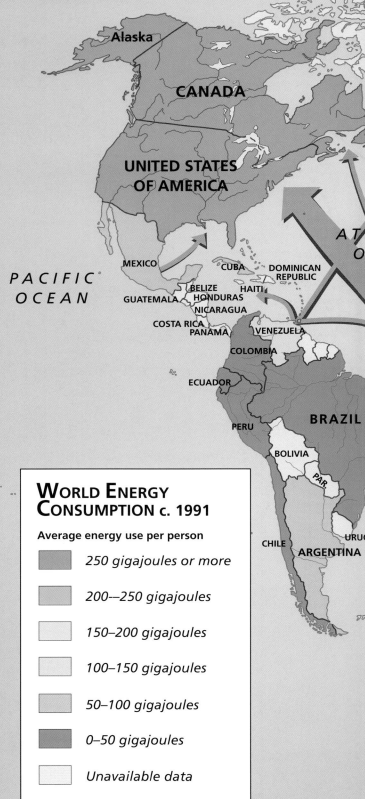

WORLD ENERGY CONSUMPTION c. 1991

Average energy use per person

250 gigajoules or more

200–250 gigajoules

150–200 gigajoules

100–150 gigajoules

50–100 gigajoules

0–50 gigajoules

Unavailable data

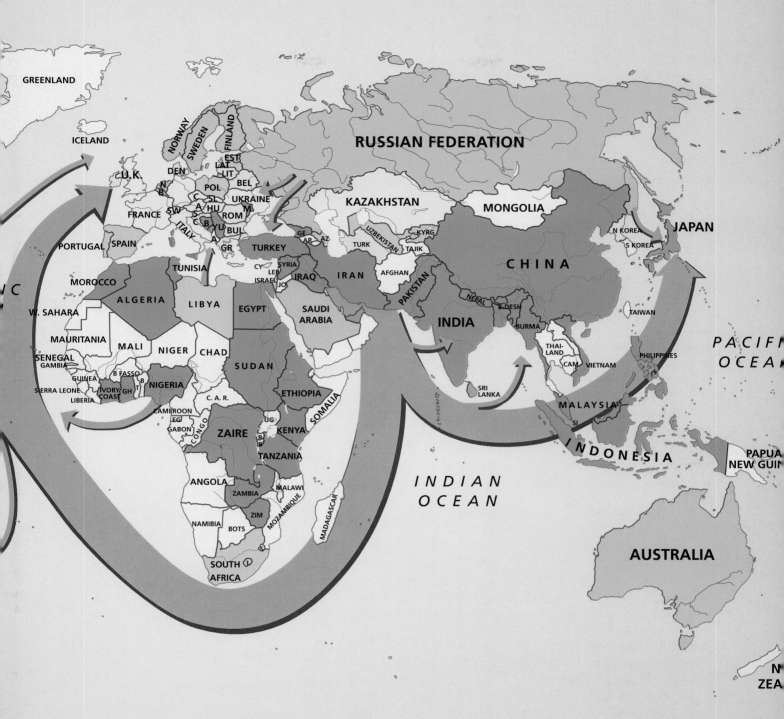

GREENLAND

ICELAND

NORWAY

SWEDEN

FINLAND

EST

LAT

LIT

U.K.

DEN

N.
B.

POL

BEL

FRANCE

SW

A

C

H

B

YU

HU

ROM

M

UKRAINE

RUSSIAN FEDERATION

KAZAKHSTAN

MONGOLIA

JAPAN

N KOREA

S KOREA

PORTUGAL

SPAIN

ITALY

GR

BUL

TURKEY

GE

AR

AZ

UZBEKISTAN

KYRG

TAJIK

TURK

AFGHAN

CHINA

TAIWAN

MOROCCO

TUNISIA

CY

LEB

ISRAEL

SYRIA

JO

IRAQ

IRAN

PAKISTAN

NEPAL

B.DESH

BURMA

PACIFIC
OCEAN

W. SAHARA

ALGERIA

LIBYA

EGYPT

SAUDI
ARABIA

INDIA

THAI-
LAND

PHILIPPINES

MAURITANIA

MALI

NIGER

CHAD

SUDAN

SRI
LANKA

CAM

VIETNAM

SENEGAL

GAMBIA

GUINEA

SIERRA LEONE

LIBERIA

B FASSO

IVORY
COAST

GH

B

T

NIGERIA

C. A. R.

ETHIOPIA

SOMALIA

MALAYSIA

SI

CAMEROON

EG

GABON

CONGO

ZAIRE

UG

R

B
B

KENYA

TANZANIA

INDONESIA

PAPUA
NEW GUINEA

ANGOLA

ZAMBIA

MALAWI

MOZAMBIQUE

MADAGASCAR

INDIAN
OCEAN

NAMIBIA

ZIM

BOTS

AUSTRALIA

SOUTH
AFRICA

N
ZEA

Major Oil Flows

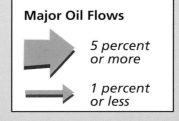

*5 percent
or more*

*1 percent
or less*

to be wealthier or more populated. At present these are China, the United States, and Australasia, although Europe also depends upon massive levels of energy. Many countries claim to be keen to find ways of reducing their energy needs, but governments are reluctant to make drastic changes that may have a detrimental effect on their productive output and therefore their economies. Scientists have developed renewable sources of energy, such as using wind power and solar energy—and the most successful of these, nuclear power—but these sources tend to be more expensive, less efficient, or arouse considerable opposition.

The Asian Tsunami

Natural disasters always present a threat to communities worldwide and on December 26 2004 a massive earthquake under the Indian Ocean triggered a tsunami which wreaked havoc across southern Asia. The quake caused the sea floor to rupture, which in turn sent a series of giant waves some 2,800 miles across the sea reaching as far as Somalia on the east coast of Africa. For those living or staying on the coasts of Sri Lanka, Thailand, Sumatra, the Maldives, the Andaman Islands, and South-East India, the first warning came when the sea was sucked back away from land exposing hundreds of feet of seabed. This was then followed by the tsunami wave, which in some places traveled around half a mile inland before retreating. The total number of dead is still not known at time of writing, but is believed to exceed 240,000 people across some thirteen countries. In addition millions lost their homes and their livelihoods, and the images sent across the globe of those in suffering prompted a massive response from governments and populations who donated large amounts in international aid.

Threats to global security

Some disasters remain the work of people rather than natural forces and the twenty-first century has already been marked by the threats posed by international terrorism. On September 11, 2001, an attack on the World Trade Center in New York proved to be a critical low point. Terrorists from the Middle East took control of four passenger airplanes and, at 8.45 am New York time, the first of these was deliberately crashed into the north tower of the Trade Center. Fifteen minutes later another plane crashed into the south tower and both buildings completely collapsed. An hour later a third plane was smashed into the Pentagon building, the US military headquarters in Washington, and just twenty minutes after that the fourth aircraft was brought down in a rural area outside Pittsburgh. The attack was carried out by nineteen hijackers who are believed to have been from Saudi Arabia and Egypt and linked to al-Qaida. Around 2,800 people are believed to have died in the attacks, a figure that includes the 260 who were aboard the planes and some 300 New York firefighters who were working to save lives in the twin towers when they both collapsed. The impact of the attack was felt not just in New York and the United States but across the globe and the call for a "war on terrorism" left many feeling a new sense of insecurity about what the future holds.

TSUNAMI
DECEMBER 26, 2004

Plate boundary

Ocean Ridge

Fault Lines

Coastline suffering major destruction

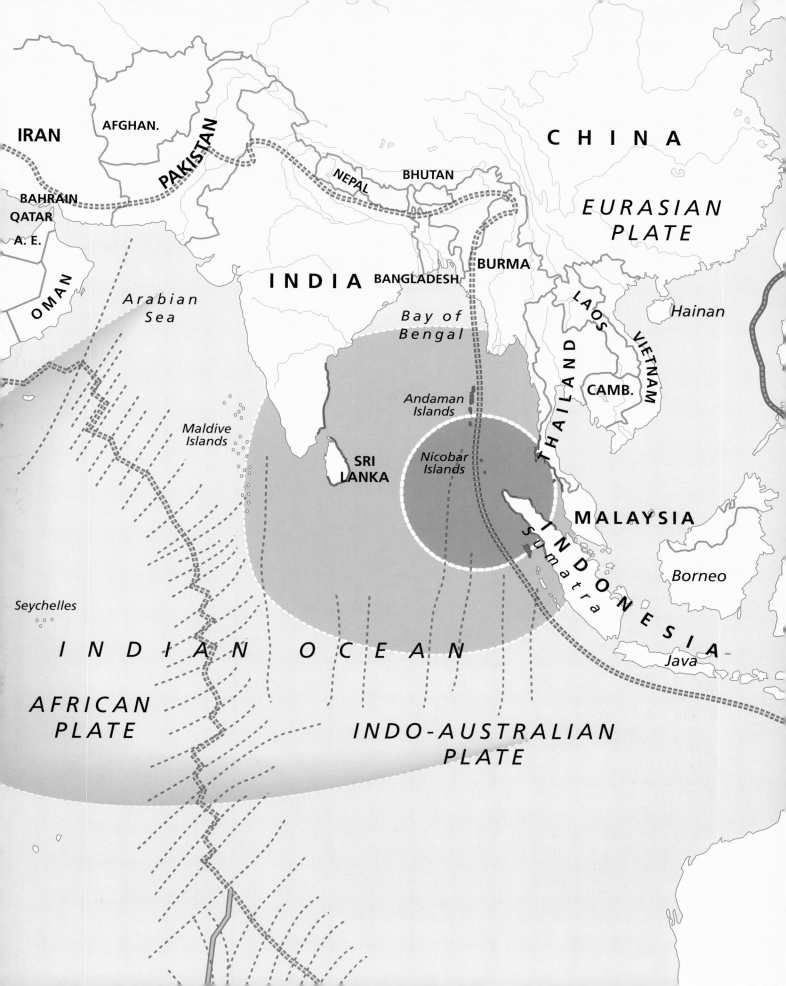

Index

Picture Acknowledgments

The Publisher would like to thank the following libraries for permission to reproduce the images listed below:

Page 10 National Geographic/Getty Images; 20 AFP/Getty Images; 21 AFP/Getty Images; 24 AFP/Getty Images;
25 Robert Harding Picture Library/Getty Images, 35 National Geographic/Getty Images; 45 Robert Harding Picture Library/Getty Images;
49 National Geographic/Getty Images; 58 Robert Harding Picture Library/Getty Images; 73 AFP/Getty Images;
76 Time Life Pictures/Getty Images; 87 Robert Harding Picture Library/Getty Images; 90 Time Life Pictures/Getty Images;
92 Lonely Planet/Getty Images; 96 The Bridgeman Art Library/Getty Images; 97 Robert Harding Picture Library/Getty Images;
100 The Bridgeman Art Library/Getty Images; 101 The Bridgeman Art Library/Getty Images; 105 Lonely Planet Images/Getty Images;
107 Lonely Planet Images/Getty Images; 117 National Geographic/Getty Images; 118 National Geographic/Getty Images;
122 The Bridgeman Art Library/Getty Images; 126 Time Life Pictures/Getty Images; 128 The Bridgeman Art Library/Getty Images;
132 Time Life Pictures/Getty Images; 136 The Bridgeman Art Library/Getty Images; 140 The Bridgeman Art Library/Getty Images;
145 The Bridgeman Art Library/Getty Images; 149 The Bridgeman Art Library/Getty Images; 151 The Bridgeman Art Library/Getty Images;
153 Lonely Planet Images/Getty Images; 164 The Bridgeman Art Library/Getty Images; 182 The Bridgeman Art Library/Getty Images;
194 Time Life Pictures/Getty Images; 199 Time Life Pictures/Getty Images; 200 Time Life Pictures/Getty Images;
214 Time Life Pictures/Getty Images; 258 Time Life Pictures/Getty Images; 272 AFP/Getty Images; 302 AFP/Getty Images;
304 AFP/Getty Images; 305 AFP/Getty Images; 307 Liaison/Getty Images

All other images © Getty Images